The Sages
Character, Context & Creativity
Volume III: The Galilean Period

מגיד
MAGGID

Binyamin Lau

THE SAGES

Character, Context & Creativity

Volume III: The Galilean Period

TRANSLATED BY

Ilana Kurshan

Maggid Books

The Sages: Character, Context & Creativity
Volume III: The Galilean Period

First Maggid English Edition © 2013
Koren Publishers Jerusalem

Maggid Books
An imprint of Koren Publishers Jerusalem Ltd.

Gila Fine, Editor in Chief

POB 8531, New Milford, CT 06776-8531, USA
& POB 4044, Jerusalem 91040, Israel

www.korenpub.com

Original Hebrew Edition © 2008 Binyamin Lau

Published in cooperation with Beit Morasha

The publication of this book was made possible through
the generous support of *Torah Education in Israel.*

Cover artwork by Ora Ruven, oraruven@gmail.com

ISBN 978 159 264 247 2, *hardcover*

A CIP catalogue record for this title is
available from the British Library

Printed and bound in the United States

The English translation of The Sages
was made possible by a generous grant from
the Jay and Hadasa Pomrenze Foundation

Contents

PART THREE:
GATES OF LIGHT – RABBI MEIR, THE "OTHER," AND OTHERS

PART FOUR:
GATES OF THE PATRIARCH – RABBAN SHIMON BEN GAMLIEL

PART FIVE: GATES OF THE MESSIAH – RABBI YEHUDA HANASI

Author's Preface

I am grateful to God that I have been privileged to complete the third volume of this series, concluding my survey of the sages of the Mishna. The warm reception accorded the first two volumes by both students of Torah and the general public inspired me to continue my study of these seminal figures whose teachings guided and shaped the soul of the Jewish people for all subsequent generations.

Over the last few years, my thinking has been significantly informed by my close consideration of the mishnaic sages. The Talmud asserts that anyone who studies the wisdom of the sages must imagine the author of each teaching standing before him or her. To my surprise, this assertion has added new depth to my learning. I have found myself enriched by the sages' worldview when contemplating sociopolitical issues such as nationalism and sectarianism or questions of culture and economics. I have also invoked the fruits of my learning in my interactions with a broad spectrum of the population, including politicians, jurists, educators, and students of Torah from all walks of life. Israeli society tends to shy away from these sources because the Talmud is not an accessible text. I have discovered that when presented appropriately, this wealth of knowledge can be introduced into the general cultural discourse. The *Sages* series is my attempt to present our traditional texts critically, in a manner that is relevant to all sectors of society. As we pray in the Rosh HaShana service, "O my Creator, grant me understanding that I may transmit my heritage."

Thankfully, I am not alone in my effort to bridge contemporary Jewish culture in all its diversity and the many layers of Jewish tradition accumulated throughout the generations. For the past ten years, I have been active in Beit Morasha in Jerusalem, a beit midrash directed by Professor Benjamin Ish-Shalom. The leaders and fellows of this institution dedicate themselves to forging a strong bond between past and present. I am also grateful to my parents for establishing a model of a Jewish, Israeli home that is tolerant of cultural and personal difference and serves the collective without encroaching on the individual. Moreover, my wife Noa – who grew up in a home devoted to the synthesis of Torah study and public service, faith and science, tradition and modernity – is the cornerstone of the home we have been privileged to build together.

This book, like its predecessors in this series, is the product of collaborative efforts. First and foremost in this collaboration are the members of the Ramban Synagogue in Jerusalem. The classes I taught in this congregation on Shabbat afternoons provided the structure for these volumes. My students at Beit Morasha helped me fine-tune several of my ideas and insights. My friend Shlomo Goldberg, the head of the circulation department of the National Library of Israel, worked long and hard to help me find all the scholarly literature related to the passages I treat in this book. Chana Amit edited the original manuscript with sensitivity and understanding, and my eldest son, Yedidya, polished the final draft.

It is a particular pleasure to introduce the English edition of *The Sages*. There is an unfortunate gulf between English and Hebrew readers. Maggid Books, under the leadership of Matthew Miller, has made it its mission to bridge this gap, bringing readers from across the Jewish world into one conversation. The translation was done by Ilana Kurshan. Her masterful work on the second volume of this series, rendering the text as clear and accessible in English as it was in Hebrew, has earned enthusiastic response from readers. The book was edited by Judy Lee and Suzanne Libenson, who distilled the text into its present shape. Thanks are also due to the editor in chief of Maggid Books, Gila Fine, who worked hard to bring the book to its finely-tuned finish.

I dedicate this book to our beloved children: "Children are a heritage from the Lord; the fruit of the womb is His reward" (Ps. 127:3). They are our portion and our inheritance. I pray that they chart their paths by following the ways of our ancestors, who always walked in the footsteps of the sages.

Binyamin Lau
Winter 2013/5773
Jerusalem

Introduction

This volume deals with the sages of the Usha generation, who are major figures in rabbinic literature. Every tractate of the Talmud features disputes involving Rabbi Meir, Rabbi Yehuda, Rabbi Yose, Rabbi Shimon, and Rabbi Elazar ben Shamua. These five sages are identified as the students of Rabbi Akiva, who ordained them before his execution:

> Rabbi Akiva had twelve thousand pairs of disciples, from Gevat until Antiparis, and they all died during one period, because they did not treat each other with respect. And the world was barren [of Torah], until Rabbi Akiva came to our rabbis in the south and taught them Torah. [They were] Rabbi Meir, Rabbi Yehuda, Rabbi Yose, Rabbi Shimon, and Rabbi Elazar ben Shamua, and it was these disciples who upheld the Torah at that time. (Yevamot 62b)

This source gives Rabbi Akiva exclusive credit for ensuring the continuity of Torah study. He towered over all his contemporaries, and his teachings sustained the next generation. As Y. N. Epstein wrote in *Introduction to the Literature of the Tanna'im*: "Akiva ben Yosef, whose name resounds from one end of the world to the other, was a giant in his own lifetime: he is the father of the Mishna – our Mishna. He marked the start of a new era for the Mishna" (p. 71).

Rabbi Akiva's brilliance nearly eclipsed the more steady-burning glow of his contemporary Rabbi Yishmael. The aggadic traditions that describe Jewish life in the wake of the failed Bar Kokhba revolt would have us believe that Rabbi Akiva's surviving students alone were responsible for the successful transmission of Torah in that tremulous time. The entire community of sages in the Usha generation is portrayed as disciples of Rabbi Akiva. All of tannaitic literature – that is, all rabbinic texts from the first and second centuries – is presented as the word of Rabbi Akiva's school: "All is according to Rabbi Akiva" (Sanhedrin 86a). But the reality was otherwise. Rabbi Yishmael, too, had students who survived the revolt and went on to teach Torah to the Jewish people.

Rabbi Yishmael is depicted as the polar opposite of Rabbi Akiva. A famous teaching ascribed to Rabbi Yishmael, that "Torah speaks in human terms," is not just a hermeneutic principle of interpreting the Torah but a fundamental aspect of his worldview. He believed that Torah study should be integrated into the human challenges of this world by learning Torah while taking part in work and the general affairs of life. Rabbi Akiva, by contrast, sought to live a life of total devotion to study in the hopes of fulfilling the principle that "You should love the Lord your God with all your soul – even if your soul is taken from you" (Berakhot 61b).

Parts I and II of this book discuss the relationship between two distinct factions among the sages in the Galilee during the generation after Rabbi Akiva and Rabbi Yishmael. The first faction consisted of Rabbi Yehuda bar Ilai and Rabbi Yose ben Ḥalafta, neither of whom were close disciples of Rabbi Akiva. They recognized Rabbi Akiva's preeminence and even quoted him frequently but based their worldview on a different set of values, a Galilean one that combined a life of Torah study with gainful employment. These two sages were also very different from one another – one was from a village and the other from a city; one was well acquainted with poverty, while the other lived among nobility – but both were firmly rooted in the affairs of this world, as we shall see.

The other faction consisted of Rabbi Shimon bar Yoḥai and

Rabbi Meir (also known as Rabbi Meir Ba'al HaNes), two students who received their rabbinic ordination directly from Rabbi Akiva. These sages were deeply ensconced in the world of Torah learning: The former concealed himself in a cave to study Torah, while the latter enveloped himself in its coruscating light. They each had a complicated relationship with their contemporaries, as the chapters about them demonstrate.

It is fascinating to consider how later generations understood the differences between these two factions, which represent the worlds of halakha and kabbala, respectively. On the one hand, the talmudic tradition ruled that the halakha follows Rabbi Yose and his colleagues, foremost among them Rabbi Yehuda. Apparently, the development of Jewish law preferred those sages who were preoccupied with the quotidian concerns of this world and spoke in human terms. In contrast, the Talmud says that the sages did not rule like Rabbi Meir, because they "could not fathom the depths of his reasoning" (Eiruvin 13b). The talmudic tradition also did not establish halakha in accordance with Rabbi Shimon, stating only that "it is good to have Rabbi Shimon to rely on in moments of urgency" (Berakhot 9a). Rabbi Meir and Rabbi Shimon bar Yoḥai became heroes of kabbala and Hasidism, but not of halakha. Their graves became popular pilgrimage destinations, the anniversaries of their deaths were commemorated as folk holidays, and the secrets of their teachings attracted many who sought higher levels of holiness and spirituality. These two senior students of Rabbi Akiva, who had also sought to penetrate inner mystical realms, had magnetic personalities that attracted the affection of the masses.

The schism between halakha and kabbala and between wisdom and prophecy has persisted throughout the generations. In the early twentieth century, Rabbi Abraham Isaac HaKohen Kook argued that the decline of prophecy and the concomitant rise of the sages saved Judaism, for prophecy trains its sights on a distant future but fails to address the mundane needs and everyday concerns of the present. He analogizes the work of the sages to that of engineers and surveyors, who take careful, measured steps, overcoming obstacles as they confront them. Nonetheless, Rav Kook said, halakhic Judaism paid a steep price for the loss of prophecy: All sense of vision vanished. In the "Zironim" section of his book *Orot*, he writes, "Over time the activity of the sages superseded that of the prophets, and prophecy disappeared. The years grew long and the principles lost their purchase, swallowed by subtleties and obscured from outside." This is a fascinating depiction of halakhic Judaism as locked in its four cubits of legal detail and lacking the broader perspective necessary to seek out God's word in this world. In our own time, we hear clarion calls to reawaken the voices of prophecy, poetry, and imagination that cry out to be heard above the measured and deliberate murmur of halakha. While I will present Rabbi Meir and Rabbi Shimon as luminaries whose examples may inspire imitation, it behooves us to take note of the significant cost exacted from a community that aspires to live apart in realms of holiness rather than walk the well-trodden paths of religious observance in this world.

The last two parts of the book deal with the two major patriarchs, Rabban Shimon ben Gamliel and his son Rabbi Yehuda HaNasi. Here we will grapple with questions of communal leadership in times of economic hardship, social inequity, cultural tension, and political struggle. For modern Jews living in the wake of the Zionist revolution, these questions offer us a way of thinking about the Jewish character of contemporary Israeli society. What constitutes a halakhic enactment for the sake of the common good? To what extent do economic considerations inform and define the limits of halakha? We will witness, for example, Rabban Shimon ben Gamliel legislate edicts concerning public responsibility for families in need, and we will examine Rabbi Yehuda HaNasi's attempt to change the law of the sabbatical year so as to alleviate the burden borne by the people in depressed economic circumstances. These two patriarchs were already resigned to the loss of Jewish sovereignty, but they continued to push for the internal political autonomy of the Jewish people within the Roman Empire. They tried to strengthen the institution of the patriarchy, which they viewed as a sort of religious monarchy presiding over worldwide Jewry. This is a middle position between a community-based model, in which authority and policy reside locally, and a national model, which attempts to vest power in a central and sovereign "royal" authority established as the successor to the Davidic dynasty. At the height of Rabbi Yehuda HaNasi's power, he faced insinuations that he harbored messianic aspirations. But his inner circle managed to chill that innuendo and refashion his image in the middle ground, so he enjoyed the honor accorded a king but was not regarded in a messianic light. As these sources teach, we have a long history of autonomy under foreign dominion. The more we can temper our messianic aspirations, the more we will improve our lives in the Land of Israel today.

The contemporary relevance of these issues speaks for itself. Anyone who studies the patriarchs of Israel is hard-pressed not to read this history in light of the national and communal issues that preoccupy Israeli society today. In spite of the temptation to "translate" my descriptions of the sages into modern terms and to accord them contemporary relevance, I have refrained from doing so beyond what I hint at in this introduction. Instead I have tried to treat the rabbinic sources as objectively as possible, confident that readers can consider the ramifications on their own terms and at their own risk.

The previous volume of this series forced me to contend with an overabundance of rabbinic sources and academic studies concerning the Yavneh period. The same problem applies to the Usha generation. My challenge was to select which of the copious relevant texts to include in this volume. I also had to reconcile the gap between the biographical images of the various sages and the literary personas constructed by the narrative sources without resorting to imaginative speculation. Here too, as in the previous volumes, I chose to combine the learning style of the traditional beit midrash, which regards rabbinic sources as trustworthy historical evidence, with the world of academic scholarship, in which every text must be scrutinized with healthy skepticism. This mingling of approaches required me to suppress my creative impulses and allow the sources to speak for themselves. Historians maintain that the difficulty of distinguishing story from history impedes our ability to write rabbinic biographies. Recent years have seen a scholarly trend of studying rabbinic *Aggada* as literature valued for its rhetorical rather than historical content. In the beit midrash where I study and teach, Beit Morasha in Jerusalem, we try to strike a balance by acquainting ourselves intimately with the various sages without surrendering the seriousness of the academy.

With the *Sages* series, I seek to make Torah accessible to several audiences. One such is religious communities like those in which I grew up, which are not accustomed to reading rabbinic texts in historical context. In traditional yeshivot, the sages of the Talmud are presented as if they all sat around a single table and debated the entire Torah simultaneously. Since the Torah is eternal, it need not be studied in its historical context. So I have tried to draw the teachings of the rabbinic sages closer to the time and place in which these masters lived. Our ability to identify the individual sages with various schools, communities, and populations enhances our ability to understand their words. This is also relevant to our own day, in which Torah study takes place in particular historical and geographical contexts and in response to specific human needs.

Another audience I seek to reach is, more broadly, the Jewish community at large. The verse "Moses commanded Torah to us, the heritage of the congregation of Jacob" (Deut. 33:4) is explained by Rashi as a charge to the entire Jewish people not to abandon its heritage. I fear for the lack of depth in the Jewish consciousness of Israeli society in particular and of world Jewry in general. Many Jews thirst to drink from the wellsprings of Jewish wisdom but struggle to understand the canonical sources of our past. It is my fervent hope and prayer that these books will be a resource for Jews the world over, so Torah will not be lost from the people of Israel.

Foreword

Above All, Literature

Avigdor Shinan

In volume III of *The Sages*, Rabbi Dr. Binyamin Lau (known to his legions of devoted students and congregants as "HaRav Benny"), chronicles the major sages who were active between the debacle of the Bar Kokhba revolt in the year 135 CE and the death of Rabbi Yehuda HaNasi at the beginning of the third century. The book introduces an illustrious cast of characters, among them Rabbi Yehuda bar Ilai, Rabbi Yose ben Ḥalafta, Rabbi Shimon bar Yoḥai, Rabbi Meir and his famous wife Beruria, and Rabbi Yehuda HaNasi. The author explores their lives and teachings, as well as their conversations with their teachers, relatives, students, and other contemporaries. The book also considers the figure of Elisha ben Abuya, known as the "other," the notorious heretic and teacher of Rabbi Meir. Also included in this volume are Rabbi Natan, Rabbi Ḥiya, and Rabbi Pinḥas ben Yair, who offer a fresh perspective on Rabbi Yehuda HaNasi's prodigious rabbinic enterprise.

The foreword to volume I of this series was written by an eminent historian of the Second Temple period, and the foreword to volume II by a leading archeologist known for his research on the Qumran Caves and the Dead Sea Scrolls. But I am neither. I approach this book as one who studies Midrash and aggadic literature from a literary perspective. The academic study of these texts requires an interdisciplinary approach that includes Jewish and world history, archeology, literature, linguistics, Jewish philosophy, and, first and foremost, talmudic philology, which demands that the scholar identify the most authentic version of each text before beginning his or her analysis. Rabbi Dr. Lau, an academic himself, proves his proficiency in each of these disciplines, but he also seeks to reach members of the yeshiva world, those who approach these texts with devotion and reverence. Does he succeed? Is it possible to conjoin a critical academic approach, which necessitates a certain objective distance, with the religious bearing of the traditional beit midrash, which seeks to bring these words ever closer to the hearts of those in search of inspiration? Rabbi Lau is well aware of this dichotomy, and he returns to it again and again, both explicitly and implicitly. We might consider, for instance, how he presents the aims of his book in his preface to the chapter on the complex figure of Rabbi Shimon bar Yoḥai:

> [My goal] is not historical reconstruction but rather clear explication of the rabbinic material so as to make it accessible to readers who would draw inspiration from the world of the sages. Verifying the historicity of the sources is beyond my capacity and purpose. I doubt whether such authentication is even possible; regardless, it is of secondary significance. The historical Rabbi Shimon is bound up with his literary personality, which ultimately determines how he has been understood and remembered.

Put more simply, we might say that the question of "what really happened" – what was a sage's life story, and what did he teach – is not Rabbi Lau's primary concern. He admits that this type of historical reconstruction is infeasible for several reasons: There is a geographical and chronological gap between these sources and the events they describe; sayings and teachings that were transmitted orally for hundreds of years are attributed to various sages, while others are quoted anonymously; manuscript copyists often abbreviated the names of various sages, resulting in false attributions (for instance, the scribal notation R"Y frequently caused Rabbi Yehuda to be mistaken for Rabbi Yose); and the most famous of the sages occasionally became associated with statements that were originally spoken by more obscure colleagues. It is also possible that multiple sages sharing the same name became fused into a single literary character – after all, could it really be that during the entire period of the Mishna there was no one else in the beit midrash named Rabbi Meir? We also confront contradictory accounts of various events, and we cannot know whether the sages had the historical consciousness to document exactly what happened, step by step, for posterity.

The talmudic sages were more concerned with prescribing proper religious belief and conduct than with factually documenting history. They were teachers and thinkers, not historians or archeologists. The events of the past were far less important to them than the lessons such events afforded the present or future. And even if there was a core "historical" version of any sage discussed in these pages, that figure is inaccessible to us, embellished, hidden, shrouded as he is under the sedimented strata of rabbinic texts: sources early and late, narrative and non-narrative, Palestinian and Babylonian. All we can do is uncover the literary construction or portrait of any sage. Thus, this volume enables anyone who would "draw inspiration from the world of the sages" to see the process by which the character of each sage was shaped and presented to impart various lessons – a goal that is not academic, but certainly educationally valuable.

It is worth mentioning, too, that in *Sages* III, in contrast to the two previous volumes, the author does not conclude each section of the book with a chapter on the contemporary relevance of the issues under discussion. Rather, he weaves a contemporary perspective into the text and footnotes when relevant.

Much of Rabbi Lau's success in this book is due to the wide net he casts over the many stories available to us about the sages and their world. Even without offering a technical definition of what constitutes a story, it is clear that rabbinic literature includes hundreds of narratives, some of which are very sophisticated literarily. In the past forty years, the academic world has made great strides in the study of such stories, while the yeshiva world has continued to dismiss this part of rabbinic literature as "assorted trinkets" compared to the "precious stones and pearls" of halakha. (See Sota 40a, from which I draw these terms.) This book, and the *Aggadata* series as a whole, reflects a welcome sea change that is taking place in the world of Torah study. Of course, literary analysis requires linguistic expertise as well as archeological and historical evidence. But the analysis of these texts also calls for close reading of each tale, paying attention to the details, the style of the language, the structure of the narrative, and the philosophical ideas at its core – as we would approach any literary masterpiece. It seems to me that the literary study of rabbinic literature is the best way to achieve Rabbi Lau's twin goals of understanding the past as it was variously depicted while treating this history with due respect and faith.

In tribute to Rabbi Lau and this book, I will now briefly discuss a few representative rabbinic narratives from the period. I will start with a story about Rabbi Yose ben Ḥalafta, the second century CE sage from Tzippori. Tzippori is currently undergoing archeological excavation, enabling us to appreciate the full splendor of this city in which Jews, Gnostics, Christians, heretics, and perhaps even Samaritans once mingled on the streets. Rabbinic sources describe nearly twenty accounts of various encounters between Rabbi Yose and a Roman matron with whom he would discuss biblical verses. One such tale appears in Genesis Rabba, in the commentary on the verse "So the Lord God cast a deep sleep upon the man, and while he slept, He took one of his ribs and closed up the flesh at that spot" (Gen. 2:21):

> A Roman matron asked Rabbi Yose: Why was woman created by theft?
>
> He said to her: Here is a parable: If a man secretly deposits an ounce of silver with you, and you return a *litra* [twelve ounces] of silver to him publicly, is that theft?
>
> She said to him: Yet why in secret?
>
> He said to her: At first He created her for him and he saw her full of discharge and blood, so He removed her from him and created her a second time.
>
> She said to him: I can confirm your words. It had been arranged that I should marry my mother's brother, but because I was brought up with him in the same home, I became ugly in

> his eyes, and he went and married another woman who is not as beautiful as I am. (Genesis Rabba 17)

As in all of these stories, it is the matron who initiates the conversation. She begins by accusing God of stealing a rib from Adam to create woman. It is noteworthy that the accusation that God is a thief appears in the context of the creation of woman in other sources as well, including Sanhedrin 39a. Rabbi Yose responds gently, without attacking his interlocutor. He invokes an analogy that will speak to a woman of means: What if she were entrusted with a small sum of silver, without witnesses present? If she were to return to the depositor a much larger sum of gold in public, could this be considered theft? The analogy is not perfect. After all, even if Adam had been provided with a beautiful woman worth her weight in gold, God took his rib without permission, whereas the man entrusts the silver to his friend *with* permission. So the matron persists. She asks her question again, this time more politely: Why the need for secrecy? Why did God conceal the creation of woman from Adam? God could have informed Adam of His plans, asked him to sign a consent form before the operation, and only then administered the anesthesia. Rabbi Yose's response, offered only when pressed, teaches that the first woman was essentially created twice. The first time, man and woman were created together, as described in Genesis 1:27: "Male and female He created them." In this verse, "male" is listed first, suggesting that Adam sat and watched how God created woman from tissue and mucous, blood and skin, bones and tendons. The sight leaves him nauseated, and thus he keeps his distance from the woman, showing no interest in her. We might conclude from this story that sometimes it is better not to witness a process, but to wait for the finished product. In any case, this is why God puts Adam to sleep before creating woman the second time, without informing anyone of His plans.

Why didn't Rabbi Yose offer this response to the matron initially? Perhaps he did not want to dishonor the Creator, who failed in His first creation of man and had to repeat His effort a second time. Presumably the tradition that the first woman was created twice was developed in order to account for the two versions of the creation story in Genesis 1 and 2. But this tradition, while appropriate for the beit midrash, was not necessarily suitable for an interfaith dialogue with a Roman matron. A religious Jew like Rabbi Yose would not want to make such a suggestion to a non-Jewish woman, so he tried first to answer her by means of a parable.

Surprisingly, the story of Rabbi Yose and the Roman matron does not end here. The matron, an affluent Roman who might be the wife of a senior government official in Tzippori, bares her heart to Rabbi Yose. She confides in him, telling him of her deepest source of personal disappointment: She did not marry the man for whom she was destined. As a child, she was betrothed to her mother's brother, who was not much older than she. But since they grew up together like brother and sister, he was not interested in her romantically. So when they reached marriageable age, he wed another woman instead. (This confirms what a psychologist once told me when I studied this story with him: "The exotic is the source of the erotic.") The matron clings to this ignominious and traumatic memory throughout her life, finally divulging it to Rabbi Yose. This story thus offers us a window into the range of Rabbi Yose's sympathetic nature as well as the breadth of his relationships with non-Jews. The episode also illustrates the general cultural milieu of Tzippori in the first few centuries of the common era. (I confess that every time I visit Tzippori and see the mosaic known as the "Mona Lisa of the Galilee" I imagine that I am looking at the Roman matron from this story, though I know this does not make sense chronologically.)

This matron figures in other stories about Rabbi Yose as well. She is portrayed as a complex figure – perhaps pagan, Christian, or Jewish by birth or by choice. She is constantly knocking on doors armed with challenging theological and exegetical questions. For instance, the Midrash relates the following story in the context of a discussion of Joseph and his encounter with Potiphar's wife:

> A Roman matron asked Rabbi Yose: Is it possible that Joseph, at seventeen years of age, with all the hot blood of youth, could act thus?
>
> Thereupon he took out the Book of Genesis and began to read the story of Reuben and Bilhah and the story of Judah and

> Tamar. He said to her: If the Bible did not suppress anything in the case of these, who were older and still in their father's home, how much more so in the case of Joseph, who was younger and his own master? (Genesis Rabba 87)

It is worth noting the suggestive parallels between Joseph (known as Yosef in Hebrew) and Rabbi Yose, and between Potiphar's Egyptian wife and the Roman matron. One exchange is presented as a seduction, and the other as an intellectual discourse – though perhaps Rabbi Yose and the matron's meeting also occurs in the privacy of the woman's home. The matron is suspicious of the biblical narrative. She does not believe a lad of seventeen could withstand the overtures of a beautiful Egyptian woman. The story strikes her as implausible. Rabbi Yose, in response, does something rather unconventional: He teaches Torah to a woman, and a non-Jewish one at that. He opens the Book of Genesis and reads her passages in which the Bible does not whitewash the sexual behaviors of other important figures: Reuben and Bilhah (Gen. 35) and Judah and Tamar (Gen. 38). He explains that if the Torah did not take pains to cover up the stories of Reuben and Judah – two adults who were still living under their father's roof or in close proximity when they committed such egregious offenses – surely the Torah would not cover up the story of a young boy hundreds of miles away from his father's watchful eye. There are many reasons for the Torah to censor the stories of Reuben and Judah, yet it did not; therefore, we can consider the Torah a credible source when it comes to documenting inappropriate sexual encounters. If the Torah relates that Joseph resisted an attempt at seduction, we can believe it.

This short text depicts Rabbi Yose as patient, levelheaded, and possessing an unusual bond with an aristocratic Roman woman. A similar characterization emerges from other tales of their encounters, with one notable exception. The Midrash relates the following story in the context of the verse "and Moses concealed his face" (Ex. 3:6), from the description of the burning bush:

> A Roman matron said to Rabbi Yose: My god is greater than your God.

> He said: How so?
>
> She said to him: When Moses beheld the serpent, immediately "he fled from before it" [Ex. 4:3]. But when God revealed Himself to Moses at the bush, he concealed his face.
>
> He said to her: May you exhale and die! When God revealed Himself to Moses at the bush, where could he flee? To heaven? To the sea? To land? Does it not say about our God, "Do I not fill heaven and earth, says the Lord" [Jer. 23:24]? Whereas in the case of your god, the serpent, a person can escape merely by running two or three paces. (Exodus Rabba 3)

Unlike most matron stories, this one begins not with a question of hers but with a cutting and provocative remark. The matron depicted as a pagan or Gnostic who is well versed in the Bible, suggests that the snake is preferable to the God of Israel. Rabbi Yose's response is uncharacteristically truculent. He curses the matron: "May you exhale and die!" He goes on to impress upon her, by way of scriptural exegesis, that the omnipresent God of Israel is profoundly different from the snake. This story appears in Exodus Rabba, a later composition than Genesis Rabba or Leviticus Rabba. Its literary style differs from that of the other stories we have seen thus far, and it depicts a very different relationship between Rabbi Yose and the matron. As such, it must be analyzed on its own terms.

We have seen that the literary approach, which takes careful note of the language used to tell these stories, affords its own opportunities for analysis. Though a narrative may be only loosely based on the reality it purports to depict, it may convey a strong moral message that transcends any era or context. Rabbi Lau's primary goal in presenting these stories is to draw out this message for his readers.

Since there can be no meaningful learning without new insight, I will now try to shed light on a story Rabbi Lau mentions only in passing in his discussion of Jewish life in Tzippori. Rabbi Lau analyzes the story as it appears in the Jerusalem Talmud, but I prefer to consider the version in Leviticus Rabba, since it is more complete and more stylistically refined. After all, literary considerations also influence one's choice of text to study.

> A story is told of a butcher in Tzippori who would feed Israel the flesh of improperly slaughtered animals and animals torn apart by beasts. Once, on the eve of Yom Kippur, he ate, drank, became intoxicated, went up on the roof, fell, and died. The dogs began licking his blood. People came and asked Rabbi Ḥanina: Is it permitted to remove his corpse from before the dogs?
>
> He answered: It is written, "And you shall be holy people unto Me; therefore you shall not eat any flesh that is torn by the beasts in the field; you shall cast it to the dogs" [Ex. 22:30]. This man robbed the dogs and also caused Israel to eat the flesh of improperly slaughtered animals and animals torn apart by beasts. Leave the dogs alone, for they are consuming that which is theirs. (Leviticus Rabba 5:6)

This story is about a butcher who deliberately sells non-kosher meat to the Jews of Tzippori. Do the people know what they are being sold? If they do, how can they permit the butcher to get away with this behavior, and how can the local rabbinic authority, Rabbi Ḥanina, keep silent? We must conclude that no one knew what was going on, and that this background information is communicated only after the fact, by way of exposition. The matter becomes known on the eve of Yom Kippur (or, in the Jerusalem Talmud's version, the eve of Shabbat), just before the beginning of the day on which the fate of all Jews is sealed for the coming year. The butcher falls off the roof after getting drunk at the pre-fast meal, and dogs gather to lick his blood. (This image may allude to the story of Jezebel in II Kings.) The strange conjunction of butcher and dogs at such a significant moment is not lost on Rabbi Ḥanina, who believes in the principle of reward and punishment and in the use of biblical verses as codes for understanding one's own circumstances. He concludes that the butcher is being punished for a sin that the community did not know about, one that has something to do with the feeding of flesh to dogs. The Bible teaches that the flesh of animals torn apart by other beasts should be fed to dogs. Rabbi Ḥanina thus concludes that the butcher is being publicly punished for the sin of feeding such flesh to the Jews of Tzippori. After all, as the Mishna teaches, "Whoever profanes the name of heaven in private will pay the penalty in public" (Mishna Avot 4:5).

Presumably if this incident had actually taken place, Rabbi Ḥanina would have found a way to deal with the corpse before the end of Yom Kippur, so the image of God would not have been publicly desecrated. But this text is interested not in what really happened, but in what we can learn from it, namely, that the principle of reward and punishment governs our world, and that the sages may understand reality by means of a close examination of biblical verses.

It seems clear to me that this type of literary analysis adds nuance and meaning to the story that would not be apparent in a more superficial reading. This is the power of the literary approach to rabbinic stories, which Rabbi Lau employs throughout this book. From story to story and from sage to sage, he offers us a fascinating and varied analysis of the period between the end of the Bar Kokhba revolt and the close of the Mishna, the period covered by *Pirkei Avot*. This tractate, the central repository of the sages' wisdom, serves as the key intertext to Rabbi Lau's series, guiding his hand and anchoring his analysis of the sages and their stories. As a person who loves humanity and works on its behalf for the sake of heaven, Rabbi Lau has drawn his readers closer to the Torah. When we conclude our reading of this volume, we might say to its author: "If you have learned much Torah, your reward will be great, and your Master can be relied upon to reward you for your labor." Would it be too much to ask for a fourth volume, dedicated to the talmudic rabbis of the Land of Israel during the third century, thereby magnifying and glorifying the Torah even further?

Part One

From Yavneh to Usha

Chapter One

The Establishment of the Beit Midrash in Usha

Rabbi Yoḥanan the Sandal Maker said: Every assembly that is for the sake of heaven will endure. Any assembly that is not for the sake of heaven will not endure. (*Mishna Avot* 4:11)

HISTORICAL BACKGROUND

In the wake of the Bar Kokhba revolt, the province of Judea became "Syria Palaestina," also known as Palestine.[1] The Jews were barred from settling in Jerusalem, which became "Aelia Capitolina," and a temple to Jupiter was built on the Temple Mount. The Jews found themselves economically and spiritually depressed. Jewish lands were expropriated, and heavy taxes were levied on the Jewish population. The Romans tried to sever any connection between the Jews and the Land of Israel.

1. S. Safrai, *In the Time of the Temple and in the Time of the Mishna* [Hebrew] (Jerusalem, 5754), vol. 1, 287–93. According to Safrai, Judea was a territory annexed to Syria and beholden to its procurator in Antioch even after the rebellion. He disagrees with those scholars who maintain that the Romans upgraded Judea and accorded it independent status. See, for instance, G. Alon, *The Jews in Their Land in the Talmudic Age*, trans. Gershon Levi (Cambridge: Harvard University Press, 1989).

For the first time since the return to Zion at the beginning of the Second Temple period, the Jewish population dwindled and the Jewish presence in Judea disappeared. Those who had not fallen in battle were taken captive or sold into slavery. Others sought escape from Roman rule and moved to Babylonia, leaving Judea desolate.[2]

In 138 CE Emperor Hadrian died and was succeeded by Antoninus Pius, who ruled until 161, during the height of the Pax Romana. Antoninus Pius never left Italy. He relied on the local rulers to administer their provinces and encouraged leaders from all parts of the empire to appeal to him directly.[3] A unit from the Sixth Legion, which had been stationed beside Megiddo, was transferred to Mauritius, a sign of relative peace in Judea.[4] Historical sources attest to the revocation of Hadrian's decree forbidding circumcision, and presumably other such decrees were also revoked during Antoninus' rule.[5]

THE ORDINATION OF SAGES DURING THE PERSECUTION

At the end of the Bar Kokhba revolt, the Jews began to fear that the chain of transmission of Jewish tradition would be forever broken. For hundreds of years the Torah had been passed down from one generation to another, but the persecution threatened to condemn the tradition to oblivion. The Talmud describes a dramatic moment in which Rabbi Yehuda ben Baba managed to safeguard the institution of rabbinic ordination:

2. A. Oppenheimer and M. D. Herr, "A Political and Administrative History from the End of the Bar Kokhba Revolt Until the Division of the Empire" [Hebrew], in *A History of the Land of Israel*, ed. M. D. Herr, vol. 5 (Jerusalem, 5745), 13–23.
3. M. Amit, *A History of the Roman Empire* [Hebrew] (Jerusalem, 5763), 500.
4. M. Avi-Yona, *In the Days of Rome and Byzantium* [Hebrew] (Jerusalem, 5722), 48.
5. See M. Stern, *Greek and Latin Authors on Jews and Judaism* [Hebrew] (Jerusalem, 1974–84), 622. Stern quotes a Roman legal document from the period which describes the revocation of the decree forbidding circumcision along with the imposition of a punishment on Jews who circumcised members of other faiths. Stern assumes that this is just one example of the revocation of all of Hadrian's decrees against the Jews. On the efforts to limit conversion to Judaism during this period, see L. H. Feldman, "Conversion and Syncretism" [Hebrew], in *A History of the Jews*, ed. M. Stern, vol. 1, *The Jewish Diaspora in the Hellenistic Roman World* (Tel Aviv, 5743), 205–7.

> The evil empire once enacted the following oppressive decrees against the Jewish people: Anyone who confers rabbinic ordination will be killed, and anyone who accepts ordination will be killed, and any town in which ordination is conferred will be destroyed, and the boundaries of a town within which ordination is conferred will be eradicated. What did Yehuda ben Baba do? He went and sat between two large mountains, and between two large cities, and between their Sabbath limit boundaries, between Usha and Shefaram, and he ordained five elders there. And they were: Rabbi Meir, Rabbi Yehuda, Rabbi Shimon, Rabbi Yose, and Rabbi Elazar ben Shamua. Rav Avya added that Rabbi Neḥemia was ordained there as well. When their enemies discovered them, Rabbi Yehuda ben Baba said to his students: My sons, run! The students said to him: Our teacher, what will become of you? He said to them: I am placed before my enemies like a rock that cannot be overturned. It was said: The soldiers did not leave the spot where they had found Rabbi Yehuda ben Baba until they had driven three hundred iron spears through him and made him into a sieve. (Sanhedrin 14a)

This story is primarily concerned not with the death of Rabbi Yehuda ben Baba, but with the preservation of the line of halakhic transmission.[6] The Talmud's term for ordination is *semikha*, which refers to the act of appointing a sage to a particular position[7] and authorizing him to adjudicate cases involving penalties.[8] Teachers need a way of entrusting their responsibility and knowledge to qualified students to enable the seamless continuity of the halakhic system. Without some

6. Rabbinic literature contains another account of Rabbi Yehuda ben Baba's death at the hands of the Romans. For more on this figure, see *Sages* II, Part Five, where I also discuss the story of his death as one of the ten martyrs.
7. See Y. Sanhedrin 1:2 (19a); H. Albeck, "Ordination and Appointment and the Court," *Tziyon* 8 (5703): 85–93.
8. This is clear from Rav Ashi's statement: "We ordain him in His name, we call him Rabbi, and we authorize him to judge cases involving penalties" (Y. Sanhedrin 1:2 [19a]). See S. Albeck, *The Courts in the Talmudic Period* [Hebrew] (Ramat Gan, 5741), 84–99.

form of ordination, there is no means of authorizing a new generation to teach and judge the public. Any rupture in the line of transmission endangers the entire Jewish future. Thus, Rabbi Yehuda ben Baba's willingness to sacrifice his own life for the sake of ensuring that a new generation of rabbis would be ordained was exceedingly consequential. He linked the generations one to another and enabled the next cohort of sages to renew the creative life of Torah even after their teachers were no longer with them.[9]

A parallel tradition relates that it was Rabbi Akiva who ordained these sages:

> Rabbi Akiva had twelve thousand pairs of disciples, from Gevat until Antiparis, and they all died during one period, because they did not treat each other with respect. And the world was barren [of Torah], until Rabbi Akiva came to our rabbis in the south and taught them Torah. [They were] Rabbi Meir, Rabbi Yehuda, Rabbi Yose, Rabbi Shimon and Rabbi Elazar ben Shamua, and it was these disciples who upheld Torah at that time. (Yevamot 62b)[10]

If we wish to harmonize these two traditions, we might say that Rabbi Akiva managed to pass on his teachings to these five disciples during the early days of the Bar Kokhba revolt, and after his death Rabbi

9. This story appears to be an aggadic tradition rather than a historical fact. After all, the Talmud also relates that Rabbi Akiva was the one who ordained Rabbi Meir. The setting of the story also seems unlikely. During the period of persecution these sages were active in Yavneh, not in the Galilee. Rabbi R. Margaliot suggests that the phrase "between Usha and Shefaram" refers to a historical period, that is, from the time the Sanhedrin was at Usha until it was in Shefaram, though this seems unconvincing. (See Margaliot, *Pearls of the Sea* [Hebrew], Sanhedrin 14a, sec. 3). S. Safrai asserts that this incident is related in rich, figurative language and has no historical grounding. See his *Time of the Temple and Time of the Mishna*, vol. 2, 604. Also see A. Oppenheimer, "Gedalia Alon Fifty Years On" [Hebrew], *Tziyon* 69 (5764), 473–74.
10. A parallel source in Genesis Rabba 61 relates that Rabbi Akiva ordained seven disciples, including Rabbi Yoḥanan the Sandal-Maker and Rabbi Eliezer ben Yaakov. See H. Licht, "On the Deaths of the Students of Rabbi Akiva," [Hebrew] in *Tura: A Collection of Articles in Jewish Philosophy*, ed. M. Ilai, presented to Professor Shlomo (Simon) Greenburg (Tel Aviv, 5749), 119–34.

Yehuda ben Baba ordained them. However, the Talmud elsewhere relates that Rabbi Akiva did not just teach Rabbi Shimon and Rabbi Meir, but also ordained them (Y. Sanhedrin 1:2 [19a]). So perhaps this ordination took place before the nation had accepted them as sages, and therefore they officially needed to be ordained again.[11] When Rabbi Yehuda ben Baba reordained them they were accepted, either because they had matured or because changed circumstances necessitated it.[12] We can conclude that all of these sources, even if they appear inconsistent with one another, attempt to link the sages of Yavneh to their successors in the Galilee.

THE SECRET ASSEMBLY IN THE RIMON VALLEY

The Jerusalem Talmud describes the first rabbinic assembly after the persecution:

> An incident is related of seven elders who came together to intercalate the year in the Valley of Rimon. Who were they? Rabbi Meir, Rabbi Yehuda, Rabbi Yose, Rabbi Shimon, Rabbi Neḥemia, Rabbi Eliezer ben Yaakov, and Rabbi Yoḥanan the Sandal-Maker. They said: How many gradations of rulings apply to holy things and heave offerings? Rabbi Meir said: Thirteen. Rabbi Yose said: Twelve. Rabbi Meir said: I heard thirteen from Rabbi Akiva. Rabbi Yoḥanạn the Sandal-Maker said: I served Rabbi Akiva standing up, whereas you served him sitting down. They said: Rabbi Yoḥanan the Sandal-Maker is really an Alexandrian. (Y. Ḥagiga 3:1 [78d])

11. *The Letter of Rav Sherira Gaon* cites a Babylonian tradition from Sanhedrin 14a according to which Rabbi Meir was ordained by Rabbi Akiva, but the people rejected him because he was too young. Also see *Dikdukei Sofrim* and Rashi's commentary on this passage. These sources suggest that ordination alone is not sufficient; a sage must also be accepted by the community.
12. S. Safrai argues that this source is far-fetched: "Who was Rabbi Yehuda ben Baba that his ordination would be regarded more highly than that of Rabbi Akiva?" See his *Time of the Temple and Time of the Mishna*, vol. 2, 604. The answer is not that Rabbi Yehuda ben Baba was regarded more highly, but rather that the historical circumstances had changed.

The intercalation of the year was a task reserved for the sages and served as a hallmark of their privileged status.[13] The assembly at Rimon attests to the sages' desire to return to routine and resume their responsibilities as leaders of the nation.

The Location

We cannot identify with certainty the location of this assembly. The Rimon Valley is thought to be located in the Lower Galilee, south of Beit Netofa, in Wadi Rimona, five kilometers northeast of Tzippori, the capital city of the Galilee.[14] But this identification is contradicted by the statement that "The year is intercalated only in Judea" (Sanhedrin 11b), which the tannaitic sage Ḥanania of Ono affirms: "If it was intercalated in the Galilee, it is ineffective." The Talmud's explanation of Ḥanania's statement is based on a biblical verse: "To His dwelling place you shall seek, and there you shall come" (Deut. 12:5). The Talmud explains, "Any matter you wish to learn should be sought out only in God's dwelling place." According to Shmuel Safrai, "It is very unlikely that the sages permitted themselves to intercalate the year in the Galilee so soon after the revolt. It is more likely that these sages, who were still largely unknown, did not dare to intercalate the year in the Galilee, but instead endangered their lives by gathering in Judea. So we should look for this Rimon Valley near the Rimon in Judea, northeast of Jerusalem and still marked on the Madaba Map."[15]

In contrast to Safrai's opinion, Ḥanania of Ono's testimony seems to support the view that the assembly took place in the Galilee, not in

13. Tannaitic literature often asserts that rabbinic ordination was a prerequisite to the sanctification of the new moon and the intercalation of the year. See Mishna Rosh HaShana 2:5–8, 4:1–4; Tosefta Sanhedrin 2:6.
14. S. Klein assumes that this was the location of the assembly based on references to the name Rimon in other sources. See Klein, *The Land of the Galilee* [Hebrew] (Jerusalem, 5727), 74.
15. S. Safrai, "The Locations of the Sanctification of the Moon and the Intercalation of the Year Before the Destruction" [Hebrew], *Tarbiz* 35 (5726), 29 (also in Safrai, *Time of the Temple, Time of the Mishna*, 250.) Also see Y. Schwartz, "The Land of Israel After the Suppression of the Bar Kokhba Revolt" [Hebrew], in *The Bar Kokhba Revolt: New Studies*, ed. A. Oppenheimer and U. Rappaport (Jerusalem, 5744), 219–20 and note 27.

Judea. Ḥanania lived at the end of Rabbi Akiva's lifetime and in the early days of Usha.[16] In parallel sources in the Tosefta and the Jerusalem Talmud, he claims that if it is impossible to intercalate the year in Judea, it is permitted to do so in the Galilee.[17] His testimony reflects a historical moment in which the sages sought to continue the line of halakhic transmission though there was no longer a Jewish presence in Judea.

The Time

The assembly took place shortly after Hadrian's final decrees and the beginning of Antoninus Pius' reign, presumably at the end of the fourth decade of the second century of the common era. A group of sages gathered in total secrecy to renew the institutions of leadership. Notably absent was Rabban Shimon ben Gamliel, who would become the next patriarch. Some of the participants had been ordained by Rabbi Akiva, including Rabbi Meir and Rabbi Shimon. Also present was Rabbi Yoḥanan the Sandal-Maker, Rabbi Akiva's right-hand man and the elder within this group.

The Atmosphere

The first discussion at the assembly was related to the laws of the Temple and the food eaten by the priests: "How many gradations of rulings apply to holy things and heave offerings?" The term "holy things" (*kodesh*) refers to meat that was designated for a sacrifice, portions of which were permitted to be eaten. The heave offering (*teruma*) is a share of the grain, vegetable, or fruit harvest that is given as a tithe to the priests. The question of "gradations of rulings" appears in the Mishna (Ḥagiga 3:4), where it is established that "There is an additional stringency in holy things as compared to heave offerings." The Talmud explains that the sages were more stringent with holy things than with heave offerings, because the meat of holy things could be eaten by anyone who brought a sacrifice,

16. We can date Ḥanania based on the few references to him in rabbinic literature. He cites a halakhic ruling that he received during the period of Rabbi Akiva's imprisonment (Gittin 66b, according to Rashi).
17. Tosefta Sanhedrin 2:13; Y. Nedarim 6:8 (40a).

whereas heave offerings were eaten exclusively by the priests, the sole experts in observing the elaborate rules of purity.

It seems strange that the sages who gathered to intercalate the year are preoccupied with the intricate question of gradations of rulings. One commentator explains that the sages' debate signals a desire to "elevate Jerusalem to the height of their joy."[18] But the numbers twelve and thirteen, which are offered as responses in the discussion, suggest a different understanding. These numbers, other experts explain, were part of the calculations concerning whether that year should contain twelve or thirteen months. The sages were trying to conceal the real issue at hand by using terms from the world of Temple worship – holy things and heave offerings – in order to prevent anyone eavesdropping on their discussion from reporting to the authorities about the true purpose of their assembly.[19]

Rabbi Akiva's spirit presides over this assembly, even though he is not physically present. The discussion is led by Rabbi Meir and Rabbi Yose, who try to anchor their views in their teacher's traditions. Rabbi Yoḥanan the Sandal-Maker intercedes and tries to put the young Rabbi Meir in his place: "I served Rabbi Akiva standing up, whereas you served him sitting down." He intends to prove that he spent more time in Rabbi Akiva's beit midrash and can therefore more reliably repeat his teachings. The other members of the assembly respond that "Rabbi Yoḥanan the Sandal-Maker is really an Alexandrian." What do they mean?

Rabbi Yoḥanan the Sandal-Maker did not grow up in Yavneh or its environs. He was a foreign transplant from Alexandria. The residents of Israel, including the sages, were not particularly enamored of these new arrivals. They used the term Alexandrian to refer to someone arrogant, coarse, boastful, loud, and impatient.[20] It is significant that they applied this derogatory label to Rabbi Yoḥanan even at a time when

18. This is the explanation of Rabbi Moshe Margalit, the Penei Moshe, in his commentary on the Jerusalem Talmud.
19. This opinion was expressed by Rabbi R. Margaliot in *Really an Alexandrian: A Book in Memory of Rabbi Yitzhak Isaac HaLevi*, ed. M. Auerbach (Benei Brak, 5724), 214–18.
20. S. Lieberman, "So It Was and So It Will Be: The Jews of the Land of Israel and the Jews of the World During the Period of the Mishna and Talmud," in *The Land of Israel in the Period of the Mishna and the Talmud* [Hebrew] (Jerusalem, 5751), 332.

the population in Israel was sparse and every additional Jewish resident counted. On several other occasions when the Mishna deplores the lack of refinement among the "Babylonians," the Talmud (that is, the Babylonian Talmud) clarifies the situation: "They were not Babylonians but rather Alexandrians; but since they [the sages] hated the Babylonians, they referred to the Alexandrians this way" (Yoma 66b; Menaḥot 100a). As this source suggests, the sages barely tolerated the Alexandrians, but they truly detested the Babylonians.

Rabbi Yoḥanan the Sandal-Maker was one of Rabbi Akiva's few surviving original students. We have already seen that he transmitted teachings from the period of Rabbi Akiva's incarceration at the hands of the Romans.[21] Another source links him with Rabbi Elazar ben Shamua in the period after the Bar Kokhba revolt:

> An incident is told of Rabbi Elazar ben Shamua and Rabbi Yoḥanan the Sandal-Maker, who were going to Netzivin to study Torah with Rabbi Yehuda ben Beteira. When they got to Sidon, they remembered the Land of Israel and raised their eyes, and the tears flowed. They rent their garments and recited this verse: "and you shall possess it and dwell in it. And you shall take heed to do all the statutes and ordinances" [Deut. 11:31–32]. They said: The duty of dwelling in the Land of Israel is equivalent to all the other commandments in the Torah. Thereupon they returned to the Land of Israel. (Sifrei, Deuteronomy 80)

At the end of the revolt, many residents of the Land of Israel made their way abroad.[22] The midrashic tradition in the Sifrei tells of two disciples of Rabbi Akiva who hesitate at the border. They find that they cannot bear to leave the land, so they return to Israel. Rabbi Yoḥanan the Sandal-Maker joins the other surviving disciples of Rabbi Akiva who assembled after the persecution and sought to renew Jewish life, first by intercalating the year, a symbol of the revival of the Sanhedrin.

21. See *Sages* II, Part Four.
22. Ibid., Part Five.

Morsels of Torah

The Jerusalem Talmud continues its account of the assembly in the Rimon Valley:

> They arose from their meeting with a kiss. And whoever in the group did not have a cloak, his fellow cut his cloak in half and gave it to him. And why did they do so? Because each of them interpreted the following verse in seven different ways: "Let me sing for my beloved a love song concerning his vineyard: my beloved has a vineyard on a very fertile hill" [Is. 5:1]. And they praised the last of them, because he had found a fine interpretation of the verse. They said it was Rabbi Shimon ben Yoḥai. And why was it so urgent? For they interpreted the verse as follows: "You shall make for yourself no molten gods" [Ex. 34:17]. What is written after that? "The feast of unleavened bread you shall observe" [Ex. 34:18]. They said: Whoever has sufficient grounds to intercalate the year and does not do so is as if he worships idols. (Y. Ḥagiga 3:1 [78d])

The Jerusalem Talmud offers us a glimpse of a ceremony that took place under trying circumstances but with all the requisite attention to detail. Several rules govern the intercalation of the year. It may be done only by the Sanhedrin, and only in the presence of the patriarch. It must be a festive event in which the sages wear their official garments and publicize the intercalation at the end. At this assembly the participants tried to attire themselves appropriately, but they were missing several cloaks. So they divided these garments among one another by cutting them.[23] It all happened with great haste. When they concluded, "they arose from the meeting with a kiss," on good terms with one another.

The Jerusalem Talmud asks about the urgency of intercalating the year at this point. The answer involves the exegesis of two adjacent but seemingly unrelated verses from Exodus 34. One verse says, "You shall make for yourself no molten gods," and the next says, "The feast

23. See A. Ehrlich, "Another Chapter in the Creation of Midrash and *Aggada*" [Hebrew], in *Teuda: A Collection of Studies of the Ḥayyim Rosenberg School of Jewish Studies*, ed. Y. Hoffman, 16–17 (5761).

of unleavened bread you shall observe." The disparate verses are linked exegetically: Anyone who can intercalate the year but does not do so (and therefore fails to observe Passover on time) is regarded as if he worships idols. In the parallel source in the Babylonian Talmud, Rabbi Elazar ben Azaria, a leader of the previous generation at Yavneh, says that anyone who spurns the festivals is regarded as an idol worshipper. Perhaps the sages who gathered in the Rimon Valley were familiar with this interpretation and reworked it to address the issue at hand.

As the Talmud relates, the sages went on to interpret a verse from Isaiah that introduces a parable about a vineyard:

> Let me sing for my beloved a love song concerning his vineyard: My beloved has a vineyard on a very fertile hill. He broke the ground, cleared it of stones, and planted it with choice vines; he built a watchtower inside it, and he even hewed a wine press in it, for he hoped it would yield grapes; but it yielded only wild grapes. And now, you dwellers of Jerusalem and men of Judah, you be the judges between me and my vineyard: What more could have been done for my vineyard that I failed to do in it? (Is. 5:1–4)

This is a song that starts joyously and ends bitterly, and the sages quote it with broken hearts. Assembled at the end of the period of persecution, they remember the glory days of the vineyard at Yavneh and lament the high hopes of the previous generation, which had dreamt of a Jerusalem of gold. They know they must rebuild the Torah world after the destruction and replant the withered vineyard, for anyone who can intercalate the year and does not do so is regarded as if he worships idols.

Rabbi Shimon bar Yoḥai displays his exegetical prowess. He is the last sage to interpret the verse under discussion, and his exegesis elicits praise from his colleagues. According to some commentaries, he was crowned head of the sages, as per the words of the famous song of the kabbalist Rabbi Shimon ben Lavi: "Bar Yoḥai – you were anointed, happy are you."[24] But it seems more likely that his colleagues were

24. H. Kolitz, *Ben HaAliya: Rabbi Shimon bar Yoḥai and His Teachings* [Hebrew] (Jerusalem, 5746), 42–49.

simply praising him for shedding light on the parable of the vineyard. His words bring the assembly to a close.

The Immortalization of the Assembly

The Jerusalem Talmud goes on to describe the sages' attempt to immortalize their assembly:

> When they were ready to leave, they said: Come and let us leave a monument to what we have done. And there was a marble stone, and each of them took a nail and hammered it in, and the nail went into the stone as into a piece of dough, and to this day it is called "the nailed marble." (Y. Ḥagiga 3:1 [78d])

The sages recognized the significance of their assembly. They knew that the responsibility for the future spiritual leadership of the Jewish people rested squarely on their shoulders.

THE ASSEMBLY AT USHA

Though the pernicious imperial decrees had been revoked, the people acclimated to the new reality only gradually. They were allowed to gather to study Torah, to intercalate the year, and to fulfill mitzvot, and slowly they resumed their routine. At this point, the leaders of the generation assembled to gather information and establish religious norms for the new era:

> At the end of the great persecution, our teachers met together in Usha, and they were Rabbi Yehuda, Rabbi Neḥemia, Rabbi Meir, Rabbi Yose, Rabbi Shimon bar Yoḥai, Rabbi Eliezer ben Rabbi Yose HaGlili, and Rabbi Eliezer ben Yaakov. They sent a message to the elders of the Galilee, saying: Whoever has learned, let him come and teach. And whoever has not learned, let him come and learn. They came together and studied and took all the necessary steps. When the time came to depart, they said: We cannot leave a place where we have been welcomed without imparting a blessing. They gave Rabbi Yehuda the honor of speaking first, because he belonged to the place, not because he was the most

> learned among them. For it is a man's place that confers distinction upon him. (Song of Songs Rabba 2:3)

Selecting the Location

The location of this assembly was not chosen at random. Usha was the home of Rabbi Yehuda bar Ilai, whom the Romans regarded as an ally, or at least as a moderate. We will consider him more fully in the pages that follow. Suffice it to say that Usha emerged unscathed from the revolt and the subsequent persecution. It was the first place to which the Sanhedrin relocated after Yavneh, as the Talmud attests:

> The Divine Presence journeyed ten journeys... and correspondingly the Sanhedrin was exiled... from Jerusalem to Yavneh, and from Yavneh to Usha. (Rosh HaShana 31a)[25]

When the fighting subsided and the decrees of persecution were repealed, the surviving leaders gathered in a stable location and proclaimed a return to Torah and rabbinic leadership. Their pronouncement reflects the enormity of their distress: "Whoever has learned, let him come teach." The paucity of qualified sages was a matter of dire concern. There was grave fear that the tradition might be lost, so the sages sought to marshal all the resources of knowledge from the preceding generations. We do not know much about the conference itself, but the midrash relates that at the closing session, permission to speak was transferred from sage to sage. Each sage offered his own words of

25. According to the printed text of the Talmud, the Sanhedrin moved from *Usha* to Yavneh and then returned to Usha. Academic scholars have corrected this version, deleting the duplication of relocations because it makes no sense. They base their emendation on several manuscripts. For another view, see D. Henshke, "From Usha to Yavneh: The Development of a Tradition" [Hebrew], *JSIJ* 1 (2002): 1–9. Henshke argues that we cannot ignore the printed version, because it is supported by textual evidence. He surveys versions of the Talmud, liturgical poems, commentaries, and material evidence, but draws no historical conclusions. There seems to be no evidence of a reawakening of Jewish leadership in Judea after the Usha period, so I concur with the version in which the Sanhedrin moved from Judea to the Galilee and then stayed there.

blessing. Their speeches were full of political overtones reflecting the new reality in which the sages found themselves.

Rabbi Yehuda's Homily

We have a record of the blessings offered by the various sages, beginning with Rabbi Yehuda bar Ilai, who was the local rabbinic authority and the host of the assembly. The midrash notes that he was not the greatest sage present, but the fact that they were in his native environs conferred on him the privilege of speaking first:

> Rabbi Yehuda came forward and expounded, "Now Moses used to take the tent and pitch it outside the camp, some distance from the camp" [Ex. 33:7]. The word "distance" is used here, and elsewhere it says, "Yet there shall be distance between you and it, about two thousand cubits by measure" [Josh. 3:4]. Just as the word "distance" in one text means two thousand cubits, this is what it means in the other text. The text goes on to say not "and it came to pass that everyone who sought Moses," but rather "and it came to pass that everyone who sought the Lord." From this we learn that receiving scholars is like receiving the Divine Presence. And you, our brothers, our teachers, eminent in knowledge of Torah, if some of you have taken the trouble to come ten miles or twenty or thirty or forty miles to hear the Torah taught, you may rest assured that the Holy One, Blessed Be He, will not withhold your reward in this world and the next! (Song of Songs Rabba 2:3)

This homily speaks directly to the situation in which the sages find themselves. Those who gather at Usha feel as if they are in exile. They are accustomed to gathering at the beit midrash in Yavneh, where Rabbi Akiva and his students were the locals. It is degrading to find themselves exiled to a place that had no role in the revolt against Rome. Rabbi Yehuda, sensitive to their frame of mind, begins his homily with a reference to Moses' retreat from the camp in order to hear the voice of God in the Tent of Meeting. He appeals to his guests' sense of displacement by referring to the need to exile oneself in order to receive the Divine Presence. He humbly tells his guests that they have come to Usha not to be near him, but to be near Torah. Usha was a place where Torah survived the persecution, which is why the sages have gathered there. Rabbi Yehuda is aware of the pain accompanying their arrival at this place, and he thanks the sages for subjecting themselves to exile so as to make their way to his place of Torah.

Rabbi Neḥemia's Homily

> Rabbi Neḥemia came forward and expounded, "An Ammonite or a Moabite shall not enter into the assembly of the Lord" [Deut. 24:4]. It has been taught: Two great peoples were excluded from entering the assembly of the Lord. Why? "Because they did not meet you with bread and water" [Deut. 24:5]. Now did Israel require them at that time? All forty years that [the people of] Israel were in the wilderness, did the well not come up for them and the manna descend for them, and were quails not always provided for them, and did the clouds of glory not surround them, and did the pillar of cloud not journey before them? And yet you say, "Because they did not meet them with bread and water"? Rabbi Elazar said: Basic courtesy requires that one who has come from a journey be met with bread and water. See now how God punished these two peoples. It is written in the Torah, "An Ammonite or a Moabite shall not enter into the assembly of the Lord." But as for you, men of Usha, who have put your food, your drink, and your couches at the service of our teachers, the Holy One, Blessed Be He, will requite you with a good reward. (Song of Songs Rabba 2:3)

Rabbi Neḥemia, the first of the guests to speak, responds to their host. We know very little about this figure. The Jerusalem Talmud (Ta'anit 4:2 [68a]) relates that a genealogical scroll found in Jerusalem lists Rabbi Neḥemia as a descendant of the biblical Neḥemia, who moved to the Land of Israel to serve as a local governor in Judea in the fifth century BCE. In any case, Rabbi Neḥemia refers to that period in Israel's history in which the people wandered through the desert without need for bread or water, because they were provided for by the manna, the well, and the clouds of God's glory. He seems to be suggesting that had the sages truly merited, they would not have needed to rely on the good graces of the people of Usha. Rabbi Neḥemia pays his respects to his hosts, but only halfheartedly. For him Usha is merely a way station. He longs to return to the days of the manna, the well, and the clouds of glory.

Rabbi Meir's Homily

> Rabbi Meir then came forward and expounded, "There was an old prophet living in Bethel" [1 Kings 13:11]. Who was he? He was Amaziah the priest of Bethel. (Song of Songs Rabba 2:3)

Rabbi Meir seeks to conjoin two historical personalities. He identifies the old prophet from the days of Jeroboam son of Nebat, who dwelled in Bethel while prophesying the city's destruction, with the figure of Amaziah, the priest of Bethel who sought to extradite the prophet Amos to Jeroboam II because of his prophecies about the destruction of Israel (Amos 7). Over two hundred years separate the two figures whom Rabbi Meir conflates.

No sooner has Rabbi Meir opened his mouth than Rabbi Yose cries out from the audience, insisting that Rabbi Meir clarify the message he seeks to deliver:

> Meir, there are broken eggs here [i.e., you have confused matters]. Who was he? He was Jonathan son of Gershom son of Moses, as it says, "Jonathan son of Gershom son of Manasseh" [Judges 18:30]. The letter *nun* in Manasseh is suspended, as if to indicate that if he were virtuous, he would be regarded as the son of Moses [Moshe in Hebrew, which is spelled like Menashe (Manasseh) but without the *nun*], and if not, as the son of Manasseh. (Song of Songs Rabba 2:3)

According to Rabbi Yose, the old prophet quoted in 1 Kings is not Amaziah but rather Jonathan son of Gershom son of Manasseh from the

Book of Judges. But this identification, too, contains a historical fallacy, since this figure lived two hundred years earlier.

Rabbi Meir continues his homily despite Rabbi Yose's interruption. He explains that the element common to both stories is the eating of "deceitful bread."[26] Rabbi Meir comments:

> Does it not then stand to reason? If this man, who deceived the other and gave him deceitful bread to eat, was nonetheless privileged to have the holy spirit rest upon him, how much more do you, our brothers, men of Usha, who have received our teachers with your food and drink and lodging, deserve to be requited by the Holy One, Blessed Be He, with a good reward! (Song of Songs Rabba 2:3)

Rabbi Meir's words reflect his sense of personal affront at having to eat "deceitful bread." As a leading disciple of Rabbi Akiva, he is a man of Yavneh, yet he is forced to come to Usha to take succor from the residents of the Galilee. His blessing is bittersweet.

Rabbi Eliezer ben Yaakov's Homily

All of these homilies bespeak the sense of exile experienced by Rabbi Akiva's disciples when they visit Usha. But Rabbi Eliezer ben Yaakov, the last to speak, voices a very different sentiment. He focuses on his sense that "this day you have become a people." He claims that the vantage point of the sages enables them to look to the future:

> Rabbi Eliezer ben Yaakov then came forward and expounded: "And Moses and the priests and the Levites spoke unto all of Israel, saying: Keep silent, and hear, O Israel – this day you have become a people" [Deut. 27:9]. Was it on that day that they received the Torah? Hadn't they already received the Torah forty years earlier? How, then, can you say, "This day"? It teaches you that since

26. For more on the conflation of the old prophet with the priest at Bethel, and on the notion of "deceitful bread," see N. Samet, "Between 'Eat Bread There' and 'Don't Eat Bread There'" [Hebrew], *Masekhet* 2 (5764): 167–81.

> Moses had repeated the Torah to them and they had received it gladly, it was considered as if they had received it that very day from Mount Sinai. Therefore, it is said, "this day you have become a people to the Lord your God." To you, then, our brothers, men of Usha, who have received our teachers so gladly, how much more does this apply! (Song of Songs Rabba 2:3)

Rabbi Yoḥanan the Sandal-Maker, who participated in the assembly in the Rimon Valley, is not mentioned among the sages at the conference at Usha, suggesting that he passed away between the two events. Alternatively, his statement in *Pirkei Avot* (4:11), "Any assembly for the sake of heaven is destined to endure," may refer to this assembly at Usha, whose sole purpose was to restore Torah to its proper place and continue Jewish life in the Land of Israel. It is also worth noting the absence of Rabban Shimon ben Gamliel, who would soon come to Usha to restore the patriarchy. Apparently he had not yet arrived.

This official gathering ushers us into a new era in which the Galilee becomes the center of Jewish leadership. With the external political front finally calm, the sages can turn their attention inward. We will take advantage of this calm equilibrium to listen closely to the voices that came forth from the beit midrash.

Part Two

Gates of Wisdom – The Heart of the Usha Generation

The Founding Generation at Usha		Rabbi Yehuda HaNasi
138–161	161–192	192–220
The Restoration of the Nation after the Destruction Antoninus Pius	The Stabilization of the Center at Usha Marcus Aurelius and Commodus	Autonomy in the Galilee Severus

Chapter Two

Historical and Political Background

THE CITY, THE TOWN, THE VILLAGE

Throughout the talmudic period, Jewish society was primarily agricultural. At one end of the spectrum was the landowning elite, which exerted influence with the Roman authorities; at the other end were the landless and impoverished masses dependent on others for support.[1]

Jews lived in cities, towns, and villages. The city was a large polis; the town was an agricultural community consisting of several hundred families; and the village was a small settlement with just a few households.

The few Jewish cities of the time included Tiberias, Tzippori, and Lod. At first, Jews were reluctant to settle in Tiberias lest they build their homes atop ancient graves.[2] Only after Rabbi Shimon bar Yoḥai purified the city could Tiberias absorb the Jewish population that had fled Judea.[3] In time it became the most important Jewish settlement in the Land of

1. Y. Cohen, *Episodes in the History of the Tannaitic Period* [Hebrew] (Jerusalem, 5738), 81–142.
2. Josephus, *Antiquities of the Jews* XVIII.
3. See below for the section on Rabbi Shimon bar Yoḥai's emergence from the cave.

Israel: It received the status of a Roman "colony" and became the new site of the Sanhedrin and other central institutions.[4] Tzippori, inhabited by Jews since before the Temple period, was home to the wealthiest sectors of society. According to Josephus, the residents of Tzippori cooperated with the Romans during the Great Revolt.[5] Finally, Lod was a major Jewish center during the Yavneh period, and it probably housed the Sanhedrin for a time after the Bar Kokhba revolt.[6] Although it was not destroyed during the revolt or the ensuing persecutions, there is no evidence of an active Jewish center at Lod after Bar Kokhba. It was not until the tenure of Rabbi Yehuda HaNasi that the Jewish community in Lod become significant again.[7]

In the other cities, the population was mixed, with a non-Jewish majority governing the major communal institutions.[8] Most Jews lived in agricultural towns, which had active communal institutions. The sages, too, generally lived in towns, near the synagogue, beit midrash, and courts. The Mishna distinguishes between villages and towns:

> Which is a large town? Whichever contains ten idlers. Fewer than this, it is a village. (Mishna Megilla 1:3)

The term "idlers" refers to those who occupied themselves with communal affairs but were otherwise unemployed. These "idlers" supervised the judicial system, administered a communal charity fund, and dealt with other public matters.[9] Each town also had an educational system, whose teachers were paid by a communal fund. According to a decree instituted by Rabbi Yehoshua ben Gamla at the end of the Second Tem-

4. A. Oppenheimer, *The Galilee in the Time of the Mishna* [Hebrew] (Jerusalem, 5751), 73–74.
5. Josephus, *The Jewish War* III. In his autobiography, Josephus speaks of the pro-Roman orientation of the inhabitants of Tzippori. Also see Oppenheimer, *Galilee in the Time of the Mishna*, 17 note 5.
6. S. Klein, *The Land of Judea* [Hebrew] (Tel Aviv, 5699), 154–61.
7. Y. Schwartz, "The Demographic History of Southern Judea After the Bar Kokhba Revolt" (PhD diss., Hebrew University of Jerusalem, 5741), 71–87.
8. Cohen, *Episodes in the History of the Tannaitic Period*, 125.
9. S. Safrai, *A History of the Jewish People in the Second Temple Period*, vol. 2 [Hebrew] (Tel Aviv, 5730), 469–78.

ple period, every community was obligated to have a school system.[10] In the classical world, only citizens attended school; the majority of the population had no access to educational institutions. In contrast, the Jewish school was open to all strata of society, regardless of political orientation or social status.

The inhabitants of each town were united by their shared obligations to supervise public services, collect taxes for communal purposes, and organize religious activities in the synagogues on Shabbat and holidays, chiefly Torah and *haftara* readings and a sermon given by the local sage.[11] Courts existed only in towns whose population exceeded a certain number, though this figure was subject to debate among the Usha sages:

> And how many should there be in a city such that it is eligible for a Sanhedrin? One hundred twenty. Rabbi Neḥemia says: Two hundred thirty, corresponding to the rulers of tens [so that each judge rules at least ten people].[12] (Mishna Sanhedrin 1:6)

The quality of Jewish life in the villages was much poorer than that in the towns, and any educational system was minimal.[13] The villages also lacked the towns' Jewish communal institutions. Until the period of the Great Assembly, it was customary to read the Torah in the towns on Mondays and Thursdays, when the markets were open and the villagers would come to town to buy and sell. The Mishna in Tractate Megilla teaches that the schedule of weekly Torah readings was determined by the market schedule. The courts, too, met on Mondays and Thursdays, a schedule dating back at least to Ezra.[14] According to

10. Ibid., 479–500.
11. S. Safrai, *At the End of the Second Temple and the Mishnaic Period* [Hebrew] (Jerusalem, 5743), 148–49.
12. This figure refers only to the men, not to all the inhabitants of the town. So a few hundred men or one hundred to two hundred families would suffice for a settlement to qualify as a town.
13. Z. Safrai, "The Village During the Period of the Mishna and Talmud" [Hebrew], in *A Nation and Its History*, ed. M. Stern, vol. 1 (Jerusalem, 5742), 193. Safrai argues that while this is an accurate description of village life in general, there were also some well-established villages whose inhabitants were more affluent.
14. Mishna Ketubot 1:1.

Ze'ev Safrai, this description of the rhythms of economic and religious life characterizes the Hellenistic period but not the Roman one, which was a time of increased prosperity.[15] Still, it is possible that practices serving a specific function during the Hellenistic era became enshrined as customs and thus survived into the Roman period as well.

FRIEND, SAGE, AND COMMONER

The social fabric changed significantly after the period of persecution. The Jewish community was no longer divided into Pharisees, Sadducees, Essenes, and other sects. The religious leadership ruled that the halakha would follow Beit Hillel and sought to foster unity "so that dispute should not proliferate in Israel."[16] Rabban Gamliel spearheaded this effort at Yavneh. He worked to create norms of Jewish conduct that would be binding upon all Jews.[17] Excluded from these norms were the Jewish Christians, who had already parted ways with the Jewish mainstream.

Jews were not divided into sects or denominations, but the sages ranked the religious status of various sectors of society, with the sages on top and the "commoners" or unlearned people (*amei ha'aretz*) at the bottom. Most Jews could be found somewhere in between. The commoners did not constitute an organized social class, nor did they come from a specific socioeconomic sector. They encompassed both rich and poor, and the residents of towns as well as villages. They regarded themselves as Jews and observed most (but not all) of the commandments. But they scorned the intellectual elite and the supreme value placed on Torah study.[18] For example, Rabbi Eliezer ben Hyrcanus' father, a wealthy villager living on the outskirts of Jerusalem, disinherited him because he wanted to learn Torah. Wealthy commoners like Hyrcanus worked the land and maintained the basic standards of Jewish observance. For the most part, they did not observe the purity laws and only pretended to

15. Z. Safrai, *Time of the Temple and Time of the Mishna*, vol. 2, 183–85.
16. S. Safrai, *History of the Jewish People in the Second Temple Period*, 382–405. Safrai views the establishment of the halakha in accordance with Hillel as a process that spanned the entire Yavneh period, from Rabbi Yoḥanan ben Zakkai until Rabbi Akiva.
17. See *Sages* 1, Part Two.
18. Cohen, *Episodes in the History of the Tannaitic Period*, 81–105.

meet the tithing requirements, which would cut into their earnings at a time when they already had to pay Roman taxes.

Sages of various generations sought to define the commoner:

> Who is considered a commoner? Anyone who does not take pains to eat his unconsecrated foods (*ḥullin*) in a state of purity. These are the words of Rabbi Meir.
>
> The sages say: Anyone who does not tithe his produce properly....
>
> The rabbis taught: Who is considered a commoner? Anyone who does not recite the *Shema* prayer in the evening and the morning. These are the words of Rabbi Eliezer.
>
> Rabbi Yehoshua says: Anyone who does not put on tefillin.
>
> Ben Azzai says: Anyone who has no tzitzit on his garment.
>
> Rabbi Natan says: Anyone who has no mezuza at the entrance to his home.
>
> Rabbi Natan bar Yosef says: Anyone who has sons and does not raise them to study Torah.
>
> Others say: Even if one read the Torah and studied Mishna but did not serve Torah scholars, he is a commoner. (Berakhot 47b)

Rabbi Meir has the strictest standard. He holds that anyone who does not eat even unconsecrated foods in a state of purity is regarded as a commoner. Presumably he also agrees with the final view, that even someone who can read the Torah and study Mishna but does not serve Torah scholars is considered a commoner.[19] The sages who disagree with him claim that commoners are those who do not tithe properly. Although these Jews observe the tithing requirement, they cut corners whenever possible.

The second half of the source quotes sages from the previous generation, those who were active at Yavneh. They are concerned with mitzvot between man and God: reciting the *Shema*, affixing a mezuza,

19. We will discuss the identification of Rabbi Meir with the viewpoint attributed to "others" when we consider this sage in his own right.

wearing tzitzit. The final sage quoted, Rabbi Natan, argues that it all comes down to education. Even if a person follows Jewish law strictly, he is still regarded as a commoner if he does not raise his children to study Torah. Eventually, the notion of a commoner became a general description of anyone who does not observe the mitzvot fully, regardless of his theology.[20]

At the opposite end of the spectrum we find the sages. It is worth noting the change in their status from the time of the Second Temple to the time of the Mishna. During the Second Temple period, the sages and those regarded as "fellows" (*ḥaverim*) were not one and the same. Rather, the fellows constituted an extreme sect with strict entrance requirements. To be considered a fellow, a person had to eat even unconsecrated foods in a state of purity. That is, even when eating ordinary food (i.e., not food that had been consecrated to the Temple), a fellow made sure he was ritually pure. In contrast, most Jews would not pay attention to their purity status before sitting down to a meal; they would concern themselves with ritual purity only when entering the Temple environs or eating of the sacrificial offerings.[21]

During the mishnaic period, sages and fellows gradually became synonymous.[22] A rabbinic tradition describes the requirements for becoming a fellow:

> He who takes upon himself four things is accepted as a fellow (*ḥaver*): not to give heave offering and tithes to a priest who is a

20. E. E. Urbach, *The Sages: Their Beliefs and Opinions* [Hebrew] (Jerusalem, 5731), 571.
21. Maimonides writes in his *Mishneh Torah* that "All that is written in the Torah and in tradition with regard to the laws of purity and impurity applies only to matters of the Temple… but unconsecrated foods carry no such prohibitions" (*Laws of Impure Foods* 15:8).
22. See A. Bickler, *The Galilean Commoner* [Hebrew] (Jerusalem, 5728), in which the author attempts to prove that the phrase "commoner" belongs to the Usha period. As many have noted, Bickler challenged the dominant Christian view that Jesus rose against the Pharisees in support of the commoners. See G. Alon, *The History of the Jews in the Land of Israel* [Hebrew] (Tel Aviv: HaKibbutz HaMe'uḥad, 5714), vol. 1, 318–21. In my opinion the reality is much simpler: The people were divided, then as now, into those who thirsted for knowledge and spirituality and those who hungered for material gain.

> commoner; not to prepare foods requiring conditions of purity for a commoner; to eat unconsecrated food in a state of purity. (Tosefta Demai 2:2)

Several sources from this period describe prerequisites for becoming a fellow,[23] but we have no evidence of any ceremony or ritual to mark one's change in status. Presumably these descriptions were intended to emphasize the separate social status of the fellows, who constituted a class apart.

THE RELATIONSHIP BETWEEN SAGES AND COMMONERS

A sage or fellow who ate unconsecrated food in a state of purity could not eat in the home of a commoner, nor could he host him in his home. Thus society became increasingly stratified, with the sages set apart from the rest of the people. Rabbinic sources cite a disagreement about the relationship between these two social classes:

> One who undertakes to be trustworthy is one who tithes what he eats, sells, and purchases, and does not accept the hospitality of a commoner. These are the words of Rabbi Meir. And the sages say: One who accepts the hospitality of a commoner is trustworthy. Rabbi Meir said to them: If he is not trustworthy concerning himself, should he be trustworthy concerning me? They said to him: Householders have never refrained from eating with one another, yet the produce in their own homes is properly tithed. (Tosefta Demai 2:2)

Rabbi Meir held that the sages and commoners could not intermingle. Anyone who undertook to be trustworthy (that is, to be a fellow) would not serve untithed produce, nor would he trust that everything he bought had already been tithed. Most important, he would decline the hospitality of a commoner. But the rest of the sages disagreed, trusting a fellow even if he accepts a commoner's hospitality. Upon hearing their dissenting view, Rabbi Meir responds with a counterargument,

23. Cohen, *Episodes in the History of the Tannaitic Period*, 83–84.

but the sages cite the tradition that "householders have never refrained from eating with one another...." This is an important tradition. It is the householders – those who are neither sages nor commoners – whose behavior determines the social norms, and not the members of one extreme group or another.

One clear marker of the relationship between sages and commoners is whether they marry off their children to one another. Rabbi Meir characteristically emerges as the extreme voice among the sages, seeking to separate those who learn Torah from those who do not:

> Rabbi Meir said: If anyone marries off his daughter to a commoner, it is as if he tied her up and put her before a lion. For just as a lion attacks its prey and devours it without shame, so too a commoner beats his wife and cohabits with her without shame. (Pesaḥim 49b)

The following *baraita*, though unattributed to any particular sage, describes the marital practices of the time:

> A man should always be prepared to sell everything he owns so he can marry the daughter of a Torah scholar. If he cannot find a daughter of a Torah scholar, he should marry the daughter of one of the great men of the generation. If he cannot find a daughter of one of the great men of the generation, he should marry the daughter of one of the community leaders. If he cannot find a daughter of one of the community leaders, he should marry the daughter of one of the charity collectors. If he cannot find a daughter of one of the charity collectors, he should marry the daughter of one of the schoolteachers. But he should not marry the daughter of a commoner, because they are vermin and their wives are insects, and regarding their daughters it is said, "Accursed is one who lies with any animal" [Deut. 27:21]. (Pesaḥim 49b)

Despite these rigid social distinctions, many other sources attest to everyday interactions between sages and commoners. For instance, Tractate

Demai deals with how fellows are to conduct themselves in the market, at home, at work, and anywhere they are surrounded by those who do not adhere to the same religious standards, particularly with regard to dietary restrictions. Several sources such as the following describe the peaceful coexistence between sages and commoners:

> If the wife of a fellow left the wife of a commoner milling in her house, and the mill ceased grinding [signifying that the commoner's wife ceased working], the house becomes impure. If the mill did not cease grinding, the house becomes impure only up to any place to which she can extend her hand and touch. If there were two [wives of commoners there], the house becomes impure in both cases, for while one is grinding, the other can wander around touching things. This is the view of Rabbi Meir. But the sages say: The house becomes impure only as far as any place to which they can extend their hands and touch. (Mishna Taharot 7:4)

Rabbi Meir does not disagree with the sages that the wife of a fellow may invite the wife of a commoner to mill in her own home. He disagrees only about the extent to which she can be trusted. It is the issue of trust between neighbors that is at stake in this mishna. Tractate Gittin (5:9) teaches that all of these laws about the relationship between fellows and commoners were taught "because of ways of peace," that is, to preserve peaceful coexistence and friendly neighborly relations.

THE CROWN OF TORAH: ALL WHO WISH MAY COME AND TAKE IT

We saw above that there were strict prerequisites to becoming a fellow. But to become a sage, a person need only devote himself to learning Torah. The following midrash became the sages' rallying cry to the nation, encouraging others to join their ranks:

> Rabbi Shimon says: There are three crowns: the crown of Torah, the crown of priesthood, and the crown of royalty; but the crown of a good name surpasses them all.

> The crown of priesthood: What is there to be said of it? Even if one were to offer all the silver and gold in the world, he could not be given the crown of priesthood, for it is said, "And it shall be unto him and to his seed after him the covenant of everlasting priesthood" [Num. 25:13].
>
> The crown of royalty: Even if one were to offer all the silver and gold in the world, he could not be given the crown of royalty, for it is said, "And David My servant shall be their prince forever" [Ezek. 37:25].
>
> Not so the crown of Torah. The toil of Torah – anyone who wishes to take it on may come and do so, as it is said, "Ho, all who are thirsty, come for water" [Is. 55:1]. (*Avot deRabbi Natan*, recension A, ch. 41)

This midrash, which we will consider in greater depth when we come to the figure of Rabbi Shimon, promotes Torah study as an activity accessible to all. Even so, it was learning Torah that distinguished the fellow from the commoner. During the rabbinic period, a fellow was anyone who wished to observe the mitzvot with additional stringency. For the most part, a fellow was merely accepting commandments that were already incumbent upon him (with the exception of his undertaking to eat unconsecrated food in a state of purity). His commitment to Torah study was what set him apart. The sages sought to become role models for the community, with all their actions guided by Torah:

> "And you shall love the Lord your God" [Deut. 6:5]. This means that the name of heaven should become beloved through you. One should read Torah, study Mishna, and serve Torah scholars, and one's dealings with people should be pleasant. What do people say about such a person? Fortunate is his father, who taught him Torah.... See how pleasant are his ways and how refined his deeds. Regarding him it is written, "God said to me: You are My servant, Israel, through whom I am glorified" [Is. 49:3].
>
> But as for one who reads Torah, studies Mishna, serves Torah scholars, but does not conduct his business transactions faithfully or speak pleasantly, what do people say about him? Woe

unto that person who learned Torah; woe unto his father, who taught him Torah. See how perverse are his deeds and how ugly his ways. Regarding him it is written, "When it was said of them, 'These are the people of God, but they departed from His land'" [Ezek. 36:20]. (Yoma 86a)

Chapter Three

Rabbi Yehuda bar Ilai: The Leading Speaker on Every Occasion

Rabbi Yehuda bar Ilai was the local authority in the new rabbinic center at Usha. According to Rabbi Y. N. Epstein, "The words of Rabbi Yehuda, 'the leading speaker on every occasion,' fill the entire Mishna. Rabbi Yehuda HaNasi [the editor of the Mishna] made extensive use of the statements of Rabbi Yehuda."[1] Rabbi Z. Frankel adds that he is the "cornerstone of the Mishna, which brims with his contributions."[2] The plethora of sources that mention of Rabbi Yehuda bar Ilai attests to his important role in the generation after the Bar Kokhba revolt.

1. Rabbi Y. N. Epstein, *Introduction to the Literature of the Tanna'im* [Hebrew] (Jerusalem, 5717), 107. The phrase "the leading speaker on every occasion" comes from the Talmud (Berakhot 33b; Shabbat 33b).
2. Rabbi Z. Frankel, *The Methods of the Mishna* [Hebrew] (Berlin, 5683), 167. Frankel argued that the phrase "the leading speaker" attests to the many halakhot quoted in his name.

HIS FATHER, RABBI ILAI, HEIR TO THE TORAH OF RABBI ELIEZER BEN HYRCANUS

Rabbi Yehuda was from the Galilee, though unlike other Galilean sages (such as Rabbi Ḥalafta of Tzippori), he was not known by where he lived.[3] His teachings bridge those of his father, Rabbi Ilai, and his teacher, Rabbi Tarfon of Lod.

Contrary to the prevailing view in Christian scholarship and among several Jewish historians as well, the Galilee was a place of Torah study and religious observance in the second century, much like Judea.[4] The customs of the Jews of the Galilee differed from those of Judea and the south, and can often be traced to Temple practices. The Jews of Judea and the Galilee were closely tied to one another during the Yavneh period. Sages from Yavneh could be found in the Galilee, and Galilean sages came to learn in Yavneh.

No one questioned that Yavneh was the most important center of Torah study and the seat of the patriarch, the spiritual leader of Israel. But not all the sages of the Yavneh generation were present at Yavneh. Rabbi Eliezer remained in Lod, where he kept strict watch over the traditions of Beit Shammai.[5] His teachings were preserved by Rabbi Ilai at a time when the other sages of the second generation at Yavneh kept their distance.[6] There was strong opposition to Rabbi Eliezer's teachings, as we find, for instance, in Rabbi Yishmael's words below:

> Rabbi Eliezer says: A dough offering may be separated from a pure batch of dough on behalf of an impure batch.
>
> They said before Rabbi Yishmael: Isn't there someone in the south who has given instruction according to this teaching?
>
> He said to them: By the clothes of my father and the gold

3. Others include Rabbi Ḥanina ben Teradion of Sikhnin and Rabbi Yoḥanan ben Nuri of Beit She'arim.
4. The Church depicted the Jews of the Galilee as ignorant commoners whose lives were devoid of Torah and Jewish content, such that Jesus saved them from their alienation from the reigning Pharisees. This claim has been discredited by Jewish scholars for decades. See A. Oppenheimer, *Galilee in the Time of the Mishna*, 16–17 notes 1–3.
5. See *Sages* II, Part One.
6. Ibid., Part Two.

> plate he bore on his brow! I will make an example of that for all who give instruction!
>
> They said to him: He has taught in the name of Rabbi Eliezer.
>
> He said to them: In that case he has something on which to rely. (Tosefta Ḥalla 1:10)

The Mishna in Tractate Ḥalla cites the teaching of Rabbi Eliezer that underlies this statement in the Tosefta. Rabbi Eliezer holds that impure and pure batches of dough may be treated as a single batch with regard to separating a portion for the priests. The sages, however, prohibit taking dough from a pure batch on behalf of an impure one, lest the two batches touch. The Tosefta relates that the students wanted to quote Rabbi Eliezer's teaching to Rabbi Yishmael, but they refrained from invoking his name. Excited by this teaching, Rabbi Yishmael swore in the name of his father's priestly garments to promulgate it. At that point his students revealed that the teaching had come from Rabbi Eliezer. Rabbi Yishmael responded, "In that case he has something on which to rely." This is a very vivid description of Rabbi Eliezer's complicated role in the transmission of Torah. Apparently he could be quoted only anonymously at Yavneh.

Rabbi Ilai was one of the few sages who preserved Rabbi Eliezer's teachings. For instance, a teaching attributed to Rabbi Eliezer in Tractate Avot is quoted by Rabbi Ilai in *Avot deRabbi Natan*:

> Rabbi Yose bar Yehuda says in the name of Rabbi Yehuda bar Ilai, who said in the name of Rabbi Ilai his father, who said in the name of Rabbi Eliezer the elder: Repent one day before you die. And warm yourself by the fire of the sages, but be careful of their coals lest you be scorched, for their bite is the bite of a fox and their sting is the sting of a scorpion, and all their words are like fiery coals. (*Avot deRabbi Natan*, recension A, ch. 15)

Rabbi Ilai is the conduit for several of Rabbi Eliezer's teachings that would otherwise be lost to us.[7] A passage from Tractate Pe'ah offers

7. We find a clear example of Rabbi Ilai's transmission of the teachings of Rabbi Eliezer

one example. This tractate deals with those taxes that every farmer is obligated to set aside for the poor, and provides the basis for the notion of a Jewish welfare state. During the rabbinic period, when Jewish society was largely agricultural, the tax burden fell primarily on those who worked the land. The various dues owed to the poor included the sheaves that fell to the ground during the gathering of the harvest (*leket*), the sheaves the gatherer forgot in the field (*shikheha*), and those that grew at the field's corners (*pe'ah*).

Chapter six of Tractate Pe'ah deals with the second category, the laws of the forgotten sheaves. This is a strange mitzva, since it can be performed only inadvertently. If the farmer forgets a sheaf of wheat in the field, he is forbidden to return to collect it, but must leave it for the poor. Of course, this applies only within reason, since a farmer could suffer serious losses if he were to forget too many sheaves. The Mishna cites a dispute between Beit Shammai and Beit Hillel regarding sheaves that were not forgotten while the harvester was working the field, but were gathered from the field and piled at a designated spot – next to a storehouse, for instance. The harvester later forgot to retrieve those sheaves from their place. Do they count as forgotten sheaves that must be left for the poor, or does the fact that they were already removed from the fields and placed elsewhere mean that they already belong to the farmer? The Tosefta quotes Rabbi Ilai, who discusses this tradition with the sages of Yavneh:

> Rabbi Ilai said: I asked Rabbi Yehoshua: Over which sheaves did Beit Shammai disagree with Beit Hillel? He said to me: By the Torah! This dispute refers to those sheaves that are near the picking ladder, grain heap, cattle, or farm tools, and that the householder forgot. But when I came and asked Rabbi Eliezer which sheaves were disputed, he said to me: Both agree that these sheaves are not subject to the restrictions of the forgotten sheaf. With regard to what do Beit Shammai and Beit Hillel disagree?

in Mishna Eiruvin 2:6. It is interesting to compare the language of this mishna ("I went around to all his disciples in search of a colleague, but I found none") with that of the midrash that follows.

> They disagree with regard to a sheaf that the householder picked up in order to take it to the city for sale, and that he placed near the fence and then forgot. For Beit Shammai say that such a sheaf is not subject to the restrictions of the forgotten sheaf, because the householder had taken possession of it. But Beit Hillel say that such a sheaf is subject to the restrictions of the forgotten sheaf.
>
> And when I came and recited these matters before Rabbi Elazar ben Azaria, he said to me: By the Torah! These matters were spoken at Sinai. (Tosefta Pe'ah 3:2)

Rabbi Ilai is receptive to the views of both Rabbi Yehoshua and Rabbi Eliezer. Rabbi Eliezer offers a clear rendering of the teaching of Beit Shammai. Rabbi Ilai then repeats Rabbi Eliezer's teaching to Rabbi Elazar ben Azaria, who served as patriarch along with Rabban Gamliel, and he responds excitedly: "These matters were spoken at Sinai." This is the end of the passage in the Tosefta. The Mishna (Pe'ah 6:2) cites only the tradition of Rabbi Yehoshua and omits the opinion of Rabbi Eliezer, though Rabbi Elazar ben Azaria clearly supports the latter.[8] This was patently a decision on the part of the Mishna's editor, Rabbi Yehuda HaNasi.

Rabbi Ilai did not just faithfully teach the traditions of Rabbi Eliezer; he also passed them on to his son, Rabbi Yehuda:

> Rebbi said: When I went to drain my measures before Rabbi Elazar ben Shamua – and some say: to drain the measures *of* Rabbi Elazar ben Shamua – I encountered Yosef the Babylonian sitting before him, and his teachings were extremely beloved to him, except one. Yosef said to Rabbi Elazar ben Shamua: My master, if one slaughters an offering with the intent to leave over some of its blood until the next day, what is the law?
>
> He said: It is valid.
>
> When Yosef made this inquiry in the evening, he said: It

8. This law appears in the Mishna, Tosefta, and Jerusalem Talmud, and then in the writings of Maimonides. See Rabbi S. Lieberman's long commentary on this passage in *Tosefta Kifshuta, Seder Zera'im* (New York, 5715), Pe'ah, 162–64.

is valid. When he repeated it in the morning, he again said: It is valid. But when he repeated it in the afternoon, he said: It is valid except that Rabbi Eliezer declares it invalid.

Yosef the Babylonian's face lit up.

Rabbi Elazar ben Shamua said to him: Yosef, it seems to me that our teachings were not in agreement until now.

Yosef said: Yes, they were! Except that I recalled that Rabbi Yehuda taught me that the offering is invalid, and I went around to all his disciples in search of a colleague [who would also remember him teaching this way], but I found none. Now that you taught me that Rabbi Eliezer states the offering is invalid, you have returned my lost teaching to me.

Rabbi Elazar ben Shamua's eyes flowed with tears, and he said: Fortunate are you, Torah students, that the words of Torah are extremely beloved to you. He applied the following verse to Yosef the Babylonian: "How I love Your Torah; all day it is my conversation" [Ps. 119:97]. Now since Rabbi Yehuda was the son of Rabbi Ilai, and Rabbi Ilai was the disciple of Rabbi Eliezer, Rabbi Yehuda taught you the opinion of Rabbi Eliezer. (Menaḥot 18a)

This story features Rabbi Yehuda HaNasi, known as Rebbi, who sought out the teachings of the previous generation. He wishes to "drain his measures," that is, to clarify any remaining obscure matters. Rebbi finds Yosef the Babylonian (also known as Isi ben Yehuda) studying with Rabbi Elazar ben Shamua, one of the earliest sages of Usha. When Yosef hears Rabbi Elazar ben Shamua give an answer that includes a teaching of Rabbi Eliezer, his face lights up. This phrase, which literally means "his face turned yellow," may signify either genuine happiness, or gloating at another's misfortune.[9] Yosef explains to his teacher, Rabbi Elazar ben Shamua, that he is happy because he now understands a teaching that he learned from Rabbi Yehuda bar Ilai. It becomes clear that Rabbi

9. Those sources that include this phrase can be interpreted either way. A prayer attributed to Rabbi Neḥunia ben HaKane expresses the teacher's fear that his students might scoff at what he has to say: "That I not err in a matter of halakha and cause my colleagues to rejoice at my expense." See *Sages* 1, Part Three, note 12.

Yehuda was transmitting his father's traditions, which had come from Rabbi Eliezer, though no one else accepted them. Yosef is pleased that Rabbi Elazar ben Shamua has not just taught him the mainstream tradition of the beit midrash, but also made reference to Rabbi Eliezer's view. This was years after Rabbi Eliezer's excommunication and death, yet he still was not viewed as a major authority. Nonetheless, as this source attests, Rabbi Ilai continued to transmit Rabbi Eliezer's traditions to his son, Rabbi Yehuda.

STUDYING WITH RABBI TARFON

Rabbi Yehuda was a student of his father, Rabbi Ilai, who was in turn a student of Rabbi Eliezer, the leading disciple of Beit Shammai during the Yavneh period. But Rabbi Yehuda was also a student of Rabbi Tarfon, another member of Shammai's school. As various sources attest, Rabbi Yehuda would visit Rabbi Tarfon in Lod to learn Torah from him, and would often stay with him for the holidays.

The Mishna in Tractate Eiruvin (4:4) attests to the close relationship between Rabbi Yehuda and Rabbi Tarfon. This source cites a disagreement between Rabbi Meir and Rabbi Yehuda regarding a person who set out on a journey before the start of Shabbat and approached a town just as the sun began to set. The man was already within the Sabbath limits of that town, but he did not know this was the case when the sun set. Rabbi Meir holds that since the traveler had not intended to spend Shabbat in that town, he may not enter. He must stay put, confining himself to a radius of two thousand *amot* from wherever he happens to be, without entering the town. However, Rabbi Yehuda holds that it is not the traveler's intention that matters, but rather where he finds himself. If he was within the town limits, he may consider himself a resident of the town and walk up to two thousand *amot* within it. Rabbi Yehuda quotes his teacher Rabbi Tarfon in support of his position:

> Rabbi Yehuda said: It once happened that Rabbi Tarfon entered though it had not been his intention (Mishna Eiruvin 4:4).

Elsewhere Rabbi Yehuda speaks of visiting Rabbi Tarfon on Purim and reading the Megilla for him when he was still a young boy:

> Rabbi Yehuda said: I was a minor, and I read it before Rabbi Tarfon in Lod, and he accepted me. (Tosefta Megilla 2:8)[10]

HIS TEACHINGS WERE NOT THOSE OF RABBI AKIVA

The sages of the Usha generation are generally associated with Rabbi Akiva.[11] But Rabbi Yehuda appears to be an exception: Although he is sometimes mentioned along with Rabbi Akiva, we never find the two studying together. Certainly he was not as close to Rabbi Akiva as were Rabbi Meir and Rabbi Shimon.[12] Nor did he tend to accept his teachings. As we have seen, Rabbi Yehuda's teachings were more closely aligned with the world of Beit Shammai, transmitted to him through his father and through his teacher Rabbi Tarfon. Beit Shammai's teachings tended to privilege action over intention when it came to the fulfillment of mitzvot, as we saw in the case of the mishna from Eiruvin. In contrast, the sages of Beit Hillel, led by Rabbi Akiva, were known for judging a person's actions based on his intentions, not on what he actually did: "These words follow the intention of the heart" (Berakhot 15b). We considered this difference of opinion when we studied the recitation of the *Shema*.[13] In studying the teachings of Rabbi Yehuda, we will see that he, too, was concerned more with action than with intention, in accordance with Beit Shammai.

10. Many sources refer to Rabbi Yehuda's study with Rabbi Tarfon. See A. Hyman, *The Legends of the Tanna'im and Amora'im* [Hebrew] (Jerusalem, 5747), s.v. "Rabbi Yehuda bar Ilai," 534–35.
11. This is how Rabbi Yoḥanan describes attributions in tannaitic literature: An anonymous mishnaic teaching is attributed to Rabbi Meir; an anonymous *Sifra* teaching is attributed to Rabbi Yehuda; an anonymous Tosefta teaching is attributed to Rabbi Neḥemia, "and all these teachings are according to Rabbi Akiva" (Sanhedrin 86a).
12. Rabbi Yehuda describes walking in the footsteps of Rabbi Elazar ben Azaria and Rabbi Akiva (Y. Berakhot 1:2 [3a], and elsewhere), suggesting that he regarded these two sages as leaders of the generation; but it does not seem that he was a primary student of Rabbi Akiva. This is the claim made by Hyman and others, albeit without substantial textual grounding.
13. See *Sages* I, Part Three.

HIS FACE WAS SHINING: HIS VIEWS ON AESTHETICS

The Talmud in Tractate Nedarim describes Rabbi Yehuda bar Ilai's appearance in a series of stories. The first describes how he looked as a child, when he studied with Rabbi Tarfon:

> Rabbi Yehuda was once sitting before Rabbi Tarfon. Rabbi Tarfon said to him: Your face is shining today! Rabbi Yehuda said to Rabbi Tarfon: Yesterday your servants went out to the field, and they brought us beets, and we ate them without salt. Had we eaten them with salt, our faces would shine all the more! (Nedarim 49b)

In this story, Rabbi Tarfon, who was rich, points out to his poor student that his face is shining. The young Yehuda responds mischievously by complaining about the food he is served in his teacher's home. His response implies that if only Rabbi Tarfon's servants bothered to season the food appropriately, his face would shine even more.

The Talmud goes on to speak of Rabbi Yehuda's ruddy complexion:

> A certain Roman noblewoman once said to Rabbi Yehuda: You are a halakhic decisor and a drunk? Rabbi Yehuda said to her: By the honor of that woman, I would be swearing falsely if I so much as taste wine the entire year, except for Kiddush, Havdala, and four cups on Passover. Furthermore, after drinking the four cups, I must bind my temples to alleviate the headache I have from Passover until Shavuot. Rather, "A man's wisdom brightens his face" [Eccl. 8:1]. (Nedarim 49b)

The third story is similar to the second, except that here Rabbi Yehuda encounters an even more confrontational interlocutor:

> A certain Sadducee once said to Rabbi Yehuda: Your face seems to be the face of either usurers or pig farmers. Rabbi Yehuda replied to the Sadducee: Among Jews, both of those occupations are prohibited. Rather, I have twenty-four rest stops between my house and the study hall, and each and every hour I enter each and every one of them. (Nedarim 49b)

Rabbi Yehuda's face shines, and others notice and wonder why. A person can develop this radiant glow as a result of negative influences, by taking advantage of others financially or by raising pigs; but one can also become radiant by living a life of balance and harmony. With Rabbi Yehuda, apparently the latter was the case. He was strict about matters of hygiene and took excellent care of his body, as sources such as the following attest:

> Rabbi Mona said in the name of Rabbi Yehuda: A drop of cold water in the eyes in the morning and washing the hands and feet in warm water in the evening are better than all the remedies in the world. He would say: A hand that is put to the eye should be cut off. A hand that is put to the nose should be cut off. A hand that is put to the mouth should be cut off. A hand that is put to the ear should be cut off. A hand that is put to the lancet puncture[14] should be cut off. A hand that is put to the penis should be cut off. A hand that is put to the anus should be cut off. A hand that is put to a barrel should be cut off. The hand causes blindness if it touches the eye; the hand causes deafness if it touches the ear; the hand generates a foul odor if it touches the mouth or nose. (Shabbat 108b–109a)

This is a delightful talmudic passage.[15] Rabbi Mona, speaking in the

14. The "lancet puncture" seems out of place, since it is not part of the body. Rashi explains that it refers to a wound caused by bloodletting. The Arukh (Rabbi Natan ben Yeḥiel of eleventh century Rome) writes similarly. H. Y. Kohut discusses this term at length and concludes that it is "a place of poking and piercing done by an instrument used for bloodletting, and it is dangerous to touch this place until it is washed. It comes from the Greek." See Kohut, *Arukh HaShalem* [Hebrew] (Hungary and New York, 1878–92), 453.
15. The mishna on which this talmudic passage comments deals with the preparation of brine (*hilmi*) on Shabbat (Mishna Shabbat 14:2). H. Albeck posits that brine was a medicinal remedy. See Albeck, *Preface to Tractate Shabbat,* final ed. (Tel Aviv, 1988), 14. A. Goldberg uses Albeck's suggestion to explain a difficult passage in the Jerusalem Talmud. According to such a contextualized reading, Rabbi Yehuda obviates the need for any such remedy by advocating proper personal hygiene. See Goldberg, *A Commentary on the Mishna, Tractate Shabbat* [Hebrew] (Jerusalem, 5736), 264–65.

name of Rabbi Yehuda, warns against touching the body in inappropriate places and spreading contamination.[16]

We also learn about Rabbi Yehuda's views on the body in a disagreement about seminal emissions documented in the Mishna:

> A person who has had a seminal emission is to contemplate the words of the *Shema* in his heart rather than say them aloud. And he need not recite the accompanying blessings, neither those preceding the *Shema* nor those following it. With regard to food, he is to recite in his heart those blessings that follow a meal, but he is not to recite those blessings that precede the meal. Rabbi Yehuda said: He recites the blessings that precede and follow the *Shema* and the meal. (Mishna Berakhot 3:4)

The Talmud pits Rabbi Yehuda's view against that of Rabbi Yehoshua ben Levi:

> Is this to say that Rabbi Yehuda maintains that one who has had a seminal emission is permitted to recite words of Torah? Did not Rabbi Yehoshua ben Levi say: From where do we know that one who has had a seminal emission is barred from reciting words of Torah? For it is written, "And you shall make them known to your children and to your children's children" [Deut. 4:9], and the Torah juxtaposes these words with "The day that you stood" [Deut. 4:10]. Just as there [at Sinai], those who experienced a seminal emission were forbidden to participate before immersing, so too here [with regard to Torah study], those who have

16. I emphasize that this passage should be understood as dealing with personal hygiene because Rashi, generally a literal reader, interprets it entirely differently. He argues that this source is the basis for washing hands to ward off the "evil spirits" that descend upon a person at night: "If one touches his eye in the morning before washing his hands, his hand should be cut off, because an evil spirit rests on his hand and will blind him." All subsequent commentators and halakhic authorities discussed this passage as relating to a spiritual rather than physical hazard. See my article "Respect the Respected: On Halakha, Kabbala, and Religious Consciousness" [Hebrew], *Granot* 1 (5761).

> experienced a seminal emission are forbidden to participate before immersing. (Berakhot 21b)

The Talmud tries to distinguish between the opinions of Rabbi Yehuda and Rabbi Yehoshua ben Levi, but the original question remains: Why does Rabbi Yehuda instruct one who has had a seminal emission to recite blessings before and after learning Torah? Rav Naḥman bar Yitzhak offers an explanation:

> Rav Naḥman bar Yitzhak said: Rabbi Yehuda equates these various blessings with the laws of *derekh eretz* [proper conduct]. (Berakhot 22a)

That is, Rabbi Yehuda argues that one who has had a seminal emission may learn the laws of *derekh eretz,* and he considers the blessings before the *Shema* to be among these laws. Thus even one who has had a seminal emission must bless before reciting the *Shema*. The Talmud then relates a particular incident in which this issue became relevant:

> Rabbi Yehuda once had a seminal emission and was walking along a riverbank with his students. His students said to him: Our master! Teach us a chapter of the laws of *derekh eretz*. Rabbi Yehuda went down and immersed in the river, and only then taught them. They said to him: Did our master not teach us that one who has had a seminal emission may study the laws of *derekh eretz*? Rabbi Yehuda said to them: Although I am lenient with others in this matter, I am stringent with myself. (Berakhot 22a)

CONTENTMENT WITH HIS LOT IN LIFE

The Talmud describes Rabbi Yehuda's economic situation:

> Rabbi Yehuda's wife once went out and purchased wool. She fashioned a fine cloak from it. When she went to the marketplace, she would wear it. And when Rabbi Yehuda went out to pray, he would wear it and pray. And when he put it on, he would recite the blessing "Blessed is He who wrapped me in this coat."

> Rabban Shimon ben Gamliel once decreed a fast, but Rabbi Yehuda did not come to the house where the sages gathered during the fast. The others said to Rabban Shimon ben Gamliel: Rabbi Yehuda did not come because he has nothing to wear. Rabban Shimon ben Gamliel sent a garment to Rabbi Yehuda, but he refused to accept it. Rabbi Yehuda showed the messenger that he had an expensive garment underneath his clothing. He said to the messenger: See what there is here! I do not wish to derive benefit from this world. (Nedarim 49b)

Rabbi Yehuda is destitute, so he appreciates the value of a good coat. Whenever he dons the coat his wife made him, he blesses, "Blessed is He who wrapped me in this coat." But he refuses the coat sent to him by Rabban Shimon ben Gamliel. In another source, too, we see that Rabbi Yehuda is reluctant to benefit from others:

> When Rabbi Yehuda went to the beit midrash, he would carry a barrel on his shoulders [to sit upon]. He said: How great is the labor that confers honor upon the one who performs it. (Nedarim 49b)

Two additional statements attributed to Rabbi Yehuda offer a sense of his extraordinary qualities:

> Rabba bar bar Ḥana said that Rabbi Yoḥanan reported in the name of Rabbi Yehuda bar Ilai: Come and see how the later generations are unlike the earlier generations. The earlier generations made their Torah study their primary occupation and their work incidental, and both endured. The later generations, which made their work their primary occupation and their Torah study incidental – neither endured.
>
> Rabba bar bar Ḥana said that Rabbi Yoḥanan reported in the name of Rabbi Yehuda bar Ilai: Come and see how the later generations are unlike the earlier generations. The earlier generations would bring their crops into their houses through the courtyard gate in order to subject the crops to tithes. The

> later generations bring their crops into their houses via the roofs, courtyards, and storage yards in order to absolve themselves of the obligation of tithes. For Rabbi Yannai said: Untithed produce does not become subject to the laws of tithes until it faces the house, as it is written, "I have removed the sacred from the house" [Deut. 26:13]. (Berakhot 35b)

There is no apparent connection between these two statements in which Rabbi Yehuda compares the earlier and later generations. The first statement relates to Rabbi Shimon's famous dispute with Rabbi Yishmael regarding the amount of time that should be dedicated to Torah and to worldly occupation.[17] Rabbi Yehuda explains that the earlier generations made their Torah study their main occupation and their work incidental, and both endured. Their work was a means of earning a livelihood, but they lived for the sake of Torah study. Therefore they were content with very little.

In the second statement, Rabbi Yehuda refers to the tithing practices of the earlier and later generations. The earlier generations gave tithes willingly, whereas the later generations sought every opportunity to evade their obligation.

Rabbi Yehuda believed that work was valuable as a means of sustenance, but he tried to strike a balance between Torah study, which should be a person's primary occupation, and the work that allows one to dedicate time to study. When we consider the Usha generation as a whole, Rabbi Yehuda stands out as a moderate on this subject. Some thought the sages should have nothing to do with worldly pursuits ("temporal life") and should devote themselves entirely to Torah ("eternal life"). At the other end of the spectrum were those who were preoccupied with daily agricultural labor and neglected the study of Torah. Rabbi Yehuda fell somewhere in between.

17. For Rabbi Yishmael's view on this matter, see *Sages* II, Part Three.

HIS RELATIONSHIP TO HUMANITY

Rabbi Akiva's beit midrash famously deemed study greater than action. Rabbi Akiva inspired his students with love of Torah, which he believed would lead to love of God. But Rabbi Yehuda had a different view:

> Rabbi Yehuda bar Ilai was once sitting and teaching his disciples when a bride passed before him. He said to his students: What is this? They said to him: It is a bride passing by. He said to them: My sons, get up and attend to the bride, for we find that the Holy One, Blessed Be He, occupied Himself with the needs of the bride, for it is said, "And the Lord God built the rib" (Gen. 2:22). Since God occupied Himself with the needs of the bride, how much more so should we. (*Avot deRabbi Natan*, recension A, ch. 4)

According to Rabbi Yehuda bar Ilai's worldview, the fulfillment of a mitzva takes precedence over Torah study. The Jerusalem Talmud articulates his position unequivocally:

> When Rabbi Yehuda would see a dead person or hear a bride being praised,[18] he would set his eyes on the disciples and say: Actions come before learning. (Y. Ḥagiga 1:7 [76c])[19]

The Talmud speaks of the intellectual distance between Rabbi Yehuda and his colleague and rival Rabbi Shimon bar Yoḥai (Rashbi):

18. The Hebrew root *k-l-s* (praise) was used originally in relation to God and then in eulogies and in reference to brides and distinguished students. See S. Lieberman, "Kalas Kilusin" [Hebrew], in *Studies in the Torah of the Land of Israel* (Jerusalem, 5751), 434 note 11.
19. The Jerusalem Talmud continues with this polemic, citing the conclusion drawn by Rabbi Akiva's students: "They voted and decided that study is greater." In *Avot deRabbi Natan* and in both Talmuds (Ketubot 17a and Y. Ḥagiga 1:7 [76c]) it is taught that action precedes study "when the number of people there is not sufficient without him [to accompany the bride to a wedding]." It seems that this is not Rabbi Yehuda's opinion. These sources seek to strike a balance between him and Rabbi Akiva. See Urbach, *Sages*, 545 note 64.

> A man said to his wife: I vow that you may not benefit from me until you give a taste of your cooked food to Rabbi Yehuda and Rabbi Shimon. Rabbi Yehuda tasted the food. He reasoned: If to make peace between husband and wife the Torah states, "Let My name, which was written in holiness, be erased in destructive waters," even where it is uncertain [that the marriage will be saved], how much more should I do so! But Rabbi Shimon would not taste the food. He said: Let the widow's children die, and let Shimon not move from his place. (Nedarim 66b)

This is a story about a man who vows to deny his wife all pleasure until she serves food to the two great sages of the generation. Rabbi Yehuda and Rabbi Shimon offer characteristic responses. Rabbi Yehuda does not mind playing along so the wife can fulfill her husband's uncomfortable mission. He agrees to taste the food so as to make peace between husband and wife.[20] But Rabbi Shimon refuses to be served, though he is aware that the welfare of the wife and children are at stake. Unlike Rabbi Yehuda, he refuses to sully his hands with the ordinary business of daily life.

HIS RELATIONSHIP TO COMMONERS AND SINNERS

Rabbi Yehuda is one of the major sages of his time, and he follows halakha stringently. But he also lives among the people and cares about their spiritual welfare. For Rabbi Yehuda, the people's observance of the Torah's laws is a prerequisite for their status as the chosen people. This is one of the novel insights that emerge from his beit midrash.

A dominant and central strain in Jewish thought, rooted in the teachings of Rabbi Akiva, is the notion that God's choice of Israel is independent of Israel's behavior: "Beloved are the Jews, who are called children of God. They are exceedingly beloved, for it was made known to them that they are the children of God, as it is written, 'You are the children of the Lord your God' (Deut. 14:1)" (Mishna Avot 3:14). According to Rabbi Akiva, the Jews were given the Torah *after* being

20. Rabbi Yehuda's reasoning appears in the Midrash in the name of Rabbi Yishmael (see Leviticus Rabba 9:104). See Urbach, *Sages*, 545 note 63.

chosen by God: "They are exceedingly beloved, for it was made known to them that they were given a precious instrument" (*Pirkei Avot* 3:14). But Rabbi Yehuda offers an alternative understanding:

> "You are the children of the Lord your God" [Deut. 14:1]. Rabbi Yehuda says: If you conduct yourselves like dutiful children, you are His children. If not, you are not His children. Rabbi Meir says: In either case, "You are the children of the Lord your God." (Sifrei, Deuteronomy 96)

Rabbi Meir, the leading student of Rabbi Akiva, rules that "In either case, 'You are [His] children,'" But Rabbi Yehuda, who is not bound to Rabbi Akiva's teachings, holds that God's choice of Israel depends on Israel's religious conduct. There is no guarantee of divine favor. God chooses us only if we uphold His Torah. Here Rabbi Yehuda follows the school of Rabbi Yishmael rather than that of Rabbi Akiva:

> "And you shall be holy unto Me" [Ex. 22:30]. Rabbi Yishmael says: If you are holy, then you are Mine. (*Mekhilta deRabbi Yishmael*, Kaspa, 2)

Rabbi Yishmael links holiness to chosenness. If we conduct ourselves with holiness, then we belong to God. As Rabbi Yehuda puts it, "If they conduct themselves like [God's] children, they are [God's] children" (Kiddushin 36a).[21]

Rabbi Yehuda's perspective on divine election does not prevent him from remaining in contact with commoners guilty of sin. Several sources describe Rabbi Yehuda's interactions with those who fail to observe the mitzvot, as the two examples below attest.

21. Urbach interprets Rabbi Elazar ben Azaria's exegesis along similar lines: "You have praised God today... and God has praised you today.... You have made Me a subject of unique praise in the world, and I will make you a subject of unique praise in the world" (Ḥagiga 3a). According to Urbach, "God's choice by Israel precedes God's choice of Israel." I disagree with his reading, since Rabbi Elazar ben Azaria seems to be describing a more reciprocal relationship. See Urbach, *Sages*, 469–70.

Those Who Gather Sabbatical Produce Are Not Ineligible to Serve as Witnesses

> And these are ineligible [to serve as witnesses]: the dice player, the usurer, those who fly pigeons, dealers in produce of the sabbatical year. Rabbi Shimon said: Initially they called them collectors of produce of the sabbatical year. When the tax collectors increased, they reverted to calling them dealers in the produce of the sabbatical year. Rabbi Yehuda said: When? When they have no trade except this. But if they have another trade besides this, they are eligible. (Mishna Sanhedrin 3:3)

The Mishna discusses those who are ineligible to serve as witnesses because they do not further the general welfare.[22] Maimonides offers the following interpretation in his commentary on the Mishna:

> They are prohibited from serving as witnesses because they are not involved in anything socially useful. It is a foundational idea of our Torah that it is not fitting for a person to occupy himself with matters of this world unless he is acquiring wisdom to perfect himself, or unless he is engaged in an occupation such as trade or commerce. It is better to do less of the second and more of the first, as the sages said: Minimize your occupation and occupy yourself with Torah.

The Mishna teaches that those who gathered produce in the sabbatical year were ineligible to serve as witnesses. This was a strong social sanction. In the Mishna Rabbi Shimon delimits this category: Only those who dealt commercially with sabbatical produce were barred from serving as witnesses. But when it came to those who gathered such produce for their own needs, the sages averted their eyes. The Talmud explains that the collection of sabbatical produce became increasingly rampant "when the oppressors increased" (Sanhedrin 26a). This is a reference

22. This is how the Babylonian Talmud explains their ineligibility. While they are not thieves, they also do not act on behalf of society, and thus they forfeit others' trust.

to those who collected the *arnona*, the royal produce tax. The Romans levied very high taxes that gravely threatened the farmers. When the economic situation reached crisis proportions, the talmudic sage Rabbi Yannai proclaimed, "Go out and plant in the sabbatical year on account of the produce tax" (Sanhedrin 26a).

Rabbi Yehuda takes these rulings one step further and teaches that even those merchants who sold sabbatical produce are not barred from serving as witnesses unless this is their sole trade. The Tosefta states:

> "Dealers in produce of the sabbatical year" refers to those who sit idly during the other six years. When the sabbatical year comes, they stretch out their hands and feet and trade the produce of sin. (Tosefta Sanhedrin 5:2)

Both Rabbi Shimon and Rabbi Yehuda recognized how difficult it was for the farmers to observe the sabbatical year. They assumed a moderate stance toward those who violated the sabbatical laws, so long as these offenders showed regard for the general welfare and did not make their living solely from their transgressions.

Taking Fertilizer Out to the Fields

Several scholars have noted that the phrase "dealers in the produce of the sabbatical year" is generally used with reference to members of the Usha generation.[23] The dire economic situation of this period made it difficult to observe the sabbatical laws properly.

The third chapter of Tractate Shevi'it deals largely with how the sages conducted their lives within the broader agricultural and municipal worlds of which they were a part. The chapter also considers issues that are not direct sabbatical prohibitions but arise in the course of general agricultural work: (1) When there is waste in the house, it is generally taken out to the fields, which serves not just to clean out the house but also to fertilize the soil. Is it permissible to take waste out to the fields during the sabbatical year? (2) Cattle are generally brought out into the fields to deposit their waste, thereby fertilizing the soil. Is it permissible

23. Apparently the first to take note of this was Bikhler, *Galilean Commoner*, 220–24.

to bring cattle out into the fields for this purpose during the sabbatical year? And if not, where can this waste be disposed? (3) It is permissible to build a house during the sabbatical year. But what if the stones used in the construction of the house are gathered from the fields, which also serves to clear them for planting? Is it still permissible to build during the sabbatical year?

The sages sought to show the people how they could go on with their lives despite the sabbatical laws. They created loopholes while also ensuring that those loopholes would not threaten the integrity of the system. The entire third chapter of Shevi'it deals with the attempt to strike this delicate balance, beginning with the opening mishna:

> From when may waste be taken out to the dung heaps? When the sinners have ceased to sin.[24] These are the words of Rabbi Meir. Rabbi Yehuda says: When the sweetening has dried up. Rabbi Yose says: When it forms knots. (Mishna Shevi'it 3:1)

This is a fascinating debate. In an agricultural society, where every house was situated next to a field, the obvious way to get rid of waste was to take it outside to fertilize the field. But it was forbidden to fertilize during the sabbatical year, since fertilizing was a corollary of planting. Nonetheless, many continued to do so, and they were not regarded as serious offenders. While some farmers worked their land with total disregard for the sabbatical laws, they must be distinguished from those who followed the biblical prohibitions relating to the sabbatical year

24. The printed text reads, "When the workers have ceased to work." (That is, *ovdei avoda* replaces *ovrei aveira*.) This is clearly an editorial gloss on the part of those who could not bear the thought that it was the sinners – those who transgressed the sabbatical laws – who determined when it was permissible to fertilize the fields. For instance, Rabbi Y. ben Malki Tzedek raises the following objection: "How can the law be determined by the sins of evildoers, and could Jews really sin so flagrantly?" The answer to his question is, of course, both yes and no: Yes, farmers would in any case transfer waste from their homes to the fields; and no, they did not regard themselves as sinning flagrantly; they were simply lenient when it came to rabbinic prohibitions. The word "sinners" appears in all the manuscripts of the Mishna that can be traced to the Land of Israel: Kauffman, Parma, Cambridge, Maimonides' commentary, etc.

(no planting, pruning, reaping, harvesting, and perhaps plowing)[25] but continued to remove the waste from their homes. They would dispose of it in what were essentially huge compost heaps in their fields. Rabbi Meir ruled that as long as sinners were working their fields, it was forbidden to transfer waste to the compost heaps. Rabbi Yehuda, who was more lax, taught that it depended on the quality of the earth. As Maimonides explains, at a certain point fertilizer no longer affects the soil. If the soil had hardened and dried up such that it could no longer benefit from fertilizer,[26] then it was permissible to take waste from the home out into the fields.

Rabbi Yehuda did not intentionally seek loopholes, but he viewed himself as a man of the people. In this sense he can be contrasted with Rabbi Shimon, who was ensconced in the world of Torah study and regarded himself as set apart from the people. Rabbi Yehuda cared about the spiritual level of all members of society, so he ruled more stringently in cases where there was a temptation to override the law. We see him ruling in this manner in the case of a Jew who worked on Shabbat: Is that Jew allowed to derive benefit from the fruits of his labor? The sages of Usha disagree:

> He who cooks food on the Sabbath, if he did so inadvertently, he may eat it. If he did so deliberately, he may not eat it. These are the words of Rabbi Meir. Rabbi Yehuda says: If he did so inadvertently, he may eat it at the end of the Sabbath. If he did so deliberately, he may not eat it at any time. Rabbi Yoḥanan the Sandal-Maker says: If he did so inadvertently, it may be eaten at the end of the Sabbath by others, but not by him. If he did so deliberately, it should not be eaten either by him or by others. (Tosefta Shabbat 2:15)

25. The sages disagreed about the force of the prohibition of plowing: Was it biblical, derived from the verse "at plowing and harvest you shall cease from labor" (Ex. 34:21), or was it rabbinic? See Mo'ed Katan 3a. In any case, rabbinic sources suggest that farmers observed the biblical prohibitions and violated only the rabbinic ones.
26. Y. Felix, *The Jerusalem Talmud Tractate Shevi'it* [Hebrew] (Jerusalem, 5747), 170.

The opinions are listed here in order of increasing stringency. Rabbi Yehuda and Rabbi Meir disagree about the person who sins inadvertently, which is the subject of the chapter. They are concerned not with the deliberate violator who flagrantly disregards the Sabbath laws, but rather with the Jew who wants to observe Shabbat but makes a mistake: Either he forgets that it is Shabbat, or he forgets that a particular activity is forbidden on Shabbat, or he simply neglects to pay attention to what he is doing.

Rabbi Meir permits such a Jew to eat the food he inadvertently cooks on Shabbat, but Rabbi Yehuda forbids him from doing so. The Talmud relates that the Babylonian sage Rav used to teach in accordance with Rabbi Yehuda when lecturing to the masses in synagogue, and in accordance with Rabbi Meir in his own beit midrash:

> When Rav ruled for his students, he would rule for them in accordance with Rabbi Meir's view. When he lectured in his public discourse, he would lecture in accordance with Rabbi Yehuda's position, on account of the commoners. (Ḥullin 15a)

Rabbi Yehuda believed that one had to rule strictly so that ordinary people would not neglect the law. Even his stringencies derived from his sensitivity to the people among whom he lived.

HIS RELATIONSHIP TO ROMAN RULE

Were Rabbi Yehuda's political views related to those of his teachers – his father, Rabbi Ilai, and Rabbi Tarfon? What was his attitude toward Roman rule?[27] In the following oft-cited source, Rabbi Yehuda extols the virtues of Rome:

> Rabbi Yehuda, Rabbi Yose, and Rabbi Shimon ben Yoḥai were once sitting together, and Yehuda ben Gerim was sitting next to them. Rabbi Yehuda opened the discussion and said: How

27. We cannot be certain how the people of the Galilee reacted to the Bar Kokhba revolt. See M. D. Herr, "From the Destruction of the Temple Until the Bar Kokhba Revolt" [Hebrew], in *History of the Land of Israel*, vol. 4 (Jerusalem, 5744), 360–61.

> admirable are the deeds of this nation! They have built marketplaces, they have built bridges, and they have built bathhouses. (Shabbat 33b)

This is the beginning of the story of Rabbi Shimon bar Yoḥai's retreat into a cave, which we will consider when discussing this sage. For our present purposes, suffice it to say that Rabbi Yehuda's laudatory description of Rome was the subject of academic debate in recent years. Some scholars sought to prove that this source lacks historical basis, arguing that Rabbi Yehuda was in fact very opposed to Roman rule.[28] They staked their claim on moral grounds, contending that no Jew could praise Rome in the aftermath of the Bar Kokhba revolt. It is hard to disagree. The destruction that followed the revolt caused a devastating crisis for the Jewish people, and Rabbi Yehuda surely felt the weight of this tragedy.

Yet even if this source is not historical, it offers us a window into Rabbi Yehuda's talmudic personality. Rabbi Yehuda was concerned with consequences rather than intentions. He recognized that Rome continued to be the ruling power following the Bar Kokhba revolt and would probably remain so for centuries. Rabbi Yehuda did not share Rabbi Akiva's commitment to issues of nationalism and statehood. While he may not necessarily have supported Rome, he also knew better than to speak out against the empire.

Rabbi Yehuda was involved in discussions concerning all aspects of Torah. There is no tractate in which his name or his teachings are not cited.[29] He deliberates on matters of social justice, taxation, torts, and ethical claims. Rabbi Yehuda also participated in legal discussions concerning the Temple and Temple worship. He figures prominently in Tractate Middot, which describes the structure of the Second Temple, its dimensions, and its architectural features. Very few sages are mentioned in this tractate, and the Talmud suggests that it may be the work

28. First and foremost among them is my teacher Yisrael Ben Shalom. See Ben Shalom, "Rabbi Yehuda bar Ilai and His Attitude Toward Rome" [Hebrew], *Tziyon* 49 (5744): 9–24.
29. Epstein, *Literature of the Tanna'im*, 106–25. Epstein attributes entire chapters to Rabbi Yehuda bar Ilai, though his name is not mentioned therein. It is clear that Rabbi Yehuda HaNasi drew heavily on his teachings.

of Rabbi Yehuda bar Ilai.[30] In his preoccupation with Temple matters, Rabbi Yehuda was part of a group of sages who were willing to endure foreign domination while clinging to the hope that the Temple would be rebuilt and God's rule restored.

RABBI YEHUDA: A SCHOLAR WHEN HE SO DESIRED

Tractate Gittin quotes a tradition in the name of Isi ben Yehuda, who sings the praises of various sages. He offers a strange description of Rabbi Yehuda: "A scholar when he so desired" (Gittin 67a). Rashi explains: "When he chose to speak carefully and deliberately, he was a scholar." *Tosafot* add that he was "even greater than Rabbi Meir. Rabbi Meir may have been the sharper one who asked more questions, but Rabbi Yehuda was the more deliberate one who was able to arrive at conclusions, as we learn from the end of Horayot (14)." The Talmud describes Rabbi Meir as a thinker of such sophistication that no one could fathom his intellectual depths. Rabbi Yehuda had no such reputation. But Isi ben Yehuda's statement suggests that if he so desired, Rabbi Yehuda could surpass even Rabbi Meir; he was just too moderate and levelheaded to do so.[31]

The Ḥatam Sofer (Rabbi Moshe Sofer, 1762–1839)[32] offers a more negative understanding of "a scholar when he so desired." His explanation is based on a story that appears elsewhere in the Talmud:

> The rabbis taught: After the death of Rabbi Meir, Rabbi Yehuda said to his students: Rabbi Meir's students are not to enter here, because they are provokers, and they come not to learn Torah, but rather to cut me down in the discussion of law.
>
> Sumakhus forced his way in. He said to them: This is how Rabbi Meir taught me the mishna: If one betroths a woman with

30. Rav Ada bar Ahava attributes Middot to Rabbi Yehuda bar Ilai, though his opinion is rejected. See Y. Yoma 2:2 (39d); Yoma 16a.
31. This is what I found in the commentary of Rabbi Yitzhak Lomrozo, author of *Zera Yitzhak* (eighteenth century, Tunisia).
32. Ḥatam Sofer, *Insights into Tractate Gittin* [Hebrew], 67b.

> his portion of an offering, whether an offering of greater or lesser holiness, he has not betrothed her.
>
> Rabbi Yehuda grew angry at his students. He said to them: Did I not say to you: Rabbi Meir's students are not to enter here, because they are provokers, and they come not to learn Torah, but rather to cut me down in the discussion of law? How can a woman come into the Temple's inner courtyard [where offerings of greater holiness are eaten]?
>
> Rabbi Yose said: Shall they say: Meir died, Yehuda became angry, and Yose remained silent? What will become of the words of Torah? Is it not possible for a person to accept betrothal for his daughter in the Temple courtyard? And is it not possible for a woman to authorize an agent to accept betrothal on her behalf in the Temple courtyard? And furthermore, what if a woman forced her way into the Temple's inner courtyard? (Kiddushin 52b)

The Ḥatam Sofer interprets this passage as follows:

> Rabbi Yehuda – "a scholar when he so desired." This can be explained according to the definition of a sage as someone who learns from all people. Rabbi Yehuda did not want to learn from the students of Rabbi Meir, for he said, "Rabbi Meir's students are not to enter here." Therefore he was a scholar "when he so desired" – that is, when he desired to learn from all people.

Rabbi Yehuda did not straddle heaven and earth, nor did he retreat into caves or penetrate mystical orchards. He recognized that the generation after the revolt needed a stable leadership that was not frenzied and charismatic, but which could navigate a steady course guided by the people's needs. Rabbi Yehuda started out as "the leading speaker on every occasion." Already then, when he welcomed the sages to the assembly at Usha, he pointed out that he was not superior to his colleagues, but that "a man's place brings him honor." While he may not have been more brilliant or learned than his contemporaries, he certainly was more grounded. The next patriarch, Rabban Shimon ben Gamliel, would choose Rabbi Yehuda bar Ilai to offer instruction in the patriarchal house (Menaḥot 104). This role befits someone who knew how to rule decisively regarding matters of uncertainty. The Talmud even suggests that the entire Usha generation was named for him:

> "Grace is false" [Prov. 31:29] – this refers to the generation of Moses. "And beauty is vain" [Prov. 31:29] – this refers to the generation of King Hezekiah. "It is a God-fearing woman who should be praised" – this refers to the generation of Rabbi Yehuda bar Ilai. They said of Rabbi Yehuda bar Ilai that six of his disciples would cover themselves with only one cloak and occupy themselves with the study of Torah. (Sanhedrin 20a)

Chapter Four

Rabbi Yose ben Ḥalafta: He Has His Reasons

TZIPPORI: CAPITAL OF THE GALILEE

The second sage of the founding generation at Usha was Rabbi Yose ben Ḥalafta. Rabbi Yose grew up in Tzippori. Tzippori enjoyed political stability for many years, in part because of its continued support for Rome, even during the Great Revolt. Unlike Rabbi Yehuda bar Ilai, who subsisted on limited means in an agrarian society, Rabbi Yose ben Ḥalafta was a wealthy man living in a bustling city. Rabbi Yehuda, as we saw, frequently interacted with Jewish farmers who had to compromise in matters of halakha on account of difficult economic circumstances. But Rabbi Yose lived among a Jewish elite exposed to the Roman culture of leisure.

Historians long assumed that the Jews kept their distance from Roman theaters and stadiums: "The Jews, guided by their spiritual leaders, the sages, viewed these forms of Roman entertainment as abominations, and kept as far away from them as possible."[1] After all, how could

1. S. Krauss, *Persia and Rome in the Talmud and Midrash* [Hebrew] (Jerusalem, 5708), 220.

a Jew enjoy a performance when he could be learning Torah? As one historian attests:

> The idolatrous character of the public space meant that Jews stayed away from cultural and educational institutions, including athletic events. The theaters, too, were bound up with the pagan cult. In general we can say that the Jews were not attracted to Greco-Roman culture, which took root in these cities. Although after the destruction of the Temple the pagan world had its allure, the activity of the sages and of other Jewish leaders succeeded in keeping the people away. The fact that the Jews were living in Roman cities meant they had to speak Greek and understand Greek wisdom. Greek was the primary language of international commerce, as well as the language of imperial and civic administration.[2]

According to some scholars, the public sermons of the sages that became increasingly popular during this period were an attempt to compete for attention, though "most of the nation preferred the sermon in synagogue to the circus shows."[3] These words were written in a particular historical context by a scholar unfamiliar with the possibility that Jews might live in major cosmopolitan cities under stable economic conditions. With the exception of German Jewry before the Nazis, the Jews of Europe never felt secure in the countries in which they lived; their sense of belonging was always precarious. Only in our present atmosphere of cultural and social emancipation can we consider this period of ancient history in a new light. We can now think more critically about Jewish assimilation in the big cities, the forms of cultural consumption in which Jews engaged during their leisure time, and their efforts to strike a balance between their fidelity to Judaism and their attraction to their non-Jewish surroundings.[4] More recent talmudic scholarship suggests that

2. Alon, *History of the Jews*, vol. 1, 83–84.
3. Y. Heinemann, *Public Sermons in the Time of the Talmud* [Hebrew] (Jerusalem, 5742), 8–9.
4. Y. L. Levine, *Judaism and Hellenism: Confrontation or Cultural Diffusion?* [Hebrew] (Jerusalem, 5760), 11–20. Levine surveys the academic literature, which ranges from those who try to trace the influence of Hellenism on Judaism (most notably

Jews who lived in Roman towns were active consumers of Roman culture. They took part in theater performances and sporting events, and even served as gladiators.[5]

The archeological evidence, too, has sharpened our sense of this period. Greek and Roman works of art were discovered in synagogues dating back to talmudic times. Archeologists found mosaics depicting the zodiac[6] in six ancient synagogues, including one in Tzippori.[7] In light of this evidence, scholars now claim that Greek and Roman culture influenced not just wealthy Jews, but also the great sages of Israel. When a particularly splendid house was discovered on the hilltop of Tzippori, filled with precious objects and decorated with a floor mosaic depicting scenes from the life of Dionysus, the Greek god of wine, archeologists and scholars immediately considered that it might have been the home of Rabbi Yehuda HaNasi; after all, who else in Tzippori would have lived so splendidly?[8] This speculation even found its way into a book by a reputable scholar of the period, who wrote that "according

S. Lieberman) to those who belittle any such influence. Naturally, this debate is between liberal and conservative Jews, which reminds us that what is at stake is not history but historiography.

5. I would argue that the first scholar to make this claim was M. D. Herr. See Herr, "Outside Influences on the Lives of the Sages" [Hebrew], in *Assimilation and Absorption: Continuity and Exchange in the Culture of Israel and the Nation of Israel – Assimilation and Rejection*, ed. Y. Kaplan and M. Stern (Jerusalem, 5749), 89–92.
6. The pagan origins of the zodiac were familiar to Jews of the time, though Josephus points out that such imagery was barred from the Temple. See Josephus, *The Jewish War* v:214. See also Y. L. Levine, *Judaism and Hellenism: Confrontation or Cultural Diffusion?* [Hebrew] (Jerusalem, 5760), 124–125.
7. Z. Weiss, "The Jews of the Land of Israel and Roman Leisure Culture" [Hebrew], *Tziyon* 66 (5761): 427–50. See also Z. Weiss, "The Culture of Entertainment and Institutions of Entertainment in the Roman Land of Israel, and as Reflected in Rabbinic Sources" [Hebrew] (PhD diss., Hebrew University of Jerusalem, 5754).
8. In considering this supposition, Z. Weiss writes as follows: "Even if the architectural plan of the house in Tzippori befits Rabbi Yehuda HaNasi, it seems that the nature of the artwork discovered would preclude the possibility that the house belonged to him. Yet this claim must be considered with an open mind…. Can we assume, not just hypothetically, that a person of Rebbi's stature would affix a mosaic like this in his front hall?" See Weiss, "Between Pagans and Jews: Toward the Identification of the Dionysus House in Roman Tzippori" [Hebrew], *Catedra* 99 (Nisan 5761): 7–26.

to recent research, the house of Rabbi Yehuda HaNasi has been identified in Tzippori."[9]

The debate about the extent to which Jews were influenced by Roman culture, which has given rise to extreme claims on both sides, must be restored to more reasonable proportions. On the one hand, the Jewish community in Tzippori clearly took full advantage of all that cosmopolitan Roman culture had to offer. On the other hand, it seems more plausible to assume that the sages who led this community kept their distance from these earthly delights. Rabbinic sources advocate distancing oneself as much as possible from Roman leisure culture. Nonetheless, these sources do reflect not the free spirit that dominated the big cities, but rather the party line of the Jewish establishment. With this more balanced understanding, we can begin to consider Rabbi Yose ben Ḥalafta, who returned to his hometown of Tzippori and became the local rabbinic authority.

THE HOUSE OF RABBI YOSE'S FATHER: RABBI ḤALAFTA OF TZIPPORI

Rabbi Ḥalafta, father of Rabbi Yose, is identified throughout rabbinic literature as one of the great sages of the Galilee. His family prided itself on a genealogy book from Jerusalem that traced Ḥalafta's lineage to Jehonadab son of Rekhab.[10] This family did not leave the Land of Israel during the Babylonian exile, because Jehonadab son of Rekhab was promised by the prophet Jeremiah that in the merit of his family's fidelity to tradition, they would never be cut off from the land (see Jer. 35).[11] The association with Jehonadab son of Rekhab is thus a sign of

9. A. Oppenheimer, *Rabbi Yehuda HaNasi* [Hebrew] (Jerusalem, 5767), 134.
10. Y. Ta'anit 4:2 (68a).
11. Scholars of rabbinic history generally base themselves on Rashi's commentary on Sanhedrin 104a ("They are the Kenites"), and argue that this family originated in Babylonia. The Talmud quotes Rabbi Yose as saying, "Rest assured that you have made me rest assured." Rashi and later commentators interpreted this statement to mean that there were negative associations with the Jews of Babylon. See Z. Frankel, *Methods of the Mishna*, 174: "He was from a family that came from Babylon." But Hyman (*Legends*, 705) quotes Rabbi Yitzhak Isaac HaLevi, *Master of the Early Generations* 1 [Hebrew] (Frankfurt, 5678), 120, which argues that Rabbi Yose's family hailed from the Galilee.

commitment to the Land of Israel and to traditional observance. These are the values that Jeremiah seeks to impart when he brings Rekhab's descendants to a wine party in the Temple, and these are the values that Ḥalafta imparts to his children.[12]

Rabbi Yose remained faithful to his father's teachings at every stage of his education, transmitting Galilean customs wherever he found himself. The Galileans were known for holding fast to their traditions, which dated back hundreds of years. The first Jews settled in the Galilee during the Hasmonean period.[13] They were rooted in their land and culture (unlike the inhabitants of Yavneh and the south, who did not fully settle into their new surroundings until the persecution precluded a return to Jerusalem). One description of a prayer offered in time of drought gives voice to this sense of rootedness:

> It once happened during the time of Rabbi Ḥalafta and Rabbi Ḥanania [Ḥanina] ben Teradion that someone passed before the ark and concluded the entire blessing, and they did not respond Amen after him. [Rather:]
>
> "Blow, priests, blow!
>
> "He who answered our father Abraham on Mount Moriah, He will answer you and heed the sound of your crying this day.
>
> "Sound the alarm, sons of Aaron, sound the alarm!
>
> "He who answered our forefathers at the Red Sea, He will answer you and heed the sound of your crying this day."
>
> And when the matter came before the sages, they said: We did not behave this way except at the eastern gate and on the Temple Mount. (Mishna Ta'anit 2:5)

This text preserves a version of the prayer for rain that differed from the version familiar to the Yavneh sages. This ceremony, performed in the

12. Jeremiah, who could not tolerate the gulf between the evil Jehoiakim and his righteous father, Josiah, sought to furnish the former with a model of family loyalty and thus brought the members of the house of Rekhab before him..
13. Nittai the Arbelite may have been the first sage to settle there. See S. Klein, *The Land of the Galilee*, 9–19.

Temple, was accompanied by shofar blasts and by blessings that have survived from a period before the Jewish prayer book was formalized.[14] It is hard to know if the custom described was brought from Jerusalem or had been preserved in the Galilee for centuries. Regardless, this source attests to the independent customs of the various regions in which Jews found themselves.

Rabbi Yose tells of several customs that were unique to the Jews of the Galilee, including strict modesty rules governing the relationship between the sexes.[15] It seems that Rabbi Yose grew up in the secure and stable world of his father's traditions, and the cosmopolitan culture of Tzippori did not interfere with his spiritual development. The following story about his childhood attests to the normality of the environment in which he was raised:

> "When you give your mouth to evil, and your tongue frames deceit" [Ps. 50:19] – When Rabbi Yose ben Ḥalafta was a boy and used to play with other boys, a man saw him and said to him: Your father should be told that you play with the boys. Rabbi Yose answered: By your life, what does it matter to you? If you tell my father, he will strike me, and you will accustom your tongue to speak slander. Hence, "When you give your mouth to evil, and your tongue frames deceit." (Midrash on Ps. 50)

Rabbi Ḥalafta was a well-known figure in the Galilee. He was among those sages who welcomed the patriarch Rabban Gamliel of Yavneh to Tiberias:

> Rabbi Yose said: There was an incident in which Rabbi Ḥalafta went to Rabban Gamliel in Tiberias and found him seated at the temple of Yoḥanan ben Nezif. In his hand was the scroll of Job in Aramaic, which he was reading. Rabbi Ḥalafta said to him: I remember that Rabban Gamliel the elder, your grandfather, was once sitting on the staircase going up to the Temple Mount. They

14. D. Levine, *Public Fasts and Rabbinic Homilies* [Hebrew] (Tel Aviv, 5761), 66–96.
15. Mishna Ketubot 1:5; Tosefta Ketubot 1:4.

> brought him a scroll of Job in Aramaic, and he instructed his sons: Put it away in storage under the course of stones. (Tosefta Shabbat 13:2)

Rabbi Yose speaks of a tradition dating back to Temple times, presumably from Rabbi Ḥalafta's youth.[16]

HOLDING FAST TO THE TRADITIONS OF HIS GALILEAN ANCESTORS

A brief passage in the Talmud offers us a sense of the confidence and trust that Rabbi Yose inspired. He studied in the Galilee, in the same beit midrash where his father had learned, and with the same teacher:

> Rabbi Yose said: When my father, Ḥalafta, went to Rabbi Yoḥanan ben Nuri to learn Torah…. (Bava Kamma 70a)

Rabbi Yose relates that his teacher, Rabbi Yoḥanan ben Nuri, also taught his father, Rabbi Ḥalafta. Even as the community in Judea was experiencing the turmoil of rebellion and persecution, the Galilee enjoyed stability. Rabbi Yoḥanan ben Nuri was the great teacher of Torah in the Galilee, and he preserved the traditions of this region. We find evidence of the uniqueness of Galilean customs in a source that describes the Rosh HaShana prayers in Usha, after the center of rabbinic leadership had relocated to the Galilee:

> When they sanctified the new year in Usha, Rabbi Yoḥanan ben Beroka passed before the ark on the first day and said it in accordance with the view of Rabbi Yoḥanan ben Nuri. Rabban Shimon ben Gamliel said: This was not the custom in Yavneh. On the second day Rabbi Ḥanina ben Rabbi Yose HaGlili passed before the ark and said the prayer in accordance with the view of Rabbi Akiva. Rabban Shimon ben Gamliel said: This was the custom in Yavneh. (Tosefta Rosh HaShana 2:11)

16. Several sources attest that Rabbi Yose was acquainted with Rabbi Akiva. See Tosefta Kelim 1:5, Ma'aser Sheni 1:13.

Rabban Shimon ben Gamliel, the patriarch in Usha who had come from Yavneh, was not familiar with Rabbi Yoḥanan ben Nuri's customs. The Mishna in Tractate Rosh HaShana describes a fascinating debate between Rabbi Akiva and Rabbi Yoḥanan ben Nuri with regard to the blessing of kingship in the *Amida* prayer of Rosh HaShana. Should this blessing be attached to the third blessing (which sanctifies God) or to the fourth blessing (which sanctifies the day)? Rabbi Akiva thought the blessing of kingship should be treated in its own right; Rabbi Yoḥanan ben Nuri held that this blessing should be added to the blessing sanctifying God's name. This Mishna is laden with religious and political significance,[17] but suffice it to say that the Galilean Jews preserved their own customs steadfastly.

Rabbi Yose lived with an awareness of his illustrious lineage and the historical traditions of his hometown. He is quoted as saying:

> In all my days I have never disobeyed the words of my colleagues. I know about myself that I am not a priest. But if my colleagues told me to go up to the platform where the priests recite the priestly blessings, I would go up. (Shabbat 118b)

Rabbi Yose believed that custom and tradition carried greater weight than any knowledge he might have possessed about himself. He had tremendous respect for the values of community and continuity.

Throughout the Talmud, Rabbi Yose is described as studying with all the great sages of Yavneh: Rabbi Yehoshua, Rabbi Akiva, Rabbi Tarfon, and Rabbi Yishmael.[18] He is often counted among the students of Rabbi Akiva, whose traditions he transmitted after the persecution.[19]

17. Y. Tabori, "The Place of the Kingship Blessing in the Rosh HaShana Prayers" [Hebrew], *Tarbiz* 48:1–2 (5739): 30–34.
18. Rabbi Yehoshua: Pesaḥim 103a; Rabbi Akiva: Pesaḥim 108a (see Reish Lakish's statement: "Rabbi Yose said in the name of Rabbi Akiva); Rabbi Tarfon: Tosefta Shevi'it 4:4; Rabbi Yishmael: Bava Kamma 54b.
19. See the discussion in the opening chapter of this book about the death of Rabbi Akiva and legacy he transmitted to his five disciples. The aggadic tradition regards all the Torah transmitted after the Bar Kokhba revolt as a continuation of Rabbi Akiva's

But as he himself attests on several occasions, his principal teachers were his father, Ḥalafta, and Rabbi Yoḥanan ben Nuri.[20]

DEBATING PHILOSOPHICAL ISSUES IN THE PARLOR OF A ROMAN MATRON

Where was Rabbi Yose during the Bar Kokhba revolt and the persecution that ensued? It seems that he never had to leave his hometown. Tzippori did not participate in the Bar Kokhba revolt, just as it had played no role in the Great Revolt. The town enjoyed peaceful coexistence with Rome, and even if some of its inhabitants were displeased with Roman rule, they did not voice their discontent. They knew to keep quiet. Perhaps this is how we ought to understand the famous story in which the sages weigh the merits of Roman rule:

> Rabbi Yehuda, Rabbi Yose, and Rabbi Shimon ben Yoḥai were once sitting together, and Yehuda ben Gerim was sitting next to them. Rabbi Yehuda opened the discussion and said: How admirable are the deeds of this nation! They have built marketplaces, they have built bridges, and they have built bathhouses.
>
> Rabbi Yose remained silent....
>
> Yehuda ben Gerim went and recounted their words, and the reports were heard by the authorities. They said: Yehuda, who praised us, he too shall be praised. Yose, who remained silent, shall be exiled to Tzippori. (Shabbat 33b)

For Rabbi Yose, Tzippori was not exile but home. Perhaps the editors of the Talmud were implying that Tzippori was a spiritual exile because of the pagan culture of the city.[21] The inhabitants of Tzippori spoke Greek

teachings, but we must not favor these sources over Rabbi Yose's own testimony as to the identity of his teachers.

20. Epstein, *Literature of the Tanna'im*, 126.

21. Scholars have debated the meaning of the phrase "Yose... shall be exiled to Tzippori." Some have tried to read the text as saying, "Yose... shall be exiled from Tzippori," but this reading is not supported by Rabbi Yose's continuous presence there. I would argue that the Babylonian Talmud is not documenting history, but rather conveying a general idea.

and frequented Greco-Roman shops and places of entertainment. Jews constituted the majority of the population, though Roman government workers also lived among them. Like any foreign occupying power, the Roman citizens in Palestine sought a suitable place to make their home. Tzippori had much to recommend it, including entertainment venues, a temperate climate, and municipal services. The Talmud speaks of the firefighting association of Tzippori, which was run by non-Jews:

> There was an incident in which the courtyard of Yosef ben Simai in Shiḥin caught fire on the Sabbath, and the men of the Roman governor of Tzippori came to extinguish it, because Yosef ben Simai was the king's treasurer. However, he did not allow them to do so on account of the honor of the Sabbath. A miracle occurred on his behalf and rain fell, extinguishing the fire. That night, he sent every member of the garrison two sela coins, and to the lieutenant among them he sent fifty. And when the sages heard of the matter, they said: He did not need to do that, for we have learned in the Mishna: A gentile who comes to extinguish the fire, they may not say to him, "Extinguish it," nor must they tell him, "Do not extinguish it." (Shabbat 121a)

As the royal treasurer, Yosef ben Simai of the town of Shiḥin was a privileged resident, and thus when a fire broke out in his home, the members of the Tzippori fire department rushed to extinguish it. Yet Yosef ben Simai, a religious Jew, did not let them carry out their work on Shabbat. Nonetheless, the flames were miraculously doused. After Shabbat he sent a tribute to the entire garrison and an even larger tribute to its lieutenant.

The Talmud includes this story because of the halakhic issue at stake: What is the law if a non-Jew comes to do work on behalf of a Jew on the Sabbath, even if the Jew has not requested his services? More relevant to our concerns is this account of an observant Jew who held a senior position in the Roman administration. (The story does not indicate if this event took place before or after the Bar Kokhba revolt.)

The cosmopolitan city of Tzippori was a place of many colorful cultural encounters. The sages often found themselves in the parlors and drawing rooms of local aristocrats, both Jewish and non-Jewish. There they frequently engaged in philosophical debate, which was an integral aspect of Roman culture. The Talmud recounts about twenty such debates between Rabbi Yose and an unnamed Roman matron. She was a wealthy lady, presumably not Jewish, who lived in a fancy neighborhood and entertained Rabbi Yose in her home. Did these conversations really take place, or are they a product of the midrashic imagination? No one has successfully answered this question, and perhaps the most compelling conclusion is drawn by historian M. D. Herr: "The question is not whether these conversations actually happened, but rather, could these conversations have actually happened? That is, what issues did the sages discuss with the great leaders of Rome, and did these issues have particular significance?"[22]

Rabbi Yehuda bar Ilai had one such encounter with a matron. She taunted him about the color of his cheeks, which she said resembled those of a drunkard. He, in turn, offered a witty rejoinder. In contrast to Rabbi Yehuda's superficial and singular encounter, Rabbi Yose's conversations with his Roman interlocutor were thought-provoking and involved. The Roman matron challenged Rabbi Yose to expose her to Jewish thought in all its depth and complexity. The topics of their conversations included fundamental questions about God's existence,[23] divine providence, Israel as the chosen people, God's relationship to Esau, the commandment of circumcision, and the biblical stories about Joseph.[24]

Did all of these conversations take place with the same Roman matron, or with several? Here, too, Herr's reflections are instructive:

> It seems that there was a preoccupation with the Roman matron, whose religious challenges and doubts typified the second century of the common era, the climax of the "failure of nerve," in

22. M. D. Herr, "The Historical Significance of the Debates Between the Sages and the Roman Elite" [Hebrew], *Proceedings of the International Congress of Jewish Studies*, vol. 4 (Jerusalem, 5729), 269–97. This quote comes from 270.
23. Exodus Rabba 3:12. Here God is contrasted with the primordial serpent. The serpent was the symbol of many ancient gods, and this dialogue deals with the question of God's origins. See Herr, *From the Destruction*, 288 note 129, which cites the relevant sources.
24. Ibid., 288–89.

> the words of G. Murray, a period in which "superstitions and foolish terror" dominated,[25] and in which people fell prey to popular trends and traditions. It is of little consequence whether these conversations took place with a single Roman matron (though it seems almost certain that this was in fact the case). It is likewise irrelevant whether this Roman matron actually existed or not. Even if she was merely imagined, she offers a window into the rabbinic imagination at a particular historical moment. This matron, who grew up in a culture of pagan Hellenism, apparently had doubts about her own faith and sought a new system of belief. Her quest led to her interest in philosophy, particularly Epicureanism, and to the history of Gnosticism, Christianity, and Judaism.[26]

We will consider one of her dialogues with Rabbi Yose in order to get a sense of the nature and tone of their exchanges:

> A Roman matron asked Rabbi Yose: In how many days did the Holy One, Blessed Be He, create His world?
>
> He said to her: In six days, as it is written, "For in six days God made the heavens and the earth" [Ex. 20:10].
>
> And from that time, what has kept Him busy?
>
> He said to her: He sits and makes matches, assigning the daughter of one man to another, the wife of one man to another, this person's money to another.
>
> She said to him: Is that so difficult? I can do it myself. I have many slaves and maidservants; I can match them up easily!
>
> He said to her: If the matter seems so simple to you, it is as difficult for the Holy One, Blessed Be He, as the parting of the Red Sea. Rabbi Yose ben Ḥalafta went on his way.
>
> What did she do? She took a thousand slaves and a thousand maidservants and arranged them in rows. She said: This

25. G. Murray, *Five Stages of Greek Religion* (New York: Anchor, 1955), 162.
26. A collection of all these conversations would serve as a sort of ancient *Kuzari*. See Herr, *From the Destruction*, 289–90. He explains that it is unclear whether the matron ultimately converted.

man will marry this woman, and this woman will marry this man. And she matched them all in one night. The next day they came to her. One had an injured brain; one had a black eye; one had a broken leg. She said to them: What happened to you?

One woman said: I don't want him.

Another man said: I don't want her.

Immediately she sent for Rabbi Yose ben Ḥalafta. She said to him: There is no god like your God. It is true: Your Torah is indeed beautiful and praiseworthy, and you spoke the truth.

He said to her: Did I not tell you that if it seems simple to you, it is as difficult for the Holy One, Blessed Be He, as the parting of the Red Sea? God matches people against their will, and against their interest. As it is written, "God restores the lonely to their homes, sets free the imprisoned, safe and sound" [Ps. 68:7]. What does "safe and sound" (*bakosharot*) mean? Weeping (*bekhi*) and song (*shirot*). He who desires his companion utters song, and he who does not weeps. (Genesis Rabba 66)[27]

In this story we are privy to a drawing-room conversation that functions as a sort of private tutorial. Unlike the beit midrash, in which the teacher asks questions and the student tries to answer them, here, in the matron's salon, it is she who asks questions and the rabbi who tries to answer them. This is an advanced lesson. The matron takes it as a given that God created the world, and asks, "In how many days did the Holy One, Blessed Be He, create His world?" Rabbi Yose answers by quoting a biblical verse: "For in six days God made the heavens and the earth" (Ex. 20:10). After this preliminary exchange, they come to the heart of the matter: What has God been doing since? The implicit premise of her question is the Aristotelian notion that although the world was created, the Creator is no longer involved in creation. The matron seeks to understand the mystery of divine providence. The question "What has kept Him busy?" is her way of asking, "Does God have any direct influence on us today?"

27. This story was a favorite among those who gave sermons during the talmudic period. See the list of parallel sources in Herr, *From the Destruction*, 288 note 131.

Rabbi Yose responds that since creation, God has been spending His time making matches: assigning the daughter of one man to another, the wife of one man to another, one person's money to another. The first category is straightforward: we would expect to find the daughter of one man matched with another man. Rabbi Yose's point is that the matchmaking is the work not of one's human parents, but of God. When Rabbi Yose then speaks of "the wife of one man to another," he is referring to cases such as a levirate marriage or the marriage of a widow. To understand the third category, in which God assigns one person's money to another, we must remember that Rabbi Yose is hosted in the matron's parlor, surrounded by splendid wealth. The Talmud relates that the matron has a thousand slaves and a thousand maidservants, though these numbers are surely exaggerated to emphasize her affluence. Rabbi Yose concludes with "this person's money to another," implying that even the matron's wealth is not really hers, since it, too, comes from God, who can just as soon take it away. This is an important lesson in divine providence.

The matron responds scornfully: You are reducing the Creator of the Universe to a mere matchmaker? Rabbi Yose replies, "It is as difficult for the Holy One, Blessed Be He, as the parting of the Red Sea." This expression is so oft-quoted that we almost forget to question why Rabbi Yose chose this particular image. In speaking of joining two people as one, why invoke this image of the sea split in two? It seems that Rabbi Yose wishes to highlight the connection between the creation of the world at the beginning of time, and God's ongoing involvement in human affairs, which may take the form of readily apparent miracles (such as the splitting of the sea) or more subtle ones (such as matchmaking). Splitting the sea –usually one uniform body of water – is a miracle. And conjoining two people as one is miraculous, too.[28]

When the lesson is concluded, Rabbi Yose returns home. But the matron is intrigued. She wishes to see if she can play God, so she rushes to match her servants and maidservants, doing so arbitrarily: This man will marry this woman, and this woman will marry this man.

28. A. Shinan, "The Splitting of the Sea" [Hebrew], in *The President's House Study Group on the Bible and Jewish Sources* (Jerusalem, 5747), 23–37.

In the morning, she makes an unexpected discovery. She had thought matchmaking would be a simple affair. After all, slaves exist to do their master's will, so surely their master can dictate whom they will marry. The matron is surprised to learn that even if she controls her slaves and maidservants, she is not the master of their emotional lives. Matchmaking requires the willed consent of others, which is beyond her control.

The midrash closes with the exegesis of a biblical verse: "God restores the lonely to their homes, sets free the imprisoned, safe and sound" (Ps. 68:7). The word for safe and sound, *bakosharot,* is interpreted by Rabbi Yose as "with weeping and song," playing on the phonemes comprising the Hebrew word. This verse describes the awakening of the individual will that is necessary for a person to escape his solitude. God conjoins man and woman and returns them to their natural state, that of Adam, who was created both male and female. Rabbi Yose's exegesis, a lesson in divine providence, is a reminder that everything depends on human willingness to participate in God's plan.[29]

BETWEEN "WAYS OF PEACE" AND "DO NOT GIVE THEM LODGING"

Not surprisingly, it was the towns and cities and not the villages that were the primary sites of cultural exchange between Jews and non-Jews. So we must treat the question of the Jews' relationships with their non-Jewish neighbors on the local level. We will consider one aspect of this dynamic, namely the laws governing the sale of land to non-Jews.

The sages of the Usha generation were divided regarding the prohibition of selling fields and homes to non-Jews:

> We may not rent houses, fields, or vineyards to them, and we do not provide them with fields on the basis of sharecropping, or of contracting to raise beasts, neither with a Jew nor with a Samaritan. Under what circumstances does this apply? In the Land of Israel. In Syria we rent them houses but not fields. In both the

29. For a literary analysis of the story, along with a scholarly bibliography, see N. Ben Ari, "Rabbi Yose and the Matron."

> Land of Israel and Syria, a person should not rent his field to a non-Jew, according to Rabbi Meir.
>
> Rabbi Yose says: Even in the Land of Israel we rent them houses and fields. Outside the Land of Israel we sell them both. (Tosefta Avoda Zara 2:8)

This is the version of the Tosefta that appears in the printed text and in the Erfurt manuscript. But in the Vilna manuscript and in the first printing, Rabbi Yose says: "In the Land of Israel we rent them houses. And in Syria we sell them houses and rent them fields."[30] The difference between these two versions is significant. Are we permitted to rent fields to non-Jews in the Land of Israel? In the Mishna, too, this matter is unclear:

> In the Land of Israel we may not rent them houses or, needless to say, fields. And in Syria we may rent them houses but not fields. And outside the Land of Israel we may sell them houses and rent them fields. This is the view of Rabbi Meir. Rabbi Yose says: In the Land of Israel we may rent them houses but not fields, and in Syria we may sell them houses and rent them fields, and outside the Land of Israel we may sell them either. (Mishna Avoda Zara 1:8)

This is the version that appears in the printed text of the Mishna, according to which Rabbi Yose teaches that it is permissible to rent houses but not fields to non-Jews (as in the Vilna manuscript of the Tosefta). But in the manuscripts of the Mishna,[31] the words "but not fields" are missing, which makes the Mishna consistent with our printed Tosefta in that Rabbi Yose permits renting both houses and fields to non-Jews.

30. There is a debate about the proper version of the Tosefta both in the printed texts and in the writings of the Rishonim. See S. Lieberman, *Tosefet Rishonim* [Hebrew], vol. 2 (Jerusalem, 5697), 189.
31. This is how the text reads in all the manuscripts of the Mishna from the Land of Israel: Kauffman, Parma, Cambridge, and the mishnayot in the Jerusalem Talmud. Rabbi Y. N. Epstein notes that this is the case but comments that "the language doesn't seem right." See Epstein, *Introduction to the Text of the Mishna* [Hebrew] (Jerusalem, 5708), 1020.

The confusion regarding the proper wording of the text reflects a lack of consensus about the issue under discussion. All agree that Rabbi Yose permits renting houses to non-Jews, which is necessary if Jews are to live side by side with others in a cosmopolitan city.[32] The issue of renting fields is more complicated, since doing so could endanger the property rights of Jews in the Land of Israel.[33] In any case, it is clear that when compared to Rabbi Meir's opinion, Rabbi Yose's ruling is more attuned to the socioeconomic reality and more conducive to peaceful coexistence.

HIS RELATIONSHIP WITH ARISTOCRATIC COMMONERS

Rabbi Yehuda bar Ilai, as we saw above, was sensitive to the plight of those Jews who sought to evade the requirements of halakha or look for lenient rulings as a result of their adverse economic situation. His contemporary, Rabbi Yose, lived among the aristocrats of Tzippori, who were also not paragons of religious observance. Rabbi Yose tried to guide his community's practice, retaining a foothold in the world of Torah even as he was drawn to more colorful settings. The Talmud describes Rabbi Yose's struggle to promote stricter observance of the Sabbath in Tzippori:

> They inquired: If a person transgressed and left a pot [of uncooked food] on an unbanked stove, what is the law? Do the rabbis penalize him [and forbid consumption of the food] or not? Come learn a proof…: When Rabbi Yose went to Tzippori, he discovered hot water that had been left on an unbanked stove, and he did not prohibit it to them. He also discovered shriveled eggs that had been left on an unbanked stove, and he did prohibit them to them. (Shabbat 38a)

32. Y. Cohen, *Episodes in the History of the Tannaitic Period* [Hebrew] (Jerusalem, 5738), 27.
33. The main issue here is the biblical prohibition of "do not give them lodging" (Deut. 7:2) and the extent to which a sage can modify this prohibition to allow for peaceful coexistence with non-Jews. See H. Burgenski, "Do Not Give Them Lodging: The Development of a Command" [Hebrew], in *Jewish Culture in the Eye of the Storm: A Volume in Memory of Yosef Aḥituv*, ed. A. Sagi (Ein Tzurim, 5762), 537–568.

This is characteristic of Rabbi Yose's style of halakhic decision-making. He does not rule uniformly in all cases, but is prepared to compromise. He permits the hot water that was left on the stove, since it may have begun cooking before Shabbat. But he forbids the shriveled eggs, since there is no chance that they were already cooked before Shabbat.

Another source attests to the lax standards of Sabbath observance in Tzippori. Here Rabbi Yose announces that he will declare any legal deed that is dated on Shabbat or Yom Kippur to be null and void. The need for such a declaration suggests that the Jews of Tzippori were conducting business on Shabbat. Upon hearing this ruling, Rabbi Yehuda reminds Rabbi Yose that he himself once accepted such a deed:

> Rabbi Yehuda said to him: Such a case came before you in Tzippori, and you declared the deed to be valid! Rabbi Yose said to him: I never declared such a deed valid. But if I did declare it valid, so I declared it valid. (Tosefta Makkot 1:3)

The following three sources speak to the Jews' sense of danger and instability in Tzippori in Rabbi Yose's day:

> 1. Rami bar Abba said: Rabbi Yose instituted in Tzippori that a woman should not walk in the street with her child behind her because of an incident that once occurred. (Sanhedrin 19a)

The Talmud does not elaborate on this "incident," though it suggests that a child was once kidnapped when walking behind his mother. Rashi preserves a more detailed account:

> The child was kidnapped and sequestered in a house. When the mother turned around and did not see her child, she began to shout and weep. One of the kidnappers then approached her and said: Come and I will show him to you. She entered the house after him, and they violated her there. (Rashi on Sanhedrin 19a)[34]

34. This tradition, preserved by Rashi, is also cited by Maimonides in his *Mishneh Torah, Laws of Forbidden Relationships,* 21:17, and then quoted in *Shulḥan Arukh, Even*

The Talmud proceeds as follows:

> 2. And Rami bar Abba said: Rabbi Yose instituted in Tzippori that women should converse while in an outhouse because of the prohibition of seclusion. (Sanhedrin 19a)

The outhouse was located outside the home, usually in an open field. A woman who went alone to the outhouse would be unprotected, and thus Rabbi Yose ruled that women should go in pairs and converse while there so as to ward off any potential miscreants.

> 3. Rabbi Yose said: There was an incident in which a girl went down to draw water from a spring, and she was violated. Rabbi Yoḥanan ben Nuri said: If the majority of the men of the town were eligible to marry into the priesthood, then she may also be married into the priesthood. (Mishna Ketubot 1:10)

This is Tzippori in all its glory. On the one hand, a young girl is violated when walking to draw water from a spring; on the other hand, the incident takes place in a town where the majority of the men are eligible to marry into the priesthood, that is, they have no bastard ancestors or other tainted lineage. And thus this girl will suffer less on account of their crime.[35]

HaEzer 22. After it became halakha, this matter took on a life of its own, with no connection to the case that had given rise to the law in the first place. In our own day, we find Jews turning to their rabbis to ask if they are permitted to walk behind their mothers, since the *Shulḥan Arukh* simply states that "it is forbidden for a woman to walk with her children behind her." See Rabbi Menashe Klein, *Responsa Mishneh Halakhot* [Hebrew], 12, 305.

35. Both Talmuds quote Rav, who adds that this incident took place "in the caravans (*karonot*) of Tzippori." This comment led to an extended discussion that continues today. Rashi and other early medieval commentators understand Rav to mean that this incident took place on a market day, when there were many caravans around, and that Rabbi Yoḥanan permitted the girl to marry based on a technical halakhic principle relating to permitted and prohibited relations. The Arukh understands *karonot* to be a Greek word for "spring." See D. HaLivni, "In the Karona of Tzippori" [Hebrew], *Sinai* 55 (5724): 121–26.

Given this background, perhaps we can better understand Rabbi Yose's stance in the following passage:

> It was taught: If one was walking outside the city and smelled a fragrance of spices, if the majority of the inhabitants are idolaters, he does not say a blessing; but if the majority of the inhabitants are Jews, he does say a blessing. Rabbi Yose says: Even if the majority are Jews, he does not say a blessing, because the daughters of Israel use incense for witchcraft. (Berakhot 53a)

Rabbi Yose recognizes that "the daughters of Israel use incense for witchcraft." Even if the majority of the town's inhabitants are Jews, that does not mean the rituals they practice are always Jewish.

We might also consider the following source about keeping kosher in Tzippori:

> An incident is told of a butcher in Tzippori who caused Israel to consume the flesh of animals that had not been properly slaughtered and were torn apart by beasts. Once on the eve of Shabbat, he drank wine, went up on the roof, fell off, and died. The dogs began licking his blood. People came and asked Rabbi Ḥanina: Is it permitted to remove him from before the dogs? He answered: It is written, "You shall not eat any flesh that is born of the beasts in the field; you shall cast it to the dogs" [Ex. 22:30]. This man robbed the dogs and caused Israel to eat the flesh of animals that had not properly slaughtered and were torn apart by beasts. Leave the dogs alone, for they are consuming that which is theirs. (Y. Terumot 8:3 [45c])

THE ATTEMPT TO ESTABLISH A COURT IN TZIPPORI

A Babylonian source sketches a map of the center of Torah learning in the Land of Israel during the time of the Mishna:

> It was taught: "Righteousness, righteousness shall you pursue" [Deut. 16:20]. This teaches that one should go after the best court available: after Rabbi Eliezer to Lod, after Rabban Yoḥanan

> ben Zakkai to Beror Ḥayil, after Rabbi Yehoshua to Peki'in, after Rabban Gamliel to Yavneh, after Rabbi Akiva to Benei Brak, after Rabbi Mattia to Rome; after Rabbi Ḥanania ben Teradion to Sikhni, after Rabbi Yose to Tzippori. (Sanhedrin 32b)

This source teaches which sages were associated with which centers of learning. Rabbi Yose, the only member of the Usha generation mentioned here, is in good company. According to this *baraita*, he established a yeshiva in Tzippori. Another source suggests that he may have tried to establish a court as well, headed by his colleague Rabbi Meir. This source, found in the Cairo Geniza, is attributed to Rabbi Sherira Gaon:[36]

> The sages left Tzippori and there was no presiding sage except for Rabbi Meir. Rabbi Yose wanted to make Rabbi Meir the head of the court. They said to him: "Her rival is at her side." He said: The exigencies of the moment demand it. They permitted him, and they invested Rabbi Meir with the authority of the head of the court, and he wrote to him: Tzippori will be established! Even a bird has found refuge. When Rabbi Meir died, Rabbi Yose ruled, and he died in Tzippori.

Rabbi Sherira Gaon begins with a description of the lack of rabbinic authority in Usha, where "there was no presiding sage except for Rabbi Meir."[37] Rabbi Meir was ordained by Rabbi Akiva, but he was not invested with the authority of patriarch. According to the historian Gedalia Alon, Rabbi Yose tried to obtain permission from Rabban Shimon ben Gamliel and the central leadership at Usha to appoint Rabbi Meir in Tzippori. At first Rabban Shimon ben Gamliel refused, on the grounds that "her rival is at her side." His use of the term "rival" refers

36. *The Letter of Rav Sherira Gaon*, Levine edition (Haifa, 5671), xxvii. This text was reconstructed by S. Klein in "Tzippori," in *Land of Israel Studies* (Vilna, 5674), 58. G. Alon endorses Klein's reconstruction. See Alon, *A History of the Jews in the Land of Israel in the Time of the Mishna and Talmud* [Hebrew] (Tel Aviv: HaKibbutz HaMe'uḥad, 5713–16), vol. 2, 72–73.
37. Rabbi Sherira Gaon makes no mention of Rabbi Shimon bar Yoḥai, who was not part of the courtroom leadership, but was more of a prophetic figure, as we will see.

to the halakhic concept of a co-wife. When a man has more than one wife, his various co-wives are considered "rivals" of one another. Rabban Shimon ben Gamliel seems to be suggesting that were Rabbi Meir to become the head of the court, his position would be perceived as threatening. But Rabbi Yose persists on the grounds that "The exigencies of the moment demand it." He speaks respectfully to the patriarch at Usha, and the respect is clearly mutual: Rabban Shimon frequently consulted Rabbi Yose, preferring his company to those of his other colleagues. Once when Rabban Shimon ben Gamliel privileged Rabbi Yehuda bar Ilai's words over his, Rabbi Yose reproached him:

> There was an incident involving Rabban Shimon ben Gamliel and Rabbi Yehuda and Rabbi Yose, who were reclining in Akko when the day became holy upon them [i.e., night fell and the Sabbath began]. Rabban Shimon ben Gamliel said to Rabbi Yose: Great one, do you wish for us to interrupt the meal [to recite the Grace after Meals] and thereby follow the opinion of Yehuda our colleague?
>
> He replied to him: Every day you cherish my words in the presence of Rabbi Yehuda, and now you wish to cherish the words of Rabbi Yehuda in my presence! "Do you mean to conquer the queen while I am in the house?" [Est. 7:8].
>
> He said to him: If so, we shall not interrupt the meal, for perhaps the students will see us acting in accordance with Rabbi Yehuda, and they will erroneously establish the halakha in accordance with his view for generations to come.
>
> They did not move from there until they had established the halakha in accordance with Rabbi Yose. (Pesaḥim 100a)

The previous source from Rabbi Sherira Gaon dealt with the appointment of judges to senior positions. It was the patriarch who made such appointments, guided by the advice of other sages. Rabbi Yose was part of Rabban Shimon ben Gamliel's inner circle, and according to Rabbi Sherira Gaon, he persuaded the patriarch to appoint Rabbi Meir to the position of the head of the court in Tzippori. But the worldly and opinionated residents of Tzippori did not readily accept this appointment. The Talmud relates that the people of Tzippori rose up against Rabbi Meir. The story begins with a halakhic discussion about whether one may greet a mourner on the Sabbath. This custom varied regionally: In the south, mourners were greeted on the Sabbath on the grounds that mourning practices are suspended on this day; but in the north this was not the case. The story unfolds as follows:

> Rabbi Yose of the house of Rabbi Ḥalafta was praising Rabbi Meir before the townspeople of Tzippori: He is a great man, a holy man, a modest man. Once he [Rabbi Meir] saw mourners on the Sabbath and greeted them.
>
> They said to him [Rabbi Yose]: Is this the man you praised?
>
> He said to them: What is the matter?
>
> They said to him: He saw mourners on the Sabbath and greeted them.
>
> He [Rabbi Yose] said to them: You should know that this was his greatness. He sought to teach us that there is no mourning on the Sabbath. (Y. Berakhot 2:7 [5b])

We can picture the situation. Rabbi Meir, the great sage from Yavneh, is not familiar with the customs in the Galilee. The people of Tzippori, notoriously intolerant, dismiss him when they see that he does not follow the local custom. They turn to Rabbi Yose and ask, "Where is that great sage you praised so highly?" Rabbi Yose knows just how to respond. He tells them that they are dealing with the great sage Rabbi Meir, who has acted as he has in order to teach them the important halakhic principle that mourning practices are suspended on the Sabbath.[38]

38. The connection between the excerpt from Rabbi Sherira Gaon's letter and the story in the Jerusalem Talmud was suggested by H. D. Mantel in *Studies in the History of the Sanhedrin* [Hebrew] (Tel Aviv, 5729), 45. Also see S. Miller, "Tzippori and the Diaspora" [Hebrew], in *The Land of Israel and the Diaspora in the Period of the Second Temple, the Mishna, and the Talmud*, ed. Y. Gafni (Jerusalem, 5764), 196–197.

RABBI YOSE'S FAMILY LIFE IN THE CAPITAL CITY OF TZIPPORI

Rabbi Yose ben Ḥalafta's family was deeply immersed in the world of Torah while also taking part in the Roman culture of Tzippori. His children's friends came from families who hobnobbed with Roman clerks and administrators. Yet his children all became rabbis, as he relates in the following source:

> Rabbi Yose said: I performed five acts of intercourse, and I planted five cedars within the Jewish people. And who are they? Rabbi Yishmael ben Rabbi Yose, Rabbi Elazar ben Rabbi Yose, Rabbi Ḥalafta ben Rabbi Yose, Rabbi Avtilas ben Rabbi Yose, and Rabbi Menaḥem ben Rabbi Yose. (Shabbat 118b)

Rabbi Yose's children are his pride and joy: He refers to them as "cedars within the Jewish people." We will consider his eldest son, Rabbi Yishmael, when we discuss Rabbi Yehuda HaNasi. First we will discuss his brother, Rabbi Elazar.

RABBI ELAZAR BEN RABBI YOSE

Traveling to Rome with Rabbi Shimon bar Yoḥai

The Talmud relates that the sages of Usha lobbied the Roman authorities to abolish any vestiges of the decrees of persecution that had followed the Bar Kokhba revolt. Although these decrees had officially been repealed by Antoninus Pius, and the sages were free to learn Torah openly, they continued to live in fear of the authorities. In the following source, the sages discuss whom to send as their representative to Rome:

> The rabbis said: Who will go and annul the decrees? Let Rabbi Shimon ben Yoḥai go, for he is accustomed to having miracles performed on his behalf. And after him, who will go? Rabbi Elazar bar Rabbi Yose.
>
> Rabbi Yose said to them: And were my father, Ḥalafta, alive, could you say to him: Give your son for execution?
>
> Rabbi Shimon said to them: And were my father, Yoḥai, alive, could you say to him: Give your son for execution?

> Rabbi Yose said to them: I will go, for I fear that perhaps Rabbi Shimon will cause punishment to befall my son.
>
> Rabbi Shimon accepted upon himself that he would not cause punishment to befall Rabbi Elazar bar Rabbi Yose [and Rabbi Yose then allowed his son to go with him]. Even so, he caused him punishment. (Me'ila 17a)

The sages choose Rabbi Shimon bar Yoḥai because he is "accustomed to having miracles performed on his behalf." But Rabbi Shimon bar Yoḥai is not from the big city, and he lacks the requisite worldliness to engage the Roman officials. The sages therefore nominate Rabbi Elazar ben Rabbi Yose to accompany him. Rabbi Elazar, who can speak the local language, will be able to help Rabbi Shimon bar Yoḥai navigate the foreign cultural milieu of Rome.

Rabbi Yose is reluctant to send his son to accompany Rabbi Shimon. He is worried not just about the dangers of the journey, but also about the prospect of entrusting his son to the care of Rabbi Shimon bar Yoḥai, who was famous for his retreat into a cave and his murderous gaze.[39] It seems Rabbi Yose's concerns were not unfounded, since the journey to Rome did in fact end in the death of Rabbi Elazar:

> As they were walking along the road, this question was asked of them: From where do we derive that the blood of a reptile is impure?
>
> Rabbi Elazar ben Rabbi Yose curled his lip and said: "And this shall be for you the impure among the reptiles" [Lev. 11:29].

39. According to an apologetic reading, Rabbi Yose was afraid of Rome's evil clutches, remarking: "How dangerous is this journey to Rome." See Kolitz, *Bar Yoḥai and His Teachings*, 55. But according to *Tosafot*, Rabbi Yose was afraid "because he [Rabbi Shimon bar Yoḥai] has a temper, and I worry that he will punish my son." In the beginning of the Jerusalem Talmud's account of Rabbi Shimon bar Yoḥai in the cave, this sage kills a Jew who violates the sabbatical law (Y. Shevi'it 9:1 [38d]). At the end of the Babylonian Talmud's account, he kills Yehuda ben Gerim (Shabbat 33b). Both these sources depict Rabbi Shimon bar Yoḥai as a zealot unafraid to commit murder in the name of justice.

> Rabbi Shimon said to him: The curling of your lips suggests that you are clearly a Torah scholar. However, let the son not return to his father! (Me'ila 17b)

It is hard to know what exactly happened to Rabbi Elazar and Rabbi Shimon en route to Rome. This account suggests that some of their fellow travelers asked them questions that were under discussion in the beit midrash, including the source of the law that the blood of a reptile is impure. Rabbi Elazar "curled his lip." Rashi explains that Rabbi Yose answered the question in a whisper, lest Rabbi Shimon bar Yoḥai conclude that he thought his own knowledge superior. Yet Rabbi Shimon bar Yoḥai, who was prone to jealous fits, took note of the young student's curled lip and cursed him. He therefore reneged on his promise to Rabbi Yose ben Ḥalafta not to punish his son. When Rabbi Elazar and Rabbi Shimon bar Yoḥai arrived in Rome, the latter was presented with the same question again:

> Rabbi Mattia ben Ḥeresh asked Rabbi Shimon ben Yoḥai in the city of Rome: From where do we derive that the blood of a reptile is impure?
>
> Rabbi Shimon bar Yoḥai said to him: For the verse states, "And this shall be for you the impure among reptiles" [Lev. 11:29].
>
> His students said to him: Bar Yoḥai has become very wise.
>
> Rabbi Mattia ben Ḥeresh said to them: It is a well-established teaching in the mouth of Rabbi Elazar ben Rabbi Yose. (Me'ila 17a)

The Roman students are impressed by the visiting rabbi's exegesis, but his host, Rabbi Mattia ben Ḥeresh, knows that the true source of this teaching is Rabbi Elazar ben Rabbi Yose. The story ends as follows:

> They went and sat in a ship, and a student named Mattia ben Ḥeresh sat with them. He began to ask them questions of halakha. He said to them: From where do we know that the blood of a reptile is more impure than its flesh?
>
> Rabbi Shimon said: They are both impure.

Rabbi Elazar said: Its blood is more impure than its flesh.

Rabbi Mattia ben Ḥeresh rose to his feet and kissed him on his mouth.

Rabbi Shimon said to him: And why didn't you kiss me?

He said: Rabbi, I kissed only the one whose lips were well ordered.

And that moment Rabbi Shimon glared at Rabbi Elazar, and he was driven to the brink of death. But Rabbi Shimon remembered the oath he had made to his father, and he calmed down.

The sailors were passing in the boat, and one trampled on the neck of Rabbi Elazar, and he choked. (Lamentations Zuta 1)[40]

The House of God in Roman Captivity

Rabbi Elazar's visit to Rome is documented in several sources, suggesting that he was there more than once. He may even have served as the official rabbinic emissary to the imperial capital, which would explain his many journeys. On his visits, he frequented Roman "museums" displaying the ruins of the Temple. Perhaps his hosts pointed out these objects as a sign of their respect for his religious affiliation.[41] The following sources refer to some of Rabbi Elazar's findings, which included the vestiges of the ark cover, the priestly headdress, and pieces of Solomon's throne:

> Rabbi Elazar ben Rabbi Yose said: I saw the ark curtain in the city of Rome, and there were several drops of blood upon it from the bull and goat offered on Yom Kippur. (Yoma 57a)

> On the priestly frontispiece it was written, "Holy to the Lord." "Holy" was written below, and "to the Lord" was written above. This is like a king who sits on his throne. And similarly,

40. *Lamentations Zuta* is a later midrash, dated approximately to the year 1000 (*Encyclopedia Judaica*, s.v. "Midrash," 1511–1512). But it was known to Rashi, who summarizes this story in his commentary on Tractate Me'ila.

41. We are also told that Rabbi Shimon bar Yoḥai saw the candelabra that had been captured (*Sifrei Zuta* 8).

> with regard to the lot marked "One for the Lord," "One" was written below, and "for the Lord" was written above. Rabbi Elazar ben Rabbi Yose said: I saw it in Rome, and the name was written on it only in a single line, as "Holy to the Lord." (Y. Yoma 4:1 [41c])

> And when Nebuchadnezzar came up and sacked Jerusalem, he carried it off to Babylon. From Babylon it was taken to Medea, and from Medea to Greece, and from Greece to Edom. Rabbi Elazar ben Rabbi Yose said: I have seen its fragments in Rome. (Esther Rabba 1:12)

Rabbi Elazar combs the parlors of Rome in search of the ruins of the Temple. This is a testament to his unique ability to live in two worlds: The outward-focused culture of Rome, and the inward-focused traditions of Judaism.

Rabbi Elazar, the Consummate Host

Another story, which figures in a collection of midrashim about the Book of Esther, showcases Rabbi Elazar ben Yose's unique personality:

> Bar Yoḥnias was asked to make a banquet for the great men of Rome. Rabbi Elazar ben Rabbi Yose was there. He [Bar Yoḥnias] said: Let us consult our fellow townsman. When he came, Rabbi Elazar ben Rabbi Yose said to him: If you intend to invite twenty guests, prepare enough food for twenty-five; and if you intend to invite twenty-five, prepare enough for thirty.
>
> Bar Yoḥnias went and prepared enough for twenty-four guests, and then invited twenty-five. They found that one guest was missing a dish. Some say it was artichokes, and some say it was date berries. Bar Yohnias brought a gold dish and set it before this guest, but he said: Can I eat gold? And do I want your gold?
>
> Bar Yoḥnias went to Rabbi Elazar ben Rabbi Yose and told him what happened. He said to him: By your life, Rabbi, I should not tell you this, for though you told me what to do, I did not do it. But why do I tell you this? Because I want to know: Has God

revealed to you scholars the secrets of the Torah, or perhaps the secrets of entertaining as well?

He said to him: He has revealed to us the secrets of entertaining as well.

He asked: How do you know this?

He said: From David, because it is written: "So Avner came to David to Hebron, and twenty men with him. And David made Avner and the men who were with him a feast" [II Sam. 3:20]. It says not simply that he made a feast for Avner, but that he made a feast for the men who were with him. (Esther Rabba 2:4)

In this source, a man named Bar Yoḥnias consults with Rabbi Elazar about the banquet he is hosting for a group of Roman aristocrats.[42] Rabbi Elazar, the son of the head of the sages, grew up in Tzippori and was familiar with its customs, so he could advise Bar Yoḥnias on how to plan the meal. When Bar Yoḥnias disregards Rabbi Elazar's advice, the evening is a colossal failure.

Who was Bar Yoḥnias? An ancient slab of marble discovered in a Jewish cemetery in Rome bears the Greek inscription "Yonias known as Akona of Tzippori." The identity of this Yonias was debated among scholars until S. Klein proved that the inscription refers to Yoḥnias of Tzippori, who was exiled to Rome.[43] This source offers further evidence that the Torah scholars of Tzippori were well integrated into Roman life and culture.

42. I disagree with Kolitz, who identifies Bar Yoḥnias as Bar Yoḥai. Kolitz writes, "Rabbi Shimon bar Yoḥai hosted a banquet for twenty-four great men of Rome, and he told Rabbi Elazar that God had revealed even the secrets of hosting" (*Bar Yoḥai and His Teachings*, 57).

43. See S. Klein, *The Land of the Galilee*, 208–9. His identification is based on a comparison of the letters, bearing in mind that the letter *ḥet* does not exist in Greek and was therefore omitted from the inscription. See the critique of Miller, "Tzippori and the Diaspora," 193–94.

THE ADOPTION OF RABBI SHIMON BAR YOḤAI'S WAYWARD SON

In addition to his five biological children, Rabbi Yose adopted a son, as a one midrash attests:

> Our sages said: All the Egyptian women's children whom Sarah nursed became converts. And do not be surprised by the matter. So you find in the case of Eliphaz son of Esau. Because he grew up in Isaac's bosom, he became righteous and was worthy of having the holy spirit rest upon him, as it is stated, "The fruit of the righteous is a tree of life" [Prov. 11:30].
>
> Rabbi Elazar ben Rabbi Shimon was the son of Rabbi Shimon bar Yoḥai. Rabbi Yose ben Ḥalafta saw him. He said to him: You come from righteous roots, but you are not a Torah scholar.
>
> He said to him: What should I do?
>
> He said to him: Do you want to learn?
>
> He said: Yes.
>
> He began teaching him one chapter, then a second, then a third. They brought him to the academy. Rebbi saw him. He said to him: You brought this one with you?
>
> He said to him: He is a child of Rabbi Shimon ben Yoḥai.
>
> Rabbi Yose brought him up to Tzippori and instructed him. The next year he brought him down with him and entered the academy. When he began to give answers there, our holy teacher applied to him the verse "The fruit of the righteous is a tree of life." Who caused him to become a Torah scholar? Was it not Rabbi Yose ben Ḥalafta? (Tanḥuma, *Vayera* 38)

This surprising story, which is inconsistent with that of Rabbi Shimon bar Yoḥai teaching his son in the cave, will be of interest when we consider the complicated relationship between Rabbi Yehuda HaNasi and Rabbi Elazar ben Rabbi Shimon bar Yoḥai. It seems that Rabbi Yose was responsible for returning Rabbi Elazar to the fold after his father, Rabbi Shimon, had withdrawn from the world. Perhaps Rabbi Elazar had been seduced by the Roman culture of Tzippori. In any case, Rabbi Yose leads the boy back to Torah and back into the world of the sages. When Rabbi

Yose brings him to the academy, the patriarch catches sight of him and reacts scornfully, "You brought this one with you?" Rabbi Yose responds that Rabbi Elazar is the son of Rabbi Shimon bar Yoḥai. Rabbi Yose's response implies that so long as Rabbi Elazar comes from righteous stock, he has the potential to bear fruit. With this, Rabbi Yose brings Rabbi Elazar back to Tzippori and studies Torah with him, enabling Rabbi Elazar to enter the beit midrash as part of the community of scholars.

We will return to Rabbi Elazar's fascinating history when we come to the chapter on Rabbi Yehuda HaNasi.

RABBI YOSE'S MERITS

The Babylonian Talmud lists nine statements attributed to Rabbi Yose, all of which reflect his most fervent wishes and desires. These statements offer insight into the milieu of this sage who lived on the border between the wealthy culture of Tzippori and the scholarly world of the beit midrash.

> Rabbi Yose said: May my portion be among those who eat three meals on the Sabbath.
>
> Rabbi Yose said: May my portion be among those who complete the Hallel prayer every day....
>
> Rabbi Yose said: May my portion be among those who pray during the redness of the sun [immediately after dawn]....
>
> And Rabbi Yose said: May my portion be among those who die of intestinal disease....
>
> And Rabbi Yose said: May my portion be among those who die on the way to perform a mitzva.
>
> And Rabbi Yose said: May my portion be among those who begin Shabbat in Tiberias and end it in Tzippori.
>
> And Rabbi Yose said: May my portion be among those appointed to seat the students in the beit midrash, and not among those appointed to stand them on their feet in the beit midrash.
>
> And Rabbi Yose said: May my portion be among charity collectors, and not among charity distributors.
>
> And Rabbi Yose said: May my portion be among those who are suspected but innocent. (Shabbat 118b)

All of Rabbi Yose's wishes relate to ordinary life and real-world affairs. He does not pray for miracles, though he aspires to the triumph of the spiritual over the physical. He wishes to eat three meals on the Sabbath, that is, to use his wealth to honor the holiest day of the week. He also wishes to complete the Hallel prayer each day, that is, to sing praises in gratitude for God's beneficence. And he aspires to pray immediately after dawn, thereby linking night to day in an awareness of God's providence. Rabbi Yose lived in a society in which it was easy to forget the source of blessing. His most fervent wish is to attune himself to the holy, and to other people.

The Talmud goes on to discuss Rabbi Yose's relationship with his wife and with his possessions:

> Rabbi Yose said: In all my days I have never called my wife "my wife" or my ox "my ox." Rather, I call my wife "my house" and my ox "my field." (Shabbat 118b)

Rabbi Yose does not think of his wife or his ox as objects that exist to serve him; he regards them as independent entities that encompass more than just their functional relationship to him. Against this backdrop, it is interesting to consider the following conversation between Rabbi Yose and his wife:

> Rabbi Yose's wife was quarreling with her maidservant. Rabbi Yose rejected her complaint in the presence of the maidservant. She said to him: How can you reject my complaint in the presence of my maidservant? He said to her: Didn't Job say, "Did I ever brush aside the case of my servants?" [Job 31:13] (Genesis Rabba 48:3)

The verse from Job that Rabbi Yose quotes is about treating all people equally:

> Did I ever brush aside the case of my servants, man or maid, when they made a complaint against me? What, then, should I do when God arises? And when He calls me into account, what should I

> answer Him? Did He who made me in my mother's womb not make him? (Job 31:13–15)

Rabbi Yose knows that his wife represents his home and hearth. He respects her, but he is not willing to insult her maidservant, who is also created in the image of God.

The Talmud, proceeding into even more intimate realms, then addresses the subject of Rabbi Yose's relationship with his own body:

> Rabbi Yose said: In all my days I have never gazed at my circumcised member.
>
> And Rabbi Yose said: In all my days the beams of my house have never seen the seams of my tunic. (Shabbat 118b)

These statements offer us a sense of Rabbi Yose's inner world. After all his encounters with the nobles and matrons of Rome, he returns to consider his own values and standards. He is consumed by the tension between the spiritual world that attunes him to holiness and the cultural world of paganism and materialism. He seeks a middle road that will allow him to be in touch with the world around him while also safeguarding the sanctity of his soul from the defilement of the body.

SILENCE, COMPROMISE, AND RECONCILIATION

The scholarly debate about the merits of Rome which we considered earlier (Shabbat 33b) may be apocryphal, but it offers a window into the personality of each sage. Rabbi Yose keeps silent, but not out of fear. We have already seen that he would walk the streets of Tzippori freely and confidently. Rather, he keeps silent because he believes in the value of compromise, as Tractate Sanhedrin attests.

The Mishna in Sanhedrin begins with the words "Property cases are decided by three judges. Cases concerning theft and damages are decided by three judges." There is a difference between the general category of "property cases" and the specific instances of "theft and damages." In property cases, the judge listens to the claims of both sides and tries to determine the facts based on witness's testimony. In cases of theft and damages, the court fines the guilty parties, and the penalty is determined by the judges. The Jerusalem Talmud opens the tractate with a midrash attributed to Rabbi Shimon bar Yoḥai:

> Are not theft and damages the same thing?
>
> We find that Rabbi Shimon ben Yoḥai taught: "And these are the ordinances that you shall set before them" [Ex. 21:1]. Some interpret this verse literally, and some interpret it in accordance with Rabbi Yose bar Ḥalafta.
>
> Two people came before Rabbi Yose bar Ḥalafta for judgment. They said to him: On condition that you render a judgment in accordance with Torah law.
>
> He said to them: I do not know what you mean by "a judgment in accordance with Torah law," but I shall judge by what you testify before me. And may He who understands thoughts exact punishment from those people [who are guilty]. Do you accept what I shall instruct you? (Y. Sanhedrin 1:1 [18a])

Rabbi Shimon bar Yoḥai interprets the words "that you shall set before them" as an imperative that judges rule in accordance with the word of God. The judge's verdict is the revelation of God's word in the world and a direct link back to Sinai. But Rabbi Yose insists that he does not know what this verse means. He is prepared to serve as judge, but not to play God.

The Jerusalem Talmud goes on to relate how Rabbi Akiva would receive those who came before him in judgment:

> When someone came to him for judgment, Rabbi Akiva would say to him: Know before whom you stand, before Him who spoke and brought the world into being, as it is said, "And both parties who have the controversy shall come before the Lord" [Deut. 19:17] – and not merely before Akiva ben Yosef! (Y. Sanhedrin 1:1 [18a])

Rabbi Akiva is the opposite of Rabbi Yose. He is fully aware of his responsibilities. He knows that a judge is not an autonomous individual, but the mouthpiece of God in this world: "God stands in the divine assembly; among divine beings He pronounces judgment" (Ps. 82:1). Rabbi Akiva wishes to be a full partner in the revelation of God's will in the world. In contrast, Rabbi Yose regards himself as only human. As he sees it, the judge must seek the truth, but this truth is not final or unequivocal. For him, compromise is not about abandoning justice, but about abandoning the certainty that only God can possess.[44]

THE VERDICT ACCORDS WITH RABBI YOSE

Rabbi Yose occupied a senior role in the beit midrash at Usha. We have already noted that Rabban Shimon ben Gamliel regarded him as a colleague and perhaps even a mentor. When the sages tried to excommunicate Rabban Shimon ben Gamliel (as we will see below), it was Rabbi Yose who intervened. Most of Rabban Shimon ben Gamliel's Torah came, if not from his father, then from Rabbi Yose.[45] And Rabbi Yose's opinion was generally accepted as halakha, as the following source attests:

> Rabbi Yaakov and Rabbi Zerika said: The halakha follows Rabbi Akiva when he disagrees with his colleague; and it follows Rabbi Yose when he disagrees with his colleague; and it follows Rebbi when he disagrees with his colleague.... Using this formulation, Rabbi Yaakov bar Idi said in the name of Rabbi Yoḥanan: In a dispute between Rabbi Meir and Rabbi Yehuda, the halakha follows Rabbi Yehuda; between Rabbi Yehuda and Rabbi Yose, the halakha follows Rabbi Yose; and it need not be said that between Rabbi Meir and Rabbi Yose, the halakha follows Rabbi Yose. For if Rabbi Meir's view does not prevail even against Rabbi Yehuda, is there any question that it would not prevail against Rabbi Yose? (Sanhedrin 46b)

44. Much has been written about the principle of compromise. See B. Lifshitz, "Two Conceptions of Compromise," in *A Collection of Weekly Parsha Pages of the Ministry of Justice*, The Department of Jewish Justice, 133, *Va'ethanan* 5763.
45. See the sources in Epstein, *Literature of the Tanna'im*, 163.

Rabbi Yose's opinion trumps that of all his contemporaries at Usha. The son of Rabbi Yehuda HaNasi once asked his father to explain this hierarchy:

> Rabbi Shimon the son of Rebbi said before Rebbi: Since Rabbi Meir and Ḥanina [Ḥanania] of Ono disagree with Rabbi Yose, why did you, Rebbi, see fit to say that the halakha accords with Rabbi Yose?
>
> Rebbi said to him: Quiet, my son, quiet. You have not seen Rabbi Yose. Had you only seen him, you would have known that he has his reasons. (Gittin 67a)[46]

Rabbi Yose frequently mediated between the various opinions of the sages of Yavneh.[47] He spent his life preaching the value of balance and restraint. When people came to him to resolve a dispute, he would tell them he didn't know the answer, and they would meanwhile arrive at a compromise.[48] His silence in the scholarly debate about the merits of Rome is characteristic: He knew how to consider the different sides of an argument and make room for every voice, without rejecting one in favor of another. Some view his silence as a sign of weakness and of a lack of assertiveness.[49] But Rabbi Yose was regarded by his contemporaries as

46. For Rashi, the phrase "he has his reasons" implies that he always provided a clear explanation of his words.
47. Epstein, *Literature of the Tanna'im*, 126. One of his means of doing so was by ruling unequivocally.
48. See the exegesis of Rabbi Yehoshua ibn Shuiv, a student of Rashba, on *parashat Mishpatim*.
49. It is no surprise that M. L. Lilienblum regarded Rabbi Yose as symbolizing all that was wrong with the traditional world. As he wrote to the editor of *HaMelitz*: "All who are weak in spirit, who lack any sort of inner genius, naturally concede and defer to others. Like Rabbi Yose ben Ḥalafta, they are prepared to go up to the platform to make the priestly benediction at the request of their colleagues, though they know they are not priests, just so as not to offend their colleagues. This is regarded as a positive attribute by the sages of the Talmud, who hold that a person should be 'exceedingly humble.' Such a stance can lead to disastrous consequences for a person who lives in the world of enterprise and action, which requires courage and fortitude." Lilienblum's letter appeared in *HaMelitz* 9:12 (5632).

the leading authority in Tzippori and in the beit midrash at Usha, and he served as the decisive voice in matters of halakha for his generation.

PARTING FROM RABBI YOSE: BETWEEN RELIGIOUS AND SECULAR

One of the first stories recounted in the Babylonian Talmud is about Rabbi Yose walking on his way and ducking inside a ruin to pray. Elijah stands guarding the entrance to the ruin. When Rabbi Yose departs, Elijah engages him in conversation. Rabbi Yose concludes: "I learned three things from him. I learned that one should not enter a ruin, and I learned that one should pray along the way, and I learned that one who is praying along the way should offer a brief prayer" (Berakhot 3a).[50]

This story, too, is characteristic of Rabbi Yose. He lived in a bustling city among people who were busy with secular affairs, but he knew how to seek out a quiet sanctuary in which to pray. His entrance into the ruin is reminiscent of Rabbi Shimon bar Yoḥai's retreat into a cave. When Rabbi Yose sought to be drawn inward, Elijah stood at the door and showed him out. As Elijah taught him, the appropriate place to pray is not in an isolated ruin, but along the way and in the public sphere. A true leader needs to find religious life amidst the secular world.

Even as Rabbi Yose sought out the spiritual realm, his feet continued treading the well-worn paths of Tzippori. The Talmud relates that when Rabbi Yose died, "the gutters of Tzippori spewed forth blood" (Mo'ed Katan 25b). The entire city wept for the death of this sage who, though bombarded by outside influences, managed to create a haven for Torah.

50. For a brief analysis of this story and a list of additional references, see the end of *Sages* I.

Chapter Five

Rabbi Elazar ben Shamua: A Guide to the Sages of His Generation

Rabbi Elazar ben Shamua said: Let the honor of your student be as dear to you as your own; and let the honor of your colleague be as dear as the reverence due to your teacher, and let the reverence toward your teacher be as dear as your reverence for God. (Mishna Avot 4:12)

THE INVISIBLE SAGE

Rabbi Elazar ben Shamua was a close friend of Rabbi Yoḥanan the Sandal-Maker, whom we first encountered at the assembly in the Rimon Valley. Together these two sages left Israel to study with Rabbi Yehuda ben Beteira in Netzivin. But they stopped when they reached Sidon, and returned on account of their great love for the Land of Israel, as per the account in Sifrei, Deuteronomy 80.[1]

1. Scholars of the rabbinic period have confused several unrelated matters in their analysis of this source, and it is difficult to sort through this material. A. H. Weiss

It is difficult to trace the biography of Rabbi Elazar ben Shamua, who is mentioned throughout rabbinic literature simply as Rabbi Elazar.[2] We have no knowledge of his childhood, education, or family. He did not participate in the Rimon assembly, nor is he mentioned in the sources that describe Usha and its sages. But he frequently transmits teachings of the founding generation at Yavneh, which suggests that he may have studied there as a colleague of Rabbi Akiva rather than as his student.[3] Though he figures in one of the two versions of the story of the students from the south who were ordained by Rabbi Akiva after the death of his 24,000 students,[4] Rabbi Elazar never directly quotes Rabbi Akiva's teachings.[5]

A GUIDE FOR HIS GENERATION

Several sources describe Rabbi Elazar as having the final word among the scholars of the Usha generation. He presided over a crowded beit midrash, as Rabbi Yehuda HaNasi attests:

wrote in his book *Dor Dor veDorshav* [Hebrew] (Vilna, 5664), vol. 2, 164: "During the persecution he fled to Netzivin, to the academy of Rabbi Yehuda ben Beteira, where he sat and expounded before him. When the persecution ended, he returned to his land, as did his colleagues." This account conflates two stories in the *Sifrei*: According to one, the students of Rabbi Yishmael left the Land of Israel amid persecution. According to the other, the students of Rabbi Akiva found themselves in the same situation but returned. On the various versions of this midrash, see M. Kahane, "The Value of Settling the Land of Israel in *Mekhilta* Deuteronomy," *Tarbiz* 62 (5753): 501–13.

2. Rashi asserts that when the Talmud refers simply to Rabbi Elazar, it means Rabbi Elazar ben Shamua (see Rashi on Shabbat 19b). The problem is that "Rabbi Elazar" is often confused with "Rabbi Eliezer," so we have no way of knowing if "Rabbi Eliezer" refers to ben Hyrcanus or ben Shamua, not to mention Rabbi Elazar ben Azaria! For attempts to resolve this confusion, see Epstein, *Literature of the Tanna'im*, 158–62.
3. Rabbi Elazar ben Shamua quotes Rabbi Yehoshua (Mishna Nazir 7:4), Rabbi Yose HaGlili (Zevaḥim 44b), Rabbi Tarfon (Tosefta Bava Kamma 1), and Rabbi Yehuda ben Beteira (Tosefta Ohalot 12:3).
4. In the Babylonian version (Yoma 62b), he is mentioned at the end. But in the parallel source from the Land of Israel (Genesis Rabba 61), there are two accounts: In the first he is listed as one of seven students, but in the second he is replaced with Rabbi Ḥanina ben Ḥakhinai. See Z. Frankel, *Methods of the Mishna*, 183–84 and note 7.
5. The Talmud relates on several occasions that "Rabbi Elazar taught in accordance with Rabbi Akiva." See Ketubot 40a; Zevaḥim 93a.

> Rebbi said: When we learned Torah from Rabbi Elazar ben Shamua, we used to sit six to an *ama*. (Eiruvin 53a)

This source suggests that students flocked to Rabbi Elazar's study hall, though we are not told where it was located. It was so crowded that students literally sat on top of one another.[6] On another occasion, Rabbi Yehuda HaNasi describes Sukkot in Rabbi Elazar's beit midrash:

> Rebbi said: When we were students studying Torah with Rabbi Elazar ben Shamua, they brought before us figs and grapes, and we ate them as a snack outside the *sukka*. (Yoma 79b)

The students ate outside on Sukkot because the *sukka* was too small to fit them all. These two sources shed light on Rabbi Elazar ben Shamua's crowded and popular beit midrash, though it is portrayed more negatively in the following passage:

> Rebbi said: When I went to learn Torah with Rabbi Elazar ben Shamua, his students joined forces against me like the roosters of Beit Bukya, and they let me learn only one thing in our mishna. (Yevamot 84a)

Rabbi Yehuda ridicules the students who gathered around Rabbi Elazar. His analogy to the roosters of Beit Bukya suggests that Rabbi Elazar's disciples were a wild bunch who did not let newcomers penetrate their circle. His beit midrash seems to have attracted many students, but its inner circle was closed to outsiders.

In a parallel version of this story in the Jerusalem Talmud, Rabbi Yehuda describes what he sought to learn from Rabbi Elazar:

6. This is an appropriate point to honor the memory of Rav Aryeh Bina, the former head of the Netiv Meir Yeshiva. We used to sit crowded in the old yeshiva beit midrash in Jerusalem's Bayit Vegan neighborhood, and he would remind us of the midrash that "no one ever said Jerusalem is too crowded." Of course it was crowded, but the miracle was that no one ever complained about it. Along similar lines, see Sanhedrin 7a, where a peddler converses with his friend about how large his bed seems when he loves his wife, and how small it seems after their passion has cooled.

> Rebbi said: I looked but did not find the teachings of Elazar ben Shamua with regard to the androgyne, for his disciples had ganged up on him. (Y. Yevamot 8:6 [9d])

An androgyne is a person of uncertain gender. The sages tried to determine the halakhic status of such an individual:

> Rabbi Yose said: An androgyne is a creature unto itself, and the sages could not decide if he is a man or a woman. (Tosefta Bikkurim 2:7)

There was a rumor that Rabbi Elazar knew of a tradition regarding the status of the androgyne. Rebbi relates that he tried to learn this tradition but could not penetrate Rabbi Elazar ben Shamua's inner circle. Ultimately this tradition reached Rebbi, who quoted it in the Mishna:

> An androgyne may marry [a woman], but may not be married [to a man]. Rabbi Elazar says: One is liable to stoning on account of [cohabiting with] an androgyne, as on account of a male. (Mishna Yevamot 8:6)

Rabbi Elazar's teachings were difficult to access, for reasons we have yet to uncover.

RABBI YOSE BEN KIPPER PRESERVES THE TORAH OF HIS TEACHER

One student who preserved and transmitted the teachings of Rabbi Elazar ben Shamua was Rabbi Yose ben Kipper:[7]

> This is a midrash expounded by Rabbi Yose ben Kipper in the name of Rabbi Elazar ben Shamua: If a man sleeps with any women included among those forbidden to him by the Bible, those women do not require a divorce document from him, except for his wife's sister, his brother's wife, and a married woman,

7. His name is spelled with both a *kaf* and a *kuf* in the various talmudic manuscripts.

> because these have a termination to their prohibition. (*Derekh Eretz*, Arayot 3)

Rabbi Yose ben Kipper was part of the Usha generation. He was sent to Babylonia by the patriarch Rabban Shimon ben Gamliel to stop Ḥanania, the son of Rabbi Yehoshua's brother, who sought to intercalate the year. We will examine this story in more detail in our chapter on Ḥanania.

When Rabbi Yose ben Kipper quotes Rabbi Elazar ben Shamua, he summarizes the opinions of previous generations. Two examples:

Watering Plants During the Sabbatical Year

> Rabbi Yose ben Kipper says in the name of Rabbi Elazar ben Shamua: Beit Shammai say: One waters all the branches, and the water falls on the root. Beit Hillel say: One may water either the branches or the root. (Y. Shevi'it 2:3 [33d])

The Jerusalem Talmud discusses a mishna in Tractate Shevi'it about watering plants during the sabbatical year. Rabbi Elazar ben Shamua does not offer a new legal opinion; rather, he teaches that Beit Shammai and Beit Hillel disagreed about the type of irrigation permissible during the sabbatical year. According to Beit Shammai, one may water only the branches, and then the water flows downward. According to Beit Hillel, one may also water the root, because this is where the plant draws its water.

This disagreement is not preserved in the Mishna, but it is quoted in the Tosefta:

> One waters saplings until the new year. Rabbi Yose ben Kipper says in the name of Rabbi Eliezer: Beit Shammai say: One waters the branches, and the water falls on the root. Beit Hillel say: One waters the branches and the root. Said Beit Hillel to Beit Shammai: If you permit the farmer to do part of the labor, permit him to do all of it. If you do not permit him to do all, do not permit him to do part. (Tosefta Shevi'it 1:5).

Note that this teaching is attributed not to Rabbi Elazar (ben Shamua), but to Rabbi Eliezer (ben Hyrcanus). This is clearly a transmission error, since Rabbi Yose ben Kipper lived many years after Rabbi Eliezer ben Hyrcanus. We also note that Rabbi Yehuda HaNasi, the editor of the Mishna, was apparently not familiar with this debate between Beit Shammai and Beit Hillel. The mishna he compiled treats the issue of watering plants during the sabbatical year as follows:

> One may water saplings until Rosh HaShana. Rabbi Elazar ben Tzaddok says: Even in the seventh year, one may water the branches but not the roots. (Mishna Shevi'it 2:4)

Rabbi Yehuda HaNasi was familiar with a dispute involving Rabbi Elazar ben Tzaddok, but he did not know of the traditions of Beit Shammai and Beit Hillel, which were preserved in the name of Rabbi Elazar.

Chopping Down Trees with an Ax on a Festival

The Mishna teaches:

> One may not chop up wood from beams, or from a beam that was broken on a festival; and one may not chop with an ax or a saw or a sickle, but only with a chopper. (Mishna Beitza 4:3)

In the Jerusalem Talmud we learn that the Mishna's general prohibition of chopping down trees with an axe is in fact a matter of dispute:

> The members of the household of Rabbi Yannai say: They may chop wood with an ax. Rabbi Hoshaya taught: They may chop wood with an ax. Shmuel said: The law accords with the view of him who says: They may chop wood with an ax. It has been taught: Rabbi Yose ben Kipper said in the name of Rabbi Elazar ben Shamua: Beit Shammai prohibits, and Beit Hillel permits. (Y. Beitza 4:3 [62c])

The disagreement between Beit Shammai and Beit Hillel was preserved in the beit midrash of Rabbi Elazar ben Shamua. Those who received this tradition from Rabbi Elazar could rely on Beit Hillel's opinion in order to rule leniently. Those who were not familiar with this tradition had no grounds for leniency.

ADDITIONAL SOURCES BEYOND THE MISHNA

Rabbi Yose ben Kipper was also a student of Rabbi Shimon Shezuri, as we learn from the following source:

> Rabbi Yose ben Kipper said in the name of Rabbi Shimon Shezuri: Regarding a crop of Egyptian beans that was planted for seed, if some of it took root before Rosh HaShana and some of it took root after Rosh HaShana, we may not separate *teruma* or *ma'aser* tithes from this new part for that old part, or vice versa, because we may not separate *teruma* or *ma'aser* tithes from the new for the old, or from the old for the new. What does one do? He piles the contents of his threshing floor into the middle, so he is found to have separated from the new portion of it for the new portion in it, and from the old portion in it for the old portion in it. (Rosh HaShana 13b)[8]

This agricultural dispute deals with varieties of beans and the time it takes for them to take root in the soil, which determines when they are tithed and the status of the crop regarding other mitzvot that apply to those who plant in the Land of Israel. There is a difference between crops planted "for seed" and those planted for food. Rabbi Shimon Shezuri suggests how farmers should tithe Egyptian beans, which are planted in different seasons. He teaches that it is permissible to separate *teruma* and *ma'aser* from the new crop for the old crop on the threshing floor by adding the old crop with its new portion to the crop already there. The basis for this law is in the Mishna:

> One may not separate the priestly portion (*teruma*) from gleanings that belong to the poor, or from forgotten sheaves that belong

8. In the Tosefta this tradition is quoted in the name of Rabbi Yose ben Kipper, who in turn is quoting Rabbi Shimon Shezuri (Tosefta Shevi'it 2:5).

> to the poor... or from the new for the old, or from the old for the new... and if he did separate *teruma,* it does not count as *teruma.* (Mishna Terumot 1:5)

In the Tosefta we learn that the opinion stated anonymously in the Mishna is actually the subject of a dispute between Rabbi Eliezer and Rabbi Akiva:

> Rabbi Eliezer says: One pays restitution for *terumot* offerings unintentionally eaten by a non-priest with produce of one kind on behalf of produce that is not of the same kind, with the stipulation that he pay restitution with choicer produce on behalf of less choice produce. How so? If he eats barley and pays restitution with wheat, or if he eats dried figs and pays restitution with dates, let a blessing be upon him.
>
> Rabbi Akiva says: One pays restitution only with produce of one kind on behalf of produce of the same kind.
>
> Rabbi Eliezer says: Just as one pays restitution with the new produce [of the present year] on behalf of the old produce [of the previous year], so one pays restitution with produce of one kind on behalf of produce of a different kind. (Tosefta Terumot 7:9)

Rabbi Akiva's statement is the basis of Rabbi Shimon Shezuri's teaching regarding a mixture of Egyptians beans, some planted for seed and some for food.

Several sources attest that Rabbi Shimon Shezuri studied with Rabbi Tarfon.[9] The following passage identifies him as a Galilean:

> My father's family was among the homesteaders of the Upper Galilee. And why were they destroyed? Because they would graze their flocks in the forests and adjudicate financial cases without a quorum of three judges. And even though they had forests next to their houses, a small field [belonging to others] was between

9. Tosefta Demai 5:22; Menaḥot 31a.

> their houses and the forest, and they would traverse it [with their animals to reach the forest].[10] (Tosefta Bava Kamma 8:14)

This testimony, in which Rabbi Shimon speaks of his Galilean roots in the days before the persecution and his study with Rabbi Tarfon, connects his teachings to the schools of Rabbi Yehuda bar Ilai and Rabbi Yose ben Ḥalafta.

HIS TEACHINGS: A MOSAIC OF OPINIONS

Rabbi Elazar ben Shamua speaks of the uniqueness of his style of learning:

> Rabbi Elazar ben Shamua says: There are three types of scholars – the hewn stone, the cornerstone, and the mosaic.
>
> Who is the hewn stone? This is the student who has studied [only] midrash. When a sage comes and asks him about midrash, he answers him. This is a hewn stone, for only one of his sides is exposed.
>
> Who is the cornerstone? This is the student who has studied [only] midrash and halakha. When a sage comes to him and asks him about midrash, he answers him; about halakha, he answers him. This is a cornerstone, for only two of his sides are exposed.
>
> Who is the mosaic? This is the student who has studied midrash, halakha, *Aggada*, and Tosefta. When a sage comes to him and asks him about midrash, he answers him; about halakha, he answers him; about Tosefta, he answers him; about *Aggada*, he answers him. And this is a mosaic, for all four of his sides are exposed. (*Avot deRabbi Natan*, recension A, ch. 28)

Now that we have taken note of Rabbi Elazar's tendency to collect and distill the disputes of prior generations and integrate them into the

10. The wording of this source is corrupt and confusing in the original Hebrew manuscripts. See Lieberman, *Tosefta Kifshuta*, Bava Kamma, 88, lines 59–60 and note 20. Also see Epstein, *Text of the Mishna*, 1261.

halakhic discussions of his day, we can appreciate his characterization of various types of scholars and their schools. Each beit midrash has its own style of learning. Some have one particularly strong area, such as midrash. Scholars in such a beit midrash do not concern themselves with matters of halakha, and are known as hewn stones. Others focus on both midrash and halakha but ignore aggada. They are described as cornerstones. Still others serve as a mosaic of the various kinds of Torah learning, with all sides exposed. This is the beit midrash of Rabbi Elazar, and thus students flock to its gates.

Only one student is not permitted to enter, and that is Rabbi Yehuda HaNasi.

THE NAME OF THE ROSE: THE EXCLUSION OF RABBI YEHUDA HANASI

Why was Rabbi Yehuda HaNasi barred from Rabbi Elazar's beit midrash? It seems that Rabbi Yehuda HaNasi's goal in approaching Rabbi Elazar and his students was to collect the many traditions they had preserved. These traditions were not familiar to him from his father's beit midrash in Usha. Against this backdrop, we can understand the following source:

> Rebbi said: When I went to drain my measures before Rabbi Elazar ben Shamua – and some say: to drain the measures *of* Rabbi Elazar ben Shamua [i.e., to extract all the knowledge he possessed] – I encountered Yosef the Babylonian sitting before him, and his teachings were extremely beloved to him, except one. (Menaḥot 18a)

Rebbi relates that he went to "drain his measures," a phrase whose meaning is unclear. Rashi understands that Rabbi Elazar ben Shamua's goal was to distill his own learning and ask about any matters that remained unclear. But he was prevented from doing so. The Jerusalem Talmud offers two explanations of why Rabbi Elazar's students did not permit Rebbi to enter their beit midrash:

> And why not? Was it so as not to reveal Ben Shamua's teachings? Or was it because Rebbi was unworthy?

> What is the difference between these two explanations? If he ordinarily would reveal what he heard, and not keep the matter in confidence. If you say that it was so he would not reveal the teachings, behold, he clearly has revealed one such teaching. So the reason is surely that he was not worthy to learn more than this one thing from him. (Y. Yevamot 8:6 [9d])

Perhaps the students denied entry to Rebbi because they did not want to reveal Rabbi Elazar ben Shamua's teachings to him. Or perhaps they felt Rebbi was not yet worthy of learning from Rabbi Elazar ben Shamua, presumably because he was still too young. In any case, Rebbi was barred, and the Mishna he compiled did not include those traditions known only to Rabbi Elazar ben Shamua.[11]

11. Hyman (*Legends*, s.v. "Rabbi Elazar ben Shamua," 207–8) debates Y. Brill, the author of *The Introduction to the Mishna* (1876), who argues along similar lines. Hyman writes:

> The author of *The Introduction to the Mishna* writes as follows: "Since the yeshiva in Lod was at odds with the other yeshivot, and was particularly opposed to the patriarch, the students did not allow Rebbi to learn Torah from them." But this claim that Rabbi Elazar ben Shamua's yeshiva opposed other yeshivot is a lie, since we have not found any indication that this was the case. And if Rabbi Elazar ben Shamua's yeshiva did indeed adopt this stance, how could Rabban Shimon ben Gamliel have sent messengers to Rebbi to learn Torah before him? But even so, this wise sage will try to understand the words of the Jerusalem Talmud. The wise sage in *Dor veDorshav*, volume 2, chapter 16 [writes,] "The reason they were so begrudging with their learning… was that Rebbi would collect all the teachings from the various *battei midrash*, and he would add to and amend them as he saw fit, which was frowned upon by Rabbi Elazar, and therefore he did not permit Rebbi to learn from him." It seems surprising that such a sage would want to blind his readers and cause the Babylonian and Jerusalem Talmuds to be lost. Did Rebbi indeed go to collect all the teachings in the various *battei midrash*?… Perhaps he had not yet even considered undertaking the great project of compiling the Mishna. And shouldn't we believe the Jerusalem Talmud, [which states] that they did not let him learn from them because he was not yet regarded as an important enough scholar?

HIS MERITS

> The disciples asked Rabbi Elazar ben Shamua: How have you attained longevity? He said to them: In all my days, I never used a synagogue as a shortcut, and I never stepped over the heads of the people of the holy nation, and I never raised my hands to offer the priestly blessing without first reciting a benediction. (Megilla 27b)

Rabbi Elazar, already an elder, attributes his longevity to his sensitivity and humility. He does not take shortcuts through synagogues, which would signify disregard for holy space. Nor does he take shortcuts that involve stepping over the heads of others, without regard for their presence. Some assume a position of dominance when they enter holy places, but Rabbi Elazar does not count himself among them.

Rabbi Elazar asserts that he does not step "over the heads of the people of the holy nation." The yeshivot were often crowded, with many students sitting close together. When a sage entered to teach, he had to walk past them to get to his place. It might have appeared as if such a sage were stepping disrespectfully over the students' heads. However, the halakha permits a sage to step over others to get to his place if he is needed by the public:

> Younger sages and disciples of sages step over even the heads of the people when the public requires them. And even though they have said: "It is not praiseworthy for a disciple of the sages to come in last," if he went out to fulfill his needs, he comes back and sits down in his place. (Tosefta Sanhedrin 7:8)

Even if it is permissible for someone of his stature to step over others' heads, Rabbi Elazar ben Shamua does not do so. He holds that "the honor of your student should be as dear to you as your own." Rabbi Elazar had exceptional respect for his students. He taught an important lesson about honoring humanity, as the following source attests:

> Rabbi Elazar ben Shamua was walking on the rocks by the sea when he saw a ship that was tossed about in the water suddenly

> sink with all on board. He noticed a man sitting on a plank of the ship, carried from wave to wave until he stepped ashore. As he was naked, he hid himself among the rocks of the sea. A caravan of Jews passed on their way to Jerusalem for the festival. He said to them: I belong to the descendants of Esau, your brother; give me a little clothing with which to cover my nakedness, because the sea has stripped me bare, and nothing was saved with me.
>
> They said: So may all your people be stripped bare!
>
> He raised his eyes and saw Rabbi Elazar, who was walking among them. He said: I observe that you are a respected elder among your people, and that you know the respect due to your fellow creatures. So help me, and give me a garment with which to cover my nakedness, because the sea has stripped me bare.
>
> Rabbi Elazar ben Shamua was wearing seven robes. He removed one and gave it to him. He also led him to his house, provided him with food and drink, gave him two hundred dinars, drove him a distance of fourteen *parsaot*, and treated him with great honor until he brought him to his home. (Ecclesiastes Rabba 11)

The midrash goes on to chronicle the fate of this Roman seafarer, who rose to greatness and remembered Rabbi Elazar's kindness.[12] For our purposes, suffice it to say that the characteristic of respect for all human beings typified and distinguished Rabbi Elazar.

THE DEPICTION OF RABBI ELAZAR BEN SHAMUA IN LATER SOURCES

In the generation after Rabbi Yehuda HaNasi, Rabbi Elazar ben Shamua developed the reputation of a great scholar. He was invoked by Rabbi Yoḥanan, a member of the next generation, who taught his students how great sages were ranked:

12. This part of the story derives from the folktale, in which everything ends happily ever after. See A. Kosman, "A Sage and the Honor of Humanity" [Hebrew], in *Men's Tractate* (Jerusalem, 2002), 87–92.

> The minds of the earlier sages were as immense as the entrance to the hall of the Temple, and the minds of the later scholars were as immense as the entrance to the chamber of the Temple, but as for us, our minds are like the eye of a needle used to mend ripped clothing. The earlier scholars – this is a reference to Rabbi Akiva. The later scholars – this is a reference to Rabbi Elazar ben Shamua. (Eiruvin 53a)

This source reflects the popular rabbinic notion of the "decline of the generations," that is, that later generations are intellectually inferior to their predecessors. Along this descending slope there are some significant signposts: Rabbi Akiva is the highest point, towering above all others. Rabbi Elazar ben Shamua is the last scholar with a truly expansive mind. "We," the scholars among whom Rabbi Yoḥanan counts himself, are "like the eye of a needle used to mend ripped clothing." The Talmud suggests another way of characterizing the difference between the earlier and later sages:

> There are those who say: The earlier generations – Rabbi Elazar ben Shamua. The later generations: Rabbi Oshaya ben Ribi. And we are like the eye of a needle used to mend ripped clothing. (Eiruvin 53a)

It is all relative. If the starting point is Rabbi Akiva, then the last sage with an expansive mind is Rabbi Elazar ben Shamua. But if the starting point is Rabbi Elazar, then the last great sage is Rabbi Oshaya. In both cases Rabbi Elazar ben Shamua is portrayed as a figure of distinction.

Chapter Six

Rabbi Shimon bar Yoḥai and His Place in the Halakhic Tradition

INTRODUCTION

In considering the figure of Rabbi Shimon bar Yoḥai (known by the acronym Rashbi), we enter into a complicated web of sources that includes laws, stories, ideas, and legends. As depicted in rabbinic sources, Rashbi was unlike any of his contemporaries, and even had an element of the divine about him. His more traditional biographers invoked poetic rhetoric to emphasize their sense of awe and reverence toward their subject, as the following examples attest:

> This holy and wondrous sage, for whose name and memory the Jewish soul lusts, is the only rabbinic sage whose name is still honored – his memory is celebrated in the village of Meron in glory and splendor and fire.[1]

1. Hyman, *Legends*, s.v. "Rabbi Shimon bar Yoḥai," 1178.

> Rabbi Shimon bar Yoḥai, the awe-inspiring lion, the divine and wondrous sage, whose name causes every Jewish heart to tremble, is the only talmudic sage whose grave it is customary to ascend to and bow down upon.... He will be honored with bonfires and celebrated with ecstatic dance and with songs composed in his honor: Bar Yoḥai, you were anointed, you are fortunate, with oil of joy from your fellows.[2]

The talmudic material about Rashbi is varied; only the later sources emphasize his mysticism. Some talmudic sources are certainly apocryphal, but they are nonetheless relevant for my purpose, which is not historical reconstruction, but rather clear explication of the rabbinic material so as to make it accessible to readers who would draw inspiration from the world of the sages. Verifying the historicity of the sources is beyond my capacity and purpose. I doubt whether such authentication is even possible; regardless, it is of secondary significance. The historical Rabbi Shimon is bound up with his literary personality, which ultimately determines how he has been understood and remembered.[3]

I shall try to focus on the non-mystical traditions about Rabbi Shimon bar Yoḥai and, in so doing, to pave the way toward a more composite sketch of this remarkable figure.[4]

RASHBI IN YAVNEH: A STUDENT OF RABBI AKIVA

We know very little about Rashbi's upbringing.[5] It seems that his father was not connected to the world of the sages but was held in high esteem

2. See the introduction to Kolitz, *Bar Yoḥai and His Teachings.*
3. O. Meir, *Rabbi Yehuda HaNasi: The Image of a Leader in the Traditions of the Land of Israel and Babylonia* [Hebrew] (Tel Aviv, 1999), introduction: "The words 'image of a leader' suggest that the subject at hand is not the historical validity of the sources."
4. The Zohar and the mystical corpus are inaccessible to me, so I do not cite these sources. For a brief introduction to the Zohar and the debates about its authorship, see the introduction by Melila Hellner-Eshed to the edition published by Am HaSefer and Yediot Books (Tel Aviv, 2008).
5. The Talmud teaches: "There were five things that Rabbi Akiva commanded Rabbi Shimon bar Yoḥai when he was in prison. Rabbi Shimon bar Yoḥai said to him: Master, teach me Torah. He replied: I will not teach you. He said: If you do not teach me, I will tell my father, Yoḥai, and he will turn you over to the authorities. He said

by the Roman authorities. His sole teacher was Rabbi Akiva. The following source describes Rabbi Shimon's journey to study Torah with him:

> Rabbi Ḥanina ben Ḥakhinai and Rabbi Shimon bar Yoḥai went to study Torah with Rabbi Akiva in Benei Brak. They stayed there thirteen years. Rabbi Shimon bar Yoḥai used to send home for news, and he knew what was happening in his house. Rabbi Ḥanina did not send home and did not know what was happening in his house. (Leviticus Rabba 21)

Elsewhere the Talmud explains that Rabbi Ḥanina ben Ḥakhinai went to Rabbi Akiva's beit midrash after Rashbi's wedding:

> Rabbi Shimon said to Rabbi Ḥanina: Wait for me until I can come with you. He did not wait for him. (Ketubot 62b)

This source describes Rashbi's spiritual quest during the early years of his marriage. The Talmud relates that Rashbi remained in close touch with his family, even though he left his wife to study Torah. In this sense he followed in the footsteps of his teacher, Rabbi Akiva, who left home to study only after obtaining his wife's permission. The ideal of the "married monk" was passed on from teacher to student, but it was only Rashbi and not Rabbi Ḥanina who knew how to strike the appropriate balance between family life and study.[6]

Rashbi's life was shaped by his love of Torah. We know of no period in his life when he dedicated himself to working, to earning a livelihood, or to any other worldly occupation. The statement attributed to him in the third chapter of Avot teaches about the right of every individual to study Torah, even if his ancestors did not:

to him: My son, more than the calf desires to suck does the cow desire to suckle" (Pesaḥim 112a). This source suggests that Rashbi's father was not part of the world of the sages but was nonetheless close to his son. Perhaps Rashbi is implying that his father opposed the revolt and did not look favorably upon Rabbi Akiva's conduct.

6. Daniel Boyarin, *Carnal Israel: Reading Sex in Talmudic Culture* (Berkeley: University of California Press, 1993). I wrote about Rabbi Ḥanina in *Sages* II, Part Three.

> Rabbi Shimon says: There are three crowns: the crown of the Torah, the crown of the priesthood, and the crown of kingship; but the crown of a good name surpasses them all. (Mishna Avot 4:13)

This mishna is elaborated upon in the following source:

> Rabbi Shimon says: There are three crowns: the crown of the Torah, the crown of priesthood, and the crown of kingship; but the crown of a good name surpasses them all.
>
> The crown of priesthood: What is there to be said of it? Even if one were to offer all the silver and gold in the world, he could not be given the crown of priesthood, for it is said, "And it shall be unto him and unto his seed after him the covenant of everlasting priesthood" [Num. 25:13].
>
> The crown of royalty: Even if one were to offer all the silver and gold in the world, he could not be given the crown of royalty, for it is said, "And David My servant shall be their prince forever" [Ezek. 37:25].
>
> Not so the crown of Torah. The toil of Torah – anyone who wishes to take it on may come and do so, as it is said, "Ho, all who are thirsty, come for water" [Is. 55:1]. (*Avot deRabbi Natan*, recension A, ch. 41)

HIS TORAH IS HIS TRADE

Rabbi Akiva was characterized by his total devotion to Torah study, which he regarded as a religious value in its own right. When asked, "Which is greater, Torah study or action?" he chose the former without hesitation. Rabbi Yishmael, in contrast, championed the value of worldly employment. As he taught, "If a person conducts business transactions honestly and people look upon him favorably, it is considered as if he has fulfilled the entire Torah."[7] The Talmud preserves the following debate between Rabbi Akiva and Rabbi Yishmael:

7. For a discussion of these sources, see *Sages* II, Part Three.

> "And you shall gather in your grain" [Deut. 11:14]. For what reason was this taught? For since it is stated, "This book of the Torah shall not depart from your mouth" [Josh. 1:8], it would be possible to think that the words are meant literally [i.e., that one should study all the time]. The Torah therefore states, "And you shall gather in your grain," that is, lead along with [Torah study] a life conducted in the way of the world [i.e., earn a livelihood]. These are the words of Rabbi Yishmael.
>
> But Rabbi Shimon ben Yoḥai says: Can it be? If a man plows at the time of plowing and sows at the time of sowing and harvests at the time of harvesting and threshes at the time of threshing and winnows at the time of the blowing wind, what will become of [the study of] Torah? Rather, [the verse must mean that] when [the people of] Israel do the will of God, their work is done by others, as it is stated, "And strangers will arise and shepherd your flocks" [Is. 61:5]. But when [the people of] Israel do not do the will of God, their work is done by themselves, as it is stated, "And you shall gather in your grain" [Deut. 11:14]. And not only that, but even the work of others is done by them, as it is said, "And you will serve your enemies" [Deut. 28:48]. (Berakhot 35b)

This source gives voice to Rashbi's attitude toward worldly occupation: "When [the people of] Israel do the will of God, their work is done by others." We have already seen how Rabbi Yehuda would walk to the beit midrash with a barrel on his shoulders so he could proclaim, "How great is the labor that confers honor upon the one who performs it." But Rashbi does not see any value in work, which he regards as a waste of time that could be better spent studying Torah. This attitude was rare during the rabbinic period, in which most sages were gainfully employed. Even the Talmud admits that total devotion to study is infeasible for most people:

> Abaye said: Many acted in accordance with Rabbi Yishmael and succeeded; those who acted in accordance with Rabbi Shimon bar Yoḥai did not succeed. (Berakhot 35b)

THE RECITATION OF THE SHEMA IN HIS BEIT MIDRASH

Another important source in the Jerusalem Talmud indicates Rashbi's attitude toward Torah study. We will cite this source in its entirety because of its centrality to our discussion:

> Rabbi Yoḥanan said in the name of Rabbi Shimon bar Yoḥai: Those like us who are constantly engaged in the study of Torah do not interrupt it even for the recitation of the *Shema*. Rabbi Yoḥanan said about himself: Those like us who are not constantly engaged in the study of Torah must interrupt our activities even for the recitation of the *Amida* prayer. (Y. Berakhot 1:2 [3b])

This passage begins by contrasting two types of Torah scholars. Rabbi Yoḥanan, one of the leading scholars in the Land of Israel in the middle of the third century, quotes Rashbi as asserting that he and his colleagues are so immersed in Torah study that they need not pause even to recite the *Shema*. In contrast, Rabbi Yoḥanan asserts that his circle of scholars is not constantly engaged in Torah study, so they pause even to recite the *Amida* prayer. This source presents a hierarchy of activities, with the *Shema* taking precedence over the *Amida*, and with Torah study taking precedence over both. The parallel source in the Babylonian Talmud is less extreme: There Rashbi and his colleagues are depicted as "engaging in Torah study and pausing for the recitation of the *Shema*, but not for the *Amida*" (Shabbat 11a). The Babylonian Talmud privileges the recitation of the *Shema*, which may be regarded as a form of Torah study that must be performed at a particular time of day. But the Jerusalem Talmud asserts that the general preoccupation with Torah study supersedes even the recitation of the *Shema* in its proper time. The Jerusalem Talmud goes on to explain the ideological basis of the dispute between the sages:

> Each man's opinion is consistent with his ruling elsewhere.
>
> Rabbi Yoḥanan is consistent with his opinion, for Rabbi Yoḥanan says: If only a person might have the opportunity to pray all day long. Why? For prayer never loses its value.
>
> Rabbi Shimon bar Yoḥai is consistent with his opinion, for Rabbi Shimon bar Yoḥai said: If I had been on Mount Sinai

> when the Torah was given to Israel, I would have asked God for two mouths, one to speak words of Torah, and one to use for all other needs.
>
> On second thought, he reconsidered and said: But the world can barely continue to exist on account of the slander that comes out of one mouth. How much worse would it be if everyone had two mouths! (Y. Berakhot 1:2 [3b])

Rashbi believes a person has to be fully engaged in Torah study. As he sees it, the mouth should ideally speak nothing except words of Torah. Any other pursuit is a distraction from learning. But when Rashbi considers how most people use their one mouth, he reconsiders his initial wish for two separate ones. He understands that not everyone in the world has his single-minded dedication.

The Jerusalem Talmud struggles with Rashbi's assertion that nothing is sufficiently important to interrupt the study of Torah:

> But does Rabbi Shimon bar Yoḥai not admit that one interrupts even the study of Torah to make a *sukka* or a lulav? And does Rabbi Shimon bar Yoḥai not hold that one who learns in order to practice acts properly, but one who learns without regard for practice does not act properly? For it would have been better for a person who learns without regard for practice not to have been born. Rabbi Yoḥanan said: It would have been better for a person who learns without regard for practice if his placenta had smothered him at birth and he had never entered the world. (Y. Berakhot 1:2 [3b])

The Jerusalem Talmud attacks Rashbi's position. What about all the other mitzvot, besides Torah study? And what about the mishnaic teaching that the purpose of study is to serve as a guide for proper action? And what about Rabbi Yoḥanan's statement that if a person learns without regard for proper action, it would be better for him not have been born at all?

These last two challenges do not seriously undermine Rashbi's position. The teaching about "one who learns in order to practice" is attributed to Rabbi Yoḥanan ben Beroka (see Mishna Avot 4:5). Rashbi does not necessarily have to accept this mishna. After all, we have already seen that Rashbi disagrees with Rabbi Yoḥanan when it comes to the relationship between learning and prayer.

In response to this barrage of challenges, the Talmud explains:

> The basis for Rabbi Shimon bar Yoḥai's teaching is that the study of Torah and the recitation of the *Shema* are both acts of study, and one does not desist from one act of study for another act of study. (Y. Berakhot 1:2 [3b])

Rashbi neglects the recitation of the *Shema* for the sake of learning Torah. But the recitation of the *Shema* is itself a form of Torah study, as per the commandment to "teach them to your children." A Jew is obligated to speak words of Torah on a daily basis, but those words need not be the *Shema* prayer. So if a person is already engaged in Torah study, he need not neglect one form of Torah study for the sake of another.

The Jerusalem Talmud presents an additional challenge:

> But behold it is taught: One who recites after this time has not lost the purpose of the action. For though he does not fulfill the obligation of reciting the *Shema*, he is like one who recites passages from the Torah. This implies that the recitation of the *Shema* in its proper time is more desirable than the study of words of Torah. (Y. Berakhot 1:2 [3b])[8]

The mishna quoted in this source, from Berakhot, concerns a person who misses the proper time for the recitation of the *Shema*. Although the sages disagree about when the *Shema* must be recited, they all agree that the prayer must be recited at a set time. The mishna teaches that if a person misses the proper time, he can nonetheless read the *Shema* as if he were simply reading from the Torah. As this source states, "the

8. For differences between the parallel versions of this text, see M. Benovitz, "Learning: The Recitation of the *Shema* in the Mishna of Rabbi Shimon bar Yoḥai" [Hebrew], *Sidra* 20 (5765): 25–56.

recitation of the *Shema* in its proper time is more desirable than the study of words of Torah." The Jerusalem Talmud then proposes two responses to this challenge, but both serve to further distance Rashbi's position from the mainstream.[9]

This passage in the Jerusalem Talmud teaches that Rashbi had his own view regarding the mitzva of reciting the *Shema*. The rest of the world saw this mitzva as "the acceptance of the yoke of heaven": It was a religious credo meant to be recited every morning and evening at fixed times. But Rashbi, who viewed this prayer as a form of Torah study, regarded the recitation of the *Shema* as superfluous for someone like himself.[10]

> Rabbi Yoḥanan said in the name of Rabbi Shimon bar Yoḥai: Even if a person did no more than recite the *Shema* in the morning and evening, he has fulfilled the mitzva of "this book of the Torah shall not depart from your mouth" [Josh. 1:8], but it is forbidden to say this before the common folk.
>
> Rava said: It is a commandment to say this before the common people. (Menaḥot 99b)

The context of this passage is a discussion of the Hebrew word *tamid*, meaning permanent. The Mishna describes a table in the Temple that had bread on it "permanently." In commenting on this mishna, the Talmud discusses the amount of time that must be spent studying Torah, invoking the following biblical verse:

> This book of the Torah shall not depart from your mouth, but recite it day and night, that you may faithfully observe all that is written in it; for then will you prosper in your undertakings, and then will you succeed. (Josh. 1:8)

9. The two responses are difficult to understand, and allow for multiple readings. This is not relevant for our purposes, but interested readers may see Benovitz, "Recitation of the *Shema*," 37–38.
10. See L. Ginzburg, *Interpretations and New Insights in the Jerusalem Talmud* [Hebrew] (New York, 5701),vol. 1, 136–37.

The most straightforward interpretation of this verse is that "day and night" refers to the entire duration of the day and night. But Rashbi interprets these words to mean that a person must merely recite the verses of the *Shema* in the morning and evening. This view is consistent with his sense that a person need not recite the *Shema* unless doing so would constitute his regular Torah study. But he himself never ceases to study Torah, so the commandment to recite the *Shema* is irrelevant to him.[11]

As we have seen, Rashbi argues that it is sufficient to recite a few biblical verses in the morning and evening in order to fulfill one's obligation to study Torah. But as we have also seen, this very same Rashbi questions what will happen to Torah study if a person spends his days engaged in worldly occupation: "If a man plows at the time of plowing and sows at the time of sowing and harvests at the time of harvesting and threshes at the time of threshing and winnows at the time of the blowing wind, what will become of [the study of] Torah?" These sources seem to contradict one another, until we realize that Rashbi regarded himself as distinct from his contemporaries. His intense devotion to Torah study led him to carve out a place for himself in the halakhic system that no one had dreamed of in previous generations. Whereas the rest of the world had merely to accept the yoke of heaven upon waking up and going to bed, Rashbi cleaved to his Creator all day long.[12]

11. A. Steinberg, "Torah with *Derekh Eretz*" [Hebrew], a collection of religious Zionist texts in memory of Dr. Yosef Burg, vol. 3 (5761), 149–162. In note 38 Steinberg cites a long list of later commentators who tried to harmonize these sources, but it seems that our proposed solution is the clearest way of making sense of them.
12. I disagree with the analysis of Y. D. Gilat, *Episodes in the Development of Halakha* [Hebrew] (Ramat Gan, 5752), 283–84. Gilat views Rashbi's stance as a continuation of a tradition that the recitation of the *Shema* is a form of Torah study. According to Gilat, the mitzva of studying Torah came first, and then the obligation to recite the *Shema* became a commandment in its own right. In contrast, I would argue that the commandment to accept the yoke of heaven is documented in many early sources and stands at the heart of the debate between Beit Shammai and Beit Hillel. Rashbi's innovation was his sense that Torah study is not necessarily bound up in the acceptance of the yoke of heaven. See Y. Knoll, "The Section That Contains the Acceptance of the Yoke of Heaven" [Hebrew], *Tarbiz* 53 (5744). Also see *Sages* I, Part Three.

RASHBI AND HIS SON: MEN OF THE HIGHER ORDER ARE FEW AND FAR BETWEEN

The following source sheds further light on Rashbi's sense of his relationship to the rest of humanity:

> Ḥizkiya said in the name of Rabbi Yirmeya, who said in the name of Shimon bar Yoḥai: I am able to exempt the entire world from the judgment that is due in the World to Come for the sins that were committed from the day I was born until now. And were my son Elazar with me, we could exempt the world from judgment for sins committed from the day the world was created until now. And were Jotham the son of Uziah with us, we could deal with all the sins that were committed and will be committed from the day the world was created until its end. And Ḥizkiya said in the name of Rabbi Yirmeya, who said in the name of Rabbi Shimon bar Yoḥai: I have seen men of the highest order, and they are few. If they number a thousand, then I and my son are among them. If they number two, then they are I and my son. (Sukka 45b)

Rashbi is keenly aware of his own uniqueness. He identifies himself and his son as belonging to an otherworldly "upper class," even though their bodies exist in the physical world. This is an unusual distinction. On the one hand, he and his son straddle the heavenly and earthly realms; but on the other hand, they must struggle with their own humanity and earthliness.[13] Along these lines, we can understand Rashbi's midrash about Torah scholars, which appears in the context of his discussion of why God did not lead the Israelites directly from Egypt into the Land of Israel:

> "For God said: The people may have a change of heart when they see war, and return to Egypt" [Ex. 13:17] – The Holy One, Blessed Be He, said: If I bring them into the Land of Israel now by the direct route, they will immediately begin seizing the fields and

13. See Maharsha, *Insights into Talmudic Stories* [Hebrew], Sukka 45b, where the phrase "men of the higher order" is interpreted in terms of the verse "and pours them over the land" (Amos 9:6).

> vineyards, and they will neglect the study of Torah. Rather, I will make them wander the wilderness for forty years, and they will eat manna and drink well water, and the Torah will have time to take root in their bodies. Based on this, Rabbi Shimon bar Yoḥai would say: The Torah was given to be expounded only by those who eat manna. Like them are those who eat the priestly offering. (*Mekhilta deRashbi* 13:17)

The Torah rightfully belongs to those who eat manna and, secondly, to those who eat the priestly offering. "Those who eat manna" refers to the Israelites in the desert, who did not need to work for their daily bread: "When [the people of] Israel does the will of God, their work is done by others." They had only to follow the Divine Presence walking before them, much like Adam in the Garden of Eden. "Those who eat the priestly offering" refers to the priests. They were obligated to engage in ritual service in order to merit the Divine Presence. For them, eating *teruma* was their reward for their work. Rashbi asserts that the Torah can be studied properly only by these two groups: the Israelites in the desert, who experienced God's presence continuously, and those who connect with the divine through their holy service. The rest of the nation is not obligated to study Torah with the same intensity. These Jews can eat of the bread of the earth and content themselves with reciting the verses of the *Shema* when they lie down at night and rise up in the morning.

WITH THE NATION IN THE FIELDS

Rashbi recognizes that "men of the higher order" are few and far between. He is aware of the needs and weaknesses of the rest of humanity, and he is therefore lenient in his public rulings.[14]

Rabbi Yehoshua Hagar-Lau has already pointed out that many of Rashbi's teachings pertain to agricultural laws. Rashbi was involved in dozens of debates in the section of the Talmud known as Zera'im (seeds), which serves as a paean to what he refers to as the "temporal life," a life of manual labor.[15] We will consider one such debate here, in

14. Z. Frankel, *Methods of the Mishna*, 181: "Rashbi is generally lenient in his rulings."
15. Y. Hagar-Lau (my uncle and teacher), "'Great Is Labor' and 'The Temporal Life' in

which Rashbi's lenient ruling dramatically altered the laws of the sabbatical year:

> Rabbi Yehuda says: *Sefihin* [anything that grows spontaneously from seeds that fell to the ground before the sabbatical year] of mustard are permitted, since transgressors are not suspected concerning them. Rabbi Shimon says: All *sefihin* are permitted except *sefihin* of cabbage, since these do not exist among wild vegetables. The sages say: All *sefihin* are forbidden. (Mishna Shevi'it 9:1)

The Torah teaches that during the sabbatical year, the farmer is forbidden to harvest his field, including the *sefihin*. But just as the fruits that grow during the sabbatical year are forbidden only to sell and not to eat, so too the *sefihin* are forbidden only to sell and not to eat, at least according to the Bible. Nonetheless, the rabbis ruled stringently and forbade eating *sefihin*, lest a person designate all his produce as such.[16] Rashbi takes the most lenient position in this mishna: He permits eating all *sefihin* except cabbage, on account of its botanical characteristics. This is further evidence of Rashbi's involvement in the real world.

Consistent with his tendency to rule leniently with regard to the masses, Rashbi offers his own reason why Shavuot is shorter than the other pilgrimage festivals:

> Passover and Sukkot, which do not fall during work seasons, are seven and eight days, respectively. The Festival of Weeks [Shavuot], which does fall during a work season, is only one day, showing that the Torah is considerate of Israel's welfare. (Sifrei, Deuteronomy 196)

In this source, the very same Rashbi who was reluctant to pray and recite the *Shema* because he felt so connected to Torah study exempts

the Teachings of Rashbi" [Hebrew] in *B'Tokhekhi Yerushalayim*, 114–54.

16. Y. Felix, "The Nature and Development of the Prohibition of *Sefiḥim* During the Sabbatical Year," in Felix, *Jerusalem Talmud Shevi'it*, 385–416.

the Jews from a week-long Shavuot holiday because they are busy working in the fields.

BETWEEN HEAVEN AND EARTH

Considering himself among the elite but also rooted in the concerns of the masses, Rashbi sometimes ran into trouble in his interactions, as the following source suggests:

> Rabbi Shimon bar Yoḥai was passing by during the sabbatical year when he saw someone gathering *sefihin*. He said to him: Are these not forbidden? Are these not *sefihin*?[17]
>
> He said to him: But isn't it you who permits *sefihin*?
>
> He said to him: But don't my colleagues disagree with me?
>
> He [Rashbi] recited the following verse about him: "One who breaches a fence will be bitten by a snake" [Eccl. 10:8], and so it came to pass. (Y. Shevi'it 9:1 [38d])

The farmer takes part in a halakhic debate. He tells Rashbi that he is relying on the sage's ruling when he gathers *sefihin*, since Rashbi permits this practice. Rashbi responds angrily. He is convinced that the farmer is simply looking for the easy way out, so he curses him, telling him he will be bitten by a snake. The story ends with the words "and so it came to pass," indicating that Rashbi's curse was effective. This story teaches the principle of "majority rule" in halakhic debates,[18] though it also serves as an example of an encounter between Rashbi, a member of the elite, and an ordinary farmer.

17. The words "Are these not *sefiḥin*?" may have been spoken by the gatherer or by Rashbi. See Epstein, *Text of the Mishna*, 709–10. This story appears in the Jerusalem Talmud immediately before that of the emergence from the cave, and it is not the first death for which Rashbi is responsible.
18. This is how the story is presented in its parallel version in the Jerusalem Talmud (Berakhot 1:1 [2a]), in the context of a debate between Rabban Gamliel and the sages regarding whether the evening prayer is optional or obligatory. See O. Meir, "The Story of Rabbi Shimon bar Yoḥai in the Cave" [Hebrew], *Alei Siaḥ* 26 (5749): 145–46.

The Midrash tells another story of a curse inflicted by Rashbi, this time during a visit to a sick man:

> Toil away over words of Torah, and do not engage in idle matters.
>
> Once, as Rabbi Shimon bar Yoḥai went about visiting the sick, he found a certain man who was afflicted with bowel sickness uttering blasphemies against the Holy One, Blessed Be He. Rabbi Shimon bar Yoḥai said to him: Empty one! You should be pleading for mercy for yourself, and instead you are uttering blasphemies!
>
> The man said: May the Holy One, Blessed Be He, remove the sickness from me and place it on you.
>
> Rabbi Shimon said: The Holy One, Blessed Be He, dealt well with me, for I neglected the words of Torah and engaged in idle matters. (*Avot deRabbi Natan*, recension A, ch. 41)[19]

This is a difficult story. Rashbi considers visiting the sick an idle matter, since it takes him away from Torah study. We must remember that Rashbi was the leading student of Rabbi Akiva, who taught that Torah study takes precedence over good deeds. But in another talmudic story about visiting the sick, we see a very different side of Rabbi Akiva:

> There was an incident in which a student of Rabbi Akiva fell ill, and none of the sages went to visit him. Rabbi Akiva went to visit him, and because they swept the floor and settled the dust on the ground before him, he recovered.
>
> The student said to Rabbi Akiva: My teacher, you have brought me back to life!
>
> Rabbi Akiva emerged and expounded: Whoever does not visit the sick is as if he sheds blood. (Nedarim 40a)

19. Solomon Schechter edited the language of this text so that it reads, "for you neglected the words of Torah and engaged in idle matters," as if Rashbi were speaking about the sick man rather than about himself. See S. Z. Schechter, *Avot deRabbi Natan* (Vienna, 5647), 130. Urbach correctly identifies Schechter's gloss as apologetic. See Urbach, *Sages*, 543 note 58.

Following his teacher's example, Rashbi visits the sick. But deep down he is convinced that he is abandoning the eternal life of Torah in favor of the temporal life of this world. His curse of the sick man reflects both his sense of himself as representing the elite few "men of the higher order," and his scorn for the coarse-minded rest of humanity, who are beholden to more mundane concerns.[20]

We conclude this section with one of Rabbi Shimon bar Yoḥai's most troublesome teachings:

> Rabbi Shimon bar Yoḥai says: An unlearned person, even if he is pious or holy or upright, is cursed unto God. (*Otzar HaMidrashim*, 512b)

According to Rashbi, a person can connect to God only through Torah study. Piety, holiness, and uprightness alone will not lead to the divine.

ESCORTING RASHBI'S SON INTO THE WORLD OF INTENTIONALITY

Rashbi includes his son among the "men of the higher order." A talmudic story recounts how his son was admitted into this elite group. The story is preceded by a description of two of Rashbi's students, Rabbi Yonatan and Rabbi Yehuda ben Gerim, who are hosted in their teacher's home:[21]

> Rabbi Yonatan ben Asmai and Rabbi Yehuda ben Gerim studied the laws of vows in the home of Rabbi Shimon bar Yoḥai. They took leave of him in the evening. In the morning they returned

20. Likewise, in the story about the man who forbade his wife from giving food to Rabbi Shimon and Rabbi Yehuda (see the chapter on Rabbi Yehuda bar Ilai), Rabbi Shimon's Torah links him to a higher realm. Rabbi Asher ben Yeḥiel ("Rosh," 1250–1327) writes in his commentary on Nedarim 40a: "Shimon will not be persuaded to dishonor the Torah."

21. We know nothing about Rabbi Yonatan. We also know little about Rabbi Yehuda ben Gerim, who, according to the Babylonian Talmud, was responsible for reporting on Rashbi to the Roman authorities, forcing him and his son to hide in a cave. This same story teaches that Rabbi Yehuda was fated to die on account of Rashbi, as we will see.

and took leave of him again. He said to them: Didn't you take leave of me last night?

They said to him: You have taught us, our master, that a student who takes leave of his teacher and ends up sleeping overnight in the same city must take leave of him once again, as it is written, "On the eighth day he let the people go" [I Kings 8:66], and it is written, "On the twenty-third day of the seventh month he dismissed the people" [II Chr. 7:10]. From this we learn that a student who takes leave of his teacher and then sleeps in the same city must take leave of him once again. (Mo'ed Katan 9a)

After this preface, the story begins:

Rabbi Shimon bar Yoḥai said to his son: These people are men of stature. Go to them that they may bless you.

He went and found them posing a contradiction between verses, as follows:

It is written, "Survey the course you take, and all your ways will prosper" [Prov. 4:26], and it is written, "She does not chart a course of life" [Prov. 5:6]. There is no contradiction. One verse refers to a mitzva that can be performed by others, and one verse refers to a mitzva that cannot be performed by others.

They sat down again and inquired: It is written, "She is more precious than rubies; all of your goods cannot equal her" [Prov. 3:15], suggesting that heavenly goods do equal her. And it is written, "No goods can equal her," suggesting that even heavenly goods do not equal her. One verse refers to a mitzva that can be performed by others, and one verse refers to a mitzva that cannot be performed by others.

They said to him: What are you doing here?

He said to them: My father told me to come to you so that you would bless me.

They said to him: May it be His will that you plant but not reap, bring in but not take out, and take out but not bring in. Let your home be destroyed and your inn be inhabited. Let your table be disturbed, and may you not see a new year.

> When he came to his father, he said to him: Not only did they not bless me, but they distressed me.
>
> He said to him: What did they say to you?
>
> He said to him: They said to me such and such.
>
> He said to him: These are all blessings:
>
> You will plant but not reap: You will raise sons who will not die.
>
> You will bring in but not take out: You will bring in brides for your sons, and your sons will not die [such that the brides would return to their homes].
>
> You will take out but not bring in: You will have daughters whose husbands will not die (such that your daughters would return to your home).
>
> Let your home be destroyed and your inn be inhabited: This world will be but a temporary dwelling place, and the World to Come will be your home, as it is written, "Their grave is their eternal home" [Ps. 49:12].
>
> Let your table be disturbed: Because you will have so many sons and daughters.
>
> And may you not see the new year: Your wife will not die, and you will not remarry. (Mo'ed Katan 9a)

Rashbi teaches his son his first lesson: When interpreting the words of others, he must listen to the implicit message, not the explicit one. Words should be judged not by their superficial meaning, but by the "intentions of the heart" (Berakhot 11a). This is a key to understanding Rashbi's teachings. Whereas his intellectual rival Rabbi Yehuda bar Ilai was interested in external deeds, Rashbi would listen closely to their inner content. It is this lesson that Rashbi seeks to transmit to his son, not literally but experientially. The message that "these are all blessings" will penetrate the young boy's heart and shape his personality for years to come.[22]

22. D. Fox, "These Are All Blessings" [Hebrew], *HaMa'ayan* 24:4 (Tammuz 5744): 1–9.

THE TEACHINGS OF RASHBI: INTENTIONS MATTER

For Rashbi, an action required proper intention in order to have value. This notion guided much of his thinking, though we will consider just the specific case of the laws of Shabbat. The Torah forbids all work on Shabbat. The rabbis explained that it is specifically "purposeful labor" (*melekhet maḥshevet*) that is forbidden by the Torah.[23] This principle is understood to mean that not just the nature of the act is taken into account, but also the intention of the one who performs it. Rabbi Shimon has a unique position regarding "purposeful labor," which stems from his ideas about the role of intention in halakha.

An Act That Is Unintended

A person may engage in a form of intentional work with unintended consequences. For instance, someone may be trying to wash his hands in the garden, and consequently he also happens to water the plants. Likewise, a person may drag a cart over an uneven surface and inadvertently create indentations in that surface, which is considered a form of plowing, an activity forbidden on Shabbat. This is referred to as "an act that is unintended." The person washing hands has no idea that he is watering the plants; and the person dragging the cart has no idea that he is plowing. But they are nonetheless performing the prohibited action. Rabbi Shimon explains his halakhic position in such a situation:

> Rabbi Shimon says: A person may drag a bed, chair, stool, or armchair to himself on the Sabbath, and it goes without saying on a festival. (Tosefta Beitza 2:18)

In the Mishna the dissenting view is attributed to Rabbi Yehuda:

> A child's cart is susceptible to impurity, and may be carried on Shabbat, but it may not be dragged except over vessels. Rabbi Yehuda says: No object may be dragged, except for the cart, because it presses. (Mishna Beitza 2:10)

23. See Rabbi Yisrael Lifschitz, *Tiferet Yisrael*, introduction to Mishna Shabbat 7, where he defines *melekhet maḥshevet*.

The disagreement between Rashbi and Rabbi Yehuda concerns their understanding of "an act that is unintended." According to Rashbi, such an act is permissible, since intentions are more significant than actions. But Rabbi Yehuda bar Ilai argues that it is the consequences that matter, and thus one is liable for such an act. However, the Talmud narrows Rabbi Shimon's ruling to only those cases in which the consequences are not inevitable. If the consequences are inevitable, the Talmud claims that even Rabbi Shimon would hold the person responsible, since one must be conscious of the inevitable consequences of his behavior.[24]

An Act That Is Unnecessary for the Thing Itself

Rabbi Shimon also maintains that "if an act is unnecessary for the thing itself, one is exempt from punishment." That is, a person may engage in an act that is forbidden on Shabbat with full awareness of what he is doing, so long as his goal is not the direct consequence of that act but rather its incidental by-product. The Talmud cites the example of a person who digs a pit because he needs the dirt. Although it is forbidden to dig a pit on Shabbat, the digger has no interest in the pit itself. He is concerned only with the dirt. According to Rashbi this person is not liable for his behavior, because it is "an act that is unnecessary for the thing itself." The sages of the Talmud, aware of this principle of Rabbi Shimon, seek the basis of his distinction. They cite a mishna in Tractate Shabbat, in which a person who hunts a reptile for the sake of using some part of it (for instance, its skin) is liable for such an act, since hunting is forbidden on Shabbat. But if the person hunts the reptile even though he has no need for it, he is not liable. This opinion is associated with Rashbi:

24. In the Talmud's lexicon, the narrow interpretation of Rabbi Shimon's ruling is paraphrased, "Can you cut off a chicken's head without it dying?" There are consequences that it is impossible to deny having been aware of from the outset. The sages expect people to act with intentionality. The rabbis further qualify this principle, arguing that if the consequences are not beneficial to the person performing the action, then Rabbi Shimon's loophole applies. The commentators debate whether Rashbi would declare such an action permissible, or would merely exempt the perpetrator from punishment. See the debate between the Arukh and the *Tosafot* in the Babylonian Talmud, Shabbat 103a.

> Who is the sage who taught this? Rabbi Yehuda said in the name of Rav: It was Rabbi Shimon, who said: One who performs an act unnecessary for the thing itself is not liable for it. (Shabbat 107b)

The Talmud explains that an example of an act that is unnecessary for the thing itself is hunting a reptile with no intention of using any part of it.

We can find examples of Rabbi Shimon's focus on intentionality and his conflict with Rabbi Yehuda in all realms of halakha.[25]

Intention in Stories About Rashbi

Rashbi insists upon the role of intention in deciding matters of halakha. His position is reflected in the stories told about him throughout rabbinic literature, where he often disagrees with Rabbi Yehuda.

> When our sages entered the vineyard at Yavneh they included Rabbi Yehuda, Rabbi Elazar ben Rabbi Yose, and Rabbi Shimon. The following question was posed in their presence: Why does this ailment start out in the innards of a person and conclude by afflicting his mouth?
>
> Rabbi Yehuda bar Ilai, the leading speaker on every occasion, answered and said: Even though the kidneys advise, the heart discerns, and the tongue articulates the words, still, the mouth concludes the process of speech.
>
> Rabbi Elazar ben Rabbi Yose said: The mouth is afflicted because through it, people eat impure things. But would you really think that eating non-kosher things would lead to such a harsh punishment? Rather, through the mouth people eat things that are improperly tithed.

25. Fox, "Blessings," cites several such examples. Also see Y. Rosenbaum, "Two Sages, Two Worlds: The Ways of Rabbi Yehuda and Rabbi Shimon" [Hebrew], in *Lifnim: A Collection of Articles for the Fifteenth Anniversary of the Mekor Ḥayyim Yeshiva*, ed. D. Guttenmacher (Jerusalem, 5760), 195–212. The Admor of Sokatchov, Rabbi Avraham Bernstein, connects the debate between Rabbi Yehuda and Rabbi Shimon regarding the laws of Shabbat to the question of whether mitzvot require intention. See his preface to *Eglei Tal* (Piotrikov, 5666).

> Rabbi Shimon answered and said: It comes from the sin of neglecting Torah study. (Shabbat 33b)

Rabbi Yehuda's explanation for the particular ailment under discussion is that "the mouth concludes the process of speech." He recognizes that many factors cause our behavior: the kidneys advise, the heart understands, and the tongue articulates. But this is all just a prelude to the critical act of speech. This is the essence of the Torah of Rabbi Yehuda, "the leading speaker." In contrast, Rabbi Shimon focuses not on speech but on the internal world of thought and intention.

Another dispute between Rabbi Yehuda and Rabbi Shimon concerns God's biblical promise to remove vicious beasts from the land:

> Rabbi Yehuda said: He will remove them from the world.
>
> Rabbi Shimon said: He will make them tranquil, so they will not injure people.
>
> Rabbi Shimon said: Under what circumstances is God praised? Is it when there are no sources of injury, or when there are sources of injury but they do no damage? You must concede that it is when there are sources of injury but they do no damage. And so it is written, "A song, a psalm for the day of rest" [Ps. 92:1] – to the One who grants the world rest from sources of injury, so that He will make them tranquil, so they will not injure people. (*Sifrei Behukkotai* 1:2)

Rabbi Yehuda interprets the verse literally. God will in fact eradicate the vicious beasts from the land. But for Rashbi, this is not enough. Rashbi does not want to see the vicious beasts eradicated; he wants to see them tamed so they are no longer vicious. This is the corrective that Rashbi, ever concerned with intentionality, seeks.[26]

26. Rabbi Yosef Razin, author of *Tzofnat Paneaḥ* (a commentary on the Torah), compares this dispute to the halakhic disagreement between Rabbi Yehuda and Rabbi Shimon regarding the commandment to nullify all leaven on Passover. Rabbi Yehuda maintains that leaven must be burned, while Rabbi Shimon holds that it it must merely be divested of those characteristics that render it prohibited. "Blessings," which elaborates on this debate.

THE STORY OF THE CAVE

The story of Rashbi in the cave has preoccupied scholars of the rabbinic period for generations. It would be impossible to narrate Rashbi's life without recounting this tale. His many years spent in a cave are considered an integral part of his identity, particularly as the author of the Zohar. To quote the lyrics penned by the kabbalist Rabbi Shimon ben Lavi: "Bar Yoḥai, into rocky caves you stepped, there you acquired your strength and glory."[27] But historical scholarship of the rabbinic period has cast doubt on the credibility of this story. The details in the Babylonian Talmud's version differ from those in the Palestinian sources. Moreover, scholars have noted that the tale, especially in its Babylonian version, seems like a work of fiction without any historical basis. As Yisrael Ben Shalom wrote, "The passage in Shabbat 33 apparently belongs to a later, post-amoraic stratum of the Babylonian Talmud, which is why it is so foreign to the spirit, atmosphere, and issues at stake in the Land of Israel during the Usha generation."[28] Yisrael Levine sought the roots of this story in classical tales about a holy man who hid in a cave for years and then emerged and purified a city: "In ancient times there was an association between holy men and caves (which included divine revelation, an annunciation before a heavenly angel, and mystical experiments). The connection between Rashbi and the cave is a testament to his uniqueness. No other sage merited having such a story told about him."[29] And Ofra Meir, writing from a literary perspective, commented, "We are still

27. Rabbi Shimon ben Lavi's song about Bar Yoḥai became popular among all Jewish communities and is sung routinely on Shabbat. The question of whether Rashbi was the author of the Zohar divides traditionalists from those scholars who insist on the composition's much later provenance. I recuse myself from this debate.

28. Y. Ben Shalom, "Rabbi Yehuda bar Ilai," 24. Ben Shalom was a student of Y. Efron, who, in the early days of the historical study of rabbinic sources, championed the credibility of sources from the Land of Israel relative to their Babylonian parallels. See, for instance, Efron's classic article "The Bar Kokhba Revolt in Light of the Talmudic Tradition: The Land of Israel vs. the Babylonian" [Hebrew], in *Bar Kokhba Revolt: New Studies*, 47–105.

29. Y. L. Levine, "Rabbi Shimon bar Yoḥai: The Bones of the Dead and the Purification of Tiberias – History and Tradition" [Hebrew], *Catedra* 22 (5742): 9–42. According to Levine, the entire Babylonian story serves to explain the elevated status of Tiberias. See especially 41–42.

far from able to answer the question of who Rashbi was as a historical personality, and who he was as a literary character. But it is clearly his literary persona that informed the traditional image of him, and even if this image is not historical, he is nonetheless a fascinating figure who has captured the imagination of our people to this day."[30]

In light of what we have learned about Rashbi thus far, we might say that the story of the cave reinforces our image of this sage as conjoining heaven and earth.[31] We need not enter in the debates about how to contextualize this tale historically.[32] Even those efforts to date stories about Rashbi to the period before or after the cave seem suspect.[33] Suffice it to say that the existence of multiple versions of this narrative

30. Meir, "Rabbi Shimon bar Yoḥai in the Cave," 145–46.

31. It is not just literary scholars who questioned the historical credibility of these accounts. Even in the traditional world of Torah study, there were those who, for religious reasons, tried to distinguish between the historical and literary aspects of this story. See Rabbi Z. Shimshoni, "The Story of Rashbi and His Son in the Cave" [Hebrew], in *Milei Me'alyuta: A Collection of Articles for the Graduates of the Hesder Yeshiva in Maale Adumim* (Elul 5758). Shimshoni opens with the following remark: "Even if we are talking about a story that we can assume actually happened, we will analyze it from a literary perspective." See also S. Ariel, "The Incident of Rashbi in the Cave" [Hebrew], *Golot* 3 (5755): 217–38. Ariel opens with his opposition to the practice of taking talmudic stories at face value: "There is a strong tendency to take these stories literally. The assumption that underlies this article is that even in such stories, there is room to dig deeper and find greater meaning, without limiting ourselves to the surface."

32. Many scholars from the Enlightenment to the modern age have broken their teeth on these efforts. It is worth considering Hyman's reflections in *Legends*, s.v. "Rabbi Shimon bar Yoḥai," 1188–89. Hyman rejects attempts to date the events of Rashbi's life as taking place before or after the cave episode. He concludes, "I have gone on at such length here in order to show that this business of recounting the lives of our holy sages has not gotten very.... Those who seek to do so will not retell their lives accurately. They will recount their own ideas, then seek evidence for their foolishness in the Talmud."

33. First and foremost among them is Moshe Konitz in his book *Ben Yoḥai* (Vienna, 5575). This book was written as a polemic against Rabbi Yaakov Emden, in an attempt to prove that Rashbi was the author of the Zohar. Konitz claimed that he proved beyond the shadow of a doubt that the original name of the sage was Rabbi Shimon, and that his name was changed to Rashbi or to Bar Yoḥai only after he emerged from the cave. Many subsequent articles were written based on his claims, but his argument has no basis in the textual evidence.

attests that it was widely known. We will refer to the version in the Babylonian Talmud, which is the most stylized and probably also the latest, with occasional reference to the Jerusalem Talmud as well.[34]

The Attitude to Rome

> And why did they call him the leading speaker on every occasion? Because Rabbi Yehuda, Rabbi Yose, and Rabbi Shimon ben Yoḥai were once sitting together, and Yehuda ben Gerim was sitting next to them. Rabbi Yehuda opened the discussion and said: How admirable are the deeds of this nation! They have built marketplaces, they have built bridges, and they have built bathhouses.
>
> Rabbi Yose remained silent.
>
> Rabbi Shimon bar Yoḥai answered him and said: Everything they built, they built only to serve their own needs. They built marketplaces in order to quarter harlots; they built bathhouses in order to beautify their own bodies; and they built bridges in order to collect tolls.
>
> Yehuda ben Gerim went and recounted their words, and the reports were heard by the authorities. They said: Yehuda, who praised us, he too shall be praised. Yose, who remained silent, shall be exiled to Tzippori. Shimon, who denigrated the Romans, shall be executed. (Shabbat 33b)

The story opens with a nod to the previous talmudic passage, which refers to Rabbi Yehuda bar Ilai as "the leading speaker on every occasion." We are then introduced to three colleagues who sit around debating the merits of Roman public works. Rabbi Yehuda begins by praising the work of the Romans. When we studied Rabbi Yehuda, we saw that he was a young student during the Bar Kokhba revolt. He spent time in Lod with Rabbi Tarfon and Rabbi Akiva. But where was he during

34. Levine's article juxtaposes the various sources from the Land of Israel. The author focuses on the purification of Tiberias, but he cites the story in its entirely. See his "Rabbi Shimon bar Yoḥai: The Bones of the Dead." Meir also presents a sophisticated and detailed analysis of the story. See Meir, "Rabbi Shimon bar Yoḥai in the Cave."

the revolt and the persecution? He certainly seems to have been aware of the political situation, as the following source attests:

> Rabbi Yehuda bar Ilai said: In former generations one would ask: What is the meaning of "The voice is the voice of Jacob" [Gen. 27:22]? The voice of the emperor Hadrian, who killed eight thousand myriads in Beitar. (Tanḥuma, *Toldot* 10)

In another source Rabbi Yehuda depicts life under Roman rule. He describes the observance of Shabbat during the persecution:

> Rabbi Yehuda said: In times of persecution, we used to bring a Torah scroll from the courtyard up to the roof, and from one roof to another, where we would sit and read from it, and no one objected. They said to him: One may not offer proof from what was done in times of persecution. (Y. Eiruvin 9:1 [25c])

Yet another source encapsulates Rabbi Yehuda's political vision:

> Rabba bar bar Ḥana said in the name of Rabbi Yoḥanan, who said in the name of Rabbi Yehuda bar Ilai: Rome is destined to fall into the hands of Persia. If in the case of the First Temple, which was built by a descendant of Shem and destroyed by the Chaldeans, the Chaldeans then fell into the hands of the Persians, then in the case of the Second Temple, which was built by the Persians and destroyed by the Romans, is it not logical that the Romans should fall into the hands of the Persians? (Yoma 10a)

All of these sources cast doubt on Rabbi Yehuda's complimentary assessment of Rome in Shabbat 33. Even more suspicious, the very exchange recorded in that passage appears elsewhere in the Talmud as part of a conversation that God conducts with the non-Jews who come to claim their place in the World to Come:

> The Holy One, Blessed Be He, said to them [the Romans]: With what did you involve yourselves?

> They said to him: Master of the Universe, we built many marketplaces, we built many bathhouses, we amassed much silver and gold. And all these we did only for the sake of the Jews, so they could involve themselves in Torah study.
>
> The Holy One, Blessed Be He, said to them: Fools of the universe! Whatever you have done has been for your own sake. You built marketplaces to quarter harlots; bathhouses to beautify yourselves; and as for the silver and gold you have amassed, it is in fact Mine, as it is stated, "Mine is the silver and the gold, says the Lord" [Hag. 2:8]. (Avoda Zara 2b)

A comparison of these two sources reveals that Rabbi Yehuda's words in Tractate Shabbat are spoken by the Romans in Avoda Zara, and Rashbi's words are spoken by God, all as part of a conversation takes place on the Day of Judgment. For this reason, Yisrael Ben Shalom argued that the discussion among the sages in Shabbat 33 is a literary construct without any historical grounding in the Usha generation.[35]

Even if this story is fictional, the storyteller seems to have captured the essence of the dispute between Rabbi Yehuda and Rabbi Shimon. As we have seen, the Talmud distinguishes between Rabbi Yehuda, who focuses on consequences, and Rabbi Shimon, who is concerned with intentions. This is the basis for their debate about Roman public works. Rabbi Yehuda notes that the Romans succeeded in repairing the world: They built splendid cities, which were comfortable for themselves and for all who inhabit them. But Rabbi Shimon cares only about intentions: "Everything they built, they built only to serve their own needs."[36] There may be no historical basis for Rabbi Yehuda's praise of the Romans, but it is consistent with his worldview as reflected in his other teachings.

In any case, this conversation reaches the ears of the Romans (presumably on account of Rabbi Yehuda ben Gerim, whom we encountered above in Rashbi's home), and Rashbi finds himself fleeing the authorities.

35. Y. Ben Shalom, "Rabbi Yehuda bar Ilai," 22.
36. This interpretation resembles that of Fox, "Blessings," 5–6.

In the Cave

> Rabbi Shimon bar Yoḥai and his son ran away and hid in the beit midrash. Every day, Rabbi Shimon's wife would bring them bread and a small pitcher of water, and they would eat. When the decrees intensified, Rabbi Shimon said to his son: The minds of women are easily swayed. Perhaps the Romans will torture your mother, and she will give us away.
>
> They went and hid in a cave. A miracle happened, and a carob tree and a spring of water were created for them. They would shed their clothes and sit covered in sand up to their necks. All day they would study together, and when the times for prayer arrived, they would dress, cover themselves, and pray. Then they would return and shed their clothes, so their clothes would not wear out. They dwelled in the cave for twelve years. (Shabbat 33b)

While it is fear of the Roman authorities that leads to the miraculous situation in which Rashbi and his son find themselves, this is not really a story about Rome. Rather, the focus is on the transformation of Rashbi and his son into angelic figures who eat out of God's hands. Under no circumstances will Rashbi desist from the study of Torah. Just as his teacher Rabbi Akiva refused to forfeit his learning, so too does his student cling to his Torah at all cost. As in the sources we considered above, he does not abandon his family, but continues learning Torah. When he flees to the cave, it is only so as to spare his wife from suffering.

So long as he remains in the beit midrash, Rashbi is connected to the real world. His food and drink are provided by his wife, not by heaven. He and his son dwell inside a structure created by human hands, and they are still bound to the material world. But when they enter the cave, they sever all connection with reality. Only prayer draws them back into the physical world. When the time comes to pray, they put on their clothes, which are manmade, and which restore their awareness of their physical bodies. As we have seen, for Rashbi, prayer exists on a lower spiritual plane than Torah study. For him, prayer belongs to the temporal world,[37]

37. We saw this in the section on Rashbi's views regarding the recitation of the *Shema*. For the notion of prayer as temporal, see Shabbat 11a.

because it is about sustenance, health, and gratitude.[38] True devotion is expressed in Torah study, an activity divorced from the physical.

Rabbi Shimon, as we have seen, dreamt about eating manna from heaven. In this story he comes ever closer to that reality.

The First Emergence from the Cave

> Elijah came and stood at the mouth of the cave. He said: Who will inform Bar Yoḥai that the caesar has died and the decree has been annulled?
>
> They [Rashbi and his son] emerged from the cave. They saw some people plowing a field and sowing crops. Rabbi Shimon bar Yoḥai said: These people are forsaking eternal life and occupying themselves with temporal life! Everywhere they cast their gaze, the object of their vision would immediately be incinerated.
>
> A heavenly voice rang out and proclaimed: Have you emerged in order to destroy My world? Return to your cave! (Shabbat 33a-b)

It is worth comparing this part of the story to the version in the Jerusalem Talmud:

> Rabbi Shimon bar Yoḥai lived hidden in a cave for thirteen years. The cave was next to a carob tree. He stayed there until his body became afflicted with a skin disease that looked like rust spots. At the end of thirteen years he said: Should I not go out to see what has happened in the world? He went out and sat in the mouth of the cave. He saw a hunter trapping birds. When Rabbi Shimon heard a heavenly echo say, "Pardoned," the bird would escape. He said: Without the intervention of heaven, even a bird does not perish. How much more so a human being! (Y. Shevi'it 9:1 [38d])

38. See Ariel, "Rashbi in the Cave," 227–28.

The storyteller in the Jerusalem Talmud focuses on the emergence from the cave, not the experience of dwelling in it or the gradual shift from the earthly realm to the heavenly. The only aspect of the cave experience that concerns the Jerusalem Talmud is Rashbi's physical condition: "His body became afflicted with a skin disease that looked like rust spots." This type of detail is irrelevant to the Babylonian storyteller, who would have been content to leave Rashbi and his son in the cave forever.[39] It is only Elijah, who comes to "return the hearts of fathers to sons," who can summon Rashbi and his son out of the cave. Elijah symbolizes the connection between the upper and lower worlds.[40] The confrontation between the cave (a symbol of the heavenly realm) and the outside world proves so fiery that the emergence from the former has fatal consequences. Rashbi and his son wonder at those who are "forsaking eternal life and occupying themselves with temporal life." They do not intend to set anything aflame. But they have become so disconnected from the rest of the world that they simply "cast their gaze," and everything spontaneously combusts. Therefore the heavenly voice chases them back into their isolated existence, lest they continue to destroy the world.

As this story teaches, God cares about both worlds. He views the outside world as "His world," and the cave as belonging to Rashbi and his son. "Men of the higher order," Rashbi and his son, are not members of this world. They dwell in the upper realm, whose contact with our own mundane reality is always dangerous and fraught.

The Second Emergence from the Cave

> They went and returned to the cave and dwelled there another twelve months, a full year in all. At that point they said to them-

39. Meir notes this in "Shimon bar Yoḥai in the Cave," 149.
40. A. Wiener, *The Prophet Elijah in the Development of Judaism* (London, 1978). Wiener argues that Elijah masquerades in these stories as a source of deliverance. I would argue that Elijah also symbolizes the encounter between worlds, much like the figure of Rashbi that I have attempted to sketch here.

> selves: The sentence of evildoers in hell lasts no more than twelve months.
>
> A heavenly voice proclaimed: Emerge from your cave!
>
> They emerged. Whenever Rabbi Elazar would destroy something through his fiery gaze, Rabbi Shimon would remedy it. Rabbi Shimon said to Rabbi Elazar: My son, the world has enough with you and me.
>
> As night began to fall on Friday afternoon, Rabbi Shimon and his son saw an old man clutching two bundles of myrtles and running home with them at twilight. They said to him: What do you need these myrtle bundles for?
>
> He answered them: They are in honor of Shabbat.
>
> They asked: But could you not have sufficed with just one bundle?
>
> He said: One is for the commandment to remember Shabbat, and one is for the commandment to observe Shabbat.
>
> Rabbi Shimon said to his son: Look how beloved the mitzvot are to the Jewish people! And they were appeased. (Shabbat 33b)

For Rabbi Shimon and his son, the Garden of Eden becomes a kind of hell. The final twelve months in the cave seem like a death sentence. Rashbi and his son realize that they sinned when they emerged from the cave, so they petition God's mercy. A heavenly voice grants them permission to emerge this second time. This sequence of events is reminiscent of the story of Elijah on Mount Horeb, when he cries out zealously, "The Israelites have forsaken Your covenant!" God teaches Elijah that the Lord is not in the wind, but in the "still, small voice" (1 Kings 19:9–14). Malbim (Rabbi Meir Leibush ben Yehiel Michel Weiser, 1809–1879) offers the following commentary:

> He showed him: When there was wind and noise and fire in the camp, God was not present, but only in the still, small voice. And from this God's messengers and prophets should learn: They need not storm or make noise or ignite a fire (as Elijah did in his

> zealotry for the Lord of hosts, when he stopped up the heavens and slaughtered the prophets of Baal), because God will send His prophets to come to Him in a still, small voice, and to draw the people with bonds of love and with soft words.

Rabbi Shimon makes his peace with the mundane. But his son is still looking down from the upper realm of the cave to the common folk below and threatening them with fire. Rabbi Shimon saves the world (and his son) when he famously teaches, "The world has enough with you and me." This is just another version of the words he spoke earlier: "I have seen men of the higher order, and they are few and far between." Rashbi understands that the entire world is not meant to live on this higher plane. There is an earthly realm where most of humanity dwells. He and his son can serve as the link between heaven and earth. They alone can support the world.

At this point they encounter an old man running with myrtle branches at twilight on the eve of the Sabbath. He is rushing to fulfill a custom, not even a mitzva. The man holds two bundles of myrtles, one corresponding to the commandment to remember Shabbat, and one corresponding to the commandment to observe Shabbat.[41] At this moment, Rashbi learns something new about the world. We have seen that he considered the fulfillment of the commandments to be less important than prayer, which was less important than the recitation of the *Shema*, which in turn was less important than the study of Torah. When Rashbi sees a Jew running with two bundles of myrtles so as to fulfill a custom, not even a mitzva, he says to his son, "Look how beloved the mitzvot are to the Jewish people!" Rashbi recognizes the merit of those Jews who live by their values, and he praises them for doing so. His face is radiant with a divine glow, but it does not blind him to the virtues of the rest of humanity.

41. Maharsha draws a connection between these two bundles of myrtles and the custom of lighting two candles on the eve of Shabbat. See his *Insights into Talmudic Stories*, Shabbat 33b.

RASHBI: BETWEEN SAGE AND PROPHET

How was Rashbi regarded by his colleagues and successors?

The Double Ordination

We have already pointed out that Rashbi studied with and was ordained by Rabbi Akiva. But when in the company of his students, Rabbi Akiva gave priority to Rabbi Meir:

> Rabbi Ba said: At first each one would appoint his own disciples to the court. For example, Rabbi Yoḥanan ben Zakkai appointed Rabbi Eliezer and Rabbi Yehoshua; Rabbi Yehoshua appointed Rabbi Akiva; and Rabbi Akiva appointed Rabbi Meir and Rabbi Shimon. He said: Let Rabbi Meir take his seat first. Rabbi Shimon's face turned pale. Rabbi Akiva said to him: Let it be enough for you that I and your Creator recognize your strengths. (Y. Sanhedrin 1:2 [19a])

This is an amoraic tradition that dates back to a time when sages would "appoint" (or ordain) their students personally. Rabbi Akiva appoints Rabbi Meir and Rabbi Shimon, two very unusual students, but he privileges Rabbi Meir. When he notices the look on Rabbi Shimon's face, Rabbi Akiva responds sensitively: "I and your Creator recognize your strengths." We will come to know Rabbi Meir's strengths in the pages that follow, but for the time being, we note that Rabbi Akiva prefers him over Rabbi Shimon.

We have already considered the story in which Rabbi Yehuda ben Baba ordained several sages, among them Rabbi Shimon and Rabbi Meir. As we learned, Rabbi Akiva ordained these students very early on, before they became known in the world. Rabbi Yehuda ben Baba ordained them later, once they had made their mark.

Rashbi was well respected at the early assemblies of the sages in the Rimon Valley and in Usha. At the Rimon Valley gathering he was the last to speak, and the sages praised him. At Usha he was regarded as their colleague.[42]

42. I do not regard the praise lavished upon Rashbi by his colleagues at Usha as an

Sending Rashbi to Rome as He Is "Accustomed to Miracles"

In our discussion of Rabbi Yose, we looked briefly at the story of how his son Rabbi Elazar was sent to Rome accompanied by Rashbi. We will now consider this story more closely. It is documented in several sources, suggesting that it probably has a kernel of historical fact.[43] The primary source is in the Babylonian Talmud, which describes how a Jew named Reuven ben Isterovli attempted to masquerade as a Roman and outwit the authorities in the hope of revoking the evil decrees against the Jews:

> For it once happened that the regime enacted a decree that the Jews not observe Shabbat, that they not circumcise their sons, and that they cohabit with menstruating women. Rabbi Reuven ben Isterovli went out and cut his hair in a pagan style in order to conceal his Jewishness, and he went and sat together with the Romans. He said to them: One who has an enemy, does he want to become poor or rich?
>
> They said to him: To become poor.
>
> He said to them: If so, let them not do work on the Sabbath, so they should become poor.
>
> They said: He has spoken well, and they annulled the decree against Shabbat observance.
>
> He then said to them: One who has an enemy, does he want him to become weak or strong?
>
> They said to him: To become weak.
>
> He said to them: If so, let them circumcise their sons on the eighth day, and they will become weak.
>
> They said: He has spoken well, and they annulled the decree against circumcision.

indication that they were crowning him "king of the sages," as Kolitz claims in his *Bar Yoḥai and His Teachings*, 42–49

43. For other sources on Rashbi's visit to Rome, see *Sifrei Zuta* 8:2; Yoma 53b. On Rabbi Elazar ben Rabbi Yose's visit, see Tosefta Yoma 2:15 (with parallels in the Jerusalem and Babylonian Talmuds and in the Midrash, as per Lieberman's *Tosefta Kifshuta*, Yoma, 239). This source describing their journey together is credible because the two sages quote the conversations between them. See S. Lieberman, *The Arukh's Commentary on Seder Mo'ed* (New York, 5722), 775–76.

> He then said to them: One who has an enemy, does he want him to increase in number or decrease?
>
> They said to him: To decrease.
>
> He said to them: If so, let them not cohabit with menstruating women.
>
> They said: He has spoken well, and they annulled the decree.
>
> Subsequently they recognized him as a Jew and reinstated the decrees. (Me'ila 17a)

These decrees are generally associated with Hadrian,[44] but in light of the other figures mentioned, this source must be dated to the end of the decrees of persecution under Antoninus Pius. The rabbinic tradition attributes the revocation of these decrees to the intervention of the sages, not to Roman benevolence. The story of Rabbi Reuven, which depicts the Roman authorities in a ridiculous light, is of course fabricated. But the decrees against Shabbat observance and circumcision have a historical basis.[45] We have historical testimony that Antoninus Pius did in fact revoke the decree against circumcision.[46] Presumably not all the decrees were revoked at once, and thus the Jews felt the need to lobby the emperor. When Reuven's attempt failed, it became necessary for the sages to send someone else:

> The rabbis said: Who will go and annul the decrees? Let Rabbi Shimon ben Yoḥai go, for he is accustomed to having miracles performed on his behalf. And after him, who will go? Rabbi Elazar ben Rabbi Yose.
>
> Rabbi Yose said to them: And were my father, Ḥalafta, alive, could you say to him: Give your son for execution?

44. See, for instance, Y. Levi, *A Confrontation of Worlds* [Hebrew] (Jerusalem, 5720), 225.
45. I have found no evidence that the Romans decreed against the observance of family purity. Although their decrees forbade religious observance in general, it seems strange that the Romans would have legislated such intimate matters, unless they went so far as to lock the gates of the ritual baths.
46. See the introductory chapter of this book.

> Rabbi Shimon said to them: And were my father, Yoḥai, alive, could you say to him: Give your son for execution?
>
> Rabbi Yose said to them: I will go, for I fear that perhaps Rabbi Shimon will cause punishment to befall my son.[47]
>
> Rabbi Shimon accepted upon himself that he would not cause punishment to befall Rabbi Elazar bar Rabbi Yose [and Rabbi Yose then allowed his son to go with him]. Even so, he caused him punishment. (Me'ila 17a)

Even if we accept that this story is entirely fictional, we must at least concede that someone from the talmudic period saw fit to describe the relationship between Rashbi and his colleagues in this manner. Rashbi is depicted as someone who is "accustomed to miracles" and is capable of killing someone with a look, presumably on account of the story of the cave. The entire cycle of rabbinic stories about Rashbi is built upon this foundational tale.

WHERE WAS RASHBI DURING THE USHA PERIOD?

The sages of the Usha generation were quite active in shaping the character of the new beit midrash and establishing the foundations of the Oral Torah. But Rashbi seems to have kept his distance from the beit midrash and from the institutions of leadership. Nonetheless, he continued to transmit Torah to his students, and his teachings are included in every part of the Mishna.[48] One tradition that appears at several points throughout the Talmud relates that he studied with Rabbi Yehuda HaNasi in Tekoa:

47. What was Rabbi Yose afraid of? An apologetic reading would suggest that he feared his son would fall into the jaws of the evil Roman Empire. Kolitz writes: "Rabbi Yose said to them: How dangerous is this trip to Rome" (*Bar Yoḥai and His Teachings*, 195–96). But also see the *Tosafot* on this passage, who explain that Rabbi Yose was afraid to send his son with Rashbi, "who was quick to anger, and I worry lest he punish my son."
48. "Though Rashbi disagreed with his colleagues on many occasions, we rarely find him engaging in discussions with them." Epstein, *Literature of the Tanna'im*, 148. Also see Z. Frankel, *Methods of the Mishna*, 182.

> Rebbi said: When I used to study Torah with Rabbi Shimon in Tekoa, we would bring oil in a wrapping cloth from the courtyard to the roof, from the roof to the shed, and from one shed to another, until we reached the spring. And there we would wash ourselves [using the oil we had carried]. (Tosefta Eiruvin 5:24)

This source is surely not referring to Tekoa in Judea, which was destroyed during the Bar Kokhba revolt. Scholars instead understand this as a reference to Tekoa in the Galilee, just south of Meron, and quite far from Usha.[49] Although Rebbi explains that he studied in Rashbi's beit midrash, we do not know which sages considered themselves students of Rashbi, aside from Rabbi Shimon ben Yehuda.[50]

Rashbi transmitted the teachings of his own teacher Rabbi Akiva:

> And this is what Rabbi Shimon would say to his students: My sons, study my teachings, because my teachings are the cream of the cream of Rabbi Akiva's teachings. (Gittin 67a)

Rashbi asserts that his teachings constitute the best of Rabbi Akiva's teachings. But when the sage Isi ben Yehuda praises Rashbi before the sages, Rashbi berates him:

> Isi ben Yehuda used to coin phrases to describe the sages.... Of Rabbi Shimon he said: He who studies much and forgets little.
>
> Afterward Rabbi Shimon came upon Isi ben Yehuda and said to him: Why do you cause my words to be despised by the sages?

49. The first to make this suggestion was S. Klein, *The Land of the Galilee*, 195-6. He demonstrates that the talmudic "Tekoa" must be located in the Galilee, not in Judea. He bases his claims on the literature of the Geonim and the Rishonim: "It seems, therefore, that Tekoa was a suburb of Meron." Also see A. Miris, "Ḥurvat Shema: The Settlement and the Synagogue" [Hebrew], *Antiquities* 5 (5732): 6–8. S. Safrai accepts this identification in *Time of the Temple, Time of the Mishna*, vol. 1, 225 note 238.
50. Hyman, *Legends*, 1177. He transmits Rabbi Shimon's traditions, but it is unclear to whom.

> Isi said to him: What have I said about you, except that you study much, forget little, and what you do forget is no more than the chaff of my learning? (*Avot deRabbi Natan*, recension A, ch. 18)

Isi ben Yehuda was a student of the Usha generation.[51] We encountered him in the chapter on Yehuda bar Ilai, where he was referred to as Yosef the Babylonian. He studied with all the leading teachers of the generation, and thus he could nickname everyone. We have already pointed out the difficulties with his dubious characterization of Rabbi Yehuda as "a scholar when he so desired." Now he refers to Rabbi Shimon as "he who studies much and forgets little." Although this is an accurate description, it infuriates Rashbi: "Why do you cause my words to be despised by the sages?" Isi responds by explaining himself: "What you do forget is no more than the chaff of my learning." But Rabbi Shimon is furious at the suggestion that he might forget anything. As he sees it, all of Rabbi Akiva's teachings are preserved in him. This image of Rashbi recalls the tragic figure of Rabbi Eliezer ben Hyrcanus, whom the sages visited just before his death:

> Rabbi Eliezer took his two arms, placed them upon his heart, and said: Woe to my two arms, which are like two Torah scrolls that are being rolled up. I learned much Torah, and I taught much Torah. I learned much Torah, but I did not diminish my teachers' knowledge even as much as a dog laps from the sea. I taught much Torah, but my students diminished my own knowledge only as much as an applicator dipped in a tube of eye powder. Furthermore, I have learned three hundred laws pertaining to a vivid white-skin affliction, and nobody ever questioned me about them at all. (Sanhedrin 68a)

Although Rashbi was not excommunicated, he does not seem to have had close connections with his colleagues. Many traditions are transmitted in his name, but they are cited not by his colleagues or students, but

51. The Talmud identifies Isi ben Yehuda as Yosef the Babylonian in Pesaḥim 113b. See Hyman, *Legends*, 151–53.

by sages of later generations. For instance, he is often quoted by Rabbi Yoḥanan, who lived decades later.[52]

It seems that Rashbi preferred the company of those in the upper realms.[53]

THE HALAKHA DOES NOT FOLLOW HIM

The halakha is only very rarely decided in accordance with Rashbi. The Talmud relates a discussion about this matter:

> Rav Aḥa bar Abba was seated before Rav Huna, and he was sitting and saying: Rabbi Mallukh said in the name of Rabbi Yehoshua ben Levi: The halakha follows Rabbi Shimon.
>
> Rav Huna said to Rav Aḥa bar Abba: Are you referring to Mallukh of Arabia? He in fact says that the halakha here does not follow Rabbi Shimon.
>
> When Rabbi Zeira went up to the Land of Israel, he encountered Rav Bibi, who was sitting and saying: Rabbi Mallukh said in the name of Rabbi Yehoshua ben Levi: The halakha follows Rabbi Shimon.
>
> Rabbi Zeira said to him: By the life of the master, I swear that I and Rabbi Ḥiya bar Abba and Rav Assi once visited Rabbi Mallukh's place, and we asked him: Did you say that the halakha here follows Rabbi Shimon? And he said to us: No, I said that the halakha does not follow Rabbi Shimon.
>
> Rav Bibi asked Rabbi Zeira: What tradition do you have in your hand on this matter? He said to him: Thus did Rabbi Yitzhak bar Ami say in the name of Rabbi Yehoshua ben Levi: The halakha follows Rabbi Shimon.

52. Rabbi Yoḥanan quotes Rashbi more than a hundred times in the Babylonian Talmud and dozens of times in the Jerusalem Talmud.
53. Hagar-Lau, "Teachings of Rashbi," 143. But Hagar-Lau links Rashbi's isolation to his emergence from the cave, which led him to withdraw from humanity. In contrast, I am suggesting that Rashbi's experience in the cave was merely a later expression of the spiritual isolation he came to on his own. Either way, Rashbi was clearly set apart from his colleagues.

> And the final decision is that the halakha does not follow Rabbi Shimon. (Ḥullin 49a)

The subject at hand is the type of deformities that would render an animal unkosher (*treif*), including a hole in its lung. Rabbi Shimon is characteristically lenient: He asserts that the animal is not considered unkosher "unless it is punctured all the way to the primary bronchus," that is, until there is a deep hole in the lung, and not just a light wound, as the sages would have it. The Talmud goes on to describe the sages' position in contrast to Rashbi's. Rav Aḥa sits before Rav Huna, the head of the academy in Sura, and listens to him quote a tradition transmitted in the name of Rabbi Mallukh and quoted in the name of Rabbi Yehoshua ben Levi: The halakha follows Rabbi Shimon. Rabbi Mallukh is not a familiar name, so Rav Aḥa asks Rav Huna: Are you referring to Rabbi Mallukh of Arabia (i.e., Yemen)? Rav Aḥa is suspicious because he himself has heard that this rabbi taught that the halakha does not in fact follow Rabbi Shimon.

The story resumes when Rabbi Zeira arrives from the Land of Israel, bearing traditions from its sages. He has heard Rav Bibi teach in accordance with Rav Huna, namely that Rabbi Mallukh said in the name of Rabbi Yehoshua that the halakha follows Rabbi Shimon. Rabbi Zeira offers an impassioned response. He relates that he went with Rabbi Ḥiya and Rav Assi, two sages from the Land of Israel in the mid-third century, to visit Rav Mallukh in person. They asked Rabbi Mallukh whether he holds that the halakha follows Rabbi Shimon, and Rabbi Mallukh said that in fact it does not. Nonetheless, when pressed by Rabbi Zeira, Rabbi Mallukh said that in practice he follows a tradition transmitted by Rabbi Yitzhak bar Ami, who quotes Rabbi Yehoshua ben Levi as saying that the halakha does follow Rabbi Shimon, and thus he permits all meat but that which is most severely punctured.

We can hear the wheels of halakhic decision-making clanking through the generations and stumbling over the question of whether the halakha follows Rabbi Shimon. At several points throughout the Mishna, Rabbi Yehuda HaNasi accepts Rabbi Shimon's position but refrains from quoting it in his name. But in the rules of halakhic decision-making presented in the Talmud, the law does not follow Rabbi Shimon:

> Using this formulation, Rabbi Yaakov bar Idi said in the name of Rabbi Yoḥanan: In a dispute between Rabbi Meir and Rabbi Yehuda, the halakha follows Rabbi Yehuda; between Rabbi Yehuda and Rabbi Yose, the halakha follows Rabbi Yose; and it need not be said that between Rabbi Meir and Rabbi Yose, the halakha follows Rabbi Yose. For if even against Rabbi Yehuda, Rabbi Meir's view does not prevail, then against Rabbi Yose, is there any question?
>
> Rav Assi said: I, too, can learn from the previous statement that in a dispute between Rabbi Yose and Rabbi Shimon, the halakha follows Rabbi Yose. For Rabbi Abba has said in the name of Rabbi Yoḥanan: In a dispute between Rabbi Yehuda and Rabbi Shimon, the halakha follows Rabbi Yehuda. Now if even against Rabbi Yehuda his view does not prevail, then against Rabbi Yose, whose opinion outweighs Rabbi Yehuda's as well, is there any question that Rabbi Shimon's view does not prevail?
>
> They inquired: In a dispute between Rabbi Meir and Rabbi Shimon, what would the rule be? Let it stand [the question remains unanswered]. (Eiruvin 46b)

This hierarchy of rulings was established during the generation of Rabbi Yoḥanan.[54] The halakha is rarely decided in accordance with the two leading students of Rabbi Akiva, Rabbi Meir and Rabbi Shimon. It is Rabbi Yehuda of the village and Rabbi Yose of the big city who are the leading halakhic decisors. This ranking reminds us that halakha is decided by those who are most rooted in the reality of this world. In the words of Psalms (115:16), "The heavens belong to God, but the earth has been given to human beings."

54. Y. Brandes, "The Halakhic Revolution of Rabbi Yoḥanan: The Laws of Halakhic Decision-Making" [Hebrew], in *In the Ways of Peace: Issues in Jewish Thought*, ed. B. Ish-Shalom (Jerusalem, 5767), 515–36.

Part Three

Gates of Light – Rabbi Meir, the "Other," and Others

The Founding Generation at Usha		Rabbi Yehuda HaNasi
138–161	161–192	192–220
The Restoration of the Nation after the Destruction Antoninus Pius	The Stabilization of the Center at Usha Marcus Aurelius and Commodus	Autonomy in the Galilee Severus

Chapter Seven

The Light of Torah

INTRODUCTION

This section focuses on Rabbi Meir, a sage renowned throughout the Jewish world. He is a complex and problematic figure known for his unique teachings and for the powerful influence he exerted on all subsequent generations, even though the halakha was not decided in accordance with his rulings.[1]

Rabbi Meir was one of the two leading students of Rabbi Akiva and one of the five students ordained by Rabbi Yehuda ben Baba, as we saw in Part One. His opinions are quoted anonymously throughout the Mishna, introduced with the phrase "others say." Everything about Rabbi Meir bespeaks otherness. In the rabbinic world, to be an "other" was to remove oneself from the mainstream, like the wicked son in the Passover Haggada, who points to the Paschal sacrifice and cynically inquires, "What does this worship mean to you?" An "other" is also anyone who challenges the consensus in the beit midrash, or who strives for a heavenly existence beyond the human realm, or who derides those scholars who worry about mundane concerns such as livelihood and subsistence.

1. I am invoking the language of Eiruvin 13b. This chapter was written with assistance from my son Yedidya.

But a person did not become an "other" unless he defined himself as such, and Rabbi Meir was the first sage to do so. Even Rabbi Eliezer ben Hyrcanus remained an insider, despite his attempts to protest and subvert the protocol of the Yavneh beit midrash headed by Rabbi Yehoshua. He did not accept the principle of majority rule or the authority of the court, and he was consequently excommunicated. But the Mishna cites his views in his name, and his students quoted him and sought out his teachings. Rabbi Meir's place in the tradition is much more complicated. On the one hand, he remained within the world of the beit midrash: He was never excommunicated, and he served variously as the head of the yeshiva, as a judge, and as a leading sage. Nevertheless, as we will see, his legacy endures as that of an "other."

Rabbi Meir's teacher was Elisha ben Abuya, the ultimate "other" in the beit midrash. It would be impossible to study this historical period without considering this exceptional figure and the implications of his life story for our own time. So our study of Elisha ben Abuya will serve as the basis of our discussion of his student, Rabbi Meir. As we shall see, Rabbi Meir was close to his teacher, but unlike him, he remained firmly rooted in the world of Torah. Although the sages retained some of his teachings in the Mishna and Talmud, Elisha ben Abuya changed his identity beyond all recognition.

Rabbi Meir's teachings also reflect those of his wife, Beruria, a rabbinical scholar in her own right. Beruria challenged her contemporaries by questioning their boundaries and definitions. She was an "other" in many senses of the term. She was not just Rabbi Meir's life partner; she also shared his longing for a world without limits.

In trying to reconstruct the lives of Rabbi Meir and his circle, we might consider an article written thirty years ago by Avigdor Shinan about a midrash on "Rabbi Meir's brother." In his literary analysis, Shinan pondered whether it is possible to use midrashic texts to construct biographies of rabbinic figures. He was interested in constructing not a historical biography, "which it is doubtful whether we can sketch even in the broadest strokes," but rather "an account of the image of the Rabbi Meir as depicted by those who succeeded him." Shinan concluded with the mandate to "try to extract from all the material... an accurate depiction, if not of the historical Rabbi Meir, then of the literary figure of Rabbi Meir as reflected in multifarious sources, some clear and some more opaque, through which we have come to know him – sources that also reflect the spiritual preoccupations of many successive generations."[2]

FROM THE SEA: RABBI MEIR'S FAMILY AND ORIGINS

In contrast to many of his contemporaries at Usha – Rabbi Yehuda bar Ilai, Rabbi Yose ben Ḥalafta, Rabbi Elazar ben Shamua, and Rabbi Shimon bar Yoḥai – Rabbi Meir is not associated with the name of his father. We know nothing about his parents, his origins, or his entry into the world of Torah study. One legend has it that he came from a family of converts descended from Emperor Nero.[3] But this midrash only further complicates our efforts to unearth Rabbi Meir's true roots.

It is not just Rabbi Meir's family that remains shrouded in mystery. He is also the only sage whose name we cannot know with certainty. The Talmud considers several possibilities:

> His name was not actually Rabbi Meir, but rather Rabbi Nehorai was his name. Then why was he called Rabbi Meir? Because he would enlighten the eyes of the sages with the law. And similarly, Nehorai was not his name, but rather Rabbi Neḥemia. And others say Rabbi Elazar ben Arakh was his name. Then why was he called Nehorai? Because he would enlighten the sages with the law. (Eiruvin 13b)

2. A. Shinan, "The Brother of Rabbi Meir" [Hebrew], in *Jerusalem Studies in Hebrew Literature* 2 (Jerusalem, 5743), 18–20.
3. This account is included in the collection of stories about the destruction of the Temple in Gittin 56a. Later commentators debated the religious significance of this historical fact. A search for the terms "Rabbi Meir" and "Nero" in a scholarly database will unearth a wealth of sources, including A. Kamina, *Studies in Bible, Talmud, and Rabbinic Literature* [Hebrew] (Tel Aviv, 5711), 180. Kamina compares the story of Rabbi Meir to that of the prophet Obadiah, who prophesies the fate of Edom. Rabbi Meir teaches that Obadiah was an Edomite convert and therefore chosen to prophesy Edom's downfall (see Sanhedrin 39b).

This source reflects the difficulty of encapsulating the extraordinary figure of Rabbi Meir.[4] The sages try to associate him with Rabbi Elazar ben Arakh, the leading student in the beit midrash of Rabbi Yoḥanan ben Zakkai, described by his teacher as an "ever-flowing fountain." According to Rabbi Yoḥanan ben Zakkai (as quoted by Abba Shaul), if all the sages were placed on one side of a scale and Rabbi Elazar ben Arakh on the other, he would outweigh them all (Mishna Avot 2:8–12). But Rabbi Elazar withdrew from his colleagues, and his Torah was lost to oblivion.[5] Perhaps the sages were trying to imply that Rabbi Meir was in danger of a similar fate.

In addition to the dearth of information about his family history and the confusion about his name, we know little about Rabbi Meir's place of origin. Among the most familiar sages, he is the only one unassociated with a specific place. One story that emphasizes Rabbi Meir's lack of roots as well as his otherness contrasts him with Rabbi Akiva:

> Rabban Gamliel said: Once I was traveling on a ship, and I saw another ship that had foundered and was sinking. I was pained by the thought of a Torah scholar who had been on that ship and was now surely lost. And who was that Torah scholar? It was Rabbi Akiva. But when I arrived on dry land, Rabbi Akiva himself came and sat and deliberated before me in a matter of law. I said to him: My son, who raised you up out of the water?
>
> He said to me: A board from the ship presented itself to me and I took hold of it, and with every wave that came upon me, I bowed my head and it passed over me. From here the sages said: If wicked people come upon a person, let him bow his head before them....
>
> Rabbi Akiva said: Once I was traveling on a ship, and I saw another ship that was sinking in the sea. I was pained by the

4. The name "Meir" is in the present tense, which sets it apart from most Hebrew names, which are in the future tense: Yitzḥak, Yaakov, Yosef. For the various names of Rabbi Meir, see the references cited in Shinan, "The Brother of Rabbi Meir," 14 note 24.
5. See *Sages* II, Part One.

> thought of a Torah scholar who had been on that ship and was now surely lost. And who was that Torah scholar? It was Rabbi Meir. But when I landed in Cappadocia, Rabbi Meir himself came and sat and deliberated before me in a matter of law. I said to him: My son, who raised you up out of the water?
>
> He said to me: One wave swept me on to the next, and the next carried me on to the next, until the sea spat me out onto dry land. (Yevamot 121a)

Rabbi Akiva and Rabbi Meir went through the same harrowing experience. Each was traveling in a ship that foundered, and each was observed by another sage who was convinced that his peer had perished. Rabbi Akiva clasped a board of the shattered ship and managed to survive the waves by going with the flow. He bowed his head so each wave passed over him. The Talmud uses the same term to describe the body language used in the *Amida* prayer (see Berakhot 28b). Rabbi Ḥanina says that "if a person bows his head, he need not bend his knees again." Bowing one's head signifies submission to the will of his Maker. Rabbi Akiva, too, seemed willing to submit to each wave that passed over him.

Rabbi Meir, by contrast, describes battling the surf: "One wave swept me on to the next, and the next carried me onto the next." He struggles against each wave, until finally the sea spits him out onto dry land. This is a different response altogether from that of his master.

Based on this story, some scholars have tried to establish Rabbi Meir's birthplace in Asia (since Cappadocia is in Asia Minor, now Turkey), but this claim lacks any firm textual grounding.[6] Rabbi Meir's true home was his rabbi's house. He and his teacher Rabbi Akiva shared a powerful bond unequaled among the other sages and their students. Rabbi Meir was one of two students Rabbi Akiva ordained, but, as we have seen, his teacher preferred him to his colleague, Rabbi Shimon bar Yoḥai.[7]

6. See A. H. Weiss' arguments against Graetz in *Dor veDorshav*, 147 note 1.
7. We lack sources linking the two disciples. For Rabbi Akiva's privileging of Rabbi Meir over Rabbi Shimon bar Yoḥai, see Y. Sanhedrin 1:2 (19a).

GARMENTS OF LIGHT: TORAH WITHOUT PACKAGING

Rabbi Meir was deeply entrenched in the world of Torah study. Only Rabbi Akiva could rival the force of his learning, and thus he was not concerned with his student's obscure family background or personal history. The sages speak of Rabbi Meir with fulsome praise:

> Rabbi Aḥa bar Ḥanina said: It is revealed and known before Him who spoke the world into being that there was no one like Rabbi Meir in his generation. Why did they not decide the halakha in accordance with his view? Because his colleagues could not fathom the depths of his reasoning. For he would assert that something impure was pure and make it seem plausible. (Eiruvin 13b)

When Rabbi Yose ben Ḥalafta tried to describe Rabbi Meir to the people of Tzippori, he used a term rarely invoked by the sages:

> A great man, a holy man, a humble man. (Y. Mo'ed Katan 3:5 [82d])

The term "holy" is used very rarely by the sages and is generally reserved for ascetics.[8] We might say that Rabbi Meir's name reflects his essence.[9] Light enveloped him and accompanied him wherever he went. In turn, he could see the light that surrounds a person and permeates the entirety of his being, as we learn from his midrash on the verse "And God made for Adam and his wife garments of skin and clothed them" (Gen. 3:21):

> In Rabbi Meir's Torah scroll it was written: garments of light. (Genesis Rabba 20)[10]

8. The Babylonian Talmud also uses this rare epithet to describe Rabbi Meir. Reish Lakish says of Rabbi Meir, "Would a holy mouth utter such a thing?" (Sanhedrin 23b).
9. See the words of Rabbi Tzaddok HaKohen of Lublin: "In the words of the Ari [Rabbi Isaac Luria, 1534–1572], a person's name is the root of his living soul" (*Pri Tzaddik*, 3, 2a).
10. Weiss, *Dor veDorshav*, 134-35 argues that "Rabbi Meir's Torah" refers to a midrash composed by Rabbi Meir. This is clearly an error, as others have explained. See

This midrash plays on the Hebrew word *or*, which may mean either "skin" (when spelled with an *ayin*) or "light" (when spelled with an *alef*). The midrash reminds us that Rabbi Meir's life, learning, and teachings are characterized by a deep and primal interiority. He was not interested in the external trappings that conceal the inner radiance. Nor did he need protection from external sources of light and heat. Even the boundary between life and death did not exist for him, as we learn from his midrash on the creation story:

> Rabbi Shmuel bar Naḥman said: I was seated on my grandfather's shoulder going up from my own town to Kefar Ḥana by way of Beit She'an, and I heard Rabbi Shimon ben Rabbi Elazar as he sat and lectured in Rabbi Meir's name: "And behold, it was very good (*tov me'od*)" [Gen. 1:31] – And behold, death was good (*tov mavet*). (Genesis Rabba 9)

The story of creation ends with an optimistic description of life: "And behold, it was very good." For Rabbi Meir, "very good" describes a reality beyond the bounds of this world.

RABBI MEIR WRITES A TORAH SCROLL

We learn from several sources that Rabbi Meir earned his livelihood as a scribe who wrote Torah scrolls. His entire life was spent amidst parchment and ink – reading, learning, writing, and originating interpretations. But unlike most scribes, who painstakingly copy from one scroll to another, Rabbi Meir could, when necessary, write Torah scrolls from memory. The Talmud relates the following anecdote in the name of Rabbi Shimon ben Elazar (ben Shamua):

> Rabbi Shimon ben Elazar said: Rabbi Meir once went to Asia to intercalate the year, and he could not find a Scroll of Esther

A. Epstein, "The Anokhi of Rabbi Meir" [Hebrew], *Beit HaTalmud* 5 (5745): 92–93. Also see Shinan, "The Brother of Rabbi Meir," 18 note 32, who provides other references as well.

> written in Hebrew. So he wrote one from memory, and then he went back and read from it. (Tosefta Megilla 2:5)

The Talmud expresses surprise at this incident. Rabbi Abahu then says:

> Rabbi Meir is different, for he is a fulfillment of the verse "Let your eyes look forward" [Prov. 4:25]. (Megilla 18b)

Rabbi Meir is different from everyone else. King Solomon's wisdom in the Book of Proverbs is quoted of him:

> For I give you good instruction; do not forsake my teaching. Once I was a son to my father, the tender darling of my mother.... Acquire wisdom, acquire discernment; do not forget and do not swerve from my words. Do not forsake her and she will guard you; love her and she will protect you. The beginning of wisdom is – acquire wisdom; with all your acquisitions, acquire discernment. Hug her to you and she will exalt you; she will bring you honor if you embrace her.... Let your eyes look forward, your gaze be straight ahead. (Prov. 4:2–3, 4–8, 25)

The rabbis understood these verses as a love song to the Torah. Thus, they associated these words with Rabbi Meir, who was ensconced in Torah. He did not need to hold a physical Torah scroll before him, because the Torah was before him always.

The midrash describes Rabbi Meir's relationship to his profession:

> "And I hated all the labor with which I labored under the sun" [Eccl. 2:18] – Rabbi Meir was a skillful scribe and used to earn three sela coins each week. He spent one sela on food and drink, another on clothing, and the third on supporting rabbinical scholars.
>
> His disciples asked him: What are you doing to provide for your children?
>
> He answered: If they are righteous, then it will be as David said: "For I have not seen the righteous forsaken, nor his descen-

> dants begging for bread" [Ps. 37:25]. If they are not righteous, why should I leave my possessions to the enemies of the Omnipresent? Therefore Solomon said, "And who knows whether he will be wise or foolish?" [Eccl. 2:19]. (Ecclesiastes Rabba 2:18)

The verses quoted from Ecclesiastes describe the despair of a man who does not know how his children will conduct themselves after his death:

> And I hated all the labor with which I labored under the sun, for I shall leave it to the man who will succeed me. And who knows whether he will be wise or foolish? And he will control all the labor that I gained by toil and wisdom under the sun; that too is futile. (Eccl. 2:18–19)

Rabbi Meir believed his children were responsible for forging their own paths. He would not feed or provide for them.

RABBI MEIR'S "BROTHER"

Although we know nothing about Rabbi Meir's father, the Midrash "adopts" a brother for him:

> "With the first light of morning" (Gen. 44:3) – Rabbi Levi said: There once was an innkeeper in the south who used to arise at night, put on his clothes, and say to his guests: Arise and go out, for a caravan is passing. They would go out, and a band of robbers would fall upon them and kill them. The bandits would then enter the inn and share the spoils with the innkeeper.
>
> Rabbi Meir once came there and was received as a guest. The innkeeper arose, dressed, and said to him: Arise and go out, for a caravan is passing.
>
> Rabbi Meir said to him: I have a brother for whom I must remain here and wait.
>
> The innkeeper asked: Where is he?
>
> He said: In the synagogue.
>
> He asked: What is his name? I will go call him.
>
> He said to him: "It was good."

> The innkeeper went out and spent the whole night calling out, "It was good," at the door of the synagogue, but no one responded.
>
> In the morning Rabbi Meir arose, put his bag on his donkey, and was about to depart. The innkeeper asked him: Where is your brother?
>
> He said to him: Behold, here he is, for it is written, "And God saw the light, and it was good" (Gen. 1:4). (Genesis Rabba 92:6)[11]

We can read this source an amusing tale mocking the credulousness of the ignorant non-Jew and praising the wisdom of the sage. Indeed, Rabbi Meir was not the first sage to cast someone plotting treachery into the very pit he had dug for others.[12] But Avigdor Shinan observes that the meaning of this tale hinges on the dialogue between the innkeeper and Rabbi Meir, who speak in two different idioms. The innkeeper speaks the language of human beings. Although malicious in his intent, he addresses his guests in terms they immediately understand. In contrast, Rabbi Meir speaks the language of Torah. The innkeeper interprets Rabbi Meir's response in literal, human terms: If he is waiting for his brother, and his brother is in the synagogue, then the innkeeper will go call him. If he becomes a comic figure in the narrative, it is not because Rabbi Meir intends to ridicule him, but rather because the reader recognizes the rhetorical gap that leads to this embarrassing predicament.

Rabbi Meir makes all his decisions based on the Torah. He escapes the innkeeper's plot not because he is aware of the scheme, but because he does not live by the scoundrel's prosaic terms. He lives by the terms of the Torah, which guides his every step. Thus he models himself on Joseph's brothers: "With the first light of morning, the men were sent off with their pack animals" (Gen. 44:3).

11. For a full analysis of this story, see Shinan, "The Brother of Rabbi Meir," 7–20.
12. From the time of Mordecai and Haman onward, Jewish storytellers were fond of this genre. The more dark and distressing their experience of exile, the more stories we find of non-Jews falling into their own traps. See Shinan, "The Brother of Rabbi Meir," 12.

Moreover, Rabbi Meir answers the innkeeper's questions with deadpan seriousness. He says he will not depart until morning, because he has a brother whose name is "it was good." When the sun at last rises, it sheds light on Rabbi Meir's response. The light to which he was referring is described in the Torah: "And God saw the light, and it was good." Shinan offers the following explanation of Rabbi Meir's invocation of this verse: "When Rabbi Meir says he is waiting for his brother, he is referring to the light of morning. But when he sets off on his way, he invokes a verse. It becomes clear that his 'brother' exists on two different planes, the sensory (i.e., daylight) and the spiritual (i.e., the light of the verse). Only a sage of Rabbi Meir's stature can perceive both of these lights simultaneously and successfully live in accordance with them."[13]

HIS EXAMINATION OF NAMES

Rabbi Meir conducted himself in accordance with his own internal standards, not external social norms, as the following story demonstrates:

> Rabbi Meir, Rabbi Yehuda, and Rabbi Yose were traveling on the road. Rabbi Meir would examine the name of the owner of the lodgings where they intended to stay, but Rabbi Yehuda and Rabbi Yose would not. When they came to a certain place, they asked for lodging and were given it. They asked the owner: What is your name?
>
> He said to them: Kidor.
>
> Rabbi Meir said to himself: Infer from this that he is a wicked man, as it is written, "For they are a generation (*ki dor*) of treachery, children in whom I have no trust" [Deut. 32:20].
>
> Rabbi Yehuda and Rabbi Yose entrusted their money purses to him. Rabbi Meir did not....
>
> The next day, Rabbi Yehuda and Rabbi Yose said to the host: Give us back our purses.
>
> He said to them: You never gave me your purses.
>
> Rabbi Meir said to them: Why did you not examine his name?

13. Shinan, "The Brother of Rabbi Meir," 17.

> They said to him: Why did you not tell us?
>
> He said to them: When I said that one should be particular about names, I meant only that suspicion was warranted, not that he was definitely wicked. (Yoma 83b)

Rabbi Meir suspects the innkeeper, even without any concrete basis. He makes it his business to examine names, meaning that he listens to the full connotation of every word and contemplates the connections between letters. The letters lead him to Torah, which serves as his key: "For they are a generation of treachery."

A MAN OF TORAH

If we are to accept the Talmud's identification of Rabbi Meir with Rabbi Nehorai, then we should consider one of his statements: "I would forsake all the trades in the world and teach sons only Torah" (Kiddushin 82a). We can add Rabbi Meir's statement in *Pirkei Avot*: "Diminish your engagement in business, and occupy yourself with Torah" (Mishna Avot 4:10).

Rabbi Meir's world is narrowly defined. He conducts himself like a surgeon equipped with a long, sharp scalpel, cutting through the world of ideas with the keen edge of his razor-sharp intellect. He does not recognize the value of other professions, nor does he seek to apply his Torah learning to other realms. He is uninterested in new horizons. Instead, he concentrates all his efforts on Torah study and regards the physical world as secondary.[14] The Talmud quotes the following pearl of wisdom in Rabbi Meir's name:

14. Every artist is familiar with this state of mind. Rabbi Yehuda Henkin, who has written many volumes of responsa, describes his work habits as follows: "When I am busy with a responsum, I ponder it when I sleep and when I wake, when I walk, lie down, and arise, and even while I am eating. I get out of bed at night to take another look at my books or to jot down an idea, because it is like a fire burning in my bones" (Introduction to *Responsa Benei Banim* [Hebrew], vol. 3 [Jerusalem, 2004]). This is an erotic description of Torah learning. The fire in his bones is the fire of human lust. (Compare this quote to Tractate Kalla 1:13, about someone who performs marital relations while standing.)

> Rabbi Meir would often say: Learn with all your heart and all your soul to know My ways, and to be industrious by the doors of My Torah. Guard My Torah in your heart, and let My fear be before your eyes, and guard your mouth from all sin. And purify and separate yourself from all trespass and iniquity, and I will be with you everywhere. (Berakhot 17a)

This is a poetic description of a man whose entire being holds fast to Torah. The Torah teaches, "And you shall love the Lord your God with all your heart" (Deut. 6:5). Rabbi Meir believes that love of God involves seeking out God's ways through the study of Torah: "To be industrious by the doors of My Torah." He holds Torah before him by day and dreams of it by night, and thus merits God's constant presence.

Maimonides describes the commandment to love God as follows:

> What is the proper way to love God? A person's love for God should be so passionate that his soul is bound up in his love of God. He must be consumed with his love, as if he were lovesick. It is like someone who cannot take his mind off a particular woman and thinks of her constantly, when he is sitting and standing, eating and drinking. So must a God-fearing person be obsessed with love for God, as we are commanded, "with all your heart and all your soul" [Deut. 6:5]. This is what Solomon meant when he said, "For I am lovesick" [Song. 2:5]. The entire Song of Songs is an allegory for this kind of love. (*Mishneh Torah, Laws of Repentance* 10:3)

AN INCIDENT WITH INDELIBLE INK: BETWEEN RABBI AKIVA AND RABBI YISHMAEL

Rabbi Meir's love song to the Torah and his fierce attachment to the parchment and letters of the Torah scroll point to his association with Rabbi Akiva. As we have already discussed, the Talmud recounts that Rabbi Meir was ordained by Rabbi Akiva:

> Anyone who says Rabbi Meir was not ordained by Rabbi Akiva is mistaken. Rabbi Akiva indeed ordained Rabbi Meir, but his colleagues did not accept him. (Sanhedrin 14a)

Several sources attest to Rabbi Meir's strong connection to Rabbi Akiva. His teacher served as both a rabbinical figure and a father figure to him, and their bond was instinctive and obvious. Rabbi Meir's relationship with Rabbi Yishmael, in contrast, was surprising. In the following story from the Jerusalem Talmud, Rabbi Yoḥanan shows his student Rabbi Elazar, who has come from Babylonia, where Rabbi Meir would sit and teach in Tiberias:

> He said to them: This is where Rabbi Meir would sit and teach and quote halakhot in the name of Rabbi Yishmael. [Rabbi Elazar asked:] But did he not quote halakhot in the name of Rabbi Akiva? He said to him: Everyone knows that Rabbi Meir was a student of Rabbi Akiva. (Y. Mo'ed Katan 3:7 [83c])

This source about Rabbi Meir's connection to Rabbi Yishmael enables us to better understand the former's uniqueness. We have already taken note of the stark contrast between Rabbi Akiva, who derived halakhot from every crown in the Torah, and Rabbi Yishmael, who believed that the Torah speaks in human terms. Rabbi Akiva was attuned to the voice of God as expressed in Torah, whereas Rabbi Yishmael was attuned to the voice of Torah as expressed in the land of the living.[15] Just as Rabbi Akiva learned from sages with very different approaches and methods – the innovative Rabbi Yehoshua and the conservative Rabbi Eliezer – so too did Rabbi Meir learn from two sages who were polar opposites, namely Rabbi Akiva and Rabbi Yishmael.

Rabbi Meir Places Vitriol in His Ink

> Rabbi Meir said: When I was studying with Rabbi Yishmael, I used to put indelible vitriol into the ink I used for writing holy scrolls, and he did not object. When I came to study with Rabbi Akiva, he forbade me from doing so. (Eiruvin 13a)

15. See *Sages* II. As I point out there, this distinction is drawn from Abraham Joshua Heschel's *Heavenly Torah.*

As we have seen, Rabbi Meir worked as a scribe. He made his ink using vitriol, a plant extract that serves as black dye. It is more durable than ink, and if added to ink it prevents the writing from being erased. The Talmud relates that when Rabbi Meir studied with Rabbi Yishmael, the latter did not object to this practice of putting vitriol in ink. But when he transferred to Rabbi Akiva's beit midrash, the sage forbade this method.[16]

The Talmud goes on to inquire which of Rabbi Meir's teachers actually told him what:

> Is it indeed so? But Rabbi Yehuda said in the name of Shmuel, quoting Rabbi Meir: When I was studying with Rabbi Akiva, I used to put indelible vitriol into the ink I used for writing holy scrolls, and he did not object. When I came to study with Rabbi Yishmael, he said to me: My son, what is your profession? I said to him: I am a scribe. He said to me: My son, take care with your work, for your work is the work of heaven. Should you perhaps omit one letter or add one letter, you might destroy the entire world! I replied to him: I have an indelible substance called *kankantom* that I put in my ink. He said to me: May we put this indelible substance in the ink used by a scribe? Has not the Torah stated, "[The priest] shall write ... and he shall blot out" [Num. 5:23]? From this we learn that the writing must be a form of writing that can be completely blotted out. (Eiruvin 13a)

The Talmud juxtaposes these two sources. According to the second source, Rabbi Meir studied with Rabbi Akiva, who saw him add vitriol to his ink but did not object. He then came to Rabbi Yishmael, who questioned him about this practice. Rabbi Yishmael interviewed Rabbi Meir when he arrived at his yeshiva, just as he would each new student. Rabbi Meir responds simply and confidently: I am a scribe. He is aware of the dignity of his profession. His teacher, who believes that the Torah speaks in human terms, offers a grave response: "your work is the work

16. The term for vitriol is *kankantom* or *kalkaltam*. Lieberman explains that these terms are interchangeable. See his *Tosefta Kifshuta*, Shabbat 11, 182 note 49.

of heaven." Every letter in the Torah is heavenly, and the scribe can destroy the world if he makes a mistake, as the following source attests:

> "Hear O Israel, the Lord is our God, the Lord is One [*eḥad*]" [Deut. 6:4] – If you make a *dalet* into a *reish,* you cause the destruction of the whole universe. It is written, "You shall bow down to no other [*aḥer*] God" [Ex. 34:14] – If you change the *reish* into a *dalet,* you bring about the destruction of the world. (Leviticus Rabba 19:2)

The student is quick to reassure his new teacher: "I have an indelible substance called *kankantom* that I put in my ink." Rabbi Meir's response suggests that writing without vitriol is dangerous, since without it the scribe is subject to the fluctuating quality and moistness of the ink. With impermanent ink, one letter can easily blend into another: A *reish* can become a *dalet,* and a *yud* can become a *vav* or *zayin*. Adding vitriol serves to prevent this from happening.[17]

The Talmud sees two problems with the story of Rabbi Meir's transfer from one teacher to another. First, it is unclear with whom he studied first. And second, it is unclear whether it was Rabbi Yishmael or Rabbi Akiva who forbade him from using vitriol. The Talmud resolves the first problem as follows:

> The sequence of study described in one source does not conflict with the sequence of study described in the other. Originally Rabbi Meir came before Rabbi Akiva to study with him, but since Rabbi Meir could not ascertain his true intent, he then came before Rabbi Yishmael and learned the traditions. And then he again came before Rabbi Akiva and studied them analytically. (Eiruvin 13a)[18]

17. We recall that Rabbi Elazar ben Arakh broke away from the sages at Yavneh and went to Emmaus, and when he returned he read from the section of the Torah that begins with "This month shall be for you," mistaking the word "month" (*ḥodesh*) for "deaf" (*ḥeresh*). See *Sages* II.
18. The Talmud uses the term *shimush* ("use") to refer to study, since studying with a

Rabbi Meir aspired to learn with Rabbi Akiva, the great scholar of his day. In contrast, Rabbi Yishmael's beit midrash offered a beginner's course. So Rabbi Meir, who wanted to jump straight into the deep end, started by learning with Rabbi Akiva. But after his learning did not progress satisfactorily, he understood that he first had to glean the fundamentals, so he turned to Rabbi Yishmael. Only after completing his studies there did he return to Rabbi Akiva's beit midrash, where he learned the more advanced practice of analytic interpretation.

Who Forbade the Use of Vitriol?
Resolving the Talmud's Contradictions

The Talmud concludes this discussion with the question of who forbade the use of vitriol. A parallel source in the Jerusalem Talmud offers one solution:

> It is written, "[The priest] shall write ... in a book" [Num. 5:23]. Is it possible that he writes with ink, red ink, ink prepared with gum, or vitriol? The Torah says, "and he shall blot out" [Num. 5:23]. Since it says, "and he shall blot out," is it possible that it may be written with any sort of liquid, or with fruit juice? How so? It must be writing that can be blotted out. And what is that writing? It is writing in ink that is not prepared with gum. And has it not been written: If it is blotted out of the scroll, it is valid? Interpret that statement in line with the following tradition, as it has been taught: Rabbi Meir said: So long as we studied with Rabbi Yishmael, we never put vitriol in ink. (Y. Sota 2:4 [18a])

The Jerusalem Talmud asserts unequivocally that it was Rabbi Yishmael who forbade the use of vitriol. The Babylonian Talmud leaves this matter unresolved.

We will try to understand the basis for this prohibition of vitriol. As we have seen, in questioning Rabbi Meir about his use of vitriol, Rabbi Yishmael quotes from the *sota* passage in the Book of Numbers. In this

sage involved being present with him and studying every aspect of his behavior, not just learning his Torah.

passage the Torah describes the ritual that a woman had to undergo if suspected by her husband of adultery.[19] As part of this ritual, the priest would pen curses in a specially prepared ink:

> The priest shall write these curses in a book, and he shall blot [it] out into the waters of bitterness. He is to make the woman drink the waters of bitterness that induce the spell, so that the spell-inducing water may enter into her to bring on bitterness. (Num. 5:23–24)

Rabbi Yishmael's exegesis relates to the writing of these curses and their erasure in the water. The Mishna in Tractate Sota elaborates on this procedure:

> He does not write on a tablet or on a papyrus or on an inadequately processed parchment, but only on a scroll, as it says, "in a book" [Num. 5:23]. He may not write with a gumlike sap or with a dye made with indelible vitriol or with anything that leaves a mark, but only with ink, as it says, "and he shall blot out" [Num. 5:23] – writing that can be erased. (Mishna Sota 2:4)

Rabbi Yishmael teaches that the type of writing referred to in the Torah must be erasable, as the following source confirms:

> One who erases a single letter of God's name violates a negative prohibition. Rabbi Yishmael says: For this reason it is written, "And you shall wipe away their name from this place" [Deut. 12:3],

19. This passage about the *sota* is one that many modern, rational scholars prefer to overlook, since it raises so many unanswerable questions. See E. Samet, *Issues in the Weekly Torah Portion* [Hebrew], 2nd series (Jerusalem, 5765), *Naso*. Samet claims that the test of the *sota* was an attempt to secure the foundations of the home, which the husband could otherwise destroy with little pretext. Samet, whose agenda is clearly pedagogical, argues that the rabbis sought to interpret the Torah in a way that would minimize the violence involved in resolving marital tension. He suggests that the *sota* passage underscores the importance of domestic tranquility, since God allows His own name to be erased for the sake of restoring harmony to a home.

> and it is written, "Do not do thus to the Lord your God" [Deut. 12:4]. But ink that is written on top of writing may be erased, since the scribe's intent was merely to correct. (Tractate Sefer Torah 5:9)

According to Rabbi Yishmael, the entire Torah was written in a script that could be erased and corrected, with the exception of the name of God, which could not be touched. Rabbi Meir did not recognize a distinction between God's name and the rest of the Torah. Elsewhere he teaches that only the *sota* passage must be written in erasable ink. (See Sota 20a.)

In the concluding sections of this chapter we will refine the distinction between Rabbi Meir, who wrote in vitriol, and Rabbi Yishmael, who objected.

Rabbi Meir and Rabbi Yishmael: Between the First and Second Tablets

In the Jerusalem Talmud, Rabbi Yehuda ben Rabbi Shimon teaches about the tablets Moses received and then broke on Mount Sinai:

> The tablets were a burden that weighed forty *se'ot*, and the writing held them up. When the writing flew off, the tablets became heavy in Moses' hands, and they fell and broke. (Y. Ta'anit 4:5 [68c])

Tablets without letters inscribed in them are like a body without a soul. The writing was the life of the first tablets, which were otherwise a dead weight in Moses' hands. Thus he could lift them only when they were inscribed. Rabbi Meir, in writing with indelible vitriol, sought to safeguard against erasure and thus fasten our grip on the Torah given on Sinai.

When Rabbi Meir arrived at Rabbi Yishmael's beit midrash and explained that he was a scribe, Rabbi Yishmael was concerned. Rabbi Meir assuaged Rabbi Yishmael by explaining that he used vitriol. As a student of Rabbi Akiva, who derived new teachings from each crown of the Torah, Rabbi Meir regarded vitriol as an elixir of life, because it ensured that anything new that was written would endure permanently. In an ever-changing world, vitriol offered a measure of stability, guaranteeing that innovation would not fade into the shadowy blankness that preceded creation. But for Rabbi Yishmael, vitriol was a potion of death. Words of Torah written in vitriol were lifeless, since they could no longer be erased. Rabbi Meir understood Rabbi Yishmael's concern that a scribe might inadvertently destroy the world as a fear that human innovation could become divorced from the crowns and letters of Torah. He explained that vitriol was his way of ensuring that his Torah was indelibly bound and sealed in sacred script. But Rabbi Yishmael's anxiety spoke to something else entirely. He lived by the second tablets, the ones written by man. The first tablets, written by God, had been forever shattered to this practice.

Who Challenged Rabbi Meir?

We have seen that Rabbi Meir championed the use of vitriol, Rabbi Akiva took note but did not object, and Rabbi Yishmael forbade him from using this substance. This reading is based on our understanding of the intellectual orientations of each sage involved. An alternative interpretation is suggested by Rabbi Abraham Isaac HaKohen Kook in a letter to his son, Rabbi Tzvi Yehuda, in which he describes a sermon he prepared for *Parashat Zakhor* 5677 about the erasure of Amalek's name and the concept of erasure in general:

> Rabbi Meir, whose colleagues could not fathom the depths of his reasoning, had a Torah scroll in which "garments of light" was written. The Jerusalem Talmud states, "Here was a messianic one," that is, the spiritual light of one such as he would illuminate the world as if the messianic light had already obliterated the wicked like smoke. He felt there was no need to prevent the use of vitriol, and indeed he felt that banning it led to great loss, for he believed that the possibility of erasure was antithetical to the refined lucidity of heavenly light that illuminates the eyes of Torah scholars with the law. So he would add vitriol to his ink on principle. But Rabbi Akiva told him the world was still beholden to the power of erasure. (*The Letters of Rabbi Abraham Isaac HaKohen Kook*, 3, 808)

According to Rav Kook, it was Rabbi Akiva who forbade Rabbi Meir from using vitriol. Of course, Rav Kook was familiar with the source in the Jerusalem Talmud, and his claim that it was Rabbi Akiva who challenged Rabbi Meir sheds light on another aspect of the relationship between them. Rabbi Akiva had forays into mysticism, but he maintained a foothold on earth. Just as his insights were linked to the crowns on the Torah's letters, his way of life was bound to tradition and to his rabbinical colleagues. Rabbi Akiva understood the power of writing that can be erased. In the words of Rav Kook, "the world was still beholden to the power of erasure." But his student Rabbi Meir, whose thinking eluded his colleagues, lost himself in mystical realms.

THE DANGER OF DEVOTION: THE CANDLE THAT BLEW OUT

Rabbi Meir's extreme devotion to Torah study led him to dangerous places without clear boundaries. He generally withstood the trials that confronted him, but those around him were not always able to do so, as we shall see.[20]

We have already considered Rabbi Yishmael's approach to the writing of the letters in the Torah:

> Rabbi Yishmael taught: Great is peace, for the Holy One, Blessed Be He, said that even His great name, written in sanctity, may be blotted out in water for the purpose of making peace between husband and wife. (Leviticus Rabba 9:9)

Peace is a fundamental value. God's name is even erased as part of the *sota* ritual for the sake of preserving peace between husband and wife.[21] Against this backdrop, the Midrash recounts the following episode:

20. For my literary analysis of this story, I am indebted to N. Hirshfeld's *Stories About Women in* Vayikra Rabba [Hebrew] (PhD diss., Hebrew University of Jerusalem, 5759), 11–42. Since then, many other articles have been written that intelligently expound on this tale, particularly from literary points of view.
21. The *sota* trial, which may seem problematic and degrading to our modern eyes, was clearly intended to restore peace to the home. See G. Hazan-Rokem, "The Triple

> Rabbi Meir used to deliver discourses on Sabbath evenings. There was a woman there in the habit of listening to him. Once the discourse lasted a long time, and she waited until the exposition was concluded. She went home and found that the candle had gone out. Her husband asked her: Where have you been? She said: I was sitting listening to the voice of the preacher. He said to her: I swear that I will not let you enter here until you go and spit in the preacher's face. (Leviticus Rabba 9:9)

The key figures in this story are the jealous husband, the learned wife, and the elderly sage.[22] It is the sage who arouses the husband's suspicions. Unlike the Temple priest who serves the woman the brew of bitter waters, the sage is not an impartial figure. Presumably the husband did not suspect Rabbi Meir of actually threatening the sanctity of his marriage, but the mere fact that his wife was drawn to his preaching late into the night was enough to extinguish the flames of marital passion in their home.[23] The woman not only attends Rabbi Meir's lengthy lecture, but she stays until the very end, which etiquette did not require.[24] Meanwhile, her husband waits at home, ablaze with passion for his wife. The Sabbath night is a time of pleasure, including marital intimacy. But the woman prefers a different flame. She chooses Torah over intimacy

Thread: On Sexuality, Partnership, and Femininity in Rabbinic Literature" [Hebrew], *Theory and Criticism* 7 (1995): 255–64.

22. Frankel writes, "His [Rabbi Meir's] attributes included love of his Creator, love of Torah, and love of man," citing this story. See Z. Frankel, *Methods of the Mishna*, 164. Hyman writes, "He was never concerned for his own honor, as long as something good should come about for his fellow." See Hyman, *Legends*, 872. M. Margaliot comments, "Rabbi Meir's great love for God's creatures is reflected in his story about one of the early preachers." See *Encyclopedia of the Sages of the Talmud and the Geonim* [Hebrew] (Tel Aviv, 5733), s.v. "Rabbi Meir," 627. The most literal reading of this story clearly suggests that Rabbi Meir was nothing but magnanimous; but, of course, Rabbi Meir himself was never satisfied with just a literal reading.
23. Hirshfeld, *Women in* Vayikra Rabba, cites several sources that draw an analogy between the candle and intimate love.
24. In the story about Rabbi Eliezer's discourse in Beitza 15b, we are told that the students left the beit midrash in the middle of his talk. This was standard practice. People were accountable first and foremost to the needs of their households rather than to the discourse or to the sage delivering it.

with her husband and returns home only after the Sabbath candles have burned out.[25] The husband views her behavior as a kind of betrayal. His patience exhausted, he seeks to clarify the nature of his wife's relationship with Rabbi Meir so as to confirm that any spark between them is strictly intellectual. The husband demands that his wife spit in Rabbi Meir's face to show that *he*, not the sage, is the true object of the woman's passion. Then the plot thickens:

> She stayed away one week, a second, and a third. Her neighbors said to her: Are you still angry with one another? Let us come with you to the discourse. As soon as Rabbi Meir saw them, he saw by means of the holy spirit all that had transpired, and he said: Is there a wise woman among you who is expert at whispering a charm over an eye? The woman's neighbors said to her: If you go and spit in his eye, you will release your husband from his vow. When she sat down before him, she became afraid and said to him: Rabbi, I am not an expert at whispering an invocation over an eye. He said to her: Even so, spit in my face seven times, and I will be cured. She did so, and he said to her: Go tell your husband: You told me to do it but once, and I spat seven times. (Leviticus Rabba 9:9)

Rabbi Meir sets up a ritual analogous to the *sota* proceedings. Here, too, the husband is jealous of his wife, and the only way to restore peace to the home is by a test involving bitter waters. The woman's act of spitting in Rabbi Meir's face is analogous to the erasure of God's name in the *sota* passage:[26]

> His disciples said to him: Should people thus abuse the Torah? Could you not have told one of us to whisper an invocation for

25. One version of this midrash makes this connection explicitly: "I heard the voice of the preacher in the synagogue, and it was pleasurable to me." See Y. D. Eisenstein, *Otzar HaMidrashim* (New York, 5675), 277. Hirshfeld, *Women in* Vayikra Rabba, cites other versions of the midrash that substantiate this claim.

26. Boyarin, *Carnal Israel.*

you? He said to them: Is it not good enough for Rabbi Meir to be like his Creator? For Rabbi Yishmael has taught: Great is peace, for the Holy One, Blessed Be He, said that even His great name, written in sanctity, may be blotted out in water for the purpose of making peace between husband and wife. (Leviticus Rabba 9:9)

Chapter Eight

Elisha ben Abuya

> *Elisha ben Abuya would say: He who learns [Torah] as a child, what is he like? He is like ink written on new paper. He who learns as an old man, what is he like? He is like ink written on erased paper.* (*Mishna Avot* 4:20)

We now turn to the relationship between Rabbi Meir and his third teacher, Elisha ben Abuya, who is known in rabbinic literature as Aḥer, the "other."

> "And you shall return unto the Lord your God" [Deut. 30:2] – Rabbi Shmuel Pargrita said in the name of Rabbi Meir: To what may the matter be compared? To a prince who took to evil ways. The king would send his tutor after him, and he would say to him: Return, my son. And the prince would send him back to his father saying: How can I return? I am ashamed to come before you. The father sent back word: Can a son be ashamed to return to his father? And is it not to your own father that you would be returning? (Deuteronomy Rabba 2:24)

In this midrash, a son is embarrassed to return home, and his father encourages him to do so. This parable becomes that much more painful and affecting when we realize that it echoes Elisha's biography. After all, the parable is taught in the name of Rabbi Meir, who repeatedly encouraged Elisha to repent and return to the fold.[1]

Rabbi Meir studied with Elisha ben Abuya, one of the great sages of his generation. No one disputes these facts. But everything else is shrouded in mystery. What drove Elisha to heresy? When did he study with Rabbi Meir? What ultimately happened to Elisha? More has been written about this sage than about any other member of his generation, for three reasons: First, he is a colorful and curious figure; second, his story raises several important philosophical questions; and third, the Talmud contains ample biographical material about him. We will not attempt a comprehensive, in-depth study of all the various aspects of his fascinating personality.[2] We will focus instead on those sources that can help us understand his influence on his student Rabbi Meir.

Several sources recount that Elisha "cut at the saplings."[3] This metaphor suggests that a teacher is analogous to a man who plants a sapling. For as long as the plant remains a sapling, it must be protected from the wind and cold, just as the teacher is responsible for the student's growth during his formative years. Generally, the sapling is not cut until it has grown into a tree, which can then be used for firewood or lumber. One who cuts at a sapling is engaging in an act of barbarous destruction by harming an entity not yet fully grown. The Jerusalem Talmud explains that Elisha ben Abuya cut at the saplings "because he would kill the

1. Rabbi Meir was famous for his parables, particularly his three hundred fox fables (Sanhedrin 38b). The Mishna states, "When Rabbi Meir died, the telling of parables ceased" (Mishna Sota 9:15).
2. Throughout this chapter I draw heavily on the doctorate of Y. Diamant-Gorman. Diamant-Gorman begins by surveying the dozens of studies of the Elisha stories and then divides the narratives into three categories: historical, philosophical-theological, and literary. See Diamant-Gorman, *Elisha ben Abuya: New Perspectives Based on Modern Research* (PhD diss., Bar-Ilan University, 5762).
3. Tosefta Ḥagiga 2:3. This phrase is generally understood as a reference to the Pardes episode, though this too lends itself to various interpretations, both ancient and modern. See Diamant-Gorman, *Elisha ben Abuya: New Perspectives*, 55–59.

young students of Torah" (Y. Ḥagiga 2:1 [77b]).[4] One of Elisha's saplings was Rabbi Meir, who ultimately became an "other" as well.

ELISHA: ONE WHO PREACHES WELL

The relationship between Rabbi Meir and Elisha ben Abuya may be understood in light of the unique personality of Rabbi Meir, who was drawn to the inner world of Torah and did not notice its external trappings. The Talmud recognizes that this was a complicated relationship:

> How did Rabbi Meir study the law from the mouth of Aḥer? Did not Rabba bar bar Ḥana say that Rabbi Yoḥanan said: What is the meaning of "For the lips of a priest guard knowledge, and men seek rulings from his mouth; for he is an angel of the Lord of hosts?" [Mal. 2:7]? If the teacher resembles an angel of the Lord of hosts, then they should seek Torah from his mouth, and if not, they should not seek Torah from his mouth. (Ḥagiga 15b)

The consensus of the beit midrash is that one's teacher is a composite of conduct and wisdom; one form of instruction cannot be divorced from the other. Rabbi Meir disagrees. He accepts Elisha's teachings but not his behavior. In so doing, he destabilizes the beit midrash. Rabbi Yoḥanan insists that a fitting teacher be like an angel, a being with no distinction between thought and action. The entire world of the sages depended on the assumption that one's Torah and identity were equivalent. Elisha ben Abuya upset that symmetry.

His Teachings: A Man of Torah and Good Deeds

> Elisha ben Abuya would say: A man of good deeds, who has studied much Torah, to what may he be compared? To a person who builds first with stones and afterward with bricks: Even

4. This same interpretation appears in the parallel sources from the Land of Israel. See Song of Songs Rabba 1:1: "How did he cut at the saplings? When he entered houses of prayer and study and observed young students excelling in their studies, he would say to them words that would shut them up."

> when much water comes and collects by their side, it does not dislodge them. But one who performs no good deeds, though he has studied Torah, to what may he be compared? To a person a builds first with bricks and afterward with stones: Even when a little water gathers, it topples them immediately. (*Avot deRabbi Natan*, recension A, ch. 24)[5]

Ironically, it is Elisha ben Abuya who emphasizes the connection between Torah and good deeds. He argues that preserving the Torah is dependent upon proper behavior, because good deeds secure a house like stones that can withstand a rush of water, whereas Torah resembles bricks that are easily toppled.

This parable is reminiscent of a statement attributed to Rabbi Elazar ben Azaria in *Pirkei Avot*:

> He would say: When a person's wisdom exceeds his good deeds, to what may he be compared? To a tree with many branches but few roots. A wind blows, uproots it, and topples it, as it is written, "He shall be like a desert shrub that never thrives but dwells unwatered in the wilderness, in a salty, solitary land" [Jer. 17:6]. But when a person's good deeds exceed his wisdom, to what may he be compared? To a tree with few branches but many roots. All the winds in the world may blow against it, yet they cannot move it from its place, as it is written, "He shall be like a tree planted by the waters that spreads its roots by the stream; untouched by the scorching heat, its foliage remains luxurious; it will have no concern in a year of drought and will not cease bearing fruit" [Jer. 17:8]. (Mishna Avot 3:17)

The sages, and Rabbi Elazar among them, are interested in the relation-

5. This is one of a series of statements attributed to Elisha ben Abuya, all of which deal with the importance of good deeds as a basis for Torah. Y. Liebes considers whether these statements date to Elisha's youth, prior to his heresy, or to his later years, when he was convinced that he could no longer repent. See Liebes, *The Sin of Elisha* [Hebrew] (Jerusalem, 5750), 56–57.

ship between wisdom and good deeds. The counterparts, the Hasidim (pious ones), focus more on the relationship between wisdom and fear of God:

> Rabbi Ḥanina ben Dosa would say: When one gives priority to reverence over wisdom, his wisdom will endure. But when one gives priority to wisdom over reverence, his wisdom will not endure. (Mishna Avot 3:9)

The sages understood that there is a correlation between a person's wisdom and his behavior. If one is wise but does not perform good deeds, his Torah will be toppled by the slightest breeze. This leaves us with the Talmud's question about Rabbi Meir: Where did he obtain license to learn Torah from a person who was wise but whose behavior undermined the foundations of everything he taught?

What Do the Pupils of Beit Rabban Say?

To persuade his teacher to repent, Rabbi Meir forcibly brought Elisha ben Abuya into a beit midrash. There, and in twelve other houses of study as well, a surprise awaited both teacher and student. There was an outcry against Aḥer's entrance and Rabbi Meir's lack of respect for proper boundaries. The outcry was voiced by children, but it was decreed in heaven:

> Rabbi Meir took hold of Aḥer and brought him to the house of study (*beit kenishta*). He said to a child: Tell me your study verse. He said to him: "There is no peace – said the Lord – for the wicked" [Is. 48:22]. He brought him to another house of study. The child said to him, "Though you wash with natron and use much lye, your guilt is ingrained before Me – declares the Lord God" [Jer. 2:22]. He brought him to another house of study. The child said to him, "And you, who are doomed to ruin" [Jer. 4:30]. He brought him to thirteen houses of study. They recited for him in similar ways. The child in the thirteenth house of study said, "And to the wicked (*u'lerasha*) God said: Who are you to recite My laws and mouth the terms of My covenant, seeing that you

> spurn My discipline and brush My words aside?" [Ps. 50:16]. That child stuttered, so it sounded as if he said, "And to Elisha (*u'leElisha*) God said…." (Ḥagiga 15a–b)

In bringing Elisha to hear young students learning their verses, Rabbi Meir is not just playing a game. Pupils' verses were regarded as a form of prophecy in the ancient world.[6] They were interpreted as a sign from heaven.

The verse uttered by the first child is from Isaiah: "There is no peace – said the Lord – for the wicked" (Is. 48:22). This verse reverses the traditional greeting: Elisha is told "there is no peace" instead of "peace be unto you." Even worse, the verse refers to "the wicked," implying that Elisha is wicked in the eyes of heaven.

The verse uttered by the second child comes from Jeremiah: "Though you wash with natron and use much lye, your guilt is ingrained before Me – declares the Lord God." No amount of purification or repentance will avail Elisha.[7] In every beit midrash he enters, the children utter similar verses. But it is the last student who seals his fate. This student utters a verse that is difficult even under ordinary circumstances: "And to the wicked (*u'lerasha*) God said: Who are you to recite My laws and mouth the terms of My covenant, seeing that you spurn My discipline and brush My words aside?" This is the divine critique of Elisha, but perhaps also of Rabbi Meir, who insists on dragging his teacher into the study hall. "Who are you to recite My laws?" – how can you be wicked yet study My Torah? The child stutters, so "and to the wicked" sounds like "and to Elisha." Now Elisha's identity is conflated with his wickedness, and he is banished from the beit midrash. Which brings us back to the Talmud's original question: How could Rabbi Meir permit himself to learn from such a teacher?

6. S. Lieberman, *Hellenism in Jewish Palestine* (New York: JTS Press, 1950). Lieberman demonstrates that the use of verses in prophecy was common among the Greeks and Egyptians as well, and was not regarded as the type of divination prohibited by the Torah.
7. In their original context, these words serve to denigrate Israel, which tries to find favor in the eyes of its enemies by whoring after foreign gods. This verse thus recalls Elisha's visit to the harlot who first condemns him to his baleful fate by calling him "other."

The Teachings of Aḥer's Daughter

The Talmud relates that Elisha ben Abuya's daughter sought economic support from Rabbi Yehuda HaNasi. He reacted with astonishment:

> He said to her: Is his seed still in the world?
>
> She said to him: Remember his Torah and do not remember his deeds.
>
> Immediately a fire came down from heaven and surrounded Rebbi's bench.
>
> Rebbi wept and said: If this happens for those who dishonor the Torah, how much more so for those who respect it? (Ḥagiga 15b)

The daughter urges Rebbi to remember her father's devotion to Torah, not his deeds. The heavenly fire exhorts Rebbi to accept her plea.[8] At this point he breaks down in tears. Rebbi believed that the wicked leave no vestige in the world, but Aḥer's daughter asserts that a person's Torah must be divorced from his deeds. When a sign from heaven validates her words, a fundamental element of his religious consciousness has been shattered, and Rebbi has good reason to cry.

Rabbi Meir's Teachings: Saving a Torah Scroll

The Jerusalem Talmud recounts a conversation between Rabbi Meir and his students that suggests that Rabbi Meir is fully aware of what he is doing when he chooses to learn from Elisha:

> They said to Rabbi Meir: If they say to you in the World to Come: Whom do you desire to visit? Will you say your father or your teacher?

8. Diamant-Gorman analyzes this dialogue and shows that, based on the various versions of the talmudic text and on the literary context of this passage, the fire is directed against Rebbi: "His approach, which conflates a person's Torah with his actions and judges them as one, does not accord sufficient weight to Torah study in its own right." See Diamant-Gorman, *Elisha ben Abuya: New Perspectives*, 140–43.

> He said to them: I will first approach my teacher, and then my father.
>
> They said to him: Will they listen to you?
>
> He said to them: Did we not learn: They save the case of the scroll with the scroll, and the case of the phylacteries with the phylacteries? They save Elisha for the merit of his Torah. (Y. Ḥagiga 2:1 [77a])

It is not surprising that Rabbi Meir prefers his teacher to his father. The only surprise is that Rabbi Meir is so confident that he will encounter Elisha in the World to Come. But Rabbi Meir believes that although Elisha has sinned, his Torah is pure. After all, the case of the scroll is saved with the scroll itself.

This question will preoccupy the sages for generations. As we have seen, the great sage of the Jerusalem Talmud, Rabbi Yoḥanan, insists that a teacher must resemble an angel of God if one is to learn from him. We will follow the continuation of this discussion.

Learning When Old, Learning When Young

> Reish Lakish said: Rabbi Meir found a verse and expounded it: "Incline your ear and listen to the words of the sages; pay attention to My wisdom" [Prov. 22:17]. It says not "to their wisdom" but "to My wisdom."
>
> Rabbi Ḥanina said: From here: "Take heed, daughter, and note, incline your ear; forget your people and your father's house" [Ps. 45:11]. (Ḥagiga 15b)

The two sages cite verses that challenge Rabbi Yoḥanan's assumption. Reish Lakish offers a daring interpretation of the verse in Proverbs: A teacher is just a mouthpiece for God's word. Even if the teacher is not an angel, the Torah he transmits is divine. Thus a student needs to heed the words of his teacher regardless of the nature of that teacher.

Rabbi Ḥanina also cites a verse that includes the words "incline your ear," but his text goes on to exhort, "forget your people and your father's house." Rabbi Ḥanina is asserting that there is no connection between the Torah that is studied and the home from which it emerges.

The Talmud considers these two conflicting views, that of Rabbi Yoḥanan and that of Reish Lakish and Rabbi Ḥanina:

> The verses contradict each other! There is no contradiction. One refers to an adult, and one to a child. (Ḥagiga 15b)

The Talmud resolves the apparent contradiction by distinguishing between mature and young learning. That which is appropriate for an adult is not appropriate for a child. Rabbi Yoḥanan's interpretation applies to the learning of a child, who cannot distinguish the teacher from what he teaches, whereas Rabbi Ḥanina's interpretation applies to the learning of a mature and discerning adult.[9]

Elisha's Teachings as an Orchard

To answer the question of how Rabbi Meir could study Torah from Aḥer, the Talmud offers three parables from the garden depicted in Song of Songs.

1. The Parable of the Date

> When Rav Dimi came, he said: They say in the west [Israel]: Rabbi Meir ate the date and threw away the pit. (Ḥagiga 15b)

Rav Dimi, who was one of those sages who would travel back and forth from the Land of Israel to Babylonia,[10] reports on how the sages in Israel

9. The *Tosafot* refer to a source in which Rav Yehuda excommunicates a teacher who has developed a reputation for improper behavior. Rabbeinu Elḥanan resolves that this source refers to a teacher of young students, thereby vindicating Rabbi Yehuda. This talmudic passage can serve as the basis for a pedagogical discussion about the character of the educator and the value of setting a personal example in educational contexts.
10. During the talmudic period, sages frequently traveled from the Land of Israel to Babylonia to transmit laws and teachings. Rav Dimi seems to be using this parable to describe Rabbi Meir's behavior. This appears to be the case in the manuscript

justified Rabbi Meir's decision to learn Torah from Aḥer: Some fruits are delicious despite their inedible pits. Rabbi Meir ate Elisha's Torah and threw away its inedible pit. Does the pit refer to Elisha's actions, in which case Rav Dimi's teaching is consistent with that of Elisha's daughter? Or does it refer to the core of Elisha's teachings, which were fundamentally unpalatable? When considered in light of the other parables, the former interpretation seems more plausible. But we must also consider the latter,[11] especially in light of Elisha's own assessment of himself.

2. The Parable of the Nut

> Rava expounded: What is written, "I went down to the nut grove to see the budding of the vale" [Song. 6:11]? Why are words of Torah compared to a nut? To tell you that just as a nut, though it is dirtied with mud and filth, its inside is not soiled, so too a sage, even though he sins, his Torah is not soiled. (Ḥagiga 15b)

This parable, too, is about a fruit with an inedible part. But here the inedible part is just on the outside. According to this understanding, Rabbi Meir learned Torah from a sage who sinned, but whose Torah escaped his taint. Although the outside became soiled, the inside remained fresh.

versions, none of which mention Rabbi Meir. See Diamant–Gorman, *Elisha ben Abuya: New Perspectives*, 146 note 469.

11. Diamant-Gorman (ibid., 147) privileges the latter explanation on the grounds that Elisha's learning was purely theoretical, never penetrating his heart. She argues that the "pit" refers to "that fundamental religious assumption that is necessary in order to learn Torah in the proper spirit. Elisha's religious standpoint was flawed from the outset, and it influenced his worldview and behavior. The phrase we use to refer to this religious standpoint is 'fear of heaven.'" In support of this claim, Diamant–Gorman quotes Rabbi Tzaddok HaKohen of Lublin, *Tzidkat HaTzaddik*, sec. 225, which distinguishes between words of Torah transmitted via the mind, and those transmitted via the heart. Diamant-Gorman's argument begs the very same educational and religious questions with which the Talmud struggles. How can Rav Dimi suggest that the sages eat a fruit that grows from a rotten pit? Surely the taste of the pit will affect the fruit!

3. *The Parable of the Pomegranate*

> Rabba bar Rav Sheila came upon Elijah. He said to him: What is the Holy One, Blessed Be He, doing?
>
> He said to him: He is reciting traditions from the mouths of all the rabbis, but He does not recite from the mouth of Rabbi Meir.
>
> He said to him: Why?
>
> He said to him: Because he learned traditions from the mouth of Aḥer.
>
> He said to him: So what? Rabbi Meir found a pomegranate. He ate the inside and threw away the peel.
>
> He said to him: Now God says: Meir My son says.... (Ḥagiga 15b)

This encounter is typical of the rabbinic literature about Elijah, who is often invoked as a mediator between heaven and earth.[12] In these encounters, God is often described as studying Torah and living the life of a Torah scholar. But here Elijah specifies that God quotes from all the sages except Rabbi Meir and Aḥer. This story thus resolves the question of whether the Torah of a sage may be studied even when his deeds discredit him. Apparently the heavenly verdict is that a sage must be regarded as an angel if his Torah is to be quoted.

Rabba bar Rav Sheila's response is quite straightforward. Knowing the parables of the date and the nut, he offers a third parable involving a pomegranate, whose peel can be discarded, leaving the delicious fruit inside. According to Rabba bar Rav Sheila, Rabbi Meir recognized that Elisha's Torah was the Torah of God, even if surrounded by an inedible peel. We have already seen that Rabbi Meir lives in a world devoid of external trappings. His Torah is "light" unencased in "skin." For him, even death can be "very good." Moreover, Rabbi Meir has a direct connection to the Torah given on Sinai, which reaches him without mediation.

12. M. Ilai, "Where Does Elijah Come From? The Origin of and Relationship to Elijah the Prophet in Rabbinic Exegesis" [Hebrew], *Tura* 3 (5754): 259–83.

Thus he could cut right through to the edible core without being stymied by the peel. The Talmud relates that God accepts this image, as per Elijah's update from heaven: Now God quotes Rabbi Meir as well.

But the sages never fully resolve the question of how Rabbi Meir could permit himself to learn Torah from Aḥer. When Rabbi Meir continues to do so, the sages label him an "other" as well, and reject his halakhic views.

ENCOUNTERS BETWEEN TEACHER AND STUDENT: THREE VIGNETTES

The Jerusalem and Babylonian Talmuds, along with the Midrash, relay several conversations between Aḥer and Rabbi Meir.[13] We will consider three such exchanges in an attempt to deepen our understanding of Rabbi Meir's personality and teachings.

Riding a Horse on Shabbat

> Aḥer was once riding his horse on Shabbat, and Rabbi Meir was walking after him to learn Torah from his mouth. He said to him: Meir, turn back, since I have already measured by the footsteps of my horse that the Shabbat boundary is here.
>
> He said to him: Then you too should return.
>
> He said to him: Haven't I already told you? I have already heard from behind the curtain, "Return, rebellious children" [Jer. 3:22] – except Aḥer. (Ḥagiga 15a)

In learning Torah from Aḥer, Rabbi Meir eats the sweet fruit of the pomegranate without regard for the bitter peel. Elisha brazenly rides his horse on the Sabbath, but Rabbi Meir hardly notices.[14] He is so absorbed in his teacher's Torah that he loses track of how far they have traveled. So

13. Many scholarly articles have been written about these conversations, which are rich in philosophical implications beyond our purview. See Diamant-Gorman, *Elisha ben Abuya: New Perspectives*, 287–96 (bibliography) and the overview in her opening chapter.
14. Riding a horse was a sign of authority in talmudic times. Commoners rode donkeys. See M. Bar, "Horse Riding in the Land of Israel During the Mishnaic and Talmudic

he is surprised to hear religious instruction from the rider: "Meir, turn back." Aḥer has kept track of the Shabbat boundary and informs Rabbi Meir that he must turn back so as not to overstep it.

Aḥer instructs Rabbi Meir to return. Rabbi Meir, playing on the Hebrew pun *ḥazor,* which means both "return" and "repent," tells his teacher that he, too, should return. Rabbi Meir also invokes this pun in his midrash about the son of the king whose father tells him to return, as we saw. (Similar language is used in the stories of Akavia ben Mehalalel[15] and Jeroboam son of Nebat.)[16] It seems that Rabbi Meir wants his teacher to have the chance to claim his place as the leader of the sages. He recognizes the brilliance of his teacher's Torah. But Elisha's bitter peel is ultimately his undoing.

Its End Is Better Than Its Beginning

The Jerusalem Talmud also includes a vignette in which Aḥer rides a horse on Shabbat with Rabbi Meir trailing behind:

> Rabbi Meir was sitting and expounding in the beit midrash in Tiberias. His master Elisha passed by riding on a horse on Shabbat. They came and said to Rabbi Meir: Behold, your master is outside. He interrupted his sermon and went out to him. (Y. Ḥagiga 2:1 [77a])

The Jerusalem Talmud depicts a much calmer scene. Although it is Shabbat, the beit midrash is in session as usual.[17] Elisha rides by on his horse

Periods" [Hebrew], *Catedra* 60 (Tammuz 5751): 28: "Riding a horse was a status symbol of rulers."

15. Mishna Eduyot 5:6. Akavia ben Mehalalel went from being the head of the court to being excommunicated.
16. The Talmud (Sanhedrin 102a) recounts that Jeroboam son of Nebat was advised to walk with God in heaven. But he lost out on this opportunity because he asked, "Who is at the helm?"
17. We know public sermons were given during the Amoraic period, but this source suggests that they were common in the Tannaitic era as well. See Y. Hyman, *Public Sermons During the Talmudic Period* [Hebrew] (Jerusalem, 5731). Frankel argues that this is the earliest record of a public sermon. See Y. Frankel, *The Methods of Aggada and Midrash* [Hebrew] (Givatayim, 5731), 569 note 42.

through Tiberias, where presumably he has errands to run.[18] The narrator seems to think it reasonable that Rabbi Meir would interrupt his sermon to greet Elisha, though it does seem somewhat embarrassing that the head of the academy finds himself torn between the holiness of Shabbat in the beit midrash and the secular world outside its walls. Nonetheless Rabbi Meir does not seem troubled.

> Elisha said to him: What were you expounding today?
>
> He said, "The Lord blessed the latter days of Job's life more than the beginning" [Job 42:12].
>
> He said to him: And how did you begin it? He said to him: "The Lord gave Job twice what he had before" [Job 42:10] – that He doubled his money.
>
> He said: Alas for things lost and not found. Akiva your master did not expound it like that. Rather, "The Lord blessed the latter days of Job's life more than the beginning" – on account of the mitzvot and good deeds he had done in the beginning.... "The end of a thing is better than its beginning" [Eccl. 7:8] – when it is good from the beginning. (Y. Ḥagiga 2:1 [77a])

The master and student delve right into a study session, without formalities and without any further ado. Rabbi Meir explains that he has been expounding a verse about Job's fate, according to which God doubled all of Job's possessions. He interprets the verse from Ecclesiastes as meaning that the end of a thing is better than its beginning. Elisha laments that Rabbi Meir seems to have forgotten Rabbi Akiva's teaching that the

18. Some readers regard this as a tense scene. Diamant-Gorman argues, "The words 'your master' reflect the mounting tension in the beit midrash" (Diamant-Gorman, *Elisha ben Abuya: New Perspectives*, 194). But I submit that Tiberias was a cosmopolitan city in which it was common to see people violating Shabbat. At the end of the second century, the city grew significantly and became a Roman colony filled with Roman citizens. During Rabbi Meir's lifetime, many Jews kept away from Tiberias because it was regarded as impure, as we learn from the story of Rashbi. Perhaps Elisha's presence outside the beit midrash was a source of tension, but it seems that no one got upset. For more on Tiberias and its inhabitants during the talmudic period, see S. Klein, *The Land of the Galilee*, 94–105.

end of a thing is good only when it is good from the beginning: "Alas for things lost and not found."[19]

Their conversation unfolds like a typical encounter between master and student. The student is asked a question, he gives an answer, he is rebuked by his teacher, and then he is given the correct answer. If it were not Shabbat and the teacher were not sitting astride a horse, this would be an unremarkable exchange. But then the conversation suddenly takes a turn. The master relates a personal memory that seems to support his interpretation of the verse they are studying:

> And this matter happened to me: Abuya my father was one of the notables of Jerusalem. On the day he was to circumcise me, he invited all the notables of Jerusalem and seated them in one house. He invited Rabbi Eliezer and Rabbi Yehoshua and seated them in a separate house. When they were eating and drinking and singing and clapping and dancing, Rabbi Eliezer said to Rabbi Yehoshua: As long as they are occupying themselves with their own business, let us busy ourselves with ours. They sat and occupied themselves with words of Torah, and from the Torah to the Prophets, and from the Prophets to the Writings, and fire came down from heaven and encircled them.
>
> Abuya said to them: My masters! Have you come to burn down my house upon me?
>
> They said to him: God forbid. But we were sitting and turning over words of Torah, and from the Torah to the Prophets, and from the Prophets to the Writings. And the words rejoiced as when they were given at Sinai, and fire enveloped them as they were enveloped at Sinai. At Sinai they were given primarily in fire: "And the mountain was ablaze with flames to the very heavens" [Deut. 4:11].
>
> Abuya my father said to them: My masters, if that is the power of Torah, then if this son of mine prospers, I will dedicate

19. A. Goshen-Gottstein, *The Sinner and the Amnesiac* (Stanford: Stanford University Press, 2000), 358 note 39.

> him to Torah. But since his intention was not for the sake of heaven, [Torah] did not prosper for that man. (Y. Ḥagiga 2:1 [77a])

Suddenly Elisha is consumed by memories of his own circumcision ceremony. Of course, these are not actual memories, but rather later realizations that serve as the key to unlocking something primal about himself. He blames his fate on his upbringing.[20] The present moment – horse, rider, Shabbat, student – fall away, leaving just an overwhelmed boy struggling to come to terms with who he is. Elisha constructs his own biographical narrative.[21] He blames his father for dedicating him to Torah without the proper intentions. In the words of Rabbi Yehuda Brandes,

> It seems that Elisha identifies a flaw in his education, which manifests itself in his personality.... This is what we would call a foundational tale. The story comes to explain how Elisha became the person he was. Perhaps Elisha, in sharing this narrative, is trying to explain to Rabbi Meir that he never felt a real connection to his studies, but always felt like an outsider to the tradition. After all, it is not the learning itself that interested him, but the fire that surrounded those who were engaged in study. There is a deep sense of alienation at the core of his being. Elisha psychoanalyzes himself and finds the roots of his own alienation in an experience that dates back almost to his birth.[22]

Gold and Glass Vessels

After Elisha "went bad," he asked Rabbi Meir the following question:

20. This is not the place to ask whether something intended for the wrong purpose can ultimately turn out for the sake of heaven. After all, we are dealing with matters of the soul, not of the intellect. Diamant-Gorman (*Elisha ben Abuya: New Perspectives*, 202) describes Elisha's account as "punctilious and genteel in a melodramatic way, arguing for an unprecedented prerequisite for the study of Torah." This is not a fair criticism.
21. On the idea of "re-biography," see M. Rottenberg, *Seventy Faces of Life: Midrashic Re-Biography as Personal Psychotherapy* [Hebrew] (Jerusalem, 5754).
22. Y. Brandes, "On Aḥer and Otherness" [Hebrew], in *The Other: Between Man, Himself, and His Fellow*, ed. H. Deutsch and M. Ben-Sasson (Tel Aviv, 2001), 402–42.

> What is written, "Gold or glass cannot match its value, nor can vessels of fine gold be exchanged for it" [Job 28:17]?
>
> He said: This refers to matters of Torah, which are as difficult to acquire as vessels of gold and vessels of fine gold, and as easy to lose as vessels of glass....
>
> He said to him: Akiva your master did not say thus. Rather, just as vessels of gold and vessels of glass can be restored even if they are broken, so a sage who has sinned can be restored.
>
> He said to him: Then you too should repent.
>
> He said to him: I have already heard from behind the curtain: "Return, rebellious children" [Jer. 3:22] – except Aḥer. (Ḥagiga 15a)

Elisha's question is drawn from chapter twenty-eight of the Book of Job, which deals with the value of wisdom. The verse "Gold or glass cannot match its value, nor can vessels of fine gold be exchanged for it" suggests that one must be willing to pay any price to acquire wisdom. Rabbi Meir, who trails behind his teacher to learn Torah from him and to encourage him to repent, explains this verse as alluding to the danger that his teacher's Torah might be lost. It can shatter like glass. This is a very pessimistic understanding of the verse, and Elisha is quick to correct his student. He offers a different interpretation in the name of Rabbi Akiva:[23] Just as gold and silver can be re-melted into new vessels, so too can sages who sin be restored. Elisha waits patiently for Rabbi Meir to offer his characteristic response: "Then you too should repent." Perhaps he quotes this interpretation just to hear Rabbi Meir utter these words and vacillate between hope and despair. Rabbi Meir is convinced that his teacher has sinned but can still repent. All he has to do is get off his high horse. But Elisha insists that while gold and silver vessels can be reshaped, their raw materials do not fundamentally change. He is who he is.

23. It is unclear whether Elisha was in fact a student of Rabbi Akiva. The only evidence we have is the story of the Pardes. It seems more likely that they were colleagues and contemporaries.

SMOOTH AND ERASED PAPER

The statement attributed to Elisha ben Abuya in *Pirkei Avot* seems undoubtedly autobiographical:

> Elisha ben Abuya would say: He who learns [Torah] as a child, what is he like? He is like ink written on new paper. He who learns as an old man, what is he like? He is like ink written on erased paper. (Mishna Avot 4:20)

According to Elisha, that which is crooked cannot be made straight. Only a child can write clearly on a fresh sheet of paper. Once a person grows older, the page is already full of erasures. This mishna contradicts the teaching quoted by Elisha in the name of Rabbi Akiva about a sage who has sinned but can still repent. Now Elisha seems to suggest that such a sage cannot repent, and even something that started out well is not guaranteed to end well. A page that is written on for the first time can never be rewritten on as clearly after it has been erased.

Elisha's statement in *Pirkei Avot* can be understood in light of Rabbi Meir's use of indelible ink (discussed in the previous chapter). Rabbi Meir, perhaps in response to his teacher's metaphor of the erasures, adds vitriol to his ink so that the writing cannot be erased. He ensures that even though Elisha has become Aḥer, his teaching is not forgotten.

RABBI MEIR'S CONVERSATION WITH NIMOS HAGARDI

> Nimos HaGardi asked Rabbi Meir: Does all wool that is placed in a dying vat come out the right color? He answered him: All that was clean on its mother's back comes out the right color. All which was not clean on its mother's back does not. (Ḥagiga 15b)

This is a baffling talmudic passage, particularly since "Nimos HaGardi" is not a Jewish name. Academic scholars identify this figure with Avnomos HaGardi, a famous philosopher of the mishnaic period.[24] The word

24. A. Shinan, *Shemot Rabba* (Jerusalem, 5744), 254.

"Gardi" may refer to his birthplace, or to the profession of weaving.[25] In any case, we need not be surprised that Rabbi Meir converses with a non-Jewish philosopher, since he never seems to concern himself with boundaries or external labels.

The passage refers to the process of dying wool. After the wool is shorn, it is placed in a vat with dye. The philosopher asks whether all the wool placed in the vat emerges with the proper degree of coloration. Rabbi Meir responds that it depends on the quality of the wool. So long as the wool grew cleanly on the sheep, it dyes well. Rabbi Meir seems to think that everything depends on a person's roots. Whether or not he will succeed as a scholar depends on his formative experiences.

We have already seen that Elisha attributes all of his problems to his father's conduct at his circumcision ceremony. Now his student Rabbi Meir suggests that indeed a person's formative moments shape his later development.[26] It seems that Rabbi Meir has internalized his teacher's Torah: The end of a thing is only as good as its beginning.

The classical commentators view this conversation as an expansion of the debate about the relationship between Torah and good deeds. Rashi writes as follows:

> *Does all wool that is placed in a dying vat come out* – Does all wool that is placed in a dying vat come out properly colored or not? That is, are all who study with the sages protected from sin by their teachings or not?
> *All that was clean on its mother's back* – All wool that did not get dirty when it was on the fleece emerges properly colored. That is, all whose faith precedes their wisdom emerge properly. So it seems to me.
>
> But the sages interpreted as follows: *All wool that is placed in a dying vat comes out* – all who went down to hell to be judged come out.
> *On its mother's back* – One-day-old wool that is not trampled

25. For more on weaving and dying in the talmudic period, see M. Ilai, *Workers and Their Craft* [Hebrew] (Givatayim, 5747): 10–11. Also see 170 note 24.
26. This is Diamant-Gorman's reading. See her *Elisha ben Abuya: New Perspectives*, 36.

> in mud will emerge properly colored. That is, if it has merits, it emerges.

Rashi reads Rabbi Ḥanina ben Dosa's teaching about faith and good deeds into the discussion of wool and dye, thereby drawing a parallel between learning and piety.

RABBI MEIR PARTS FROM HIS TEACHER

The world is indifferent to the fate of Aḥer. No one takes interest in him, and he loses his influence on others. Rabbi Meir recognizes this reality, but it is important to him that Elisha's teachings gain him entry into the World to Come. The last battle Rabbi Meir wages is an attempt to save his teacher's soul:

> Years later Elisha became sick. They came and said to Rabbi Meir: Behold, your teacher is sick.
>
> He went, desiring to visit him, and found him sick. He said to him: Will you not repent?
>
> He said to him: If one repents, is it accepted?
>
> He said: Is it not written, "You return men to dust" [Ps. 90:3]?[27] Until life is crushed to dust, it is accepted.
>
> At this point Elisha wept and passed away and died.
>
> Rabbi Meir rejoiced in his heart and said: It seems that my teacher died repenting. (Y. Ḥagiga 2:1 [77a])

Elisha is afflicted with an unusual disease. The Talmud uses the term *hivish* (literally: "he went rotten"), which suggests a moral judgment as well as a physical diagnosis. Rabbi Meir comes to visit his teacher and to plead with him to repent. Elisha responds with a question suggesting that Rabbi Meir has made inroads in his heroic attempt to save his master's soul: "If one repents, is it accepted?" Rabbi Meir expounds on a verse from Psalms, and for the first time, Elisha does not refute his

27. The second half of this verse, which is not quoted here, is also relevant: "You decreed: return, you mortals."

homily.[28] This encounter between them serves as a sort of rite of passage in which the teacher learns from the student and the student uses his authority to protect his teacher. Elisha weeps. His tears recall those of penitent Elazar ben Dordaya, who cried "until his soul departed from him" (Avoda Zara 17a). His defiance, pride, and brash self-confidence are replaced by weakness and despondency.

Rabbi Meir cannot know with certainty what has transpired in his teacher's heart. But he suspects that he has died repenting. Even after his teacher's death, Rabbi Meir will continue working to ensure that Elisha's soul merits entry into the World to Come.

The Fire on the Grave

> After they buried him, a fire came down from heaven and burned his grave. They came and said to Rabbi Meir: Behold, your teacher's grave is burning. He left, desiring to visit it, and found it burning. What did he do? He took his cloak and spread it upon it. (Y. Ḥagiga 2:1 [77a])

A fire from heaven may be a sign of divine approval or revelation.[29] But this fire is not an auspicious one. The heavens are waging a battle against Rabbi Meir. Fire descends to burn the sinner Elisha. It no longer seems possible for Rabbi Meir to sustain the hope that Elisha died while repenting. After all, if he had truly repented, the heavens would not be raging.

Rabbi Meir decides to try one last time. This time he is fighting against divine fire, which threatens to burn him as well. He takes off his cloak, the garment that marks him as a sage.[30] In spreading out his cloak over Elisha's grave, Rabbi Meir is taking responsibility for protecting his teacher. As Ruth said to Boaz, "and you will spread your cloak

28. Goshen-Gottstein points this out. See his *Sinner and Amnesiac*, 172.
29. This is the case with the fire that surrounded Rabbi Eliezer and Rabbi Yehoshua during Elisha's circumcision ceremony, as well as the fire that surrounded Rabbi Yoḥanan ben Zakkai during Rabbi Elazar ben Arakh's wondrous homily (see Ḥagiga 15a).
30. See Chapter One on the sages who gathered in the Rimon Valley, where not everyone had the proper cloak. This garment marked a Torah scholar.

over your servant" (Ruth 3:9). The cloak covers the burning grave, but the cloak itself does not catch fire. This miracle inspires Rabbi Meir's greatest homily:[31]

> He said: "Stay the night..." [Ruth 3:13]. "Stay the night" – in this world, which resembles night. "Then in the morning" – this is the World to Come, which is completely morning. "If he redeems you, good" – this refers to the Holy One, Blessed Be He, who is good, as it says, "He is good to all, and His mercy is upon all His creatures" [Ps. 145:9]. "But if he does not want to redeem you, I will redeem you myself, as God lives!" [Ruth 3:13]. And it was extinguished. (Y. Ḥagiga 2:1 [77a])

Rabbi Meir interprets the verses from Ruth radically. He invokes Ruth's words to Boaz on that magical night on the threshing floor to address his master, Elisha, who lies dead before him. He is Boaz, Elisha's soul is his Ruth, and God is the redeemer. In the biblical story, the redeemer is banished from the city. He redeems neither the field nor Ruth. Boaz takes on this responsibility himself, becoming the hero of the story. Rabbi Meir challenges God: If He redeems Elisha's soul, good. And if not, Rabbi Meir will do it. Don't ask how.

And with that, the fire is extinguished.

31. For more on the meaning of this homily, see J. L. Rubenstein, "Elisha ben Abuya: Torah and the Sinful Sage," *The Journal of Jewish Thought and Philosophy* 7:2 (1997): 165.

Chapter Nine

Beruria: A Sage and a Woman

When we studied the figure of Rabbi Ḥanina ben Teradion, a leader of the Jews living in Judea during the Bar Kokhba revolt, in volume two of *The Sages,* we took note of his daughter's involvement in Torah study. Beruria studied with her father and took an active role in scholarly debates. Was there a special Galilean custom whereby women studied Torah? It is unlikely, since we have no evidence of other women like Beruria. So we must assume that Beruria was one of a kind, and that her unique personality drew her to Torah study.

BERURIA IN HALAKHIC LITERATURE

Rabbi Shimshon of Kinun, one of the last of the Tosafists, wrote in *Sefer HaKeritut,* "There is a woman who disagrees with the sages like a sage herself." The early medieval commentators (Rishonim) as well as some of the later ones (Aḥaronim) did not hesitate to identify Beruria as a *Tanna,* a sage of the mishnaic period.[1] She was also included among

1. See the responsa of Maharal of Prague [Hebrew], sec. 193; and *Responsa Binyamin*

the sages dating from the mishnaic and talmudic periods. But because Beruria was a woman, her status as a sage was a source of great tension, if not in Beruria's own lifetime, then certainly for those scholars who succeeded her. Although she was counted among the sages of her generation, the fact that she was a woman inevitably meant she was also regarded as a sexual being.[2]

A BOOK OF YOḤASIN IN HER HANDS

According to talmudic tradition, Beruria was a leading scholar of halakha in Israel:

> Rabbi Simlai came before Rabbi Yoḥanan. He said to him: Let the master teach me the Book of Yoḥasin. Rabbi Yoḥanan asked him: Where are you from? He said: From Lod. And where is your dwelling place? In Nehardea. He said to him: We do not expound on the Book of Yoḥasin to residents of Lod or Nehardea, and certainly not in this case, given that you are from Lod and your dwelling place is in Nehardea.
>
> Eventually, Rabbi Simlai pressured him and he agreed. Rabbi Simlai said to him: Let us learn it over the course of three months. Rabbi Yoḥanan took a clump of earth and threw it at him. He said to him: If Beruria, wife of Rabbi Meir and daughter of Rabbi Ḥanania ben Teradion, who would learn three hundred rulings a day from three hundred masters, nevertheless did not finish it in three years, do you think you will be able to finish it in three months? (Pesaḥim 62b)

Ze'ev [Hebrew] (Rabbi Binyamin Ze'ev Arta, sixteenth century Greece): "We find a woman who is mentioned in the *baraita* as disagreeing with the sages.... There is a woman in the Talmud who exists on the border of the *Tanna'im*, who disagrees with the other sages as a *Tanna*, and they concede to her opinion."

2. See Daniel Boyarin, *Carnal Israel*, 183–97; B. Bakun, "How Do We Tell the Story of the End of Beruria's Life?" [Hebrew], in *To Be a Jewish Woman*, ed. M. Shilo, collection B (Jerusalem, 2003); Hyman, *Legends*, s.v. "Beruria"; M. Margaliot, *Encyclopedia of the Sages of the Talmud and the Geonim* [Hebrew] (Tel Aviv, 5733), s.v. "Beruria"; Nissim ben Jacob ibn Shahin, *An Elegant Composition Concerning Relief After Adversity*, trans. William M. Brinner (Yale University Press, 1977), in *Yale Judaica Series*, vol. 20.

This story seems plausible. Rabbi Simlai is a familiar talmudic figure. He was indeed from Lod, and he was sent to Netzivin by Rabbi Yehuda Nesiya, grandson of Rebbi.[3] According to this source, he was interested in learning the Book of Yoḥasin. Rashi explains that this text was a collection of tannaitic expositions on the biblical Book of Chronicles. Yet Rashi's identification is unconvincing. Why would Rabbi Simlai want to learn a midrash on this book specifically? And why did Rabbi Yoḥanan respond so harshly? Why would he care whether Rabbi Simlai learned such a midrash? Maharsha (Rabbi Samuel Eidels, 1555–1631, Poland)[4] offers an alternative explanation:

> "The Book of Yoḥasin" cannot be referring to a list of which families had illustrious lineage and which did not, because it says in the tenth chapter of Yoḥasin that it is permissible to study this book only once every seven years. If so, how could Beruria complete it in three years? Thus Rashi has explained that this is not the case, but that the Book of Yoḥasin is a tannaitic commentary on the Book of Chronicles, according to the lineages of the tribes and their families. (Maharsha, *Insights into Talmudic Stories*, Pesaḥim 62b)

According to Maharsha, the most obvious explanation is that the Book of Yoḥasin refers to the "black books" that list all those families that assimilated and whose children's lineage is therefore suspect. Such genealogical matters were a source of anxiety for the sages, who devoted the tenth chapter of Tractate Kiddushin to this subject. But as Maharsha explains, Rashi rejects this account because the Talmud teaches that it is permissible to study this book only once every seven years. How, then, could Beruria have studied it for three consecutive years? Rashi concludes that Sefer Yoḥasin must refer to a commentary on the biblical Book of Chronicles, which is composed of genealogical lists.

3. Hyman, *Legends*, s.v. "Rabbi Simlai," 1150–51.
4. Maharsha's talmudic commentary was printed in the Talmud and was therefore widely distributed.

The obvious explanation, which Rashi rejects, seems like the most plausible reading of this story. We will briefly consider the section of Kiddushin that describes the study of the Book of Yoḥasin:

> Rabbi Yoḥanan said: I swear by the sanctuary that it is in our power to reveal which families in the Land of Israel are genealogically tainted! But what can I do? For behold, great people of the generation are intermixed with them.
>
> Rabbi Yoḥanan agrees with Rabbi Yitzhak, for Rabbi Yitzhak has said: Once a genealogically tainted family is mixed with Israel, it is mixed….
>
> It was taught: There was yet another tainted family whose identity the sages did not want to reveal. But the sages do transmit it to their children and students once every seven years, and some say twice every seven years. (Kiddushin 71a)

As this source implies, the sages had a genealogy book in their possession. However, they did not want to reveal it to the public, because those families that were genealogically tainted were intermixed with many great men of the generation. There was an unspoken understanding that if a family were regarded as genealogically pure, no one would go back to examine the genealogical records.[5] So instead the sages would pass this book down from disciple to disciple and study it only once (or twice) every seven years.

Perhaps Rashi rejects this identification of Sefer Yoḥasin as a genealogical record because his reading was informed by a parallel version of this story in the Jerusalem Talmud:

> Rabbi Simlai came before Rabbi Yonatan and said: Teach me *Aggada*. He said to him: I have a tradition from my ancestors that we should not teach *Aggada* to Babylonians or to southerners,

5. The discovery of tainted lineage can lead to very awkward and painful situations. After a period of persecution such as the Bar Kokhba revolt (or the Holocaust, in our own time), such discoveries are all too common.

> for they are coarse-minded and know little Toraḥ. And you are from Nehardea and you live in the south! (Y. Pesaḥim 5:2 [32a])

The Jerusalem Talmud explains that Rabbi Simlai wanted to learn a book of commentary, not a book of genealogy. But the dialogue between Rabbi Simlai and Rabbi Yoḥanan is very similar in the two texts (particularly when we consider that Lod is in the south,[6] and that "Yonatan" in the Jerusalem Talmud often corresponds to "Yoḥanan" in the Babylonian Talmud).[7] Perhaps Rashi read the Babylonian Talmud in light of the Jerusalem Talmud, and therefore explained that the text Rabbi Simlai sought to learn was a commentary on the Book of Chronicles.[8]

The source in the Jerusalem Talmud does not mention Beruria, which raises the question of whether she was a fictional construct of the Babylonian Talmud.[9] Yet even if we prefer the version in the Jerusalem Talmud for historical reasons,[10] Beruria remains one of the great Torah scholars of her generation and a role model for generations to come.

BERURIA SPEAKS WELL

Beruria is depicted as a peer of the other talmudic sages, participating fully in halakhic conversations:

6. On the interchangeability of "Lod" and "the south," see S. Klein, *The Land of the Galilee*, 249–51.
7. Many years ago I learned from Rabbi Yaakov Zussman that the Babylonian Talmud "adopted" many students of Rabbi Yoḥanan and attributed their teachings to Rabbi Yonatan.
8. It seems that the author of *Sefer Hasidim* (Margaliot ed., sec. 297) was familiar only with the source in the Jerusalem Talmud: "Rabbi Simlai came before Rebbi. He said to him: Teach me *Aggada*. He said to him: I have a tradition to teach *Aggada* neither to Babylonians nor to southerners, because they are coarse-minded and know little Torah. And you are from Nehardea and you live in the south! And you are young, and we do not reveal the wondrousness of *Aggada* to young people, lest they react dismissively. And we also don't teach *Aggada* to commoners, lest they believe it, nor do we teach it to anyone who would disparage it."
9. Y. Monikondum, "Beruria as an Analogical Figure: A Foil to Rabbi Meir" [Hebrew], *Derekh Aggada* 2 (5759): 37–38, and bibliographical note 3.
10. This is the approach of Y. Efron in *Scholarship of the Hasmonean Period* [Hebrew] (Tel Aviv, 5740), 131–95, and of his successor Y. Ben Shalom.

> A door bolt: Rabbi Tarfon declares it impure, and the sages declare it pure. And Beruria says: One removes it from this door and hangs it on another on the Sabbath. When these matters were reported before Rabbi Yehuda, he said: Beruria spoke well. (Tosefta Kelim, Bava Metzia 1:6)

Beruria is depicted as a student of Rabbi Yehuda (ben Baba),[11] who compliments her for having "spoken well." This is a common way for a teacher to praise a student. For instance, Rabbi Yoḥanan ben Zakkai invokes this phrase when he hears that Ḥanan HaKohen disagreed with Rabbi Dosa ben Hyrcanus (Mishna Ketubot 13:1), and Rabbi Yehoshua speaks these words to his student Rabbi Akiva (Mishna Nazir 7:4). It seems that Rabbi Yehuda addresses Beruria as he would respond to any male student who has offered a compelling argument, suggesting that Beruria did not stand out in a world of men. If she had something to say, she would say it, and her words were well received.

HER ENCOUNTERS WITH THE SAGES

Beruria continued to deepen her Torah knowledge. She soon became a mature scholar in her own right who posed a threat to the community of sages. The Talmud offers an amusing account of how Beruria used to supervise the Torah scholars to ensure that they studied properly:

> Beruria saw a student who was reciting in a whisper. She kicked him and said to him: Does it not say, "Ordered in full and safeguarded" [II Sam. 23:5]? If Torah is ordered in all 248 of your limbs, it will be safeguarded; and if not, it will not be safeguarded. (Eiruvin 53b)

11. This source is clearly referring to Rabbi Yehuda ben Baba and not to Rabbi Yehuda bar Ilai, who was Beruria's contemporary. Rabbi Yehuda ben Baba, a member of the previous generation, speaks these words about the daughter of Rabbi Ḥanina ben Teradion in Tosefta Kelim, Bava Kamma 4:17. For the full quote, see *Sages* II, Part Four.

Beruria is depicted as an impatient Talmud scholar who resembles a typical member of a (Babylonian) beit midrash.[12] She has full command of the Bible, which she teaches to other students by means of brute force. The Talmud describes a conversation between Beruria and one of the sages, although it is not a matter of Torah that they are discussing:

> Rabbi Yose HaGlili was walking down a road when he met Beruria. He asked her: Which is the road we take to Lod?
>
> She said to him: Foolish Galilean, did not the sages say: Don't indulge in excessive conversation with a woman? You should have said: Which to Lod? (Eiruvin 53b)

Much scholarly ink has been spilled about this exchange. Perhaps most compelling is the claim that Beruria is upset with Rabbi Yose HaGlili for speaking to her about mundane matters rather than words of Torah.[13] She regards herself as a fitting interlocutor for the sages, so she reacts angrily when Rabbi Yose is interested only in asking her for directions. She tells him that if he regards her merely as a woman (and not as a sage), he should heed the rabbinic dictum not to engage in excessive conversation with a woman, and should ask his question in two words rather than four. With this encounter, Beruria begins to be perceived as a woman, not just as another one of the young students.[14] The scholars in the beit midrash do not know how to deal with her. She can no longer study with them lest the sages be tempted by her, because "it is forbidden to uncover the nakedness of an engaged young woman."[15]

Beruria continues to study Torah, but at home.

12. Y. Ben Shalom, "And I Took Two Staffs, One of Which I Named Favor and the Other Unity" [Hebrew], in *Generation to Generation: A Collection of Studies in Honor of Yehoshua Efron*, ed. A. Oppenheimer and A. Kasher (Jerusalem, 5755), 235–50.
13. Y. Henkin, *Responsa Benei Banim*, vol. 4, 104.
14. Hyman states that the encounter between Beruria and Rabbi Yose HaGlili takes place "while she is still a young woman" (*Legends*, 294). I would instead say that it takes place when she is *already* a young woman, since she now begins to experience the conflict between her identities as a woman and as a Torah scholar.
15. R. Leibel, "The Beruria Incident" [Hebrew], *Granot* 2 (5762): 135–43. Leibel explores this insight thoroughly. Her treatment is fictional, but she offers a legitimate reading of the sages' ambivalence toward Beruria.

BERURIA AND RABBI MEIR

We do not have many talmudic sources regarding the relationship between husbands and wives. But we are privy to a few conversations between Beruria and Rabbi Meir:

> A heretic in Rabbi Meir's neighborhood used to distress him using biblical verses. Rabbi Meir prayed to God that the heretic should die.
>
> Beruria said to him: How can you wish he should die? Is it because it is written, "Let sins (*ḥataim*) desist from the earth" [Ps. 104:35]? Does it say "sinners" (*ḥotim*)? It says "sins" (*ḥataim*)! Furthermore, look at the end of the verse, "and let evildoers be no more" – since sin will desist, evildoers will be no more. You should pray that he repent.
>
> Rabbi Meir prayed for him, and he repented. (Midrash on Ps. 104)

The verse that Beruria cites literally means that sinners will desist from the earth. As she notes, the word for sinners, *ḥataim,* can be mistaken for the similar word "sins" (*ḥotim*). But given that the verse has a parallel structure ("Let *ḥataim* desist from the earth, and let evildoers be no more"), *ḥataim* must mean "sinners" in this context.[16] Yet Beruria offers a creative alternative reading of both halves of the verse: *Ḥataim* refers to sins, which will desist from the earth when sinners repent. At that point, as the second half of the verse teaches, there will be no more sinners, because they all will have repented.[17]

In this source Rabbi Meir is portrayed not as his wife's intellectual equal, but as her student. Whereas she knows how to offer a brilliant exegetical reading, he is a scribe caught up in the literal meaning of the biblical words. Rabbi Meir, generally depicted as a precise, literal reader who contains all of Torah within him, is treated like a young disciple with

16. Beruria changes the vocalization of the word to turn sinners (*ḥotim*) into sins (*ḥataim*). Her exegesis is even harsher than the literal meaning of the verse.
17. A parallel exegesis can be found in Berakhot 10b, where the evildoers are bad neighbors rather than heretics.

much still to learn. Interestingly, Beruria's attitude toward her husband is identical to Aḥer's attitude toward him in all their exchanges. Beruria, like Aḥer, poses an intellectual challenge to Rabbi Meir.

Consider the gender dynamics of this story. In Greek culture, woman is regarded as impetuous and chiding, whereas man is her even-keeled counterpart, seeing the big picture and cooling his wife's temper. For instance, Plato writes, "When it comes to all the injustice that needs to be corrected, we must understand first and foremost that no evildoer is willfully evil... and so you must stop and cool your wrath, and not berate the evildoer excessively, as women are wont."[18] In the story of Beruria and Rabbi Meir, these dynamics are reversed. Rabbi Meir is consumed by his own suffering and wishes to rid himself of it in the simplest manner possible – by eradicating the one who is responsible. Thus, somewhat impetuously, he prays for the heretic to die.[19] Beruria keeps her cool and teaches her husband that there is another way of alleviating his distress while also benefiting the world at large. By the end of the story, Rabbi Meir has learned from his wife to pray for the heretic to live.

Generations later, Rabbi Naḥman of Breslov offered an exegesis very similar to Beruria's:

> Know that every person must be judged favorably, even someone thoroughly wicked. You must seek out the good in him, for in that little bit of goodness he is not evil. When you find the good in him and judge him favorably, you effectively make him into a good person and can lead him to repentance. And this is the meaning of the verse "A little longer and there will be no evildoer; you will look at where he was, and he will be gone" [Ps. 37:10].... You must seek out the little bit of good in him, that place where he is not wicked.... And by means of finding that part of him which is not wicked, and judging him favorably, you truly elevate him so that his merits outweigh his faults, until he repents.... And

18. Plato, *Laws*, 731:3–4. Quoted in Monikondum, "Beruria as an Analogical Figure," 43.
19. In the parallel version in Berakhot, too, Rabbi Meir prays for the death of those who are distressing him.

this is what it means to "look at where he was" and find that "he will be gone." (*Likkutei Moharan* 282)

BERURIA'S BRILLIANCE AS A TORAH SCHOLAR

A certain heretic once said to Beruria: It is written: "Sing out, O barren one who has not given birth" [Is. 54:1]. But should she sing because she has not given birth?

Beruria said to him: Fool! Look to the end of the verse, where it is written: "For the children of the desolate one are more numerous than the children of the inhabited one, said the Lord." What, then, is meant by the phrase "O barren one who has not given birth"? It means, let the congregation of Israel sing out, for Israel is like a barren woman in that she has not given birth to children destined for hell, as you have. (Berakhot 10a)

This story appears in the Talmud just prior to the conversation between Beruria and Rabbi Meir about wicked neighbors. Apparently one of the heretics who used to distress Rabbi Meir using biblical verses also caused trouble for Beruria.[20] As this story suggests, the heretics sought to undermine their Jewish neighbors by dismissing them as "carnal Israel." The sages had to defend their claim to the Bible and their right to interpret it against the rising Christian tide.[21] Here too, Beruria demonstrates her exegetical aptitude. Once again she insists that her interlocutor consider the verse in its entirety. The happiness of the barren woman is all relative: "the children of the desolate one are more numerous than the

20. One of the talmudic stories speaks of neighbors rather than heretics, but in the parallel text in the Midrash on Psalms, infidels are responsible. Babylonian culture was no longer familiar with troublesome heretics, and thus the Babylonian Talmud transformed the heretical neighbor into an ordinary thug.

21. Against this backdrop, we can understand the wonderful story of Rabbi Safra's arrival in the Land of Israel and his failure to pass the tax-exemption test that is posed to him by the Babylonian authorities (see Avoda Zara 4a). The test comprised a series of questions about biblical verses, which Rabbi Safra could not answer. The authorities nearly charged him with tax evasion, until the sages of the Land of Israel came and explained to the clerks that "we who live among you apply ourselves to the study of Torah; they [the Babylonians] are not interested."

children of the inhabited one." She compares Israel to a woman who is happy despite her barrenness, since at least she is not raising children destined for hell.

Here too, Beruria is depicted as a brilliant, quick-witted sage who has mastered the subtleties of the biblical text and excels in its exegesis. Like her husband, the heretics learn from her.

THE LORD HAS GIVEN, AND THE LORD HAS TAKEN AWAY: THE LOSS OF THE SONS

> It is told of Rabbi Meir that while he was sitting and expounding in the beit midrash on Shabbat, his two sons died. What did their mother do? She left them both lying on their bed and spread a sheet over them.
>
> At the close of Shabbat, Rabbi Meir came home from the beit midrash and asked her: Where are my two sons?
>
> She said: They went to the beit midrash.
>
> He said: I looked for them in the beit midrash but did not see them.
>
> She handed him the cup of wine for Havdala, and he ended Shabbat. Then he asked her again: Where are my two sons?
>
> She said: Sometimes they go someplace. They will be back presently. She served him his meal and he ate. After he recited the Grace after Meals she said to him: Master, I have a question to ask you.
>
> He replied: Ask your question.
>
> She said: Master, some time ago a certain man came by and deposited something with me. Now he has come to reclaim this deposit. Should I return it to him or not?
>
> He said: My daughter, is not one who holds a deposit obligated to return it to its owner?
>
> She said: If not for your opinion on the matter, I would not give it back to him.
>
> What did she do then? She took him by the hand, led him up to the children's room, brought him to the bed, and removed the sheet, so that Rabbi Meir saw them both lying dead on the

> bed. He burst into tears, saying: My sons, my sons! My masters, my masters! My sons biologically, and my masters who enlightened me with their Torah learning.
>
> At this point Rabbi Meir's wife said to him: Master, did you not just now tell me that we must return a pledge to its owner?
>
> He said: "The Lord has given, and the Lord has taken away; blessed be the name of the Lord" [Job 1:21].
>
> Rabbi Ḥanina said: In this manner, she comforted him and brought him solace, and hence it is said: "A woman of valor, who can find?" [Prov. 31:10]. (Midrash on Prov. 31)

This is a difficult story that speaks to Beruria's extraordinary self-control. She is the protagonist, while Rabbi Meir assumes a secondary role. It is she who guides the conversation when he is looking for his sons. Eventually she leads him into their bedroom, where she occupies a position of strength and he of weakness.[22] She speaks to her husband like a student addressing a teacher, though in actuality these roles are reversed. It is she who teaches Rabbi Meir a lesson: that a parent may be responsible for a child only until the "Owner of the deposit" returns to claim what is rightfully His.

Though Beruria is depicted as a mother in the story's opening lines, she addresses Rabbi Meir as a sage and speaks to him of matters of Torah. And he, at first depicted only as a sage, is shaken terribly as a father by the story's conclusion. In contrast to our understanding of these characters at the beginning of this chapter, here Beruria is depicted as ensconced in words of Torah, whereas Rabbi Meir is caught up in matters of the heart. Her metaphor for death went on to become a dominant motif in Jewish words of comfort and condolence.

BERURIA'S SISTER: "GOD OF MEIR, ANSWER ME"

In another talmudic story about this couple, Beruria sends Rabbi Meir to liberate her sister from the brothel in which she was imprisoned:

22. S. Faust, "The Death of Rabbi Meir's Sons" [Hebrew], *Makor Rishon*, 5 Nisan 5766.

> Beruria, the wife of Rabbi Meir, was another daughter of Rabbi Ḥanina ben Teradion. She said to her husband: It is a disgrace to me that my sister dwells in a brothel.
>
> Rabbi Meir took a measure of gold dinars and went to the brothel. Along the way he said: If a forbidden act has not been performed with her, then a miracle will be performed for her. But if she has performed a forbidden act, a miracle will not be performed for her.
>
> Rabbi Meir went and disguised himself as one of the Roman horsemen. He said [to his sister-in-law]: Submit to me.
>
> She said to him: The way of women is upon me.
>
> He said to her: I shall wait for you.
>
> She said to him: But many girls here are more beautiful than I am!
>
> Rabbi Meir said to himself: Conclude from this that she has not performed any forbidden act, and that she responds in this manner to all the men who come here. (Avoda Zara 18a)

Elsewhere in the Talmud we learn the background to this story. Beruria's family was sentenced to execution because her father, Rabbi Ḥanina ben Teradion, remained openly committed to Torah study during the decrees of persecution. Rabbi Ḥanina was burned at the stake, his wife was slain, and his daughter was consigned to a brothel, all in accordance with Roman judiciary protocol.[23] Presumably Beruria herself was spared because she was regarded as a member of her husband's family rather than her father's.

As with every story featuring Beruria and Rabbi Meir, she is the dominant player, whereas he is more passive. Only when she is not around does he emerge as an independent agent. In this story, Beruria sends her husband to liberate her sister from the brothel, because she cannot bear the disgrace of her sister's predicament. At this point, she leaves the scene and is replaced by Rabbi Meir, who takes on a more active role in her absence. He asserts that his rescue of Beruria's sister is

23. See *Sages* II, Part Five, note 15, where I quote Lieberman, who shows that these punishments accorded with Roman judiciary practices.

conditional upon her behavior: If she has not sinned, she will be saved. He enters the brothel anonymously, and concludes from his conversation with his sister-in-law that she deserves a miraculous rescue.

> Rabbi Meir went to his sister-in-law's guard and said to him: Give her to me!
>
> He said to him: I am afraid of the government.
>
> He said to the guard: Take this measure of dinars, and distribute half to the Roman authorities, and the other half shall be yours.
>
> The guard said to him: But when the dinars are exhausted, what shall I do?
>
> Rabbi Meir said: Say, "God of Meir, answer me," and you will be saved. (Avoda Zara 18a)

Once the coins are all spent, a miracle will take place. The guard will be protected by the magic words "God of Meir, answer me," which will guarantee him immunity. But why do these words have such power?

We cannot but notice that this story begins rather formulaically: A Jew sets out to bribe a non-Jewish guard. But then it takes a surprising turn when Rabbi Meir introduces God into the conversation. So long as he is preoccupied with mundane affairs – neighbors, heretics, brothel guards – he is not sure how to conduct himself, and tends to respond passively. But when he is freed from matters of this world, he is able to reach great spiritual heights. The magic words he shares with the prison guard will serve as a charm for all who merit his blessing.[24]

24. In 1991, Professor Y. Sheintuch of the Department of Yiddish Language and Literature at the Hebrew University published an article in which he showed that author Y. Dinur began each of his compositions with an acronym for Rabbi Meir's magic words. Dinur, who was known as Ka-Tzetnik, used this charm in the concentration camps and refused to reveal to anyone what it meant: "Who would have believed that these four letters would keep me alive in Auschwitz for two years?" (T. Segev, "The Trip of Ka-Tzetnik" [Hebrew], *Koteret Rashit*, 28 Iyar 5747, 18).

Chapter Ten

The Torah of Rabbi Meir: Light from Darkness

We have witnessed the force of Rabbi Meir's unique personality. Both Elisha ben Abuya and Beruria knew how to relate to him. But his encounters with more ordinary individuals occasionally proved disastrous, as the following three stories demonstrate:

1. SEDUCED BY SATAN

> Rabbi Meir used to scoff at sinners. One day Satan appeared to Rabbi Meir disguised as a woman on the far side of the river. There was no ferryboat, so he grasped onto a rope and proceeded to cross. When he reached the middle of the rope, Satan released him from his grip. Satan said to Rabbi Meir: Had they not proclaimed in heaven: "Be cautious of Rabbi Meir and his Torah learning," I would have made your life worth just two *me'ah* coins! (Kiddushin 81a)

The term "sinners" commonly refers to the sexually licentious. For Rabbi Meir, a man of Torah, it is inconceivable that anyone would want to preoccupy himself with lowly matters of the flesh when he could engage in lofty matters of the spirit. Thus he scoffs at sinners. Satan seizes the opportunity to try to seduce him in the guise of a woman standing on the opposite side of the river. Rabbi Meir falls right into his trap, making no attempt to look before he leaps. With no ferry to bring him to the object of his desire, he engages in a feat of athletic prowess to reach her. The story concludes with Satan's asserting that if not for divine intervention, he would have humiliated Meir by leading him to sin.

This tale serves as a prelude to the Talmud's most disturbing story about Rabbi Meir.

2. THE BERURIA INCIDENT

After the story of Rabbi Meir's magic words, the Talmud offers two accounts of what happened next. According to one, described at length, the Roman authorities cracked the code of the magic words, and Rabbi Meir became a wanted man in the Roman Empire. Exiled from his home, he found shelter in a brothel (once again). Some say Elijah the Prophet then disguised himself as a prostitute and embraced him. Rabbi Meir survived this trial but decided to flee to Babylonia, where he would be outside Roman jurisdiction. This is one ending to the story. But the Talmud offers an alternative account, according to which Rabbi Meir fled because of "the Beruria incident." Rashi elaborates where the Talmud does not:

> *The Beruria Incident* – She once disparaged the sages' dictum that the minds of women are easily swayed. Rabbi Meir warned her: By your life, ultimately you will acknowledge the truth of their words! He ordered one of his disciples to test her fidelity, and after many days of resisting his overtures, she finally consented. When the matter became known to her, she hanged herself, and Rabbi Meir fled the Land of Israel out of shame.

This is a very difficult and painful story. How could Rabbi Meir, so ensconced in Torah, deliberately lead his wife into sin? How could he drive her to such a terrible death?

Coming to Terms with the Beruria Incident

There have been many attempts to make sense of this terrible story. Some readers have insisted on the danger of granting women entry into the world of Torah, which should be the exclusive province of men. Rabbi Aharon Hyman concludes his chapter on Beruria as follows: "And thus Rabbi Meir demonstrated the wisdom behind the sages' dictum in Sota 20a that 'Anyone who teaches his daughter Torah teaches her licentiousness.'"[1] Rabbi Yehuda Henkin, who argues that the Beruria incident could not possibly have occurred as Rashi describes it, nonetheless concludes that Beruria, the lone and lonely woman Torah scholar, permitted one of her husband's students to seduce her from time to time.[2] The Ḥida (Rabbi Ḥayyim Joseph David Azulai, 1724–1806) uses this story as the basis for an elaborate homily about why it is better to rule like Rabbi Eliezer that "Anyone who teaches his daughter Torah teaches her licentiousness" than to rule like the three hundred rabbis who taught Beruria Torah:

> In the beginning they reasoned that the halakha does not follow Rabbi Eliezer, and they would teach the Oral Torah to girls, a consequence of which was Beruria. But after what happened to Beruria, the sages agreed in the first chapter of Avoda Zara that the halakha follows Rabbi Eliezer. (*Responsa Tov Ayin*, 4)

The Ḥida's reading is remarkable. True, he argues during the time of the halakhic dispute about teaching Torah to girls, the halakha did not follow Rabbi Eliezer. But after the Beruria incident, the sages removed women from the world of Torah learning on the grounds that it was impossible to disassociate their sexuality from their intellectual life. The Ḥida does not say anything about Rabbi Meir's role in this dreadful story. Daniel Boyarin, following in the footsteps of the Ḥida, argues that "Beruria's

1. Hyman, *Legends*, 295.
2. Henkin, *Benei Banim*, vol. 4, 104–5 note 4: "This story contains a kernel of truth in that Beruria had no one to speak with in matters of Torah, since other women of her day were not learned. Thus she was all too pleased for one of the young students to pay her a visit from time to time."

story is generated...out of the matrix of the Babylonian understanding of Rabbi Eliezer – namely, that there is an essential nexus between a woman studying Torah and the breakdown of the structure of monogamy...a demonstration that there is an intrinsic and necessary connection between a scholarly woman and uncontrolled sexuality."[3] Rachel Adler also interprets the Beruria incident as a way for men to come to terms with the fact that a woman could also be a Torah scholar.[4]

At the end of the nineteenth century Rabbi Yosef Ḥayyim, the Ben Ish Ḥai, offered an impressive apologetic reading:

> This student was not a sexual being, and he had no sexual desire, though she did not know this – because one can be asexual without its being externally apparent. He seduced her into permitting him to come to her home when she was bathing, and to bathe with her – not for the sake of engaging in sin, but because he convinced her that he needed to bathe with a married woman as a sort of talisman. And she fell for it. When she came in to bathe, he followed her. He disrobed and stood naked before her, even before seeing her flesh. When she saw he was castrated, she said to him: What is this about? And he told her what had happened – that his master had instructed him to try to seduce her on account of what she had said about the sages. Then he dressed and left. And although she had not in fact committed any sin, heaven forbid, but had only gone so far as to grant him permission to bathe with her, she was embarrassed to show her face to her husband, Rabbi Meir. Her shame drove her mad, and she hanged herself. She was not regarded as one who committed suicide willfully, because she was not of sound mind when she did so. Her husband fled to Babylonia in an act of self-imposed

3. Boyarin, *Carnal Israel*, 191.
4. Rachel Adler, "The Virgin in the Brothel and Other Anomalies: Character and Context in the Legend of Beruria," *Tikkun* 3 (1988). Boyarin had Adler's article before him, and their approaches are similar.

> exile to atone for what he had done to her. (Rabbi Yosef Haim, *Ben Yehoyada*, Avoda Zara 18)[5]

The Ben Ish Ḥai judges Beruria favorably, arguing that she committed suicide not because she had sinned, but because she drove herself insane. When it comes to Rabbi Meir's behavior, the Ben Ish Hai refers merely to "what he had done to her," sparing this sage from censure. The attempt to lure another person into sexual sin is generally regarded as the work of Satan, as we saw in an earlier story about Rabbi Meir.[6] Yet it seems that Rabbi Meir was so well regarded by the rabbis that they could not subject him to more critical appraisal. So they smoothed over what he had done by invoking phrases such as "Rabbi Meir, who cared more for the words of the sages than for his own body and soul and for the bodies and souls of the members of his household, asked one of his loyal students to try to lead his wife into sin."[7] The criticism in this statement is implicit, if subtle: Rabbi Meir cared more for the teachings of the sages than for the lives of his family.

In an article summarizing much of the scholarly literature about Beruria, Brenda Bacon offers an entirely different reading. Instead of Rashi's explanation of "the Beruria incident," she cites a story from a composition by Rabbeinu Nissim ben Yaakov, the head of the academy in Kirouan in the tenth century. The work was written in Arabic, and we can assume that it was not known to Rashi. According to Rabbeinu Nissim, the talmudic passage concludes as follows:

> Rabbi Meir went and took his wife and all his possessions and went to live in Iraq.[8]

5. Bakun, "How Do We Tell the Story?" 126 note 4.
6. A similar story is told of Rabbi Mattia ben Ḥeresh, whom Satan tried to lead into sexual sin. See *Yalkut Shimoni* I:161.
7. Hyman, *Legends*, 295.
8. Rabbeinu Nissim ben Yaakov, *Ḥibbur Yafeh Min HaYeshua* [Arabic] (Jerusalem, 5630), 30. This work was written to inspire the Jewish community of the time by presenting talmudic tales of hope and salvation. Rabbeinu Nissim tells the story of the rescue of Beruria's sister from the brothel and the tale of Rabbi Meir's exile, but he makes no mention of Rashi's reading of the Beruria incident.

This is a much happier ending. The family stays together, escaping to safer shores. Bacon concludes her article on this positive note: "It seems to me that in our generation, we should tell Rabbeinu Nissim's version of the Beruria story. It more befits Beruria's character, and it appears to be based on an ancient tradition known to the Babylonian Geonim."

Interpreting the Story of Rabbi Meir and Beruria

In light of my analysis of the sources, Bacon's words seem unconvincing. Rabbeinu Nissim's conclusion does not seem to fit the personalities of these characters, given their tense relationships and their attempts to drive themselves beyond what is humanly possible.

Whereas the Beruria incident appears only in Rashi's marginalia, the story of Rabbi Meir and Satan is documented in the Talmud. But the similarities between the two seduction stories necessitate a conjoined reading.[9] Rabbi Meir, like his wife, nearly succumbed to sexual temptation. He scoffed at sinners, thinking himself immune to sin; but Satan showed him that he, too, was only human. If not for divine intervention, Rabbi Meir would have fallen hard.

Unlike Rabbi Meir, Beruria prevents herself from sinning. She resists the student's overtures for "many days," and even when she consents, she does not know she is sinning. Only afterward does the matter become "known to her." So she sins unknowingly, in contrast to Rabbi Meir. Moreover, it is Rabbi Meir who plays the role of Satan in the Beruria incident. Unlike her husband, who was saved by divine intervention, Beruria has no one to save her. She takes responsibility for her own actions and kills herself. Even if suicide is not considered a legitimate recourse in Jewish tradition, we cannot help but see an element of heroism in Beruria's reaction. Certainly she is in good company. We have several stories of talmudic heroes who committed suicide in response to their circumstances: the launderer who killed himself after the death of Rabbi Yehuda HaNasi, Ketiya bar Shalom, the man who executed Rabbi Ḥanina ben Teradion, Elazar ben Dordaya, and Yakim

9. Monikondum, "Beruria as an Analogical Figure," 57–59. Throughout her article, Monikondum emphasizes the tension between Beruria and Rabbi Meir. I was strongly influenced by her reading.

Ish Tzerurot.[10] In contrast, Rabbi Meir flees on account of his shame. Is fleeing in shame regarded by the sages as an appropriate response? Would not true repentance entail owning up to one's sin and declaring, like Cain, that it is too great to bear?

Both Beruria and Rabbi Meir fell into sin. Both were put on trial, she by her husband and he by Satan. These stories, rather than casting shadows on Beruria, serve to warn us about Rabbi Meir's terrible radiance.

Shmuel Moldar, a nineteenth century Dutch Jew, wrote a eulogy for Beruria, excerpted here:[11]

> Woe to the woman of valor! Woe to you, O learned one
> How was your wisdom confounded?
> Ah! You will wither like a leaf.
>
> Would that the heavenly hosts would pardon me
> My soul was lifted from its fetters
> But the sound of its motions sings praise.
>
> God is good to all. Why should the spirit
> Of human beings quarrel forever?
> God's mercy will rest also on me.

3. RABBI MEIR'S FALL: THE CENSORED VERSION

Rabbi Meir also figures in the Jewish folk tradition, where we find a story about another woman who succumbed to sin much like Beruria. This story did not find its way into the canon of rabbinic literature but

10. See S. Safrai, "The Relationship Between Halakha and Aggada," in *From Generation to Generation: From the End of the Biblical Period Until the Closure of the Talmud* [Hebrew] (Jerusalem, 5755), 228–29. Safrai writes of various suicides that are regarded favorably in the Talmud, despite the halakhic prohibition of taking one's life. He does not mention the Beruria incident, since it appears only in Rashi's commentary.

11. Excerpted from Shmuel Moldar's poem "Beruria the Daughter of Rabbi Ḥanina ben Teradion." The poem was published in the 1850s, then republished with an introduction and notes by Y. Friedlander: "Beruria the Daughter of Rabbi Ḥanina ben Teradion," in *New Studies on Dutch Jewry* [Hebrew] (Jerusalem, 5741), 125–63.

nonetheless survived for hundreds of years. We will quote this story in full in order to complete the picture:[12]

> There was once a sage by the name of Rabbi Meir who would travel to Jerusalem each year on the festival. He took lodgings with Rabbi Yehuda the butcher. Rabbi Yehuda's wife was beautiful and very modest, and she faithfully guarded Rabbi Meir's honor whenever he would ascend to Jerusalem.
>
> A few years went by and Rabbi Yehuda's wife died. Rabbi Yehuda married another woman. Yehuda instructed his new wife: If another sage named Rabbi Meir seeks lodgings here, be mindful of his honor when you provide him with food, drink, and a place to sleep – for this is what my first wife would do for him.
>
> When the time came for the festival, Rabbi Meir went to Jerusalem as usual and stood in the entryway of Rabbi Yehuda's inn. Rabbi Yehuda's wife came down to greet him, but he did not recognize her. He said to her: Smile, call for the wife of my friend Rabbi Yehuda.
>
> She said to him: Master, I am the wife of Rabbi Yehuda, for his first wife passed away and he married me.
>
> Rabbi Meir began to cry and wished to turn around. The woman took hold of him and said: Come, my master, for my husband instructed me that when you come here, I must treat you very well and be mindful of your honor, and offer you food and drink and a place to sleep. I will do as my husband charged me, and I will honor you even more than his first wife.
>
> Rabbi Meir said to her: I am not permitted to enter here when the master of the house is not present until he gives me permission.
>
> Rabbi Meir went outside and immediately bumped into Rabbi Yehuda, who said to him: My master Rabbi Meir, my first

12. A. Shinar, "Rabbi Meir's Learning as Presented in Aggadic Literature" [Hebrew], in *Research in Judaic Studies* (Haifa, 5736), 259–66. Shinar cites the entire story and analyzes it as a work of folklore.

wife has died and this is my second wife. I warned her to be mindful of your honor, my master Rabbi Meir.

Rabbi Meir then went to Yehuda's home, where Yehuda's wife prepared food and drink for him and treated him very well. Rabbi Yehuda went to his place in the market as usual.

Rabbi Meir was very good-looking. What did Rabbi Yehuda's wife do? She cast her eyes upon Meir and her heart desired him. That night she served him wine until he could not tell his right hand from his left. That night was Purim eve, and when she saw that he was drunk, she took off all his clothes and slept with him until the morning. Rabbi Meir was not aware of any of this.

In the morning he went to the synagogue. When he returned, she served him food and drink and spoke with him and entertained him. Rabbi Meir was rather surprised at how comfortable she seemed, and at the liberties she took. He lowered his eyes because he did not want to look at her.

She said to him: Why aren't you looking at me?

He said to her: Because you are another man's wife, and I would be sinning against my friend Yehuda.

She said to him: But didn't you sleep with me last night?

He said to her: Heaven forbid! I have not seen you or slept with you or with anyone who looks like you in my entire life.

She said: You slept with me all night, and now you pretend you are more modest than I?

He said to her: By your life, you are speaking lies!

She said to him: If you don't believe me, I will tell you about your birthmarks. She had seen a red mark on his right shoulder, and a scab in his nostril.

When he heard this, Rabbi Meir realized he had sinned. He felt deeply embittered, and he cried out and put ashes on his head and said: Woe that I have lost my world! This is the reward for all the Torah I have learned? Now how can I ever fix matters? He decided to go to the great yeshiva in Babylon and subject himself to whatever they decreed. He returned home crying out and weeping the whole way, and he tore his clothes and put ashes on his head.

He ran into a non-Jewish neighbor who said to him: Rabbi Meir, what happened to you?

He said to him: I must ask that you please go to my town and tell my family that robbers came upon me and seized all my possessions.

The neighbor went and did as Rabbi Meir had bid. Immediately his family members rushed out to Rabbi Meir, and he told them what had happened to him. They said to him: What do you intend to do? He said to them: I will go to the head of the academy in Babylon, and I will do whatever they demand of me.

His family members said to him: You acted unwittingly. God will forgive your sin, but do not make it public, because you will cast aspersions on our family.

He said to them: If I were to listen to you, God would not forgive me.

What did Rabbi Meir do? He went to the head of the academy and told him what had happened. He said to him: I came before you so that I might take upon myself whatever you decree.

The head of the academy said to him: I will inquire as to your punishment and tomorrow I will tell you what to do. The next day Rabbi Meir came back to the head of the academy, who said to him: I have inquired into your punishment, and I see that you deserve to be devoured by a lion.

He said to him: I will accept this as a heavenly decree, and he authorized the head of the academy to proceed accordingly.

The head of the academy called two strong men and told them to take Rabbi Meir to the lion's den and bind his hands and legs and cast him there. He told the men to hide there in one of the trees and observe what the lions did. If the lions killed Rabbi Meir, the men were to bring his bones to the head of the academy, who would then lionize him for accepting the heavenly decree.

The men took Rabbi Meir and did as the head of the academy had commanded.

In the middle of the night a lion approached Rabbi Meir, roared at his side, and then left him there and went off on his way, leaving Rabbi Meir unscathed.

> The next day the men related this matter to the head of the academy, who said to them: Do this again for a second night.
>
> In the middle of the night a lion approached Rabbi Meir, sniffed him, turned him over, and then left him there unscathed.
>
> The next day the men returned to the head of the academy and told him what had happened. He said to them: Do this one more night, and if the lions once again don't harm him, then he is a truly righteous man undeserving of divine punishment, and you should bring him before me.
>
> In the middle of the night a lion came, roared and growled by his side, knocked him with his teeth and extracted one of his ribs, and ate an olive-size portion of his flesh.
>
> The next day they went and relayed the matter to the head of the academy, who said to them: Bring him before me. Since the lion ate an olive-size portion, it is as if he devoured him entirely.
>
> The men went and brought Rabbi Meir before him, and the head of the academy instructed the doctors to heal him. Rabbi Meir asked forgiveness of the head of the academy, who said to him: Happy are you, Rabbi Meir, for you are a truly righteous person.
>
> When Rabbi Meir returned home, a heavenly voice came forth and said: Rabbi Meir merits life in the World to Come.

This is a typical folktale: It is anachronistic, and it combines supernatural elements such as lions with the power to reveal the divine will.[13] According to the story, Rabbi Meir is not a truly righteous person because in fact he sinned, and thus the lions nibble at his flesh. According to another version of the tale in *Ḥibbur Yafeh Min HaYeshua,* the heavenly voice says to Rabbi Meir, "Do not fear, Rabbi Meir, because no sin has befallen you. That evil woman deceived you. Do not worry, for your reward will be very great."[14] This statement is more characteristic of folktales, which generally end on a positive note.

13. Ibid., 263 note 15. Shinar demonstrates that this motif is universal in folkloric literature.
14. Rabbeinu Nissim ben Yaakov, *Ḥibbur Yafeh Min HaYeshua* [Arabic] (Jerusalem, 5630): 28. Quoted in Shinar, "Rabbi Meir's Learning," 265.

Over the course of many centuries, the stories of Beruria and Rabbi Meir unfolded in parallel. Yet the sages of Israel ensured that the version about Rabbi Meir's fall was forgotten, and only Beruria's story was preserved in the Talmud's pages.

RABBI MEIR IN EXILE: REBELLION AGAINST THE AUTHORITY OF THE PATRIARCH

According to several rabbinic sources, Rabbi Meir left the Land of Israel. The Babylonian Talmud narrates that he was exiled to Babylon. Another textual variant relates that he reached "Asia," which is interpreted as Ezion-gaver, known today as Eilat.[15]

Rabbi Shimon ben Elazar, a student of Rabbi Meir, attests that his teacher went "to intercalate the new year in Asia" (Tosefta Megilla 2:8). Intercalating the year was the province of only the most senior of the sages.[16] For instance, when Rabban Shimon ben Gamliel heard that Ḥanania (also referred to as Ḥanina in the talmudic text), a nephew of Rabbi Yehoshua, was intercalating the year in Babylon, he immediately sent messengers to instruct him to desist, since his action was regarded as an attempt to undermine the centralized authority of the patriarch in the Land of Israel.[17] Now Rabbi Meir engages in the same subversive act – he intercalates the year in Asia. The background to this incident is the story of Rabbi Meir's flight from the yeshiva in Usha, which we will discuss in the next part of this book. For now, we will consider just one source related to this affair:

> They wished to excommunicate Rabbi Meir. He said to them: I will not listen to you until you tell me who gets excommuni-

15. S. Klein identified Asia as Ezion-gaver based on classical sources. See Alon, *History of the Jews*, 320–21. And see Y. Elitzur, "The Boundaries of the Land of Israel in Jewish Tradition: Ancient Geography" [Hebrew], in *Me'inot: Studies in Education and Pedagogy*, vol. 5 (Jerusalem, 5715), note 1.
16. S. Safrai, *Time of the Temple, Time of the Mishna*, vol. 1, 247–58. Safrai discusses intercalating the year and the tension between Judea and the Galilee, but he does not reference this source from the Tosefta.
17. See Part Four, especially Chapter Fourteen.

> cated, for what reasons, and for how many offenses. (Y. Mo'ed Katan 3:1 [81c])

This description, though cryptic, makes sense in light of the Tosefta cited above. The attempt to excommunicate Rabbi Meir was clearly linked to his mission to intercalate the year.[18] Upon hearing what was happening in Asia, Rabban Shimon ben Gamliel ordered that Rabbi Meir leave the yeshiva in Usha. This extreme measure was equivalent to taking a fish out of water, or, more accurately, taking the water away from the fish. Rabbi Meir left the Land of Israel, which was heartbreaking for this sage who had said, "All who live in the Land of Israel – the Land of Israel atones for them."[19] He was banished, but he took his teachings with him.

FROM THE SEA HE CAME, AND TO THE SEA HE WILL RETURN: RABBI MEIR'S WILL

Rabbi Meir's many journeys were coming to an end. He was far from his home and from his native land, and he had neared the end of his life. Just before his death, he issued the following instructions regarding his burial:

> Rabbi Meir was dying in Asia. He said: Go tell the people of the Land of Israel: Your Messiah is coming.[20] Even so, he said

18. Z. Frankel, *Methods of the Mishna,* 290 note 1. Also see G. Libson, "For What Reasons Do We Excommunicate?" [Hebrew], *HaMishpat HaIvri Annual* 2 (5735): 309.
19. Sifrei, Deuteronomy 32. Recall that Rabbi Meir was one of those students of Rabbi Akiva who, unlike the students of Rabbi Yishmael, did not leave the Land of Israel during the persecutions following the Bar Kokhba revolt.
20. This is the version that appears in several sources from the Land of Israel and in all the manuscripts, and thus we must assume it is authoritative. Rabbi L. Ginzburg (quoted in G. Alon, "Rabbi Meir's Will" [Hebrew], in Alon, *Studies in the History of the Land of Israel During the Second Temple and the Period of the Mishnah and Talmud* [Tel Aviv: HaKibbutz HaMe'uḥad, 5717–18], vol. 1, 322–23) argues that the term translated above as "your Messiah" is grammatically incorrect in Aramaic and all other languages, so the text must be referring to *meshikhta* (your rope) rather than *meshiḥun* (your Messiah). Rabbi Meir is implying that Asia, too, is linked as if by a rope to the Land of Israel, and must be considered part of it. Ginzburg asserts that even though Rabbi Meir believed Asia would be regarded as part of the Land of Israel in messianic times, he wanted to be buried at sea, since the sea marked the

> to them: Place my bier on the seashore, as it is written: "For He has founded it upon the seas, and established it upon the rivers" [Ps. 24:2]. (Y. Kilayim 9:3 [32c])

Rabbi Meir was cast to the far south. His will instructed the inhabitants of the Land of Israel to lay him to rest on the shores of the Holy Land, lest he be buried outside it.

Gedalia Alon, following in the footsteps of Rabbi L. Ginzburg, argued that Rabbi Meir's entire will is a eulogy for the Land of Israel. The land known as Asia was not regarded as part of the Land of Israel when it came to many halakhic matters. So Rabbi Meir was heralding the Greater Israel of messianic times. As Alon explains, "Rabbi Meir did not think Asia/Eilat was impure land, but he also did not regard it as part of the Land of Israel proper. Thus he was concerned that his coffin not be placed in its soil for even an hour."[21]

However, this reading of Rabbi Meir's will does not do justice to the great sage. As we have seen, Rabbi Meir had tremendous force of personality. His stormy temperament tossed him from wave to wave until he was spat out upon dry land. He spent the majority of his life on the shores of Tiberias, and he was buried on the banks of the Red Sea. So we must assume that his final words were not about Greater Israel, but rather about his tempestuous relationship with its inhabitants.

Rabbi Meir turned to the people of the Land of Israel to fight his final battle: *You banished me because you thought the Land of Israel was the place of the Divine Presence. But I avow to you that your Messiah is present among you.* His use of the term Messiah was a derogatory reference to the patriarch who had banished him from the yeshiva,

border of the land. This is a lovely reading, but it is not grounded in the text. Alon took it even further, basing his claims on a later version found in *Yalkut Mekhiri.*

21. Alon, *History of the Jews*, vol. 1, 325. This interpretation assumes that Rabbi Meir had nothing but praise for the people of the Land of Israel. Many have commented on the agendas of scholars such as Alon, who wrote during the early years of the State of Israel. On Alon in particular, see Oppenheimer, "Gedalia Alon Fifty Years On," 468–69. In the words of A. Z. Melamed: "In one hand he held a dagger, which bore the burden of his comrades in the war of defense and conquest. In the other hand he held a pen to write his scholarship."

Rabban Shimon ben Gamliel. Rabbi Meir is telling the people that the patriarch is not his leader, but theirs.[22] We will see in the pages that follow that the term Messiah was used to refer to the patriarchy during the tenure of Rabbi Yehuda HaNasi, son of Rabban Shimon ben Gamliel. Rabbi Meir tells the inhabitants of the Land of Israel that he has nothing to do with them or with their Messiah. But neither will he cast his lot with Asia, because it is impure on account of its non-Jewish inhabitants.[23] So he is not buried in either soil. The sea that spewed him out will eventually absorb him once again.

As we have come to expect of Rabbi Meir, the light of Torah continues to illuminate his path. His will quotes a verse about God's dominion over the sea: "For He has founded it upon the seas, and established it upon the rivers." If the Land of Israel spews him out, the sea will swallow him up. So he instructs that his coffin be placed by the water.

OTHERS SAY: RABBI MEIR'S PLACE IN RABBINIC TRADITION

> At first each one would ordain his own disciples to the court. For example, Rabbi Yoḥanan ben Zakkai ordained Rabbi Eliezer and Rabbi Yehoshua; Rabbi Yehoshua ordained Rabbi Akiva; and Rabbi Akiva ordained Rabbi Meir and Rabbi Shimon. He said: Let Rabbi Meir take his seat first. Rabbi Shimon's face turned pale. Rabbi Akiva said to him: Let it be enough for you that I and your Creator recognize your strengths. (Y. Sanhedrin 1:2 [19a])

22. Z. Frankel offers a different but related interpretation. See his *Methods of the Mishna*, 164 note 7: "And perhaps we must say as follows: The fact that I have to die outside the Land of Israel is on account of your Messiah, that is, Rabban Shimon ben Gamliel, who was responsible for Rabbi Meir's departure from the land. Rabbi Meir used 'Messiah' as a derogatory term, suggesting that the patriarch thought of himself as highly as the Messiah."
23. Interestingly, according to rabbinic tradition, the patriarchy had a representative in Asia, as we learn from Rabban Shimon ben Gamliel's statement during the destruction of Beitar: "The only ones who remain here are I, and the son of my brother in Asia" (Sota 49b). The author of *Seder HaTanna'im veHaAmora'im* (pp. 60–61) also writes of a member of the patriarchal family who was born in Asia at the beginning of the third century.

Rabbi Akiva ordained Rabbi Meir in his youth, but then the rabbinic order was thrown into disarray by the persecutions that followed the Bar Kokhba revolt. When the sages convened at Usha after the persecutions, they conferred the title of sage upon Rabbi Meir. He was held in great esteem in the Galilee, which became a source of tension when Rabban Shimon ben Gamliel came on the scene. The rivalry between the two sages led to Rabbi Meir's banishment from the beit midrash and then from the Land of Israel. The other sages tried but failed to reconcile the two. Rabbi Meir apologized, but Rabban Shimon ben Gamliel would not capitulate. In his role as patriarch, he sealed Rabbi Meir's fate by removing him from the world of Torah learning.

Years later, Rabban Shimon ben Gamliel conceded that Rabbi Meir's teachings could be cited in the beit midrash, but not in his name. Anyone who wanted to quote Rabbi Meir would have to do so by invoking the phrase "others say." And thus his teachings link Rabbi Meir back to his own teacher – he is known as "others say" and his teacher is known as "Aḥer," the other.

Sumakhus

> The rabbis taught: After the death of Rabbi Meir, Rabbi Yehuda said to his students: Rabbi Meir's students are not to enter here, because they are provokers, and they come not to learn Torah, but rather to cut me down in the discussion of law.
>
> Sumakhus forced his way in. He said to them: This is how Rabbi Meir taught me the mishna: If one betroths a woman with his portion of an offering, whether an offering of greater or lesser holiness, he has not betrothed her.
>
> Rabbi Yehuda grew angry at his students. He said to them: Did I not say to you: Rabbi Meir's students are not to enter here, because they are provokers, and they come not to learn Torah, but rather to cut me down in the discussion of law? How can a woman come into the Temple's inner courtyard [where offerings of greater holiness are eaten, and accept a portion for her betrothal]?

> Rabbi Yose said: Shall they say: Meir died, Yehuda became angry, and Yose remained silent? What will become of the words of Torah? Is it not possible for a person to accept betrothal for his daughter in the Temple courtyard? And is it not possible for a woman to authorize an agent to accept betrothal on her behalf in the Temple courtyard? And furthermore, what if a woman forced her way into the Temple's inner courtyard? (Kiddushin 52b)

Sumakhus is but one of Rabbi Meir's many orphaned disciples throughout the Land of Israel. The sages of Usha disagree as to whether they should be allowed back into the rabbinic conversation. Rabbi Yehuda bar Ilai is convinced that Rabbi Meir's disciples have no place in Usha. But Sumakhus, famous for transmitting Rabbi Meir's teachings, forces his way in nonetheless.[24]

We can learn about Sumakhus' worldview and about his relationship to his teacher Rabbi Meir from the few teachings attributed to him in the Talmud:

1. The law of half damages: Jewish law recognizes a category of punishment known as "half damages." The two Talmuds disagree about whether this punishment is a fine or just an ordinary monetary penalty.[25] But no one argues about whether this category of punishment exists, except Sumakhus.[26]

2. Money of dubious status: Judges need a means of arbitrating between two disputing parties. But in some cases, there is no way to determine who is right. Sumakhus establishes the

24. Eiruvin 13b.
25. In the case of an innocuous (non-goring) ox alone, Sumakhus accepts the notion of half damages. See Y. Florsheim, "Half Damages: Fine or Monetary Penalty? A Historical Overview" [Hebrew], in *Religious Zionism Anthology*, vol. 4 (5762), 471–77.
26. Bava Kamma 17b–18a. The Talmud cites another source suggesting that Sumakhus, too, accepts the law of half damages, but it immediately calls this source into doubt.

principle that "money of dubious status is divided equally."[27] One classic example is the first mishna in Bava Metzia: "Two are holding on to a *tallit*. One says, 'It is all mine,' and the other says, 'It is all mine.'" In such a case the judge does not try to arbitrate, but simply rules that the two parties divide the contested article equally, thereby precluding the violence of "might makes right."

3. The recitation of the *Shema*: Rabbi Meir ruled that only the first verse of the *Shema* requires special concentration. This matter is disputed between Beit Hillel and Beit Shammai. Rabbi Meir agrees with Beit Hillel and argues that one's concentration must be focused on the verse that coronates God as Ruler of the universe. Sumakhus further asserts that "all who prolong the last letter of the word 'One' (*eḥad*) will have length of days and years" (Berakhot 13b).

When considered in conjunction, these three teachings reflect Sumakhus' commitment to truth. His need to live with perfect conviction leads him to oppose the notion of half damages; either the person must pay damages, or he need not. On the other hand, he rules that when there is no way to determine the truth, the two parties must divide the contested item equally. He also rules that a person must prolong the word "One," which attests to the affinity between Rabbi Meir's beit midrash and the transcendent light of divine unity: Anyone who prolongs the last word of the *Shema* cultivates an awareness that everything has its foundation in God's oneness. This is the essence of the Torah of Rabbi Meir, who was famous for ruling that the pure was impure and vice versa. Living in a world of unity, he recognized that everything

27. On the use of halakhic principles to resolve monetary disputes, see Y. Sherlo, "'All the Ways of Man Seem Right to Him, But the Lord Probes the Mind': Preliminary Studies on Resolving Matters of Doubt" [Hebrew], in A. Weitzman, ed., *The Old Will Be Renewed: A Collection of Articles in Memory of Eli Klodin and Uri and Ḥayyim Pell* (5749), 11–67.

has its source in the same divine creation, so further distinctions are irrelevant.

Rabbi Meir rules that the impure is pure because he is connected to a transcendent unity. But Rabbi Yehuda bar Ilai sees the situation differently. While the Torah belongs to the supernal realms, we are inevitably confronted with uncertainty and doubt when we try to overlay it onto this world. Our world is one not of unity, but of difference and distinction.

Rabbi Yehuda bar Ilai wishes to prevent Sumakhus from entering the beit midrash because, as a student of Rabbi Meir, he is a "provoker" who "comes not to learn Torah, but rather to cut me down in the discussion of law." He is concerned that Rabbi Meir's students are converting their master's otherworldly sensibility into a sport and a pastime rather than engaging in true Torah study. He worries that their learning has become pedantry, since for every thesis it is possible to find an antithesis. This is a world of chaos rather than light.

Rabbi Shimon ben Elazar and the Ugly Man

Another important student of Rabbi Meir was Rabbi Shimon ben Elazar ben Shamua. We have already discussed Rabbi Elazar ben Shamua, noting that his beit midrash denied entry to Rabbi Yehuda HaNasi. It comes as no surprise that Rabbi Elazar's son was a close disciple of Rabbi Meir in Tiberias.

> Rabbi Shimon[28] could not find grounds for releasing his vow until one of the sages of the Galilee came to him. Some say it was Rabbi Shimon ben Elazar. He took him from here and put him there, and took him from here and put him there, until he put him in the sun, where he began picking lice from his garments.

28. In the parallel source in the Jerusalem Talmud (Mo'ed Katan 3:1 [81d]), this sage is referred to as "Rabbi Shimon ben Rebbi," identifying him as the son of Rabbi Yehuda HaNasi. This makes sense chronologically, since Rabbi Shimon ben Elazar was a contemporary of Rebbi, so he would have been an elder during the time of Rebbi's son.

> They said to him: If you had known that the elder would do this to you, would you have taken such a vow?
>
> He said to them: No.
>
> Then he released the vow.
>
> They said to the elder: How did you know to handle the matter in this way?
>
> He said to them: Many years ago I served Rabbi Meir in his second flight. And some say [that he said]: Rabbi Meir's staff was in my hand, and it taught me knowledge. (Y. Nedarim 9:1 [41b])

This story deals with how a person can get out of a vow he has made. This is a complicated matter, since on the one hand, a person is obligated to fulfill his vows; but on the other hand, he should not hasten to make a vow he will be unable to fulfill. The sage who is responsible for releasing individuals from their vows must do so by finding some "opening" through which to revoke the vow. However, this opening cannot be dependent on a new reality that was not present when the vow was made. It is against this halakhic backdrop that our story appears in the Talmud.

Rabbi Shimon, son of Rabbi Yehuda HaNasi, could not find grounds for releasing his vow until he came before one of the elder sages of the Galilee, possibly Rabbi Shimon ben Elazar. The latter helped release him from his vow by dragging him from place to place and ultimately forcing him to stand in the sun, where the elder began cleaning his clothes. It is not difficult to imagine Rabbi Shimon's predicament: He came before the sages to be released from his vow, and found himself caught up in bureaucratic complications; when he finally manages to be seen by a real person, that person is attending to his clothes while keeping Rabbi Shimon waiting in the sun. Rabbi Shimon ben Elazar waited until Rabbi Shimon had reached the limit of his tolerance, and then asked him, "If you had known that this was the procedure for being released from a vow, would you have taken your vow?" The outraged Rabbi Shimon cries out, "Of course not!" And on this basis, Rabbi Shimon ben Elazar releases him from his vow.

At that point Rabbi Shimon turns to the elder and asks where he learned this approach. The text quotes two answers, which are really one. Rabbi Shimon ben Elazar served Rabbi Meir during his second flight. The first flight may have been his escape after Rabbi Yehuda ben Baba ordained him. But the second flight was undoubtedly Rabbi Meir's flight to Babylon after the Beruria incident.[29] Rabbi Shimon ben Elazar attests that he held Rabbi Meir's staff in his hand, signifying the close connection between master and disciple.[30]

Rabbi Shimon transmits many teachings in the name of his own master, Rabbi Meir, and often argues with the Samaritans.

In one notable story he almost forgets himself:

> Rabbi Shimon ben Elazar[31] was coming from Migdal Gedor, from his teacher's house. And he was riding on a donkey and traveling along a riverbank, and he was exceedingly happy [and felt very proud of himself][32] because he had studied much Torah.
>
> An exceedingly ugly man chanced to meet him. He [the

29. This is the explanation offered by Rabbi David Frankel, author of the Korban HaEda commentary on the Jerusalem Talmud. Rabbi Moshe Margalit, author of the Penei Moshe commentary, explains simply that Rabbi Shimon ben Elazar said, "in the past I served Rabbi Meir."
30. Hyman erroneously argued that Rabbi Shimon ben Elazar could not have been the son of Rabbi Elazar ben Shamua, "because we know Rabbi Elazar lived a long life, and Rebbi was his student. So could Rabbi Elazar's son, who was a friend of Rebbi, not have quoted a single teaching in his father's name?" (Hyman, *Legends*, s.v. "Rabbi Shimon ben Elazar," 1157). This weak contention can be refuted in one of two ways: Either Rabbi Elazar taught the Torah of earlier masters, or Rabbi Yehuda was not part of his beit midrash. But it is clear from many sources that Rabbi Shimon ben Elazar was the son of Rabbi Elazar ben Shamua. See Z. Frankel, *Methods of the Mishna*, 211 note 6. Frankel explains why that Talmud refers to him as "ben Elazar" rather than as "ben Rabbi Elazar."
31. The version in the printed text is corrupt. The Munich manuscript and the parallel in *Avot deRabbi Natan* (recension A, ch. 41) read "Rabbi Shimon ben Elazar." N. Ben Ari considers the variant texts in her article "Rabbi Elazar ben Rabbi Shimon and the Ugly Man" [Hebrew], Da'at website, 5764. She notes the corruption in the protagonist's name but nonetheless entitles her article "Rabbi Elazar ben Rabbi Shimon," which would suggest an entirely different historical context.
32. The words in brackets do not appear in the manuscripts and were added by the editor in light of the story's conclusion, as noted in Ben Ari, "Rabbi Yose and the Matron." The shift from happiness to ugliness is even more dramatic without this editorial gloss.

> ugly man] said to him: Peace be upon you, my teacher. But he did not return the greeting. He said: Empty one! How ugly is that man. Could all the people of your city be as ugly as you? He said to him: I don't know. But go tell the craftsman who made me: How ugly is this vessel you made.
>
> When he [Rabbi Shimon ben Elazar] realized he had sinned, he dismounted his donkey, prostrated himself before him, and said to him: I have spoken out of turn to you. Forgive me." He [the ugly man] said: I will not forgive you until you go to the craftsman who made me and tell him: How ugly is this vessel you made.
>
> He [Rabbi Shimon ben Elazar] traveled behind him until he reached his city. The people of his city came out to greet him. They said to him: Peace be upon you, teacher, teacher, master, master. He [the ugly man] said to them: Whom are you calling "teacher, teacher"? They said to him: [We are addressing] this man who is traveling behind you. He said to them: If that one is a teacher, may there not be many like him in Israel! They said to him: Why? He said to them: He did such and such to me. They said to him: Forgive him nonetheless, because he is a man of great Torah knowledge. He said to them: For your sakes I forgive him, provided that he does not make a habit of doing this.
>
> Rabbi Shimon ben Rabbi Elazar immediately entered the beit midrash and expounded: A person should always be soft as a reed, not hard as a cedar. (Ta'anit 20a–b)

Much ink has been spilled on this story.[33] Rabbi Shimon ben Elazar comes riding on a donkey from his master's house, overflowing with joy because of all the Torah he has learned. This is an apt description of a student of Rabbi Meir, whose beit midrash near the Sea of Galilee

33. Major articles about this story include Y. Frankel, *The Aggadic Story: Unity of Form and Content* [Hebrew] (Tel Aviv, 2001), 189–97; A. Kosman, "Rabbi Shimon ben Elazar and the Damaged Man" [Hebrew], in *Masekhet Gevarim* (Jerusalem, 2002), 73–82; and Ben Ari, "Rabbi Yose and the Matron."

enabled students to reach great intellectual heights.[34] From the vantage point of such a student, the ordinary "man on the ground" seemed small and insignificant. So Rabbi Shimon ben Elazar was still "on a high" after studying with Rabbi Meir. He left the beit midrash and passed a body of water, presumably either the Yarmuk or the Jordan. The beautiful pastoral landscape blended with the beauty of the Torah he had learned, perhaps inspiring him to hum some verses from Psalms 19: "The heavens proclaim the glory of God, and the sky proclaims His handiwork.... The Torah of the Lord is perfect, renewing life."[35] Suddenly "An exceedingly ugly man chanced to meet him." This encounter comes as a surprise. How did ugliness intrude upon this scene of aesthetic perfection?

As if that weren't disruptive enough, the ugly man proceeds to greet Rabbi Shimon ben Elazar: "Peace be unto you, my teacher." How could such an ugly man offer words of peace? Rabbi Shimon does not acknowledge these words. Instead he shoots back: "Empty one! How ugly is that man. Could all the people of your city be as ugly as you?" He addresses the ugly man, but he ought to be directing his cries to heaven. If creation includes ugliness, then perhaps we can no longer trust in one God who creates light as well as darkness, peace as well as evil.[36] The world collapses into a dichotomy with beauty and perfection on the one hand, and emptiness and chaos on the other. Suddenly Rabbi Shimon

34. This geographical description is an approximation at best. Z. Frankel locates Migdal Gedor in the area of Ḥamat Gader, near Tzemaḥ. He therefore assumes that the protagonist was riding by the banks of the Yarmouk, near the Sea of Galilee – a very pleasant journey. Ben Ari, in "Rabbi Yose and the Matron," comments that "Migdal Gedor may be identified with Hirbat Um Kiq on the other side of the Jordan, over the Yarmouk." The version in *Avot deRabbi Natan* refers not to a river but to the seashore, which S. Klein identified near Tiberias in *Sefer HaYishuv* [Hebrew] (Jerusalem, 5699), 8. Menaḥem Katz points out that the Babylonian version, edited between the two great rivers of Babylon, not surprisingly states that he was riding along the banks of a river, perhaps referring to the Jordan or the Yarmouk. See Katz, *In the Paths of Aggada* [Hebrew] (Jerusalem, 5759), 8.
35. This chapter of Psalms uniquely juxtaposes the harmony of creation with that of Torah. These are two forms of perfection that only human action can defile.
36. Rabbi Shimon ben Elazar was well versed in heretical works. See H. Shalem, "Rabbi Shimon ben Elazar: His Personal Story and Public Roles" [Hebrew] (M.A. thesis, Bar-Ilan University, 5745).

finds himself entertaining theological dualism: "The kingdom of Benei Tzedek is in the hands of the minister of light. They will walk in ways of light. The kingdom of sin is in the hands of the minister of darkness. They will walk in ways of darkness."[37]

The ugly man, who is not even granted a name, is the victim of Rabbi Shimon's crisis of faith. He offers a response that is very much to the point: "Go tell the artist who made me: How ugly is this vessel you made!" This is an instance of role reversal: The scholar who has just come from the beit midrash is supposed to know that God creates both good and bad, beautiful and ugly. Instead he must learn this lesson from an ordinary, anonymous man on the street. The answer he receives cuts like a knife through his heart: The ugly man challenges Rabbi Shimon's religious worldview as well as his Creator.[38] In response, Rabbi Shimon tries to mend his ways. But the ugly man, like the unbending cedar, refuses to accept the sage's apology. In the story's final lines, Rabbi Shimon enters the beit midrash and declares, "A person should always be soft as a reed, not hard as a cedar." This ending leaves the reader confused: Who is the reed, and who is the cedar? Everything has become its opposite. While one leaves Rabbi Meir's beit midrash with a sense of sheer joy, the encounter with the real world serves to complicate matters significantly.

CONCLUSION: THE END OF THE PASSAGE IN EIRUVIN

We opened our study of Rabbi Meir with an extended passage in Tractate Eiruvin that relates to his period of study with Rabbi Yishmael and Rabbi Akiva. We now return to consider the end of that passage:

> Rabbi Aḥa bar Ḥanina said: It is revealed and known before Him who spoke the world into being that there was no one like

37. *Community Rule Scroll* (*Serekh HaYaḥad*), Licht ed., 92. Also see Urbach, *Sages*, 142 note 7. Urbach quotes many sectarian sources that express the fundamental principles of dualism.

38. This worldview is particularly interesting when it informs halakhic literature. Rabbi Eliezer Waldenberg was asked whether plastic surgery was permissible. He concluded based on this story that a person who complains to God about his appearance is dishonoring his Maker. See *Responsa Tzitz Eliezer* 11:41.

> Rabbi Meir in his generation. Why did they not decide the halakha in accordance with his view? Because his colleagues could not fathom the depths of his reasoning. For he would assert that something impure was pure, and make it seem plausible. (Eiruvin 13b)

Rabbi Meir's Torah was illuminated by an otherworldly light. It did not belong to this messy, complicated world. The Torah of this world is that of Rabbi Yishmael, who famously asserts that the Torah speaks in human terms.

Rabbi Akiva's teachings reached Rabbi Meir and were then transmitted to Rabbi Yehuda HaNasi, who incorporated them into the Mishna: "An unattributed mishna is the teaching of Rabbi Meir" (Sanhedrin 86a).[39] Despite the tension between Rabban Shimon ben Gamliel and Rabbi Meir, Rabbi Yehuda HaNasi remained committed to the latter's teachings:

> Rebbi said: If I am a sharper thinker than my colleagues, it is only because I saw Rabbi Meir from behind. Had I seen him from the front, I would have been an even sharper thinker. As it is written, "And your eyes will watch your Guide" [Is. 30:20]. (Eiruvin 13b)

We cannot help but read this story in light of Moses' request to see God after the golden calf episode (Ex. 33). God accedes, but only partially: "You will see My back, but My face must not be seen."

Rabbi Meir, in this sense, resembles his Creator.

39. "And this is meant literally: Rebbi relied heavily on Rabbi Meir's teachings and followed his halakhic opinion unless otherwise specified." Epstein, *Literature of the Tanna'im*, 96.

Part Four

Gates of the Patriarch – Rabban Shimon ben Gamliel

The Founding Generation at Usha		Rabbi Yehuda HaNasi
138–161	161–192	192–220
The Restoration of the Nation after the Destruction Antoninus Pius	The Stabilization of the Center at Usha Marcus Aurelius and Commodus	Autonomy in the Galilee Severus

Chapter Eleven

Historical and Political Background

In the introduction to Part One of this book we discussed the reign of Antoninus Pius, which marked the beginning of a new period of Roman rule. Antoninus Pius was succeeded by Marcus Aurelius, then Julius Commodus, and then Septimius Severus, all part of the Antonine dynasty. During the reign of the first three of these emperors, Rabban Shimon ben Gamliel served as patriarch. We will consider each of these periods below.

ANTONINUS PIUS

Antoninus Pius reigned during a period of unity and tranquility in the Roman Empire. In the year 155, an anonymous lecturer in Asia Minor observed:

> The empire was a confederation of free cities in which democracy prevailed. Small cities expanded, new cities were founded, disputes between individuals subsided, and everyone was preoccupied with how to become more beautiful and attractive.

> Cities included gymnasiums, fountains, gates, temples, stores, and schools. The affairs of the emperor were administered in perfect harmony, like a choir under the conductor's baton. The government was a form of universal democracy in which the best man won.[1]

These words were clearly intended to ingratiate the speaker with the authorities; he conveniently neglects to mention the farm laborers and slaves at the lowest strata of society.

This atmosphere resulted in tranquility in the Land of Israel as well. Antoninus made no attempt to penalize the Jews for the Bar Kokhba revolt or to exile them from their land. As a result, the sages could regain their bearings and reestablish the major centers of Jewish leadership.

MARCUS AURELIUS

The reign of Marcus Aurelius (161–180) marks the end of the enlightened rulers. Aurelius was a Stoic philosopher interested in questions about the nature of reality. But the peace that had characterized his predecessors' reign came to an end as the Parthians in the east strove to expand their kingdom. In a war that lasted from 162 to 165, the Romans defeated the Parthians in an impressive victory.[2] Aurelius transferred his forces from Europe to Syria, where most of the fighting took place. At the end of the war a terrible plague took tens of thousands of lives, both soldiers and citizens. During the following years, the emperor was preoccupied by a great war in northern Italy (169–175). Meanwhile the northern border was vulnerable to attack by German tribes, whose incursions into Roman territory took a heavy toll on the empire's soldiers and citizens.

In 175, Aurelius' eastern general, Avidius Cassius, rebelled against the caesar and declared himself emperor. He was supported by the local Roman legions, including those in the Land of Israel. The rebellion was

1. This is a quote from a speech delivered in Greek in Asia Minor in 155 and published as "To Rome." See M. Amit, *A History of the Roman Empire,* [Hebrew] (Jerusalem, 5763), 508–9.
2. During this period Rabbi Shimon bar Yoḥai taught, "If you see a Parthian horse tied to the graves of the Land of Israel, anticipate the arrival of the Messiah" (Lamentations Rabba 1:3).

suppressed after a few months, and Aurelius journeyed eastward to quiet the region. He traveled from Egypt to Syria via the Land of Israel. A fourth century historian described the caesar's passage through the Holy Land and the repulsion he felt for the Jews: "He was overcome by disgust for the odious, restless Jews, and cried out: 'O Marcomanni, O Quadi, O Sarmatae! I have finally found people more despicable than you!'"[3] It is unclear what gave him such a negative impression of the Jews, but this much is certain: Despite the Talmud's colorful stories about his debates with Rabbi Yehuda HaNasi, and despite the emperor's philosophical leanings, we must conclude that Marcus Aurelius never engaged with a rabbi in enlightened conversation.[4]

COMMODUS

Commodus' father endorsed his reign (180–192), so he ascended the throne unchallenged. The twelve years of his reign were a low point in Roman imperial history. Historian Moshe Amit notes that "It is difficult to think of a starker contrast than that between the personality and imperial conduct of Marcus Aurelius and that of his son Commodus."[5] Commodus was preoccupied by his own whims and fancies: His reign was notorious for its gladiatorial games, corruption, and exceptional

3. This quote, originally in Latin, is from Ammianus Marcellinus, the last of the great Roman historians, who wrote in the mid-fourth century. The Marcomanni and Quadi were Germanic tribes that invaded the Roman Empire in 167. The Sarmatae were a Slavic tribe from the area that is now Poland. Marcus Aurelius' comment about the Jews is quoted in several sources, among them Amit, *The History of the Roman Empire*, 526; and Oppenheimer and Herr, "Political and Administrative History from the Bar Kokhba Revolt Until the Division of the Empire," 23.
4. I write these words in response to I. Zlotnick's article "The Identification of Antoninus, Friend of Rebbi" [Hebrew], *Sinai* 11 (5707): 136–37. Zlotnick performs complicated calculations involving imperial chronology and rabbinic *Aggada* in an effort to demonstrate that Rebbi was the contemporary of Marcus Aurelius, known in rabbinic literature as Antoninus the philosopher. As Zlotnick writes, "All the emperors known as Antoninus were blackguards and reprobates, and Rebbi could not bear to associate with them. The only exception was Antoninus the philosopher, his contemporary. Only he could become Rebbi's associate." Apparently Zlotnick was unfamiliar with Marcus Aurelius' attitude toward the Jews and with his statement quoted above.
5. Amit, *The History of the Roman Empire*, 615.

cruelty, reminiscent of the dark days of the emperors Caligula and Nero. He was thought to foreshadow the empire's decline into anarchy.

Commodus was murdered in 192 and succeeded by the Roman senator Pertinax, who in turn was murdered just three months later. The victor in the struggle for succession was Septimius Severus, who seized power in 193 but was challenged by Pescennius Niger, the ruler in the east. The eastern provinces were split between Severus and Niger. Though the Roman legions and residents of Palestine were also divided, the Jews did not take sides. After four years of fierce contest, Severus emerged triumphant.[6]

6. This struggle for succession is far more fascinating than my brief overview suggests. See Amit, *The History of the Roman Empire*, 630–40.

Chapter Twelve

Rabban Shimon ben Gamliel's Early Years

Following the repeal of the Hadrianic decrees, the sages redirected their attention to religious matters during the reign of Antoninus Pius. They founded a beit midrash at Usha and began the work of reviving the Torah learning of the Yavneh generation. Their early gatherings, which we read about in the introductory chapter, were not attended by representatives of the patriarchal family, presumably for political reasons. At Yavneh Rabban Gamliel had enjoyed a close relationship with the Roman authorities.[1] But during the period of persecution, the Romans forbade

1. This close relationship does not necessarily mean that the Roman Empire officially recognized the patriarchy. Nonetheless, many scholars have shown that Rabban Gamliel was recognized as the Jewish people's legal representative to the Roman authorities. For more on his status, see D. Goldblatt, "The Origins of the Patriarchy in the Land of Israel" [Hebrew], in *Studies in the History of the People and Land of Israel* (Haifa, 5738), vol. 4, 89–102. Goldblatt argues that Rabban Gamliel, his son Rashbag, and their family were issued de facto leadership by the authorities. This problematic claim can be verified only by means of a closer examination of the full matrix of relations between Rome, the patriarchy, and the community of sages.

the Jews from fulfilling mitzvot and outlawed any institutions that might be regarded as a sign of autonomy, including the patriarchy.[2] With the waning of the battle cries and the rise of a new imperial dynasty, the institution of the patriarchy was rehabilitated and the patriarch assumed the mantle of national leadership.

RABBAN SHIMON BEN GAMLIEL'S CHILDHOOD

Rabban Shimon ben Gamliel, who became known by the acronym Rashbag, studied with his father Rabban Gamliel in Yavneh. Since he was being groomed to succeed his father as patriarch, he received a Hellenistic education:

> They permitted the house of Rabban Gamliel to teach its sons Greek, because they had dealings with the government. (Tosefta Sukka 15:8)[3]

The Babylonian sources add important information about the house in which Rabban Shimon ben Gamliel was raised and educated:

> And is Greek wisdom really prohibited? But Rabbi Yehuda has said that Shmuel stated in the name of Rabban Shimon ben Gamliel: I can apply to myself the verse "My eyes cause me grief at the fate of all the maidens of my city" [Lam. 3:51]. A thousand young men were in the household of my father. Five hundred of them studied Torah and five hundred studied Greek wisdom, and no one remains from them except myself here and the son of my father's brother in Asia.
>
> They say: Rabban Gamliel's household was different, for its members had dealings with the Roman government.
>
> As it is taught: One who cuts his hair in the Komi style – this is among the ways of the Amorites. Nevertheless, the

2. See G. Alon, *History of the Jews*, vol. 2, 70.
3. It seems that it was forbidden to teach Greek in schools, but not to study it. See S. Lieberman, *Greek in Jewish Palestine; Hellenism in Jewish Palestine* (New York: JTS Press, 1994); and Lieberman, *Tosefta Kifshuta*, Sota, 768.

> sages permitted Avtolmos bar Reuven to cut his hair in the Komi style, because he had dealings with the Roman government. And they permitted the members of Rabban Gamliel's household to speak the language of Greek wisdom, because they had dealings with the Roman government. (Bava Kamma 83a)

This source suggests that there was a separate educational system for the children of diplomats, even if the numbers cited by Rabban Shimon ben Gamliel are probably exaggerated. This school had two tracks: Half the students learned Torah, and half learned general subjects.

This source also teaches about the type of Roman haircut that was forbidden to Jews, with the exception of the patriarchal family. Avtolmos bar Reuven was not from the patriarchal family and is not mentioned in other rabbinic sources. Presumably he was one of those five hundred students who studied in the school for diplomatic families. His father, Reuven, campaigned for the revocation of the Roman decrees of persecution early in the reign of Antoninus Pius:

> For it once happened that the regime enacted a decree that the Jews not observe Shabbat, that they not circumcise their sons, and that they cohabit with menstruating women. Rabbi Reuven ben Isterovli went out and cut his hair in a pagan style in order to conceal his Jewishness, and he went and sat together with the Romans. (Me'ila 17a)[4]

The special dispensations granted to the patriarchal family are mentioned in another source as well:

> Three matters were permitted to the household of Rebbi: They [the members of Rebbi's household] may look in a mirror; they may cut their hair in the Komi style; and they may teach their

4. We considered this source in Chapter Six. Given that the name Reuven occurs very rarely in rabbinic sources, the connection between father and son does not seem too far-fetched, especially when considered against the backdrop of the diplomatic education that the son received.

> children Greek, because they have dealings with the government. (Y. Shabbat 6:1 [7d])

The sages were surrounded by Roman culture. They were also susceptible to an alternative eastern culture, often described as the culture of Medea. For Rabban Shimon ben Gamliel, a man of the west, the east was exotic and alluring. This is expressed in his midrash on the verse "And Jacob sent and called Rachel and Leah to the field" (Gen. 31:4):

> Rabban Shimon ben Gamliel said: There are three things I like about the Medeans: They do not tear meat with their teeth and eat, but cut it and eat it; they kiss not on the mouth but on the hand; and they take counsel only in a field, as it says: "And Jacob sent and called Rachel and Leah to the field." (Genesis Rabba 74)

RASHBAG DURING THE PERSECUTION

Rabbinic sources suggest that the patriarchal house, along with its special diplomatic school, was located in Beitar during the war.[5] Of all the children of the diplomats, only a handful survived the persecution. In the source from Bava Kamma cited above, Rashbag relates that only he and his brother in Asia survived. In the following source he speaks of the traumas of Beitar that he experienced in his youth:

> Rabban Shimon ben Gamliel says: There were five hundred schools in Beitar. The smallest of them had no fewer than five hundred children. They said: If the enemy comes against us, we shall go forth against them with these quills and gouge their eyes out.
>
> On account of the sins that caused the tragedy, they wrapped each one of the children in his scroll and burned him, and out of them all, I alone have survived. He recited this verse about himself: "My eyes cause me grief at the fate of all the maidens of my city" [Lam. 3:51]. (Y. Ta'anit 4:5 [69a])

5. G. Alon, *History of the Jews*, vol. 2, 39.

Rabban Shimon ben Gamliel describes the schools of Beitar with their hundreds of students who clutched their books to shield themselves from the enemy. Yet the Romans wrapped them in their scrolls and burned them, and only Rashbag survived.

Where was Rashbag during the period between the rebellion and assembly at Usha? This question has preoccupied historians of the period, most of whom agree that he was forced into hiding. But why did he emerge when he did? Was it because the people wanted a leader from the patriarchal family whose lineage extended back to King David? Or was it because the Romans wanted a Jewish leader who was inclined toward accommodation and cultural openness rather than national and religious struggle?[6]

6. Most Israeli scholars assume that Rashbag was forced into hiding. See A. Oppenheimer, "The Jewish Leadership: The Sanhedrin and the Patriarchy," in *History of the Land of Israel*, vol. 5, 83. The other view, that Rashbag was appointed as a de facto leader, is espoused by Goldblatt, "Origins of the Patriarchy," 98.

Chapter Thirteen

Domestic Disputes in the Beit Midrash

Even before Rashbag came on the scene, the sages began restoring Jewish life after the revolt and the persecution. But the people held out for a leader who would represent their interests to the Roman authorities. Rashbag presented himself as a religious, social, and political leader, as was his father. He sought to restore the patriarchy to its former glory.[1] The patriarchy had served as the official Jewish leadership since Temple times. Although the beit midrash continued to develop independently, the sustained presence of the patriarchal leadership inspired confidence and optimism.

Sometime after the establishment of the beit midrash at Usha, Rashbag assumed leadership. We have no historical accounts of public reaction to the restoration of a member of the patriarchal line to a leadership position. Rashbag was not coronated, nor were trumpets or shofar

1. E. E. Urbach, "Status and Leadership in the World of the Sages," in *The World of the Sages* (Jerusalem, 5748), 324.

blasts sounded to signify his inauguration. He arrived at Usha without fanfare, but great drama was enacted behind the scenes.

Before Rashbag came to Usha, the sages had already established a division of labor among themselves. The people regarded the sages as a self-sufficient leadership. Yet the patriarch served additional roles, added another perspective, and acted with a greater sense of responsibility. Raised in the home of Rabban Gamliel and educated in the diplomatic school, Rashbag knew that a sense of hierarchy was necessary to maintain the stature of the patriarchy, so he established a few rules of protocol:

> When the patriarch enters, everyone rises and does not sit down until he says to them: Sit down.
>
> And when the head of the court enters, they set up two rows for him, one on one side and one on the other side, through which he enters, and he sits down in his place.
>
> When a sage enters, one rises as another sits down, until the sage comes in and sits down in his place.
>
> Younger sages and disciples of sages step over even the heads of the people when the public requires them.
>
> And even though they have said: "It is not praiseworthy for a disciple of the sages to come in last," if he went out to fulfill his needs, he comes back and sits down in his place.
>
> Younger sages and disciples of sages turn their heads toward their fathers when they are capable of understanding the proceedings.
>
> If they are incapable of understanding the proceedings, they turn toward the people.
>
> Rabbi Elazar ben Rabbi Tzaddok says: At a feast they place them by their fathers. (Tosefta Sanhedrin 7:8–9)

Rabbi Yoḥanan, who lived during the second half of the third century, attests that these protocols were established during Rashbag's tenure and reflect the early activities of the new patriarch.

> Rabbi Yoḥanan said: This mishna was taught in the days of Rabban Gamliel: Rabban Shimon ben Gamliel is the patriarch (*nasi*);

> Rabbi Meir is the [greatest] sage (*hakham*); Rabbi Natan is the head of the court (*av beit din*). (Horayot 13b)

According to the Tosefta, there is a difference between these three leadership positions. The patriarch represents the nation to the Roman government. He is responsible for the administrative autonomy of the Jews within their province of the Roman Empire. The head of the court, second-in-command to the patriarch, is the judicial authority. The role of the sage is unclear. According to the Babylonian sources, this individual was responsible for the curriculum and for the proceedings of the *beit din* (court).[2] According to the Palestinian sources, however, this title may have applied to any ordained rabbis who were permitted to rule on matters of law, as distinguished from their younger disciples.

The Tosefta quoted above suggests that in Rashbag's time, changes were instituted in the way various leaders entered the court so as to emphasize each one's status in the leadership hierarchy. When the patriarch entered, the whole audience would stand, and no one was permitted to take his seat until the patriarch gave dispensation. When the head of the court entered, the people formed two rows, allowing him to pass. When a sage entered, each member of the audience would stand until he passed.

RABBI MEIR'S DEPARTURE FROM THE BEIT MIDRASH: THE JERUSALEM TALMUD'S VERSION

Rabbi Meir regarded Rashbag's new protocols as personally humiliating.[3] The Jerusalem Talmud relates:

2. D. Goldblatt, "The Story of the Conspiracy Against the Second Rabban Shimon ben Gamliel" [Hebrew], *Tziyon* 49 (5744): 362–64.
3. According to Z. Frankel, "This was an ad hoc appointment created specifically for Rabbi Meir. For Rabbi Meir was the greatest sage of his generation, but Rashbag had already been appointed patriarch on account of his lineage, and Rabbi Natan had been appointed as head of court because he was the son of the Babylonian exilarch. So they established a new position, that of sage, and gave this title to Rabbi Meir. We have already discussed the role of the sage, who was responsible for pursuing all avenues of inquiry in the court and for evaluating all the instruction concerning any question brought before the sages, in all its aspects and ramifications." See Frankel, *Methods of the Mishna*, 163.

> Rabbi Meir would learn. When he came to the beit midrash, all the people would watch him enter and stand before him. When they heard the announcer teach the new decree of the patriarch, the people wished to modify their conduct accordingly. Rabbi Meir grew furious and left the beit midrash. He said to them: I have heard that we increase in holiness and don't decrease. (Y. Bikkurim 3:3 [65c])

Rabbi Meir was accustomed to everyone rising when he entered the beit midrash. But then Rabban Gamliel instituted a new law revising the protocol: Each member of the audience would stand only long enough to allow Rabbi Meir to pass. Rabbi Meir stormed out of the beit midrash. He asserted that "we increase in holiness and don't decrease," meaning that no one should be demoted on account of a new protocol.

THE ATTEMPT TO OVERTHROW RABBI MEIR: THE BABYLONIAN TALMUD'S VERSION

The Babylonian Talmud offers a somewhat different account of this incident. The story is lengthy, so we will divide it into sections and consider each in turn.

The Conspiracy

> When Rabban Shimon ben Gamliel entered the beit midrash, everyone would stand up before him. When Rabbi Meir and Rabbi Natan entered, everyone would stand up before them.
>
> Rabban Shimon ben Gamliel said: Should there not be a distinction between my honor and theirs? He instituted this teaching. That day Rabbi Meir and Rabbi Natan were not there.
>
> When they came the following day, they saw that the scholars were not standing before them in the usual manner. They said: What is going on?
>
> They said to them: This is what Rabban Shimon ben Gamliel instituted.
>
> Rabbi Meir said to Rabbi Natan: I am the sage and you are the head of the court. Let us initiate something for our ben-

> efit. What should we do to him? Let us say to him: Teach us Tractate Uktzin; for he does not have it fully mastered. And since he has not mastered it, we shall say to him, "Who shall utter the mighty acts of God? Who can declare all of His praise?" [Ps. 106:2] – Who is fitting to utter the mighty acts of God? One who can declare all of His praise. And with that argument, we shall remove Rabban Shimon ben Gamliel from office, and I shall become the head of the court and you the patriarch. (Horayot 13b)

This story could appear only in the Babylonian Talmud. In Babylonian Jewish culture, the authority to serve as a leader was invested only in those who had mastered all aspects of talmudic and halakhic literature. One's status was a function of his learning. The Babylonian storyteller depicts Rabbi Meir as a sage who wishes to advance by shaming his colleague. He colludes with Rabbi Natan, whom we will discuss in a subsequent chapter, and together they try to disgrace Rabban Shimon ben Gamliel.[4]

The Uktzin Test

The test that the sages prepare for the patriarch reflects a tradition deeply entrenched in Babylonian talmudic culture. One entrance requirement for the most advanced classes in the beit midrash was a mastery of Tractate Uktzin. Another source sheds light on this tractate's significance:

> Rabba proclaimed a fast [in time of drought]. He appealed to God's mercy, but the rain did not fall. They said to him: But would not the rain fall when Rabbi Yehuda declared a fast? He said to them: What can I do? If it is learning that brings rainfall, we are more learned than they were. For in Rabbi Yehuda's day, they would study only Seder Nezikin, whereas we learn all six orders. And when Rabbi Yehuda reached Tractate Uktzin, he would say: I see this was difficult for Rav and Shmuel. Whereas we teach thirteen classes on Tractate Uktzin. And yet when Rabbi Yehuda removed one sandal [to signify the beginning of the fast],

4. Goldblatt, "Story of the Conspiracy," 362 note 330.

> immediately the rain would fall. Yet we cry out all day long, and no one answers us. (Ta'anit 24a–b)

This is an amoraic story laden with intense self-awareness and self-criticism. The students learn on a very high level, yet they cannot cause the rain to fall as it did in the time of their predecessors, who were not as learned. The bar is set by Uktzin, considered the most challenging tractate. By means of this tractate, Rabbi Meir and Rabbi Natan attempt to overthrow Rashbag.[5]

Rabbi Yaakov Rescues the Patriarch

> Rabbi Yaakov ben Karshi overheard [Rabbi Meir and Rabbi Natan's plot]. He said: Perhaps, heaven forbid, the matter will lead to Rabban Shimon's disgrace. He went and sat behind Rabban Shimon ben Gamliel's upper chamber and learned Tractate Uktzin aloud. He recited and reviewed it, recited and reviewed it.
>
> Rabban Shimon ben Gamliel said: Perhaps, heaven forbid, there is something amiss in the beit midrash. He set his mind to the matter and studied Tractate Uktzin.
>
> The next day they said to him: Come, master, teach us Uktzin.
>
> Rabban Shimon began expounding the tractate. After he finished he said to them: If I had not learned the tractate yesterday, you would have disgraced me. He thereupon instructed that Rabbi Meir and Rabbi Natan be expelled from the beit midrash. (Horayot 13b)

This Babylonian account is a further elaboration on the story in the Jerusalem Talmud, which offers a more general description of the anger of Rabbi Meir (without reference to Rabbi Natan) after his honor

5. Goldblatt argues that the reference to Tractate Uktzin serves as additional evidence that this story is a later Babylonian reworking rather than a contemporaneous testimony.

is insulted. The plot of the two sages and Rabbi Yaakov's intervention recall the story of Megillat Esther, in which Mordecai overhears Bigthan and Teresh scheming to overthrow the king.

This account depicts the difficult situation in which Rashbag finds himself. Having joined an already functioning institution, he has to assert his position by establishing a new leadership structure. Rashbag establishes rules pertaining to entry into the courtroom, but this new protocol provokes his colleagues.

Rabbi Meir and Rabbi Natan are not minor sages; they are both leaders of the beit midrash. The sage who comes to Rashbag's rescue, Rabbi Yaakov ben Karshi, is less well known. He was certainly not one of the leading sages of the Usha generation, as we shall see when we consider him in his own right.

A DOOR SLAMMED SHUT, OR EXCOMMUNICATION? A COMPARISON OF THE REMOVAL OF RABBI MEIR AND RABBI NATAN

After Rabbi Yaakov saved the patriarch from embarrassment, the latter expelled Rabbi Meir and Rabbi Natan from the beit midrash. We learn from other sources that expulsion from the beit midrash was often a form of excommunication.[6] In our story, though, Rabbi Meir and Rabbi Natan refuse to accept that they have been excommunicated:

> From outside, Rabbi Meir and Rabbi Natan would write questions on a tablet and throw it inside. The sages of the beit midrash would answer any question they could. If the sages could not answer a question, Rabbi Meir and Rabbi Natan would write the answers and throw them inside. (Horayot 13b)

6. This was what Rabbi Ḥiya assumed when Rabbi Yehuda HaNasi expelled him. We will consider this source when we discuss Rabbi Yehuda HaNasi. Libson tries to prove that Rashbag did in fact excommunicate Rabbi Meir and Rabbi Natan: "It is clear that the punishment of anyone who challenged the authority of the patriarch would be removal from the beit midrash, which constitutes excommunication." See Libson, "For What Reasons Do We Excommunicate?" 311. Goldblatt counters that this motif of sending someone out of the beit midrash is also a Babylonian trope. See Goldblatt, "Story of the Conspiracy," 359–61.

This interlude demonstrates that Rabbi Meir and Rabbi Natan did not regard themselves as excommunicated. They saw themselves as an inextricable part of the beit midrash, regardless of any punishment they had officially received. Some scholars assume that this story is the backdrop to the following passage in the Jerusalem Talmud:[7]

> They sought to excommunicate Rabbi Meir. He said to them: I will not listen to you until you tell me who gets excommunicated, for what reasons, and for how many offenses. (Y. Mo'ed Katan 3:1 [81c])

Rabban Shimon ben Gamliel wished to establish his own authority. But he could not ignore the stature of the sages of the Usha beit midrash, with Rabbi Yose ben Ḥalafta of Tzippori at their helm.

No Teaching Shall Be Stated in Their Names: The Punishment Imposed by Rashbag

> Rabbi Yose [ben Ḥalafta] said to his colleagues: Torah is outside and we are inside?
>
> Rashbag said to them: We shall allow them to enter the beit midrash, but we will penalize them in that no Torah teaching shall be quoted in their names.
>
> They referred to Rabbi Meir as "others" and to Rabbi Natan as "some say."
>
> The following was revealed to Rabbi Meir and Rabbi Natan in their dreams: Go appease Rabban Shimon ben Gamliel. Rabbi Natan went, but Rabbi Meir did not go. Rabbi Meir said: The contents of dreams are meaningless.
>
> When Rabbi Natan went, Rabban Shimon ben Gamliel said to him: Granted, your father's golden belt helped you to become head of the court, but shall we also make you patriarch? (Horayot 13b)

7. Z. Frankel, *Methods of the Mishna*, 290 note 1; Libson, "Grounds for Excommunication," 309.

Each figure in this story plays a role, like actors in a drama: Rabbi Meir does not give in; Rabbi Natan seeks reconciliation; and Rabbi Yose ben Ḥalafta serves as mediator. Rashbag is prepared to reinstate Rabbi Meir and Rabbi Natan, but only on the condition that their teachings not be quoted in their names. Rabbi Meir will be referred to as "others" (appropriate for the student of Aḥer, the Other), and Rabbi Natan will be referred to as "some say."

This source, with its discussion of how sages are quoted, seems to bear witness to an early stage in the redaction of the Mishna, which we will discuss in the chapters ahead.

The Patriarchal House: No Forgiving, No Forgetting

The next source considers the memory of the attempted revolution at Usha:

> Rebbi taught the following lesson to Rabban Shimon his son: Others say: If it were a substitute offering, it would not be offered.
>
> His son said to him: Who are these others whose waters we drink, but whose names we do not mention?
>
> Rebbi said: These are people who sought to eradicate your honor and the honor of your father's house.
>
> Rabban Shimon quoted: "Their love, their hate, their jealousy have already perished" [Eccl. 9:6].
>
> Rebbi quoted back: "The lives of the enemy have ended, but their ruins remain forever" [Ps. 9:7].
>
> Rabban Shimon said to Rebbi: Those words apply only where the enemies' deeds were effective, but the deeds of these rabbis were not effective.
>
> He then taught the following version to Rabban Shimon: They said in the name of Rabbi Meir: If it were a substitute offering, it would not be offered.
>
> Rava said: Even Rebbi, a humble man, taught: They said in the name of Rabbi Meir. But he did not say: Rabbi Meir said. (Horayot 14a)

Many years after the dispute between Rashbag and the sages, Rebbi sat with his son and taught him a law in the name of "others." In this account, Rebbi's son innocently inquires about the identity of the "others," since it is wrong to drink the waters of Torah without acknowledging their source. His father answers that these "others" sought to uproot the patriarchy. Now Rebbi and his son begin to argue. The son quotes a verse from Ecclesiastes to argue that the feud has already been forgotten and is no longer relevant. Rebbi responds by quoting a verse from Psalms that appears in a chapter about how God exacts justice upon the wicked, a very difficult source given that it is the sages of Israel who are described as wicked. Rebbi's choice of quotation suggests that there can be no forgetting in such a feud. The son answers that hatred lives on only in those cases where the enemy succeeds, yet the sages of Israel clearly surrendered to the patriarchy. At that point Rebbi partially concedes. He teaches the law by alluding to Rabbi Meir without crediting him directly: "They said in the name of Rabbi Meir."

Chapter Fourteen

The Threat from the Diaspora

The new patriarchy established the central beit midrash at Usha as the sole legitimate substitute for the Great Court in Jerusalem. Usha was chosen because its local sage, Rabbi Yehuda bar Ilai, had appeased the Roman authorities. Rashbag, the new patriarch, respected the existing leadership. He appointed Rabbi Yehuda bar Ilai as his adviser, presumably on account of Rabbi Yehuda's connection to Usha.[1] In addition, he appointed Rabbi Natan head of the court on account of his important Babylonian forebears, which gives us a window into Rashbag's strategy of cultivating relationships with Jewish communities abroad. Rashbag was also close to Rabbi Yose, the rabbi of the important Galilean city of Tzippori.[2]

Two members of the founding generation were noticeably absent from Usha: Rashbi had already departed for the next world. (His son was adopted by Rabbi Yose, who initiated him into the beit midrash.)

1. E. E. Urbach, "From Judea to the Galilee" [Hebrew], in *World of the Sages*, 342.
2. Z. Frankel, *Methods of the Mishna*, 194; Epstein, *Literature of the Tanna'im*, 163.

And Rabbi Elazar ben Shamua kept his distance, opting instead to reside in Tiberias. The patriarch tried to include Rabbi Meir, but the latter responded to the change in status among the sages with fury and abandoned the beit midrash. He may have set up a rival beit midrash, perhaps in Tiberias with Rabbi Elazar ben Shamua. Despite these complications, the patriarch seems to have asserted his authority over the majority of the population. The Talmud tells of his frequent travels throughout the Land of Israel, accompanied by the great sages of his day.[3]

With Usha replacing Yavneh as the new beit midrash, and with the new leadership structure secured, the patriarch could now turn his attention to the next challenge, which we might refer to as the eastern front.

ḤANANIA, NEPHEW OF RABBI YEHOSHUA: THE BEIT MIDRASH IN BABYLONIA

Ḥanania's Descent to Babylonia

Rabbi Yehoshua's nephew Ḥanania appears in a midrash that describes the centers of Torah learning at the end of the tannaitic era:

> Our rabbis taught: "Righteousness, righteousness, shall you pursue" [Deut. 16:20]. This teaches that one should go after the sages to the place of the yeshiva to have his case adjudicated. For example, after Rabbi Eliezer to the town of Lod, and after Rabban Yoḥanan ben Zakkai to the town of Bror Ḥayil, after Rabbi Yehoshua to Peki'in, after Rabban Gamliel to Yavneh, after Rabbi Akiva to Benei Brak, after Rabbi Mattia to Rome, after Rabbi Ḥanania ben Teradion to Sikhni, after Rabbi Yose to Tzippori, after Rabbi Yehuda ben Beteira to Netzivin, after Rabbi [Ḥanania the nephew of Rabbi] Yehoshua[4] to the Diaspora, after Rebbi to Beit She'arim, and after the sages to the chamber of hewn stone. (Sanhedrin 32b)

3. Urbach, "Judea to Galilee," 343 note 367.
4. This bracketed addition is according to the Munich manuscript. See *Dikdukei Sofrim*.

Ḥanania grew up in the Land of Israel and went to Babylonia after the Bar Kokhba revolt, as the following midrash relates:

> An incident is told of Rabbi Yehuda ben Beteira, Rabbi Mattia ben Ḥeresh, Rabbi Ḥanania the nephew of Rabbi Yehoshua, and Rabbi Yonatan, who were traveling out of the Land of Israel. When they came to Puteoli and remembered the Land of Israel, they raised their eyes heavenward, letting their tears flow, rent their garments, and recited the verse "When you have occupied it and are settled in it, take care to observe all the laws and rules that I have set before you this day."[5] Thereupon they returned to the Land of Israel. (Sifrei, Deuteronomy 80)

According to this midrash Ḥanania went to Babylonia along with a group of sages, some of whom hoped that by traveling abroad, they could continue to devote themselves to learning Torah without having to get involved in political affairs.[6] But Ḥanania seems to have gone to Babylonia for different reasons entirely:

> Ḥanina the nephew of Rabbi Yehoshua came to Capernaum, and the heretics worked a spell on him and set him riding upon a donkey on Shabbat. He went to his uncle Yehoshua, who anointed him with oil, and he recovered from the spell. Rabbi Yehoshua said to him: Since the donkey of that wicked person has roused itself against you, you cannot reside in the Land of Israel. So he went down from there to Babylon, where he died in peace. (Ecclesiastes Rabba 1)

This is a strange story. Ḥanania goes to Capernaum, where he is bewitched by the Christians – referred to as heretics – into riding a donkey on Shabbat. He returns to Rabbi Yehoshua, who anoints and

5. This is a combination of Deuteronomy 11:31 and 11:32. See M. Kahana, "The Virtue of Residing in the Land of Israel According to *Mekhilta Devarim*" [Hebrew], *Tarbiz* 62 (5753): 501–13.
6. See *Sages* II, Part Five.

heals him but informs him that since he has been tainted by heresy, he cannot remain in the Land of Israel. So he heads to Babylonia, where he dies in peace.

Is this a true story?[7] Is it suggesting that Ḥanania converted and then attempted to repent and return to the fold?[8] Rabbi Hyman explains this incident as follows:

> The heretics lured him with their deception and their promise of fraternity. They ensnared him in their net until he believed them that the Messiah had already arrived to repair the world. According to the sages, he rode a donkey on Shabbat. But Rabbi Yehoshua in his great wisdom showed his beloved nephew that the heretics spoke vain lies. Rabbi Yehoshua feared that "All who go to her cannot return" [Prov. 2:19], so he said to him that since the donkey of the wicked had roused itself against him, he could not remain in the Land of Israel. He was correct in sending Ḥanania to Babylonia, where there were no heretics, as is well known.[9]

The midrash is based on the verse "All who go to her cannot return" (Prov. 2:19). Rabbi Yehoshua suggests that anyone who has had contact with heresy cannot return to his normal routine. Heresy is a sort of addiction from which one can be weaned only in stages.[10] Maharal (Rabbi Judah Loew, 1520–1609, Prague) discusses this process:

7. Several scholars have written about the relationship between this midrash and the early one concerning the four sages who left the Land of Israel. Some point to the Talmud's description of Ḥanania's descent to Babylonia and his return to the Land of Israel during the days of Rabbi Yehoshua (Sukka 20b). According to this source, Rabbi Ḥanania went to Babylonia twice. But Tractate Sota suggests otherwise. See Y. Gafni, *The Jews of Babylonia During the Talmudic Period* [Hebrew] (Jerusalem, 5751), 80 note 111.
8. R. Asaf, *Caught in the Brambles* [Hebrew] (Jerusalem, 5766), 136–51. Asaf describes the conversion of Rabbi Schneur Zalman of Liadi's son Moshe, as chronicled in Hasidic tales.
9. Hyman, *Legends*, 504.
10. See M. Hirshman, *Kohelet Rabba 1–4: Introduction, Critical Edition, and Commentary* [Hebrew] (PhD diss., New York, 1983).

> The reason is known to the wise and to the sages, especially when it comes to these particular sins – heresy and illicit sexual liaisons. Heresy harnesses the evil impulse in service of other ends, and the person who succumbs to it becomes a new person and cannot return to his former self.... He cannot escape alive unless he departs from this world. (Maharal, *Insights into Talmudic Stories*, Avoda Zara, 40)

Why was Ḥanania banished from the Land of Israel? According to Hyman, he needed distance from that which had ensnared him. Nahmanides (Rabbi Moshe ben Nahman, 1194–1270, Spain) offers a more theological explanation:

> The Jewish people's closeness to God is what leads to their exile and punishment. This is all the more true of those who merit to dwell in God's land. They are like the king's advisers. If they honor the king properly, then all is well. But their rebellion is the gravest sin, because they are essentially making war with the king in his own palace and provoking him to his face. How does the king respond? He banishes them from his palace and makes trouble for them wherever they go. (Sermon for Rosh HaShana)[11]

The Struggle for Hegemony

The persecution that followed the Bar Kokhba revolt was thought to mark the end of Jewish life in the Land of Israel. Until the rabbis established the beit midrash at Usha, there was concern that the new center of Jewish learning would be established outside of Israel. Rabbi Akiva, for instance, went to intercalate the year in Nehardea:

> Rabbi Akiva said: When I went down to Nehardea to proclaim a leap year, I met Neḥemia, a resident of Beit Deli. He said to me: I

11. Nahmanides, "Sermons of Nahmanides" [Hebrew], in *The Letters of Nahmanides*, Chavel ed. (Jerusalem, 5723), 251–52. Also see A. Ravitzky, "Land of Fear and Trembling" [Hebrew], in *Engraved on the Tablets* (Tel Aviv, 5759); and my *A Nation Apart: Homeland and Diaspora* [Hebrew] (Tel Aviv, 5766).

> heard that except for Rabbi Yehuda ben Baba, they do not allow a woman to marry in the Land of Israel on the evidence of one witness. And I said to him: This is so. He said to me: Tell them in my name: You know that the country is overrun by troops. I have a tradition from Rabban Gamliel the Elder that one may allow a woman to marry on the evidence of one witness. And when I came and related the matter before Rabban Gamliel, he rejoiced at my words and said: We have found a colleague for Rabbi Yehuda ben Baba. (Mishna Yevamot 16:7)

This mishna teaches that Rabbi Akiva had to leave the borders of the Roman Empire in order to intercalate the year. He went to Nehardea, where there was an active Jewish community.[12] In the years after the rebellion, once the center at Usha was established under the leadership of Rashbag, Ḥanania tried to establish himself as the Jewish leader responsible for intercalating the year. His attempt is documented in both the Jerusalem and the Babylonian Talmuds.

1. The Jerusalem Talmud's Version

> They do not intercalate the year abroad, and if they do, it is not intercalated. This applies when they can intercalate in the Land of Israel. But if they cannot intercalate in the Land of Israel, then they do intercalate the year abroad.
>
> Jeremiah intercalated the year abroad. Ezekiel intercalated the year abroad. Barukh the son of Neriah intercalated the year abroad. Ḥanania the nephew of Rabbi Yehoshua intercalated the year abroad.
>
> Rebbi[13] sent him three letters with Rabbi Yitzhak and Rabbi Natan. In one he wrote: To his holiness, Ḥanania. And in

12. See Y. Gafni, *Jews of Babylonia*, 78–79. Also see A. Burstein, *The Problem of Intercalating the Year in the Diaspora* [Hebrew], *Sinai* 38 (5716): 32–46.
13. Although the Talmud says Rebbi, it is actually referring to Rebbi's father, Rashbag. The name "Rebbi" is a title used to refer to the patriarch in the Land of Israel. See Z. Rabinovitch, *The Gates of Torah of the Land of Israel* [Hebrew] (Jerusalem, 5700), 275, quoted in Alon, *History of the Jews*, vol. 2, 76 note 145.

one he wrote: The kid goats you have left behind have become rams. And in one he wrote: If you do not accept our authority, go out to the thorny wilderness, and be the slaughterer of the sacrifice with Neḥunyon the sprinkler.

He read the first and heeded it, the second and heeded it. But when he read the third, he wanted to disgrace the messengers.

They said to him: You cannot, for you have already treated us with honor.

Rabbi Yitzḥak stood up and read in the Torah: These are the festivals of Ḥanania the nephew of Rabbi Yehoshua.[14]

They said to him: "These are the festivals of the Lord" [Lev. 23:4].

He replied: They are for you.

Rabbi Natan rose and read from the Prophets: For from Babylonia will Torah go forth, and the word of the Lord from Nehar Pekod.

They said to him: "For from Zion will Torah go forth, and the word of the Lord from Jerusalem" [Is. 2:3].

He said to them: For you.

Ḥanania went and complained about them to Rabbi Yehuda ben Beteira in Netzivin. He said to them: After them, after them!

He said to him: Do I not know what is over there? What tells me that they are masters of calculating the calendar as I am? Since they are not so well informed as I am in calculating the calendar, let them listen to what I say.

And since they are masters of calculation as much as you, you must listen to them.

He rose and mounted his horse. Places he reached, he reached. And the ones he did not reach observed in error. (Y. Sanhedrin 1:2 [19a])

This passage begins with the assertion that "They do not intercalate the year abroad, and if they do, it is not intercalated." This is an attempt to

14. The manuscripts read, "These are the festivals of the Lord Ḥanania, nephew of Rabbi Yehoshua." The words "the Lord" are a scribal error, as noted in the Zussman edition.

preserve the status of the Great Court as the source of authority for the entire Jewish people. The Jerusalem Talmud then qualifies this statement: If it is impossible to intercalate the year in the Land of Israel, then they do it abroad. The Jerusalem Talmud cites several examples from the Bible: Jeremiah, Ezekiel, and Barukh the son of Neriah, all prophetic figures. Also included in this list is Rabbi Ḥanania the nephew of Rabbi Yehoshua, who stands out as a rabbinic rather than biblical figure. The text deliberately presents him in this context so as to capture the reader's attention.[15] The midrash then relates a story about Ḥanania's experience of intercalating the year. The patriarch sends three letters in the hands of two sages. This story, though harsh, is not without humor as the messengers, Rabbi Yitzhak and Rabbi Natan, make light of Ḥanania's attempt to present Nehar Pekod as an alternative to Jerusalem.

The messengers present each letter separately. Presumably Ḥanania does not receive them all on the same day, since he reacts to each in turn. The first letter says, "To his holiness, Ḥanania," and he is pleased to see that he has been accorded the respect due to him. The second letter informs him that there are rams in the Land of Israel, thanks to him: "The kid goats you have left behind have become rams." He continues to treat the messengers respectfully. But then he receives the third letter, which reads like an ultimatum: "If you do not accept our authority, go out to the thorny wilderness, and be the slaughterer of the sacrifice with Neḥunyon the sprinkler."

This third letter paints a very different picture. Ḥanania is told that either he may accept the authority of the sages in the Land of Israel, or he must "go out to the thorny wilderness." This cryptic message alludes to the parable of the thorn in Judges 9, in which the lowly thorn, though devoid of gifts, would be king.[16] The rest of the sentence is equally difficult for Ḥanania to digest: "be the slaughterer of the sacrifice with Neḥunyon the sprinkler." The sages are mocking Ḥanania,

15. This is a well-known literary technique in which the narrator captures the reader's attention by relating three similar sentences followed by a fourth that is completely different and surprising. For the use of this technique in the Bible, see Y. Zakovitch, *On Three and On Four* [Hebrew] (Jerusalem, 5739).

16. This is how the Korban HaEda explains this line in the Jerusalem Talmud, Tractate Nedarim.

who wishes to establish his own Temple in Babylonia, by alluding to the Temple of Onias (Neḥunia) built in Egypt during the Second Temple period.[17] Ḥanania is offended by their words. But his community, who took its cue from his initial response, has already come to respect these messengers and even honors them with the reading of the Torah and *haftara* on Shabbat.

Now we come to the third act of the comic drama. Rabbi Yitzḥak stands up and begins reading from the Torah. He deliberately distorts the original biblical verse: Instead of saying, "These are the festivals of the Lord," he says, "These are the festivals of Ḥanania." The people rush to correct him: "the festivals of the Lord." Rabbi Yitzḥak laughs and says, "They are for you." That is, for us they are the festivals of the Lord, but if you intercalate the year, then your festivals will be holy no longer to the Lord, but to Ḥanania.

Rabbi Natan stands up to read from the Prophets, and he, too, distorts a verse: "For from Babylonia will Torah go forth, and the word of the Lord from Nehar Pekod." The people rush to correct him: "For from Zion will Torah go forth, and the word of the Lord from Jerusalem." Rabbi Natan responds, "That is the case for you."

The next scene takes place in the beit midrash of Rabbi Yehuda ben Beteira in Netzivin, the first house of study established outside Israel.[18] Rabbi Yehuda ben Beteira's response, "After them," implies that the only true center of halakhic authority is in the Land of Israel. Ḥanania continues to scoff at the sages of Israel. But Rabbi Yehuda ben Beteira does not take his side. He travels throughout the Babylonian Diaspora in an effort to undo the damage Ḥanania caused in intercalating the year. As the Talmud relates, those places he did not reach continued to observe in error.

17. The Korban HaEda comments, "Do what the high priest Neḥunia ben Shimon did when he built an altar in Egypt." The Penei Moshe understands Neḥunia to refer to Neḥunia the Babylonian exilarch, but this explanation has no textual corroboration.
18. For more on Rabbi Yehuda ben Beteira and his yeshiva in Netzivin, see *Sages* II, Part Five.

2. *The Babylonian Talmud's Version*

When Ḥanina the son of the nephew of Rabbi Yehoshua went down to the Diaspora, he would intercalate the year and establish months outside the Land of Israel, which is prohibited. The sages sent two scholars after him, Rabbi Yose ben Kipper and the son of the son of Zekharya ben Kevutal. When he saw them, he said to them: Why did you come?

They said to him: We came to study Torah.

Rabbi Ḥanina announced: These men are the great ones of the generation, and their forefathers served in the Temple! As we learned in a mishna: Zekharya ben Kevutal says: Many times I would read before him in the Book of Daniel.

Rabbi Ḥanina would rule a particular thing impure, and they would deliberately rule it pure. He would rule something forbidden, and they would rule it permitted. He announced regarding them: These men – they are worthless. They are of desolation!

They said to him: You have already built, and you can no longer demolish. You have made a fence, and you can no longer breach it.

He said to them: Why when I rule something impure do you rule it pure? And why when I rule something forbidden do you rule it permitted?

They said to him: Because you are intercalating years and establishing months outside the Land of Israel.

He said to them: But did not Akiva ben Yosef intercalate years and establish months outside the Land of Israel?

They said to him: Leave Rabbi Akiva aside, for he left no one equal to him in the Land of Israel.

He said to them: But I too have left no one equal to me in the Land of Israel!

They said to him: The kid goats you left behind have become rams with horns. And the sages have said to us: Go and say to him in our name that if he obeys us, very well; but if not, he will be excommunicated. And say to our brothers in the Diaspora: If they obey us, very well; but if not, let them go up

> to a mountain and let Aḥiya build an altar, and let Ḥanina play the harp, and let them deny God and say: They have no portion in the God of Israel!
>
> Immediately the entire nation moaned with weeping and said: Heaven forbid! We do have a portion in the God of Israel!
>
> But why all this? For it is stated, "For from Zion will Torah go forth, and the word of the Lord from Jerusalem" [Is. 2:3]. (Berakhot 63a)

The Babylonian Talmud was clearly familiar with the Jerusalem Talmud's version, which it modifies and reworks.[19] The sages have different names, and they are the descendants of those who served in the Temple. The figures in the Babylonian version are also more confrontational. In the Jerusalem Talmud's version, biblical verses are read with cynicism as a way of subtly criticizing Ḥanania. But in the Babylonian Talmud, the sages directly challenge Ḥanania's authority. The last part of the story, which parallels the Jerusalem Talmud's command to "go out to the thorny wilderness," refers to the establishment of an alternate temple outside Jerusalem.

In the Babylonian Talmud's version, the Babylonian community responds with a rousing cry of repentance: "We do have a portion in the God of Israel!"

IN BABYLONIA THE HALAKHA FOLLOWS ḤANANIA

In the Jerusalem Talmud's version, the sages did not forgive or forget Ḥanania's attempt to intercalate the year.[20] This story came to represent the threat posed by the Diaspora to the Jewish community in the Land of Israel, which had lost its prominence after the Bar Kokhba revolt.[21]

19. Yonah Frankel thinks otherwise. He cites this story as an example of a tradition that exists independently in both talmudic texts. See Frankel, *Aggadic Story*, 51–52. I think the Babylonian tradition is not independent, however, because the mention of the altar at the end clearly refers to the third letter in the Jerusalem Talmud's version.
20. The Jerusalem Talmud goes on to involve Ḥanania in the terrible fate of the captive Babylonian girls who fell into Shmuel's hands in Ketubot 23a. See V. Noam, "The Case of a Story Taken Captive" [Hebrew], *Jerusalem Studies* (5763): 9–21.
21. The argument between the historians Graetz and HaLevi is quoted in Gafni, *Jews of Babylonia*, 80 note 113.

Even if Ḥanania was forced to scale back his attempt to undermine the hegemony of the sages of Israel, this was merely one lost battle in a war that had only just begun. As the Babylonian leadership and scholarship gained force, Ḥanania became an increasingly important figure. He was regarded as the source of Babylonian Jewry's customs and traditions, as the following examples attest.

Praying for Rain Outside the Land of Israel

The Mishna in the first chapter of Tractate Ta'anit cites a dispute regarding the proper time of year to begin praying for rain. One opinion is that one should not begin praying until the seventh day of the month of Ḥeshvan out of concern for the pilgrims returning from Babylonia. This is very considerate of the Mishna, though it is clear who espouses this position. The Talmud responds to the Mishna:

> It was taught in a *baraita*: Ḥanania says: And in the Diaspora, [they begin praying for rain] sixty days after the autumnal equinox. Rav Huna bar Ḥiya said in the name of Shmuel: The halakha accords with Ḥanania. (Ta'anit 10a)[22]

Hot Food on Shabbat

The Mishna's ruling about placing a cooked dish on the stove on Shabbat is ambiguous. According to one opinion, it is permitted to return a dish to the stove only if it was already cooked before Shabbat. A more lenient view allows for the dish to be left on the stove so long as it was heated even minimally. The dispute in the Talmud revolves around the Mishna's statement that "one may not place":

22. See the responsa of Rosh [Hebrew], 4:10, regarding the status of Babylonia vs. the Land of Israel in talmudic passages relating to geography: "We always follow the Babylonians when they disagree with the sages of the Land of Israel in matters of halakha, because the Babylonian Talmud is the dominant one. This is the case in matters of permitted vs. prohibited, liable vs. exempt, and pure vs. impure. But when it comes to matters that are historically contingent, the matter depends upon the era, time, and place."

> They inquired: Is the meaning of the phrase "one may not place" that one may not return food to the stove on Shabbat, but one may leave food on it even if the stove was neither shoveled nor banked with ash? This is the view of Ḥanania. For it was taught: Ḥanania says: If any food has been cooked to the level of Ben Drosai's food, then it is permitted to leave it on the stove before Shabbat, even though the stove is neither shoveled nor banked. (Shabbat 36b)

According to Ḥanania, if the food has just begun cooking, such that only the most ill-mannered and vulgar people (such as the infamous bandit Ben Drosai) would find it palatable, it is considered sufficiently cooked; one may place it on the stove before Shabbat so that the dish continues cooking once Shabbat begins. (This is the halakhic source for the permissibility of cholent, a dish that is not fully cooked before Shabbat but continues cooking after sunset.)

The halakhic authority Rabbi Shimon Doran of fifteenth century Algiers explained in his *Sefer HaTashbetz* (part 4, column 3, section 8):

> Rabbi Sherira Gaon wrote that the halakha follows Ḥanania, and this is what Rashi wrote as well, and these are his words: We leave our dishes on stoves with an uncovered fire, relying on the ruling of Ḥanania, since the unattributed mishna reflects his opinion. And this is what the Rosh ruled as well. Since there are many opinions regarding this matter, and since the Jewish people want to be able to enjoy Shabbat, they will not listen to anyone who rules more stringently. Therefore we should let them be and permit them to follow Ḥanania's ruling.

During talmudic times, Shmuel regarded Ḥanania as the local halakhic authority for the Jews of Babylonia, and he followed his rulings. And the rabbinic academy in Nehardea followed Shmuel, even though the Mishna and the Jerusalem Talmud did not. Thus Ḥanania became the authority for the Jews of Babylonia and helped them establish their autonomy vis-à-vis the sages of the Land of Israel.[23]

23. Gafni, *Jews of Babylonia*, 81.

Chapter Fifteen

Rabbi Natan: A Babylonian Sage in Usha

Unlike Ḥanania, who left the Land of Israel for Babylonia, Rabbi Natan brought the Torah of Babylonia to the Land of Israel. We have already encountered Rabbi Natan as Rabbi Meir's partner in the dispute with the patriarch. He appears as a member of the first generation of sages at Usha, but he was actually born in Babylon. Hence he was referred to as "Rabbi Natan the Babylonian."

The sages of the Land of Israel looked down upon the Jews of Babylonia for failing to heed King Cyrus' decree permitting their return to the Land of Israel in 520 BCE.[1] When they wanted to cast aspersions on someone, they would refer to him as "the Babylonian." For instance,

1. This is apparent in several sources, mostly from the Land of Israel. See S. Lieberman, "So It Was, and So It Will Be," in *Studies in the Torah of the Land of Israel* [Hebrew] (Jerusalem, 5751), 331–38. It is also the subject of Reish Lakish's famous criticism of Rabba bar bar Ḥana: "God hates you" (Yoma 9b). Also consider Rabbi Yehuda HaLevi's criticism of his own practice of praising the Land of Israel while living in the Diaspora.

this is how the Mishna describes the bridge built in Jerusalem to bring the goat to the wilderness on Yom Kippur:

> And they made a ramp for him [the person leading the goat] because of the Babylonians, who would pull the hair of the person leading the goat and say to him: Take and go forth, take and go forth. (Mishna Yoma 6:4)

The Talmud attests in the name of Rabba bar bar Ḥana:

> They were not Babylonians but rather Alexandrians; but because they [the sages] hated the Babylonians, they used to refer to them this way. (Yoma 66b)

THE HISTORY OF BABYLONIAN JEWRY

After the destruction of the Temple, many sages began visiting Babylonia and investing in its Jewish life, as we saw with the case of Rabbi Akiva's intercalation of the year. But we do not have precise information about the centers of Jewish settlement in Babylonia prior to the Temple's destruction. Josephus writes about a Jewish kingdom that was active in Nehardea under the leadership of two brothers, Hasinai and Hanilai.[2] His account of the conversion of the kings of Adiabene (*Antiquities* XX: 17–96) presupposes an active Babylonian community during the time of the Temple, since it is inconceivable that such a conversion could take place in the absence of an active Jewish presence.

We also know that Herod sought to strengthen his kingdom by glorifying the Hasmonean line and strengthening foreign presences. He appointed Ḥananel the Babylonian to the position of high priest and helped a group of Babylonian immigrants establish themselves in the Land of Israel by offering them a tax exemption and a land grant. It seems that Benei Beteira, who were active in Hillel's day, were among these Babylonian immigrants. Hillel himself came from Babylonia, and stories about him refer to Babylonian intellectual traditions – though

2. *Antiquities* XVIII:310–79. Also see Gafni, *Jews of Babylonia*, 61–64.

of course these sources were reworked by later generations.[3] The most significant Babylonian figure of the Temple period is Rabbi Yehuda ben Beteira, of whom it was said, "You are in Netzivin, but your net is cast over Jerusalem" (Pesaḥim 3b).

RABBI NATAN ARRIVES IN THE LAND OF ISRAEL

Many sources speak of Rabbi Natan's Babylonian origins. He probably immigrated to the Land of Israel around the time of the Bar Kokhba revolt, at which point he offered the following exegesis on martyrdom:

> Rabbi Natan says: "Of those who love Me and keep My commandments" [Ex. 20:6] refers to those who dwell in the Land of Israel and risk their lives for the sake of the commandments. Why are you being led out to be decapitated? Because I circumcised my son to be a Jew. Why are you being led out to be burned? Because I read the Torah. Why are you being led out to be crucified? Because I ate unleavened bread. Why are you receiving a hundred lashes? Because I performed the ceremony of the lulav. And it says: "Those with which I was wounded in the house of my friends" [Zech. 13:6] – these wounds caused me to be beloved by my Father in heaven. (*Mekhilta deRabbi Yishmael, Yitro,* Masekhta deBaḥodesh 6)

As Rabbi Natan faithfully documents, the Romans killed Jews for violating the ban on castration by circumcising their sons. Learning Torah was regarded as an even greater threat, because it was a way for Jews to influence public opinion and begin rallying for the next revolt; thus, anyone who was caught studying Torah was burned at the stake. Likewise, the observance of Passover was understood to symbolize the very freedom that the Romans found so threatening; thus, anyone caught celebrating this day was crucified. But a Jew caught carrying a lulav was merely beaten.[4]

3. Gafni, *Jews of Babylonia,* 70–76.
4. S. Lieberman, "Religious Persecution," in *Studies in the Torah of the Land of Israel,* 351–52.

Where was Rabbi Natan during the revolt? Perhaps he was still in Babylonia and came to the Land of Israel only after the revolt, as a sign of his identification with the inhabitants of the land. He spoke very passionately of Israel, using singular expressions like the following:

> Rabbi Natan said: There is no love like the love of Torah; and there is no wisdom like the wisdom of the Land of Israel; and there is no heroism like the heroism of Persia; and there is no licentiousness like the licentiousness of the Arabs; and there is no crassness like the crassness of Ilem; and there is no hypocrisy like the hypocrisy of Babylonia, as it is written, "And he answered: To build a shrine for it in the land of Shinar" [Zech. 5:11]; and there is no witchcraft like the witchcraft of Egypt. (*Avot deRabbi Natan*, recension A, ch. 28)

According to the Tosefta, when Rabbi Natan learned that the first fruits brought by Agrippa, a descendant of Herod, were accepted by the priests and that Agrippa was greeted as a brother, he responded harshly:

> They said in the name of Rabbi Natan: The Jews became liable for destruction because they flattered Agrippa the king. (Tosefta Sota 7:16)

Another source relates that Rabbi Natan traveled to distant coastal towns, perhaps those of ancient Greece:

> Rabbi Natan said: Once I went to visit the coastal towns, and a woman came before me who had circumcised her first son and he died, her second son and he died, and now she brought her third son before me. I saw that he was red, and I told the woman: Wait for him until his blood is absorbed into his flesh. She waited for him until his blood was absorbed into his flesh and then she circumcised him, and he lived. And they called him Natan the Babylonian after me. On another occasion I traveled to the province of Cappadocia, and a woman came before me who had circumcised her first son and he died, her second son and he died,

> and now she brought her third son before me. I saw that he was green. I looked closely at him and did not see in him any covenantal blood. I said to the mother: Wait for him until he is full-blooded. And she waited for him and then she circumcised him, and he lived. And they called his name Natan the Babylonian after me. (Shabbat 134a; Tosefta Shabbat 15:8)

This passage grapples with difficult questions about the boundary between medicine and mysticism. Rabbi Natan is presented as someone who has discovered the underlying cause of a medical condition. He instructs mothers of the afflicted to wait to circumcise their sons until their blood is absorbed into their flesh.[5]

When the court was established at Usha, Rabbi Natan was named head of court, second only to the patriarch. As we have seen, he received this distinguished title on account of his father, who had held an important position in Babylonia. According to Rabbi Sherira Gaon, his father was the Babylonian exilarch. But other sources suggest that his father may simply have been part of the Jewish coterie that was close to the Babylonian rulers.[6]

BABYLONIAN TEACHINGS IN THE LAND OF ISRAEL

Rabbi Natan brought Babylonian teachings to the Land of Israel. The following two sources attest to the differences between the intellectual traditions of Babylonia and those of the Land of Israel.

Shofar Blasts to Herald the Sabbath

> The rabbis taught: On Friday afternoon we sound six blasts of the shofar [to announce the arrival of Shabbat]. The first is meant to

5. Several later commentators sought to identify the diseases that affected the blood of the infant. Perhaps anemia was responsible for the green child, and hemophilia for the red one. See A. Steinberg, *Halakhic and Medical Encyclopedia* [Hebrew] (Jerusalem, 5753), s.v. "Circumcision," 684–90.
6. Rabbi Sherira Gaon points to Rashbag's use of the term "Kamara" to refer to Rabbi Natan. This term sounds like "Kamar," the belt worn by the exilarch when standing before the Persian kings. See Gafni, *Jews of Babylonia*, 96–97.

> stop people from performing labor in the fields. The second is to stop labor in the city and to stop shops from doing business. The third proclaims that it is time to light the Shabbat candles. These are the words of Rabbi Natan. But Rabbi Yehuda HaNasi says: The third is to signal that it is time to remove *tefillin*.
>
> After this third blast, the blower would wait enough time to roast small fish over the fire, or enough time to stick bread to the wall of an oven and bake it there. And then he would sound a *tekia*, a *terua*, and another *tekia*, and rest.
>
> Rabban Shimon ben Gamliel said: What should we do about the Babylonians, for they sound just a *tekia* and a *terua*, and then they rest after sounding this *terua*? Can it be that they would sound just a *tekia* and a *terua*? That makes for just five blasts. Rather, it must be that the Babylonians would sound a *tekia*, then another *tekia*, and finally a *terua*, and then they would rest after sounding this *terua*. The Babylonians are retaining their ancestors' customs. (Shabbat 35b)

The Mishna describes the shofar blasts that were sounded to herald the Sabbath. Rabbi Natan transmits the Babylonian custom, and Rabbi Yehuda HaNasi transmits the custom of the Land of Israel. As the passage attests, Rashbag is exasperated by the Babylonian custom: "What should we do about the Babylonians, for they sound just a *tekia* and a *terua*, and then they rest after sounding this *terua*? Can it be they that would sound just a *tekia* and a *terua*?" He complains that the Babylonians greet the Sabbath with a *terua* (a cry of alarm) rather than a *tekia* (a calming cry). But he accepts that "The Babylonians are retaining their ancestors' customs."

This is a classic example of how Rabbi Natan brought traditions and teachings with him from Babylonia.[7]

7. Epstein, *Literature of the Tanna'im*, 169. But see Gafni's reservations in his *Jews of Babylonia*, 90.

The Tip of the Letter *Yud*

> If one says, "Write a *get* and give it to my wife," "Divorce her," "Write a letter and give it to her" – then they may write and give it to her. "Dismiss her," "Provide for her," "Deal with her according to the law," "Deal with her as is proper" – then it is as if he said nothing. (Mishna Gittin 6:5)

This mishna discusses the case of a man who wishes to write a bill divorcing his wife. (In mishnaic times, a woman's consent was not needed in order to divorce her.) Is the language used by the man a sufficiently clear sign of his desire to sever all ties with her? In the case of the first few expressions, the answer is yes; but the latter expressions do not constitute a proper divorce proceeding.

The phrase "Dismiss her" is written as *Patteruha* in all the printed editions of the Mishna. But in the manuscripts from the Land of Israel it appears as *Pitruha*, with the letter *yud*.[8] The Talmud discusses this terminology:

> It was taught: Rabbi Natan said: If the husband said, *Patteruha* (dismiss her), his words are upheld. If he pronounced it *Pitruha*, he said nothing.
>
> Rava said: Rabbi Natan was a Babylonian, and he thus differentiated between the pronunciations of *Pitruha* [a Hebrew word that connotes release from debts] and *Patteruha* [an Aramaic word that connotes divorce]. But the *Tanna* of our Mishna, who was from the Land of Israel, did not differentiate between the two pronunciations. (Gittin 65b)

The root *p-t-r* was not considered acceptable divorce parlance in the Mishna of the Land of Israel. When Rabbi Natan first encounters this Mishna, he responds by distinguishing between *Patteruha* (which was deemed acceptable) and *Pitruha* (which was not). Rava, a later authority,

8. This is the case in the Kauffman, Parma, Cambridge, and Munich manuscripts. See *Dikdukei Sofrim*, Gittin, Feldblum ed. (New York, 5726).

explains that the linguistic distinction reflects a geographical one. This is an excellent example of how the language used by a sage can attest to his origin and cultural background.[9]

The language of the various early biblical translations also sheds light on this matter. Onkeles translated the Bible's "book of divorce" (*sefer keritut*) as *get pitturin*. In contrast, Targum Pseudo-Yonatan translates *sefer keritut* as *sefer terukhin*, and Targum Neophyti translates it as *iggeret shevukin*. All three of these terms appear in the Mishna (Gittin 9:3), suggesting that halakhic discourse influenced the biblical translations. The Mishna's invocation of all three terms used in the Targum also serves for some scholars as evidence of the early dating of these translations.[10]

THE TEACHINGS OF REBBI AND THE TEACHINGS OF RABBI NATAN

During talmudic times, wealthy individuals were reluctant to bequeath their property to their daughters. After all, a daughter would bring all her possessions with her into her husband's home, and if she were to predecease him, her husband would inherit her. Fathers did not want to risk losing their possessions to their sons-in-law. So the sages instituted a "sons' *ketuba*" as a sort of insurance policy: If a woman were to die before her husband, her children (i.e., her father's grandchildren) would inherit her dowry. This "sons' *ketuba*" encouraged fathers to relinquish their daughters' dowries more willingly.

> If he did not write for her, "Male children whom you will have by me will inherit the money of your *ketuba*, besides what they share with their brothers," he is liable, because this is a condition of the court. (Mishna Ketubot 4:10)

This mishna deals with the case of a man who did not write a "sons'

9. See Y. Breuer's discussion of this case in "*Patteruha/Pitruha*," *Leshoneinu* 5756. For a succinct version, see Gafni, *Jews of Babylonia*, 87–89.
10. The halakhic authorities relied on Targum Onkeles in formulating the *get*. See *Responsa Binyamin Ze'ev*, which addresses the question of the terms *peturin* and *pitturin*. The author decides in favor of *peturin* (without the *yud*), supported by Targum Onkeles.

ketuba" for his wife. Will his children still inherit their mother? The mishna answers in the affirmative, because this is a condition stipulated by the court.

The mishna spells out the language of the "sons' ketuba": "Male children whom you will have by me will inherit the money of your *ketuba*, besides what they share with their brothers." The term "inherit" signifies that the money the sons receive constitutes a bequest rather than a present, which is an important legal distinction. Money for a bequest is collected only from unpledged property, that is, property that has not been pledged by a debtor in payment for the debt. In contrast, money for a present is collected from both pledged and unpledged property. The mishna above, which specifies that the "sons' *ketuba*" is an inheritance, reflects the opinion of Rabbi Yoḥanan ben Beroka, one of the great students of Rabbi Yehoshua of Yavneh. The Talmud elaborates:

> Rabbi Natan said to Rebbi: You taught your mishna in accordance with the opinion of Rabbi Yoḥanan ben Beroka. For we learned in a mishna: If a husband did not write for his wife the stipulation that "the male children you will have by me will inherit the money of your *ketuba* in addition to their share of my estate that they will inherit with their half brothers," the husband is nevertheless obligated to honor this arrangement, because it is an automatic stipulation instituted by the court.
>
> And Rebbi said to Rabbi Natan: We read the mishna as follows: They will take. But Rebbi said afterward: I was possessed by childishness and dared to reply impudently to Rabbi Natan the Babylonian. (Bava Batra 131a)

The two interlocutors here are Rabbi Natan, part of the founding generation at Usha, and Rabbi Yehuda (Rebbi), the young son of the patriarch. Rabbi Natan asks Rabbi Yehuda if he teaches the mishna in accordance with Rabbi Yoḥanan ben Beroka, as per the wording quoted above: "Male children whom you will have by me will inherit the money of your *ketuba*, besides what they share with their brothers." Specifically Rabbi Natan wants to know if Rebbi holds that the sons receive the money as a bequest rather than a gift. Rebbi responds that in fact they read the mishna as "they will take," meaning that the sons receive the money as a gift. Later Rebbi admits to having made a mistake: "I was possessed by childishness," he says, perhaps a reference to the significant age difference between himself and the much older Rabbi Natan. Rebbi mistakenly thought that the sons receive the money as a gift, but Rabbi Natan taught him that it is in fact a bequest.

A comparison to the parallel source in the Jerusalem Talmud sheds further light on this conversation:[11]

> Rabbi Zeira (Rabbi Yasa) said in the name of Rabbi Yoḥanan: Rebbi asked Natan the Babylonian: What is the reason that they said the law follows Rabbi Yoḥanan ben Beroka's ruling?
>
> He said to them: Did you yourself not teach that if the husband did not write for his wife this stipulation, the male children will inherit?
>
> He said to them: I said not that they will inherit, but that they will take [as a gift].
>
> He came to his father [Rashbag]. He said to him: You have insulted Natan the Babylonian. You have a case here not of a gift, but of a bequest.
>
> Rabbi Yose ben Rabbi Bun said: He said to him: I erred in what I taught you. This is the case not of a gift, but of a bequest. (Y. Ketubot 4:11 [29a])

Now the story becomes clearer. The young Rebbi asks the elder sage Rabbi Natan why the sages ruled in accordance with Rabbi Yoḥanan ben Beroka (the minority opinion) in the matter of the sons' *ketuba*. Rabbi Natan responds: "Didn't you yourself teach the mishna in Ketubot in accordance with Rabbi Yoḥanan, that is, that the sons inherit?" Rebbi responds with the impudence and confidence of youth: "I said not that they will inherit, but that they will take [as a gift]." He insists

11. I used a version of the Jerusalem Talmud informed by Epstein's notes in his *Text of the Mishna*, 12. He reworked the print version based on the Babylonian Talmud version, his own reasoning, and other findings.

that the elder sage misquoted the mishna.[12] Rebbi relates this incident to his father, who grows furious at him: "You have insulted Natan the Babylonian."

Rabbi Natan was correct. A later *Amora*, Rabbi Yose ben Rabbi Bun, clarifies Rashbag's statement to his son. Rashbag had initially taught that the sons' ketuba was like a gift, so he taught his son Rebbi that "they will take." But once he heard Rabbi Natan, he corrected himself and taught that this *ketuba* is a bequest rather than a gift.[13]

RABBI NATAN IN RABBINIC TRADITION

Rabbi Natan is rarely cited in halakhic discourse, in keeping with Rashbag's injunction in the story about the rebellion in the court. One notable exception is the mishna (Berakhot 9:5) that speaks of the need to disregard law in time of crisis: "It is a time to act for the Lord; they violated Your teaching" (Ps. 119:126).

Rabbi Natan's teachings were incorporated into the Mishna, but no one went on to quote him by name. He seems to have suffered the fate described in the *Mekhilta*: "For as long as a sage is alive, his wisdom endures. When a sage dies, his wisdom dies with him" (*Mekhilta deRabbi Yishmael, Yitro*, Masekhta deAmalek 2).

12. The Babylonian version of the story uses the word *yasbun* instead of *yatlun*, which has the same meaning and simply reflects geographical linguistic differences.
13. The Talmud (Ketubot 55a) relates that the people of Pumbedita taught the mishna as "they will inherit," whereas the people of Mata Meḥasia taught, "they will take."

Chapter Sixteen

Gathering Halakhic Sources at Usha

In the previous chapter, we witnessed Rabbi Natan and Rebbi preoccupied with determining the proper wording of the Mishna under the watchful eye of Rabban Shimon ben Gamliel. This was the primary enterprise of the beit midrash at Usha. This was also the original task that the sages had taken upon themselves at their founding meeting: Anyone who knew of a halakhic tradition was instructed to share it in the beit midrash, where the sages sought to gather all the material from the earliest days of the Oral Torah and create the first halakhic corpus in Jewish history.

The difficult experience of the persecution that followed the Bar Kokhba revolt impelled Rashbag and his colleagues to gather and compile all the sources from prior generations.[1] Rashbag sought to create an

1. Y. Taborsky wrote of the tendency to gather and codify sources in the wake of a crisis period. See his "Maimonides' *Mishneh Torah*: Its Agenda and Purpose" [Hebrew], *Proceedings of the Israeli National Academy of the Sciences*, 5:1 (5732): 13–14. Also see his book *Introduction to Maimonides' Mishneh Torah* (Jerusalem, 5751), 56.

authoritative Mishna that would incorporate the views of all the various *battei midrash*, with halakhic sources organized by subject.[2] His work laid the foundations for that of his son Rabbi Yehuda HaNasi, the editor of the Mishna: "Rebbi added and deleted, examined and checked through all the mishnayot ... he combined sources from Rabbi Meir and Rabbi Yehuda, Rabbi Yose and Rabbi Shimon and Rabbi Elazar; pair by pair, he added to the mishnayot. In some places he would add the words of his colleagues and others."[3] So there were two stages in the compiling of the Mishna. First the sources were collected during Rashbag's tenure, and then they were edited and reworked by Rebbi and his contemporaries.[4]

Did Rashbag merely devise a way of preserving earlier sources, or did he lay the groundwork for the book of laws that would accompany the Jewish people for generations? The historian Arnold Toynbee (who famously referred to the Jewish people as a "living fossil") describes the historical processes that lead to codification. He argues that the demand for such collections is greatest just before social catastrophe, when a reasonable period of time has elapsed since the laws' original codification. According to Toynbee, codification is a sign of attenuation; a depressed cultural spirit that leads to the collection and codification of sources, as opposed to the flourishing creativity of those who originally wrote and developed these sources.[5] But Rashbag's enterprise suggests just the opposite. His compilation was accompanied by a spirit of optimism and renewal that followed (rather than preceded) a terrible crisis. The generation that survived the destruction of Beitar awoke to a new spirit of creativity with Torah at its heart.

2. Epstein, *Text of the Mishna*, 224.
3. Ibid.
4. I attempt to strike a balance between the scholarly opinions of Epstein (in *Text of the Mishna*) and H. Albeck (in his *Introduction to the Mishna* [Hebrew], [Jerusalem, 5727]). For a description of this debate, see M. Elon, *Jewish Law* [Hebrew] (Jerusalem, 5733), 865–66.
5. A. Toynbee, *A Study of History* VII (London 1954): 279.

Chapter Seventeen:

The Enactments at Usha: The Responsibility of the Part for the Whole

Rashbag's inauguration began a new chapter in Jewish history. The establishment of a center of learning in the Galilee organized around the patriarchy led to several rabbinic enactments. Of course, such enactments had been made throughout Jewish history, particularly during the Second Temple period, when the sages instituted many laws for the sake of the common good.[1] But the Usha enactments were unprecedented in terms of their high concentration over such a brief period.[2]

1. Elon, *Jewish Law*, 865–66.
2. Scholarly research suggests that some of the Usha enactments were in fact instituted in later generations. See Alon, *History of the Jews*, vol. 2, 153; Mantel, *History of the Sanhedrin*, 365–369. The enactments at Usha were traditionally understood as dating back to the same period. See Rashi on Bava Metzia 35a and Rashbam on Bava Batra 50a. I treat all the Usha enactments as if they were from a single period, not because I believe this approach is historically accurate, but because I am interested

These enactments were an expression of the sense of responsibility felt by the Jewish leadership, which sought to strengthen and unite the nation after the destruction.

New Jewish communities arose after the Bar Kokhba revolt, along with new ways of life. As a result of Hadrian's decrees and the ensuing economic decline, foundational questions about the structure of Jewish life came to the fore. This was the period of Antoninus Pius' reign and Rashbag's tenure, a time of political calm that led to the development of municipal autonomy among the various Jewish communities. The values and principles that underlie communal life were established in Usha. We will survey some of these principles below, paying careful attention to the tension between the responsibility of the individual for the family unit and the responsibility of the community for its members.[3]

PROVIDING FOR CHILDREN

> In Usha the sages enacted that one should support his sons and daughters when they are minors. (Ketubot 49b)

This enactment seems like a strange principle to codify legally; of course parents are responsible for their children's welfare. The need for such an ordinance reflects the enormity of the economic crisis in the years following the Bar Kokhba revolt. Parents found themselves driven to neglect their children, who became the responsibility of the community.

in the talmudic tradition that presents Usha as a place in which such enactments were fashioned and instituted. See my introduction to this volume.

3. This section relies heavily on the work of Ze'ev Safrai. See his book *The Jewish Community in the Land of Israel During the Period of the Mishna and Talmud* [Hebrew] (Jerusalem, 5735). For a more succinct version, see his article "The Jewish Community in the Land of Israel During the Period of the Mishna and Talmud" [Hebrew], in *Jewish Community*, ed. Y. Gafni (Jerusalem, 5761), 147–68.

PROVIDING FOR ELDERLY PARENTS

> In Usha the sages enacted that if one bequeaths all his possessions to his children, he and his wife may be supported by them. (Ketubot 49b)

If elderly parents transfer all their property to their children and grant them the right to administer their affairs, it is obviously the moral obligation of the children to support their parents. What sort of society must enshrine this obligation legally? Apparently during the Usha period, the sense of moral responsibility was insufficient, so the legal enactment was necessary as well.[4]

SETTING LIMITS ON CHARITY

> In Usha they enacted that one who gives away [his money to charity] may not give away more than a fifth. (Ketubot 50a)

At first there seems to be no connection between the enactments about providing for children and elderly parents and this statute limiting the amount of money that may be given in charity. But as Rabbi Yehuda Brandes notes, the enactments at Usha served to strengthen the sense of private responsibility so public funds could be used for public purposes. As Brandes writes, "A father is beholden to his sons, and sons are beholden to their father. Along similar lines, a person is not permitted to give away all his money in charity, because the responsibility to provide for one's family takes precedence."[5] This enactment was necessitated by the rise of a sect that advocated disregarding all material pursuits and relying on the grace of heaven – which generally meant the grace of public funds. This stance is represented by Elazar Ish Birta:

4. Y. Brandes, *Practical Aggada* [Hebrew] (Jerusalem, 5766), 236. Brandes speculates about the environment and social conditions that would give rise to a need for such an enactment.
5. Ibid., 240.

> Whenever the administrators of the charity funds saw Elazar Ish Birta coming, they would hide from him, because he would give them everything he had. One day he was going to the market to purchase a dowry for his daughter. The administrators of the charity saw him coming and went and hid from him. He went and ran after them and found them. He said to them: I adjure you to tell me, for what charity are you now collecting? They answered: To marry off an orphan boy to an orphan girl. He said to them: By the Temple service! They take precedence over my own daughter. He took everything he had and gave it to them. He was left with one *zuz*. He went and bought some wheat and brought it home and tossed it in his granary. His wife came and said to her daughter: What did your father bring home? She said to her mother: Whatever he brought home, he tossed in the granary. She went to open the door to the granary and saw that it was filled with wheat overflowing through the hinges of the door, and the door would not open because of the wheat that was pressing against it. His daughter went to the beit midrash and said to her father: Come and see what the One who loves you has done for you. He said to her: By the Temple service! This grain shall be like consecrated property to you, and you have no more share in it than any other poor person in Israel. (Ta'anit 24a)

Rabbi Elazar Ish Birta, also known as Rabbi Elazar Ish Birtuta,[6] hands over his possessions to the charity collectors and leaves his own daughter destitute. He abandons all sense of familial responsibility as if rejecting the notion of private property altogether. This stance was very popular among the early Christians, who emphasized the importance of charity and dismissed material possessions. As poverty spread, charity was increasingly championed.[7] But the abandonment of personal responsibility had the potential to undermine the welfare services of a Jewish community still trying to rebuild and renew itself. So the rabbinic leader-

6. *Dikdukei Sofrim*, 142.
7. E. E. Urbach, "Religious and Social Trends in the Sages' Teachings About Charity," in *World of the Sages*, 97–124.

ship at Usha instituted this enactment to prevent people from choosing piety at the expense of their family's basic needs.

PUBLIC RESPONSIBILITY FOR PRIVATE WELFARE

In addition to issuing enactments about taking responsibility for one's family, Rashbag developed communal services and cultivated a sense of public responsibility. The tannaitic sources offer a detailed overview of the ideal Jewish community, in which public responsibility is expressed in terms of civic duties rather than civic rights.[8] By the end of the second century, the Mishna speaks of a charity fund as a familiar communal institution.[9] This fund was to provide food for those who had no relatives to come to their aid. The Mishna actually refers to two such services: the charity fund (*kuppa*), which provided weekly sums of money to poor residents of the city; and a collection plate (*tamḥui*), which offered daily provisions to impoverished out-of-towners. Maimonides describes the welfare institutions founded during this period:

> Every city with Jews must appoint a charity collector.... Each poor person is given enough food for seven days, and this is known as the charity fund. The city also appoints collectors who go around to each courtyard and collect bread and foodstuffs, both fruit and coins, from anyone who volunteers them. In the evening they distribute these among the poor, giving each poor person enough for the next day; this is known as the collection plate. The collection plate is collected daily, while the charity fund

8. This is an important distinction that we must bear in mind when considering relationships among citizens in the modern state in light of the traditional network of relationships in Jewish communities in prior historical eras. We have shifted from a discourse of responsibilities to one of rights. See Y. Breuer, *Signposts* [Hebrew] (Jerusalem, 5742), 57–86; M. Zilberg, *This Is the Way of the Talmud* [Hebrew] (Jerusalem, 5722), 66–72; H.H. Cohen, *Individual Rights in the Bible and Talmud* [Hebrew] (Tel Aviv: Broadcast University, 1988); *The Law* [Hebrew] (Jerusalem, 5752), 512–13.
9. Mishna Pe'ah 8:7: "One who has enough food for two meals should not take from the collection plate. One who has enough food for fourteen meals should not take from the charity fund."

> is collected weekly. The collection plate is for any poor people around, while the charity fund is for the poor of the city alone.[10]

It seems the charity budget was drawn from municipal taxes collected by designated charity collectors. The Talmud specifies the minimum period of residence that would obligate a person to pay taxes as a citizen of a particular city or town, as Maimonides outlines:

> Once a person has resided in a town for thirty days, he is obligated to contribute to the charity fund along with the other residents. Once he has resided there for three months, he must contribute to the collection plate. Once he has lived there for six months, he must pay for the clothing of the town's poor. Once he has lived there for nine months, he must pay for the burial of the town's poor and attend to all their burial needs.[11]

A city's tax requirement is determined not by the residents' ability to give, but by the needs of the city's poor. Yet each resident's charity burden is assessed according to wealth. Moreover, the public is required to contribute to the charity fund even if the basic needs of the poor exceed twenty percent of the community's funds, in contrast to the limits on private donations that we saw above in the Usha enactments.

RANSOMING CAPTIVES

The Mishna in Tractate Gittin lists a series of enactments whose purpose is "for the benefit of society," that is, to ensure that society runs smoothly. One such enactment is the following:

> Captives must not be ransomed for more than their value, for the benefit of society, and must not be helped to escape, for the benefit of society. Rabban Shimon ben Gamliel says: For the benefit of captives. (Gittin 4:6)

10. Maimonides, *Mishneh Torah, Laws of Gifts to the Poor,* 9:1, 2:6.
11. Ibid. 12, based on Bava Batra 8a.

Rashbag refers to the ransoming of captives in his discussion of a man's responsibilities to his wife:

> If he did not write for her, "If you be taken captive, I will ransom you, and I will take you back to me for my wife"; and for a priest's wife, "I will return you to your town" – he is liable, because this is a condition of the court. (Ketubot 4:8)

That is, even if the husband does not specify in the *ketuba* that he will ransom his wife if she is captured, he is obligated to do so. (A priest is forbidden from marrying a captive, so he is obligated to ransom his wife but not to take her back into his home.) Furthermore, the husband is not permitted to redeem his wife using her *ketuba* money.

The phrasing of this enactment, which contains the same Aramaic wording as the *ketuba*, indicates that it dates back to the Second Temple period, after the return of the Babylonian exiles, when Aramaic was the vernacular.[12] The enactment was necessary to prevent women from remaining in captivity any longer than necessary, and to place the responsibility for a wife's ransoming squarely on her husband's shoulders.[13]

The Talmud relates:

> The rabbis taught: If a woman was captured and the abductors demanded from the husband even up to ten times her worth, he must ransom her the first time this happens. From then on, he ransoms her if he wants to, and he does not ransom her if he does not want to. Rabban Shimon ben Gamliel says: Even the first time, one may not ransom captives for more than their value for the benefit of society. This implies that we do ransom a wife for up to her value, even though her ransom payment exceeds the value of her *ketuba*.
>
> But this contrasts with the following: If a woman was

12. Rabbinic sources attribute the *ketuba* to Shimon ben Shetaḥ in the first century BCE See *Sages* I.
13. Y. Cohen, *Rabbinic Enactments Relating to Money Within Marriage* [Hebrew] (Jerusalem, 5757), 390.

> captured and the abductors demanded from her husband ten times the value of her *ketuba,* he must ransom her the first time this happens. From then on, he ransoms her if he wants to, and he does not ransom her if he does not want to. Rabban Shimon ben Gamliel says: If her ransom was equivalent to her *ketuba,* he must ransom her. But if not, he need not ransom her. Rabban Shimon ben Gamliel subscribes to two leniencies. (Ketubot 52b)

The first source attributes to Rabban Shimon ben Gamliel the view that a wife may be ransomed for even more than her *ketuba* payment, thereby allowing the husband to redeem her if he so desires. In the second source, Rabban Gamliel asserts that the husband is not obligated to ransom his wife unless her ransom does not exceed her *ketuba* payment, thereby exempting the husband who does not wish to redeem his wife. As these sources attest, Rashbag allows for a lenient interpretation of the important mitzva of ransoming captives for the sake of economic considerations and for the welfare of society.[14]

14. It is important to distinguish between the Talmud's laws about ransoming captives and the difficult question that has often arisen in the State of Israel concerning the release of prisoners of war in exchange for terrorists. The latter is a public issue with its own host of considerations.

Chapter Eighteen

Rabbi Yaakov ben Krushai: Defender of Rashbag

Rabbi Yaakov says: This world is like a corridor to the World to Come. Prepare yourself in the corridor so that you may enter the banquet hall.

He would say: One hour of penitence and good deeds in this world is better than all of life in the World to Come. And one hour of spiritual calm in the World to Come is better than all of life in this world. (Mishna Avot 4:16)

The figure known in rabbinic literature as Rabbi Yaakov is Rabbi Yaakov ben Krushai, whom we will now consider.[1]

HIS TEACHING IN AVOT

Rabbi Yaakov's statement in *Pirkei Avot* is so widely quoted that we may not realize he was the first to articulate this notion. But until Rabbi Yaakov, no one spoke of this world as a corridor to the next.[2]

1. Hyman, *History*, 770.
2. The Tosefta also uses this phrase: "They proclaim that this world leads to the World

We can trace the evolution of the idea of the World to Come, which did not originate with the Usha generation. According to the Bible, the reward for doing mitzvot is granted in this world: "that you may fare well and live long" (Deut. 22:7). The Mishna likewise states that "Whoever performs one mitzva is rewarded, and his days are prolonged, and he inherits the land" (Mishna Kiddushin 1:10).[3] The idea of reward and punishment in another world appears as early as the time of Hillel, a hundred years before the destruction of the Temple: "If he has acquired words of Torah, he has acquired the World to Come" (Mishna Avot 2:7).[4] Beit Shammai and Beit Hillel disagree about the fate of souls after death (Tosefta Sanhedrin 13:3), but Rabbi Akiva and his circle make frequent mention of the World to Come.[5] In this sense Rabbi Yaakov's teaching that "this world is like a corridor to the World to Come" is merely the development of a well-known rabbinic idea. But the sages who discussed the World to Come as a place of reward and punishment assumed that there is retribution in this world as well. Rabbi Yaakov, in contrast, speaks of this world as merely a gateway to a future world.

to Come as a corridor leads to a banquet hall" (Tosefta Berakhot 6:21). We do not know if this statement predates Rabbi Yaakov's words in Avot, since it was corrected by censors, which could have happened at various historical moments.

3. Epstein argues that this mishna predates Rabbi Yaakov's statement in Avot and extends the biblical notion of reward and punishment. He writes, "How ancient is the end of this mishna…'and he inherits the land,' meaning the Land of Israel [!], as the Torah states, 'that you may fare well and live long… in order that you may fare well and inherit the land.'" The language of the mishna is reminiscent of Isaiah 57:13: "But those who trust in Me shall inherit the land." This is a far cry from the fifth chapter of Avot, where we are told that Abraham's disciples enjoy this world and inherit the World to Come. Our mishna makes no mention of reward in the World to Come, just as the Torah and Prophets speak of reward only in this world. See Epstein, *Text of the Mishna*, 53.
4. Even prior to Hillel, the Book of Maccabees quotes those who died in sanctification of God's name as saying that "One cannot but choose to die at the hands of men and to cherish the hope that God gives of being raised again by Him. But for you there will be no resurrection to life!" (II Maccabees 7:13).
5. Heschel argues in *Heavenly Torah* that the notion of the World to Come was developed in the beit midrash of Rabbi Akiva and does not appear in the sources associated with Rabbi Yishmael. Urbach disagrees in "The Laws of Inheritance and the Eternal Life," in *World of the Sages*, 248 note 60.

Presumably he belonged to the generation after Rabbi Akiva, and the horrors experienced by the previous generation led him to focus on the importance of an eternal realm instead of this transient world.

HIS LIFE AS A BACKGROUND TO HIS TEACHINGS

Rava discusses the mishna that states that whoever does a mitzva is rewarded with longevity:

> Whose view does this follow? It follows the view of Rabbi Yaakov, who said: The reward for fulfilling a mitzva is not given in this world. For it was taught: Rabbi Yaakov says: Of all those commandments that are written in the Torah along with their reward, there is not one upon which the resurrection of the dead is not dependent. Regarding the mitzva of honoring one's father and mother, it is written, "that you may live long, and that you may fare well" [Deut. 5:16]. Regarding the mitzva of sending a bird away [from its nest before taking its offspring], it is written, "that you may fare well and live long" [Deut. 22:7]. But what of one whose father said to him: Climb up the tower and fetch me some young birds. The son climbed up the tower, drove the mother bird away, and took the bird's offspring, and on his way back he fell and died. Where is his good life? And where is his long life? Evidently, "that you may fare well" refers to the world that is entirely good, and "that you may live long" refers to the world that is entirely long. (Kiddushin 39b)

Rabbi Yaakov raises the vexing question of whether there is divine justice in this world. He concludes that no reward is granted in this world. The Talmud continues to debate Rabbi Yaakov's ideas until Rav Yosef comes on the scene:

> Rav Yosef said: Had Aḥer interpreted that verse as Rabbi Yaakov, the son of his daughter, did, he would not have sinned.
>
> What happened with Aḥer? Some say: He saw an incident similar to the one witnessed by Rabbi Yaakov. And some say: He saw the tongue of Ḥutzpit the announcer as it was being dragged

> by a pig. He exclaimed: The mouth that spoke pearls of wisdom should lick the dust?! He thereupon went out and sinned. (Kiddushin 39b)

This is an astonishing text. It links the terrible experiences of the generation of the persecution with the teaching of Rabbi Yaakov. It also teaches us that Rabbi Yaakov's grandfather was Elisha ben Abuya, the most notorious heretic.[6] The Talmud seems to suggest that after the decrees of persecution, there were two options: To believe that all reward and punishment take place only in the World to Come, or to become a complete heretic. The Mishna adopts the former view, and the World to Come assumes an important role in rabbinic theology.

THE IMPACT OF HIS TEACHING ON JEWISH THOUGHT

Rabbi Yaakov's teaching about this world's insignificance exerted a strong influence on Jewish thought for generations to come. Here are three examples:

> Our ancestors received from the prophets the tradition that this world is to the World to Come like a corridor before a royal castle. A person has to prepare himself in the corridor before he enters the castle and appears before the king. This is explicit in the words of the sages: "This world is like a corridor to the World to Come. Prepare yourself in the corridor so that you may enter the banquet hall." They also received the tradition that life in the World to Come is like light, without food or drink or business dealings and without anything of this world, except the redemption of the righteous on account of the glory of the Creator. Hence their statement that the World to Come has no eating, drinking, reproduction, or commerce; rather, righteous people sit with their crowns on their heads and bask in the glory of the divine presence. (Rabbi Saadia Gaon, *Book of Beliefs and Opinions*, article 9)

6. Hyman argues that this reputed relationship is historically implausible. See his *Legends*, 770.

Rav Saadia Gaon endows Rabbi Yaakov's teaching with a historical pedigree, rooting it in the early prophetic traditions of the Jewish people.

> The good that awaits the righteous in the life of the World to Come is that life that is devoid of death and that good that is devoid of evil. That which is written in the Torah, "that you should fare well and live long" is understood by tradition to mean "that you may fare well" in the world that is entirely good, and "that you may live long" in the world that is entirely long, that is, the World to Come. The reward of the righteous is that they are privileged to enjoy this goodness, and the payment exacted from the wicked is that they are not privileged to enjoy this life, but they are cut off and die. Anyone who does not merit this life dies without receiving an eternal afterlife. Instead he is cut off on account of his wickedness, and is lost like an animal. This is the cutting-off that is mentioned in the Torah, such as when it is written, "that soul shall be utterly cut off." According to a tradition, we learn that the words "cut off" refer to being cut off from this world, and that the word "utterly" comes to include [being cut off from] the World to Come. That soul which was separated from its body in this world will not merit life in the World to Come, but is cut off from there as well. (Maimonides, *Mishneh Torah, Laws of Repentance* 8:1)

> Our sages of blessed memory have taught us that man was created for the sole purpose of rejoicing in God and deriving pleasure from the splendor of His presence; for this is true joy and the greatest pleasure that can be found. The place where this joy may truly be derived is the World to Come, which was expressly created to provide for it; but the path to the object of our desires is this world, as our sages of blessed memory have said, "This world is like a corridor to the World to Come." (Rabbi Moshe Ḥayyim Luzzato, introduction to *Mesillat Yesharim*)

We have just quoted three pillars of Jewish thought from the Middle Ages to the eighteenth century who accepted Rabbi Yaakov's teaching as a given. The previous mishna, from the school of Rabbi Yishmael, which taught that reward and punishment are granted in this world, was supplanted by the teaching of the school of Rabbi Akiva. Rabbi Yaakov's view that a person is granted retribution in the heavenly and not the earthly realm became the accepted Jewish outlook. Thus we conclude yet another chapter in the establishment of Rabbi Akiva's teachings as the foundation for Jewish religious life and thought.

Part Five

Gates of the Messiah – Rabbi Yehuda HaNasi

The Founding Generation at Usha		Rabbi Yehuda HaNasi
138–161	161–192	192–220
The Restoration of the Nation after the Destruction Antoninus Pius	The Stabilization of the Center at Usha Marcus Aurelius and Commodus	Autonomy in the Galilee Severus

Chapter Nineteen

Historical and Political Background

Much ink has been spilled about Rabbi Yehuda HaNasi and his intellectual legacy.[1] He was a patriarch of Israel and the editor of the Mishna, one of the most canonical works in the history of the Jewish people. In the pages that follow, I seek to listen closely to the many sources about him in an effort to develop a composite sense of this important figure.

Rabbi Yehuda HaNasi, known simply as Rebbi, served as patriarch during the final two decades of the second century and the first two decades of the third. He first assumed this mantle during the reign

1. For background on Rabbi Yehuda HaNasi's Mishna, see Z. Frankel, *Methods of the Mishna*, 201–8. For a selection and discussion of the sources from a literary perspective (distinguishing between Babylonian and Palestinian sources), see Meir, *Yehuda HaNasi: Image of a Leader*. Meir is interested not in the historicity of the sources, but rather in the composite figure that emerges therefrom. Oppenheimer, in contrast, who published a biography of Rabbi Yehuda HaNasi, seeks to reconstruct the sage's life and period through a study of the sources. On the difference between their two approaches, see Oppenheimer, *Rabbi Yehuda HaNasi*, introduction.

of Commodus, the "black stain" on Roman imperial history.[2] In the year 192, Commodus was murdered and Septimius Severus assumed the throne. For four years there was a fierce struggle between Severus and his rival, Pescennius Niger. Niger's followers were concentrated in Samaria and its capital, Shekhem (Nablus), while supporters of Severus were primarily in the Galilee. The Sixth Legion, stationed in Megiddo, was loyal to Severus, whereas the Tenth Legion, stationed in Jerusalem, backed Niger. Fortunately, the Jews pinned their hopes on Severus, who proved the victor. After assuming the throne, he visited the Land of Israel on multiple occasions. During one visit, he revoked the harsh decrees Niger had imposed.[3]

Severus reigned until 211 and was considered one of the strongest emperors of the period. Unlike his predecessors' regimes, his rule was based on the army rather than the senate, resulting in a more unified government. He was born in Africa and his wife Julia Domna was born in Syria. An enlightened woman well versed in Greco-Roman culture, she often accompanied her husband on diplomatic missions.[4] According to Roman historians, the two spoke a Canaanite-Phoenician dialect, suggesting that Severus knew Hebrew. Although he was a tough military man, Severus ran an efficient political system with the help of his wife.

The reign of the Severans was a good time for the Jews. We can assume that Rebbi's friend Antoninus, who figures prominently in rabbinic sources, was part of the Severan dynasty. As historian M. D. Herr argues,

> The general political questions that 'Antoninus' raises in his dialogues with Rebbi are characteristic of the end of the second century and the beginning of the third. These include questions about the relationship with the senate, the imperial treasury, imperial succession, the conduct of the emperor's family members, etc. The legends about Rebbi's friendship with Antoninus,

2. See Part Three, Introduction.
3. See M. D. Herr, "The History of the Caesars" [Hebrew], in *History of the Land of Israel*, vol. 5, 30.
4. Amit, *The History of the Roman Emperors*, 640–45. Herr, "History of the Caesars," 25.

> while obviously exaggerated, are based on the Roman Empire's official recognition of the patriarch in Rebbi's time. They also reflect the emperors' genuine interest in the Torah of Israel and their affinity for the people of Israel, which also explains the stories about Antoninus' interest in conversion.[5]

Severus was succeeded by his son Caracalla. He assumed the throne in 211, after murdering his brother. Caracalla reigned until his own murder in 217. The annals of Roman imperial history relate that his father beat him when he was seven because he took interest in Judaism.[6] For seven years, he concentrated all his attention on the northern front and left his mother, Julia Domna, to administer interior affairs. His reign foreshadowed the decline of the Roman Empire.

5. Herr, "Debates Between the Sages and the Roman Elite," 295.
6. Amit, *The History of the Roman Emperors*, 669–75. The story appears in *Augustan History, The Lives of Caracalla.*

Chapter Twenty

Rabbi Yehuda HaNasi's Coming-of-Age

Rebbi was the first patriarch who did not have to secure his own position. His grandfather Rabban Gamliel had arrived in Yavneh after Rabban Yoḥanan ben Zakkai left Jerusalem and established a new beit midrash there. The sages who gathered around Rabban Yoḥanan ben Zakkai were the core of the generation's scholars. Rebbi's father, Rabban Shimon ben Gamliel, arrived in Usha following the Bar Kokhba revolt. He established the patriarchy and initiated the massive project of editing the Mishna, which Rebbi would spearhead. Rebbi was born into a new reality, one that was politically quiescent but religiously invigorating.

Rebbi grew up in Usha surrounded by sages. He felt a responsibility to continue the patriarchal line. He first learned in the *battei midrash* of his father and of Rabbi Yehuda bar Ilai, and he grew up with Rabbi Yose, the latter's son. Several sources discuss the early years of Rebbi and Rabbi Yose, focusing on their unusual experiences and accomplishments.[1]

1. Sources describing the conversations and activities of the great sages of Israel tend to be read as if the protagonists were born fully formed and never changed. But only by

UNDER THE WATCHFUL EYE OF RABBI YEHUDA BAR ILAI

> Rebbi and Rabbi Yose bar Ilai would bring a basket [of dried figs] into the house by way of the roof. Rabbi Yehuda ben Rabbi Ilai saw them and said: Look how different you are from your ancestors! Rabbi Akiva would buy three kinds of produce with a *peruta* coin in order to remove the tithes from each kind, while you bring the basket into the house by way of the roof! (Y. Ma'asrot 3:1 [59c])

This passage is related to a mishna (Ma'asrot 3:1) that deals with a worker who transports figs from the field to a drying area. May the worker eat from the fruit that has not yet been tithed? Yes, as long as it is still in the field. But once collected from the field, the figs are regarded as untithed produce (*tevel*) and must be tithed before eating. The mishna teaches that unlike fruit brought into the yard, fruit brought in through the roof is exempt from tithing. Against this backdrop, the story in the Jerusalem Talmud describes two friends who sneak a basket of figs through the roof so as to avoid having to tithe them. Rabbi Yose's father catches them in the act and rebukes them: "Look how different you are from your ancestors!" Whereas Rabbi Akiva sought any way possible to fulfill the mitzva of tithing, these two boys try to evade the tithe however they can.

RIPENING FIGS

> Rebbi and Rabbi Yose ben Rabbi Yehuda entered a field to eat late-ripening figs, and the guard shouted at them. Rabbi Yose ben Rabbi Yehuda refrained [from taking the figs]. Rebbi said to him: Eat, since the owners have already given up on them. (Y. Demai 1:1 [21c])

The mishna deals with fruit that is dealt with leniently when it comes to tithing. The case involves a field of figs and grapes that are

considering sources from various stages in a sage's life can we appreciate the stature he eventually attained.

watched by their owner. The fig season passes, and some fruit remains unharvested on the trees. The owner guards his field because he is still interested in the grapes. Though he has no interest in the figs, it is forbidden to take them from his field. The owner's right to his produce depends not on which fruit he is cultivating primarily, but rather on the degree to which he keeps watch over his field. Against this backdrop, the Talmud cites the story above. Two friends enter an orchard to eat figs after the harvest season. The guard yells at them, and Rabbi Yose draws back. But Rebbi encourages his friend to keep eating, claiming that the figs are considered ownerless once the harvest season has passed.

These two stories describe two close friends who share in the adventures and escapades of youth.

EATING VEGETABLES AFTER THE SABBATICAL YEAR

The Mishna in Tractate Shevi'it (6:4) deals with vegetables picked right after the sabbatical year and therefore presumably planted when planting was prohibited. The sages wished to forbid the purchase of this produce at the beginning of the eighth year as well. But as the Mishna teaches, Rabbi Yehuda HaNasi declared these vegetables permissible immediately after the sabbatical year. This was one of several lenient rulings of his relating to the sabbatical year. The Jerusalem Talmud cites the following story related to this ruling:

> Rebbi and Rabbi Yose bar Yehuda went down to Akko and were hosted by Rabbi Manna. They said to him: Rabbi, cook us a vegetable stew! Instead he made them meat. The next day they again said to him: Cook us a vegetable stew! Instead he made them chicken.
>
> Rebbi said: It appears that he learned from Shmuel.[2]
>
> Rabbi Yose ben Rabbi Yehuda said to him: He did not learn from Shmuel. Rather, why did he serve us wine rather than vegetables? Because he is one of the students of Rabbi Yehuda, and Rabbi Yehuda said: It is forbidden to purchase vegetables

2. There have been some scholarly attempts to associate Rebbi with Shmuel. See Hyman, *Legends*, s.v. "Shmuel," 1123.

immediately after the sabbatical year in the border areas of the Land of Israel.

When Rebbi and Rabbi Yose bar Yehuda came to Rabbi Yehuda, they related this incident to him. Rabbi Yehuda said: You should have followed my custom. (Y. Shevi'it 6:4 [37a])

This story has puzzled many scholars. According to some, Rebbi and Rabbi Yose bar Yehuda were establishing a matter of law by eating vegetables in the border lands just after the sabbatical year.[3] But this reading does not explain Rabbi Yehuda bar Ilai's instruction to his son to follow his custom.

In any case, this story depicts Rebbi and Rabbi Yose bar Yehuda as close childhood companions. At the time they do not yet have any official roles; they are known only as the sons of famous sages. They ask the lesser-known Rabbi Manna to prepare a vegetable stew, but he serves them meat. Rabbi Manna does not argue with his guests, but his actions indicate that he cannot fulfill their request. The story resumes the next day when the two young men once again ask for vegetable stew; this time Rabbi Manna serves them chicken. Rebbi responds disparagingly, identifying Rabbi Manna as a student of Shmuel.[4] Rabbi Yose instead posits that Rabbi Manna is following the teaching of his father, Rabbi Yehuda.[5] They relate this incident to Rabbi Yehuda, who instructs the two to follow his ruling and refrain from eating vegetables right after the sabbatical year.

When they go on to become communal leaders, Rebbi and Rabbi

3. S. Safrai, "The Mitzva of Shevi'it After the Destruction of the Second Temple" [Hebrew], in *Time of the Temple, Time of the Mishna*, vol. 2, 453.
4. The identity of Shmuel in this passage has puzzled scholars. Most commentators identify him as the Babylonian talmudic sage Shmuel, but this does not make sense chronologically if Rebbi is still just a young man. Some scholars assume that Shmuel was the name of Rebbi's doctor and Rebbi is therefore suggesting that Rabbi Manna serves them meat rather than vegetables because he is concerned for their health. See Bava Metzia 85b, where he is known as Shmuel Yarhina'a.
5. Felix, *Jerusalem Talmud Shevi'it*, vol. 2, 93, as per the commentary of the Penei Moshe and Rabbi Eliyahu Pardo.

Yose often disagree in matters of law. Rabbi Yose bar Yehuda is mentioned rarely in the Mishna, but often in the Tosefta and in *baraitot*.[6]

THE FRIENDSHIP OF REBBI AND RABBI ELAZAR BEN RABBI SHIMON: LOVE AND JEALOUSY

In the chapter about Rabbi Yose ben Ḥalafta in Tzippori, we saw that he adopted Rabbi Elazar ben Rabbi Shimon bar Yoḥai and brought him to the beit midrash, where he became close to Rebbi. Both Rabbi Elazar and Rebbi stood out for their intellectual acumen. At some point the members of the beit midrash wished to promote them, as the Talmud recounts:

> When Rabban Shimon ben Gamliel and Rabbi Yehoshua ben Korḥa would sit in the beit midrash on benches, Rabbi Elazar ben Rabbi Shimon and Rebbi [their students] sat before them on the ground. The students asked and answered. They [the other rabbis] said: We drink their waters, yet they sit on the ground? So they made benches for them and elevated them from the ground.
>
> Rabban Shimon ben Gamliel said to them: I have only one fledgling among you, yet you seek to take it away from me? So they lowered Rebbi onto the ground.
>
> Rabbi Yehoshua ben Korḥa said to them: Shall he who has a father [Rebbi] live, but he who has no father [Rabbi Elazar ben Rabbi Shimon] die? They lowered Rabbi Elazar ben Rabbi Shimon as well. He became disheartened. He said: They think he is like me.
>
> Until that day, whenever Rebbi would say something, Rabbi Elazar ben Rabbi Shimon would support him. But from then on, whenever Rebbi would say: I have an objection to raise, Rabbi Elazar ben Rabbi Shimon would say to him: This is the answer to your objection, and this is the refutation of your answer, which lacks substance.
>
> Rebbi became disheartened. He came and told his father [what had happened]. His father said to him: My son, do not be

6. Epstein, *Text of the Mishna*, 172–74.

> distressed, for he is a lion son of a lion, while you are a lion son of a fox. (Bava Metzia 84b)

A parallel version of this story appears in the Jerusalem Talmud:

> The canes of a weaver – Rebbi declares them exempt. Rabbi Elazar ben Rabbi Shimon declares them liable. Rebbi said to Rabbi Elazar: So I learned from your father. He said to him: I served my father while standing up, whereas you served him while seated.
>
> But was Rebbi the student of Rabbi Shimon bar Yoḥai [the father of Rabbi Elazar]? Was he not the disciple of Rabbi Yaakov? Rather, this is what he said to him: I served my father while standing up, whereas you served your teacher while seated.
>
> When Rabbi Elazar ben Rabbi Shimon entered the beit midrash, Rebbi's face would darken. His father said to him: And that is well and good. This one is a lion son of a lion, while you are merely a lion son of a fox. (Y. Shabbat 10:5 [12c])

Both of these sources express the tension between these two sages who are forging their own paths toward leadership.[7] The Babylonian Talmud's description of the benches provided by the sages underscores this tension. The Babylonian version clearly privileges Rebbi, who is depicted as a victim of Rabbi Elazar's jealousy and pettiness. The Jerusalem Talmud instead focuses on Rabbi Elazar's pride in preserving the traditions of his father, Rabbi Shimon bar Yoḥai, and his interest in keeping his distance from his rival, Rebbi.

According to the Babylonian source that we studied in the chapter on Rabbi Yose ben Ḥalafta, Rabbi Elazar was appointed by the Romans to catch Jewish thieves. In stark contrast to his father, who despised the Romans and their rule ("Everything they built, they built only to serve their own needs"), Rabbi Elazar joined the Roman administration. The Talmud recounts his adventures at great length, depicting him as a fan-

7. In addition to the versions in the Babylonian and Jerusalem Talmuds, the story appears in *Pesikta deRav Kahana* 11, Mandelbaum ed., 200; and Ecclesiastes Rabba 11.

tastical, larger-than-life figure who can be understood only by invoking literary[8] and philosophical[9] scholarship.

Rabbi Yehuda HaNasi is aware of his friend's force of personality. There is tremendous strain between these two figures, who must keep a respectful distance from one another. When Rabbi Elazar's widow is offered Rebbi's hand in marriage, she responds, "A vessel used for the sacred should be used for the secular?"[10] With her razor-sharp wit, she locates Rabbi Elazar in the realm of the sacred and Rebbi – for all his grandeur and glory – in the realm of the secular.

BEIT SHE'ARIM BEFORE AND AFTER REBBI

Rebbi only grew in stature. The nation looked on at its leader, who kept his distance. Just as Moses pitched his tent outside the Israelite camp, Rebbi moved from his home in Usha to establish a center of Jewish life and learning in Beit She'arim.[11]

Josephus points out that Beit She'arim belonged to Berenice, the daughter of King Agrippa I. It was not a major center of settlement prior to the Bar Kokhba revolt, but was regarded as a town or even a large village.[12] The Tosefta relates that during the Usha period, the ashes of a red heifer was found in Beit She'arim (Tosefta Para 5:6), suggesting that it was a town of priests or of others who were stringent about purity

8. Rabbi Elazar ben Rabbi Shimon is beloved among literary scholars. See Boyarin, *Carnal Israel*; Y. Ben-Aharon, "Legends of Pumbedita" [Hebrew], *Mahberet Shedemot* 12 (2000): 11–14, 31–34; O. Meir, "Vinegar Son of Wine: Between Tradition and Innovation" [Hebrew], *Dappim leMehkar beSifrut* 4 (1988): 9–18; E. Yassif, "Story Cycles in Rabbinic *Aggada*" [Hebrew], *Jerusalem Studies in Hebrew Literature* 12 (5750): 103–45; D. Shoshani, "Rabbi Elazar ben Rabbi Shimon and the Thieves: A Story of Sin and Atonement" [Hebrew], *JSIJ*: 1–21.
9. E. Levinas, *Nine Talmudic Readings* [Hebrew] (Jerusalem, 5761), 117–45.
10. Y. Shabbat 10:5 (12c); *Pesikta deRav Kahana, Beshallaḥ* 24; Bava Metzia 4a.
11. According to rabbinic tradition, the Sanhedrin moved from Usha to Shefaram before relocating to Beit She'arim. Shefaram is described in a handful of sources as a well-organized, midsize Jewish settlement. See S. Safrai, "Jewish Settlement in the Galilee and the Golan" [Hebrew], in *The Land of Israel from the Destruction of the Temple to the Muslim Conquest*, ed. C. Bars et al. (Jerusalem, 5742), 154.
12. Josephus identifies Beit She'arim as both a town and a village. See *The Life of Flavius Josephus*, 24. B. Mazur argues that by and large Beit She'arim is described as a village. See B. Mazur, *Beit She'arim*, vol. 1 (Jerusalem, 5718), 15 note 14.

matters even after the destruction of the Temple.[13] Rebbi's move to Beit She'arim was probably on account of his close relationship with the emperor Antoninus Pius, who, according to the Talmud, bequeathed him towns and villages.[14] So Rebbi transferred to Beit She'arim, bringing with him the Sanhedrin and the other institutions of leadership.

The oldest extant ruins in Beit She'arim date from the Herodian period. The archeological evidence suggests that the town was permeated by Hellenistic culture. Most of the inscriptions found there are in Greek, some in a high literary style. A network of intricately decorated caves attests to the wealth of those Jews who chose to live near the patriarch.[15] These caves are mentioned in the Jerusalem Talmud in a passage about transferring graves from one place to another.[16]

Rabbi Yehuda relocated to Beit She'arim presumably to establish an independent center that was not beholden to the culture and traditions of Usha. As the authority in Beit She'arim, he had a certain stature, especially since the sons of the other Usha sages were not there with him.

WITH RABBI YISHMAEL, THE SON OF RABBI YOSE

We have already discussed Rebbi's close friendship with Rabbi Yose ben Rabbi Yehuda and his complicated bond with Rabbi Elazar ben Rabbi Shimon. Now we will consider his relationship with Rabbi Yishmael,

13. S. Safrai, "Beit She'arim in Talmudic Literature" [Hebrew], in *Time of the Temple, Time of the Mishna*, vol. 2, 182–93.
14. Y. Levine, "The Period of Rabbi Yehuda HaNasi" [Hebrew], in *The Land of Israel from the Destruction of the Temple to the Muslim Conquest*, ed. C. Bars et al (Jerusalem, 5742), 102. Levine argues that the Romans seized the property of the Herodians and returned it in the form of a gift to the patriarchy.
15. For an up-to-date description of the place and its artifacts, see C. and D. Amit, *Signposts: Traveling with the Sources in the North of Israel* [Hebrew] (Jerusalem, 5764), 76–87.
16. Y. Mo'ed Katan 3:5 (82c). Lieberman argues that this passage should read, "Like us from Caesarea, who are buried in Beit She'arim." Lieberman explains that the residents of Caesarea were concerned about purity matters and wanted to be buried where they would not have to worry about contamination. Presumably they chose Beit She'arim because it was the most lavish burial site. See S. Lieberman, "Corrections in the Jerusalem Talmud" [Hebrew], *Studies in the Torah of the Land of Israel*, 167.

the son of Rabbi Yose ben Ḥalafta of Tzippori. We have no evidence that Rebbi studied with Rabbi Yishmael or with Rabbi Yose. Although Rabbi Yose was one of the senior sages at Usha, he does not seem to have been a formative figure in Rebbi's education. After Rabbi Yose's death, Rabbi Yishmael became the authority in Tzippori, where he continued to promulgate his father's teachings. Rebbi and Rabbi Yishmael lived near one another, but in separate jurisdictions: Rebbi in Beit She'arim, and Rabbi Yishmael in Tzippori. There was some tension between them, as the following story attests:

> One time in the market of Tzippori, Rabbi Yishmael granted support for a woman whose husband had gone abroad. What difference does it make that this took place in the market?[17] Rather, the woman came from the market. Rebbi heard it and said: And who told Yishmael that the husband had not sent her adequate means of support? Those who stand in the place know this.[18] (Y. Ketubot 13:1 [35d])[19]

The Talmud deals with the case of a woman whose husband abandoned her and went abroad. The woman claims she is entitled to assistance from the communal charity fund, and the court seizes the husband's property. Rebbi rules that only a widow is entitled to such financial support, whereas Rabbi Yishmael ben Rabbi Yose holds that a married woman whose husband has abandoned her is also entitled. The story relates that Rabbi Yishmael granted her support from the communal charity fund in Tzippori. When word of this ruling reached Beit

17. The language of the Jerusalem Talmud is difficult. I used the version that appears in the Leiden manuscript as it is printed in the edition of the Academy for the Hebrew Language (Jerusalem, 5761). The medieval commentators suggested several emendations.
18. The phrase "those who stand in the place know this" perplexed many commentators. The Korban HaEda instead reads "servants and maidservants," understanding this line as meaning, "Who said the husband did not leave his wife servants and maidservants?"
19. I explained this line as per S. Lieberman, *Yerushalmi Kifshuto* (Jerusalem, 5695), 18–19.

She'arim, Rebbi objected: "Who told Yishmael that the husband had not sent her adequate means of support?"

In the Babylonian parallel to this story, their disagreement is presented more starkly:

> The case came before Rebbi in Beit She'arim, and he did not grant her support. The case came before Rabbi Yishmael in Tzippori, and he granted her support. (Ketubot 107b)

Evidence of the tension between these two sages can be found throughout the Talmud. Rebbi repeatedly refuses to follow the teachings of Rabbi Yose, the father of Rabbi Yishmael. Their disagreements are presented slightly differently in the Palestinian and Babylonian sources.

> Rebbi would praise Rabbi Ḥama, the father of Rabbi Hoshaya, in the presence of Rabbi Yishmael ben Rabbi Yose. Rabbi Ḥama, the father of Rabbi Hoshaya, asked during a session before Rabbi Yishmael ben Rabbi Yose: If a woman examined herself with a hand that had not been inspected, or if she sat herself down in a filthy place, what is the law? He said to him: In accord with whose opinion do you ask me this question? Is it in accord with the opinion of the master, or in accord with the opinion of the disciple? Yishmael said to him: Father said it is deemed to have the status of a bloodstain, while Rebbi says it is deemed tantamount to a drop of menstrual blood. Rabbi Yishmael said to Rebbi: Is this the one you were praising? (Y. Nidda 2:1 [49d])

Rebbi praises Rabbi Ḥama, the father of Rabbi Hoshaya, in the presence of Rabbi Yishmael. Rabbi Ḥama is not a familiar figure in the Galilee, so Rebbi must introduce him to the sages. In their first encounter, Rabbi Ḥama asks Rabbi Yishmael a question of halakha. The question deals with the laws governing a woman who checks herself to see if she is ritually pure following her menstrual period. She sees blood on a cloth or on her hand, but she cannot be certain of the source of the blood. It is possible that the blood is on account of an injury rather than menstrual blood, in which case it would not render her ritually impure. Rebbi and

Rabbi Yose disagree about this case. Rabbi Yishmael asks Rabbi Ḥama where he stands: Do you agree with my father or with Rebbi? According to the Jerusalem Talmud, Rabbi Yishmael turns to Rebbi and says, "Is this the one you are praising? How can you praise someone who asks me about a matter that you and my father disagree on?" The conclusion of the story is clearer in the Babylonian Talmud. Here Rabbi Yishmael seeks to uphold his father's view and to dismiss Rebbi's ruling.

> Rabbi Yishmael said: Is this the one you are praising as a great man? How can you reject the master's teaching and listen to his student? Rabbi Ḥama bar Bisa reasoned: Rebbi is the head of the academy, and he is surrounded by many students, so his teachings must be sharper. (Nidda 14b)

RABBI YISHMAEL VISITS REBBI'S ACADEMY

The following talmudic story describes Rebbi's position in Beit She'arim. The passage begins with a conversation among sages in the beit midrash:

> For Rabbi Ḥiya and Rabbi Shimon ben Rebbi were sitting. One opened with the statement: When one prays, he must direct his eyes downward, as it is said, "My eyes and my heart shall ever be there" [1 Kings 9:3]. The other opened with the statement: When one prays, he must direct his eyes upward, as it is said, "Let us lift our hearts with our hands to God in heaven" [Lam. 3:41]. Just then Rebbi came to them. He said to them: What are you busy with? They said to him: With prayer. He said to them: Thus my father said: When one prays, he must direct his eyes downward and his heart upward in order to fulfill these two verses. (Yevamot 106b)

Rabbi Ḥiya and Rabbi Shimon ben Rebbi are important members of Rebbi's circle. Here they consider the question of how to direct one's gaze in prayer. Rabbi Yishmael ben Rabbi Yose teaches his father's view: One's eyes should be directed downward, and one's heart upward. As Maimonides explains (*Mishneh Torah, Laws of Prayer* 5:4), one who casts his eyes downward appears to be looking at the ground, expressing a sense of effacement and surrender. In contrast, one who casts his eyes upward expresses yearning and a desire to approach the exalted. Rabbi Yishmael's solution, quoted in the name of his father, is an attempt to bridge these two positions.[20]

> Just then Rebbi came to the academy. Those who were light ran and sat in their places. Rabbi Yishmael ben Rabbi Yose, because of his weight, was treading as he went. Avdan said to him: Who is this one who treads on the heads of the holy people? He said to them: I am Yishmael, son of Rabbi Yose, who has come to learn Torah from Rebbi. He said to him: And are you worthy of learning Torah from Rebbi? He said to him: And was Moses our master worthy of learning Torah from the mouth of the Almighty? He said to him: Are you Moses? He said to him: And is your master God? (Yevamot 106b)

This source depicts the beit midrash when the patriarch enters. The sages sit in rows and the patriarch sits before them in a great chair. Those who are close to the patriarch gather in the front rows. Rabbi Yishmael, a heavy man, seems to be treading on people's heads.[21] Avdan, Rebbi's companion, witnesses Rabbi Yishmael's comportment and reacts disparagingly: "Who is this one who treads on the heads of the holy people?" Rabbi Yishmael's response is brief and to the point: "I am Yishmael, son of Rabbi Yose, who has come to learn Torah from Rebbi." Avdan then responds arrogantly, reflecting the elitist, confrontational culture of the rabbinic academy: "And are you worthy of learning Torah from Rebbi?" Rabbi Yishmael remains cordial: "And was Moses our master worthy of learning Torah from the Almighty?" Only when Avdan continues brashly ("Are you Moses?") does Rabbi Yishmael match his tone: "And is your master God?" Although Rebbi's glory has made him into a god-

20. U. Ehrlich, *All My Bones Shall Proclaim: The Body Language of Prayer* [Hebrew] (Jerusalem, 5759), 97–105.
21. See Y. Frankel, *Studies in the Intellectual World of the Aggadic Story* [Hebrew] (Tel Aviv, 5741), 78–82. Frankel analyzes this story. He cites the halakha that "The sons of sages and the students of sages may even tread on people's heads when the people need them."

like figure, Rabbi Yishmael possesses much knowledge that Rebbi has yet to acquire. As the master of his own father's teachings, he has much to offer Rebbi's beit midrash. The story continues:

> Just then a *yevama* [a widow eligible for levirate marriage] came before Rebbi. Rebbi said to Avdan: Go out and check her [to see if she is an adult, and therefore eligible to perform *halitza* and extricate herself from the marriage]. After he went out, Rabbi Yishmael said to Rebbi: Thus my father said: "Man" is written in this passage. But as for a woman, whether an adult or a minor [she may perform *halitza,* and therefore she need not be checked]. Rebbi said to Avdan: Come back. You are not needed. The elder has already given instruction. (Yevamot 106b)

Rebbi, both a great man and a humble one, knows he does not have all the answers. He knows that many collections of teachings have not yet reached him. So he is grateful to Rabbi Yishmael for bringing his father's teachings to his attention. When he says, "The elder has already given instruction," he is referring to Rabbi Yose, whose teachings have just been transmitted through his son Rabbi Yishmael.

Avdan has already departed to check the *yevama,* but in the meantime, he has been rendered superfluous by Rabbi Yishmael. Nonetheless, Avdan returns to his seat beside Rebbi, and the story continues:

> Avdan was treading as he came. Rabbi Yishmael ben Rabbi Yose said: He whom the holy people need – let him tread on the heads of the holy people. He whom the holy people do not need, how can he tread on the heads of the holy people? Rebbi said to Avdan: Stand in your place. (Yevamot 106b)

Rabbi Yishmael succeeds in demonstrating to Avdan that while his rabbi may resemble Moses, he is most certainly not God.

Chapter Twenty-One

Rabbi Pinḥas ben Yair: Hasid and Sage

The leadership of the patriarch was absolute and unimpeachable. But in addition to the patriarchal leadership, there were pious individuals known as Hasidim, who had no formal communal roles but served as models of honesty and integrity. Rabbi Ḥanina ben Dosa functioned in this capacity during the period of Rabban Yoḥanan ben Zakkai. And it was Rabbi Pinḥas ben Yair who did so during Rabbi Yehuda HaNasi's tenure.

Rabbi Pinḥas was the nephew of Rabbi Shimon bar Yoḥai (Shabbat 33b). He was the most prominent Hasid from the Usha period until the era of Rabbi Yehuda HaNasi. While he did not take part in the halakhic creativity of the beit midrash, he made great strides in teaching people how to serve God:

> Rabbi Pinḥas ben Yair says: Alacrity leads to cleanliness; and cleanliness leads to purity; and purity leads to abstention; and abstention leads to holiness; and holiness leads to humility; and humility leads to fear of sin; and fear of sin leads to saintliness;

> and saintliness leads to divine inspiration; and divine inspiration leads to the resurrection of the dead; and the resurrection of the dead will be heralded by Elijah of blessed memory, Amen. (Mishna Sota 9:15)

This sequence, which begins with alacrity and ends with the messianic resurrection of the dead,[1] established a model of spiritual ascent and religious devotion for generations. It was the basis for *The Paths of the Just* by Rabbi Moshe Ḥayyim Luzzato, the eighteenth century scholar known as Ramḥal, who in turn served as the inspiration for the *Musar* movement. Note that Rabbi Pinḥas ben Yair makes no mention of Torah study; his path to spiritual ascent privileges action, on the assumption that action is greater than study.[2] This was to change in the Middle Ages, when the rabbis insisted that Torah study could not be omitted from the individual's path to spiritual perfection and gave it priority above all else.[3]

Tractate Demai of the Jerusalem Talmud includes eight stories about Rabbi Pinḥas ben Yair, all of which require further study in order to gain a comprehensive sense of this figure.[4] The most famous of these stories describes Rabbi Pinḥas ben Yair's powerful influence over those around him, including, remarkably, his donkey:[5]

1. This version appears at the end of the printed text of the Mishna. Classical commentators and contemporary scholars alike have established that this passage is a *baraita* tacked on to the end of the Mishna. For the classical commentaries, see *Melekhet Shlomo* and *Tosefot Yom Tov*. For the scholarly literature, see Epstein, *Text of the Mishna*, 976–977. The *baraita* appears with slight variations in both Talmuds: Y. Shekalim 3:4 (47c); *Avoda Zara* 20b. On the various versions of the *baraita* and the superiority of the Babylonian text, see S. Safrai, "Hasidism and Men of Action" [Hebrew], in *Time of the Temple, Time of the Mishna*, vol. 2, 532–34.
2. I am alluding here to the famous dispute between Rabbi Akiva and Rabbi Tarfon about whether study or action takes precedence. See S. Safrai, "Hasidism and Men of Action," 532–34.
3. Torah study appears first in this list in several manuscripts of Avoda Zara 20b as well as in some printed versions. See *Dikdukei Sofrim*, Avoda Zara, sec. 20.
4. R. Nissim, *The Image of the Hasid* [Hebrew], *Alei Siaḥ* 12–14 (5742): 135–54.
5. Different versions of this story appear throughout the aggadic literature. For an analysis and assessment of the various versions, see O. Meir, "The Donkey of Rabbi

> Rabbi Pinḥas ben Yair's donkey was stolen by brigands. It spent three days with them but would not eat anything. They said: Eventually it will die and render our cave forbidden to us.[6] So they sent it away, and it went to its master's house. On entering there it brayed. Rabbi Pinḥas ben Yair said: Open up for that poor creature and give it something to eat, for it has not eaten in three days. They brought it barley, but it would not eat. He said to them: Has it been tithed? They replied: Yes. They asked: Have you separated *demai*? They said: No, for didn't you teach us that when one purchases grain for cattle, flour for tanning hides, or oil for lighting or for anointing vessels, these commodities are not liable to *demai*? He replied to them: But what can we do? She is extra-stringent with herself. (Genesis Rabba 60)

This story addresses the divide between the Hasid and the man of law. According to the letter of the law, a person must tithe his produce even if it is intended merely as animal feed. However, it is permissible to feed one's animal *demai*, produce whose status with regard to tithes is uncertain. The other members of Rabbi Pinḥas ben Yair's household acted according to the letter of the law. But Rabbi Pinḥas, a Hasid, went beyond the letter of law, as did his donkey, which refused to touch any produce that had not definitely been tithed. In this source, the Hasid is depicted as simple but straight as a rail, a characterization reinforced by the following story about Rabbi Pinḥas:

> Rabbi Pinḥas ben Yair was once traveling to ransom captives. He came to the Ginai River and said to it: Ginai, split your waters for me, that I may cross through you. The river replied: You are

Pinḥas ben Yair" [Hebrew], in *Studies in Aggada and Jewish Folklore* (Jerusalem, 5743), 117–37.

6. This line makes no sense. See Genesis Rabba, Albeck ed., 648, note on line 4. Meir reads this line as saying, "Eventually it will die and make our cave smell foul." See Meir, "Donkey of Rabbi Pinḥas ben Yair," 117–37. Perhaps this story is about people who were stringent about purity matters and therefore did not want a corpse in their cave, yet had no qualms about committing theft. This tendency to be strict about matters of holiness but lax about ethical concerns is familiar to us from other sources.

going on your way to perform the will of your Maker, and I too am flowing to perform the will of my Maker. If I split for you, you may or may not successfully accomplish your mission. But so long as I do not split, I will certainly accomplish the will of my Maker. Rabbi Pinḥas ben Yair said to the river: If you do not split, I decree upon you that water shall never again flow through you. The river split for him.

A certain man with him was carrying wheat used to bake matza for Pesaḥ. Rabbi Pinḥas ben Yair said to the river: Split for this one too, for he is engaged in a mitzva. The river split for him too.

An Arab merchant had accompanied them. Rabbi Pinḥas ben Yair said to the river: Split for this one too, so that it not be said: Is this how they deal with traveling companions? The river split for him too.

Rabbi Yose said: How great is Rabbi Pinḥas ben Yair! He is greater than Moses and the six hundred thousand Jews for whom the Red Sea split. For whereas there, the water split only once, here it split three times.

Rabbi Pinḥas ben Yair arrived at a certain inn where they poured barley for his donkey to eat. The donkey did not eat it. They sifted the barley, but he still would not eat it. They cleaned the barley, but he still would not eat it. He said to them: Perhaps the barley is untithed? They tithed it and the donkey ate it. Rabbi Pinḥas ben Yair said: This poor creature is going to perform the will of its Maker, and you feed it untithed produce? (Ḥullin 7a)

The stories about Rabbi Pinḥas ben Yair in the Babylonian Talmud serve to teach that it is impossible to stop a Hasid on his way to perform a mitzva.[7] In this sense the Hasid resembles Elijah, who was able to make nature conform to his will. We have already considered the figures of Ḥoni HaMe'agel and Rabbi Ḥanina ben Dosa as depicted in the Palestinian sources and reworked in the Babylonian Talmud.[8] There we argued that the Babylonian Talmud was not satisfied with the Pales-

7. Meir, "Donkey of Rabbi Pinḥas ben Yair," 129–31.

8. See *Sages* I.

tinian sources' depiction of the Hasid as one who tries to withdraw from this world and negate himself. Instead, the Babylonian sources portray the Hasid as an individual preoccupied with the relationship between human action and divine decree. The same is true of Rabbi Pinḥas ben Yair. In the Palestinian sources, he comes across as a pious ascetic who requests nothing of God or of the world. But in the Babylonian sources, he demands that miracles be performed on his behalf.

RABBI PINḤAS BEN YAIR AND RABBI YEHUDA HANASI: THE ENCOUNTER BETWEEN THE HASID AND THE SAGE

In the Jerusalem Talmud's collection of sources about Rabbi Pinḥas ben Yair, we find this foundational story about his relationship with Rabbi Yehuda HaNasi:

> Once Rabbi Yehuda HaNasi wanted to annul the sabbatical year. Rabbi Pinḥas ben Yair went to him. Rebbi said to him: How do the crops fare? He said to him: The endives are fine. Rebbi again asked him: How do the crops fare? He said to him: The endives are fine. Rebbi understood that Rabbi Pinḥas did not agree with him about annulling the sabbatical year.
>
> Rebbi said to him: Would the master care to eat a light meal with us today? He said: Yes. While coming to eat, he saw Rebbi's large team of mules standing outside. He said: Do the Jews support all of these? May I never see his face from this moment on! Rebbi's attendants heard him and went and told Rebbi what had happened. Rebbi sent out attendants after him, wanting to appease him. They caught up with him near the town. Rabbi Pinḥas ben Yair said: My fellow townspeople, draw near! The townspeople came down and surrounded him so Rebbi's attendants could not reach him. The attendants said to them: Rebbi wants to appease him. The townspeople left him and went away. Rabbi Pinḥas ben Yair said: My son, draw near to me! Fire descended from heaven and surrounded him. They went back and told Rebbi what had happened. He said: Since we were not privileged to have our fill of him in this world, may we be privileged to have our fill of him in the World to Come. (Y. Demai 1:3 [22a])

This story relates to Rabbi Yehuda HaNasi's enactments, including his attempts to rescind the sabbatical year or at least to mitigate its impact so as to relieve the economic strain.[9] The decision is up to the patriarch, but he is dependent on the moral support of the Hasid. The Jerusalem Talmud describes a climactic encounter between the two. The story begins with a cryptic and laconic conversation about the status of the crops. Rebbi understands from this exchange that Rabbi Pinḥas ben Yair does not support his policy with regard to the sabbatical year. Perhaps Rebbi was hinting that if the sabbatical year were to be observed, there would be no crops to eat. Rabbi Pinḥas ben Yair responds that in fact the endives are growing well. After two rounds of this dialogue, Rebbi understands that he will not receive Rabbi Pinḥas' endorsement. He invites him to eat a light meal at his home, an attempt to publicly demonstrate that the two are not at odds. Rabbi Pinḥas agrees in principle. But then he notices Rebbi's many white mules, a sign of the patriarch's prodigious wealth. Rabbi Pinḥas is suddenly uncomfortable and breaks off all connection with the patriarch. The rest of the story describes Rebbi's failed attempt to reconcile with the Hasid. The story ends with Rebbi's resigned acceptance that they will never come to terms with one another in this world.

The Babylonian Talmud cites a version of this story that makes no mention of the sabbatical year. After Rabbi Pinḥas splits the river, he encounters Rebbi:

> Rebbi heard that Rabbi Pinḥas ben Yair was passing by. He went out to greet him. Rebbi said to him: Would you like to dine with me? Rabbi Pinḥas ben Yair said: Yes. Rebbi's face became radiant.

9. Gedalia Alon argues that Rebbi attempted to rescind the sabbatical year completely. See Alon, *History of the Jews*, vol. 2, 154–55. S. Safrai agrees in *Time of the Temple, Time of the Mishna*, vol. 2, 446–48. Y. Felix, in contrast, cannot accept that Rebbi would rescind the sabbatical year altogether, and contends instead that he wished to permit the eating of *sefihin*, crops planted inadvertently by seeds that fell during harvesting. See Felix, "Jerusalem Talmud Tractate Shevi'it: The Parameters of the Prohibition of *Sefihin* and Rebbi's Enactments Regarding the Sabbatical Year" [Hebrew], in *Festschrift for Rabbi Y. D. Soloveitchik* (5745), 370–400.

> Rabbi Pinḥas ben Yair said to him: Did you think I was prohibited by a vow from benefiting from Jews? On the contrary, the Jews are all holy, but some want to share what they have but lack sufficient resources, and some have sufficient resources but do not want to share them with others. As it is written: "Do not eat the bread of a miser, and do not desire his delicacies. For like one whose soul is embittered, so is he: eat and drink, he says to you, but his heart is not with you" [Prov. 23:6–7]. But you, Rebbi, sincerely want to share what is yours, and you have the resources to do so. However, right now I am rushing to perform a mitzva. When I return, I will come in to visit you.
>
> When Rabbi Pinḥas ben Yair came back, he entered Rebbi's home through a door flanked by white mules. He said: The Angel of Death is in this one's house, and I should dine with him?
>
> Rebbi heard and went out toward him. He said to Rabbi Pinḥas ben Yair: I will sell the mules.
>
> Rabbi Pinḥas ben Yair replied: "You shall not place a stumbling block before a blind person" [Lev. 19:14].
>
> Rebbi said: I will abandon them and set them loose in the forest.
>
> Rabbi Pinḥas ben Yair replied: You will thereby increase the harm they cause.
>
> I will cut their hooves!
>
> You would cause suffering to a living creature.
>
> I will kill them.
>
> There is a prohibition not to destroy wantonly.
>
> As Rebbi pleaded with him excessively, a mountain rose between them. Rebbi wept and said: If even during the lifetime of the righteous it is so, how much more so will it be after their deaths! (Ḥullin 7b)

The Babylonian Talmud attributes the parting of ways between Rebbi and Rabbi Pinḥas ben Yair not to their disagreement about the sabbatical year, but rather to Rebbi's remarkable wealth and Rabbi Pinḥas' determination to disassociate from anything that smacked of luxury or excess.

Chapter Twenty-Two

Rebbi and Rabbi Ḥiya: From Mishna to Baraita

Rabbi Yehuda HaNasi became famous for his project of compiling the Mishna, though the work was initiated by his father. In response to the political crisis around him, Rabban Shimon ben Gamliel began collecting teachings of the sages from the Second Temple period until his own day. Rebbi started out by helping his father and then continued to work on this enterprise as an adult. It is impossible to exaggerate the significance of this work or its centrality in the Jewish canon. The Mishna shaped Torah study from its inception: It is the basis for the two Talmuds and the foundation of halakha.

The organization of the Mishna into orders, tractates, and chapters bespeaks an extraordinary feat of literary architectonics. Many scholarly studies have dealt with the creation of the Mishna, its structure and agenda, its language and content. Scholars have debated whether Rebbi sought to create a legal canon in which he chose among dissenting views, or whether he simply wished to present to the student the full range of halakhic opinions without deciding among them.[1] In recent years there has been a resurgence of interest in the literary study of the Mishna, including attempts to determine the rhythm of the orders, tractates, chapters, and even individual mishnayot.[2]

Alongside the Mishna we also have records of statements by the sages that were not included in the Mishna or were appended to it. They are known as *baraitot*, from the Aramaic word for "external." The project of collecting and organizing all the *baraitot* is traditionally attributed to Rabbi Ḥiya the Great. In this chapter we will consider Rabbi Ḥiya and his relationship to the patriarch.

RABBI ḤIYA'S ARRIVAL IN THE LAND OF ISRAEL

The Talmud relates that Rabbi Ḥiya came from Babylonia to the Land of Israel with his sons, thereby saving the land from becoming a spiritual wasteland:

> When Torah was forgotten from Israel, Ezra came from Babylonia and reestablished it. It was again forgotten and Hillel the Babylonian came and reestablished it. It was again forgotten and Rabbi Ḥiya and his sons came and reestablished it. (Sukka 20a)

This source associates Rabbi Ḥiya with Hillel and Ezra. Like them, Rabbi Ḥiya arrived in Israel and made a significant impact, as the following source confirms:

1. This is an old dispute between Albeck and Epstein. See E. E. Urbach, "Introduction to the Mishna and to One Hundred Years of Its Scholarship" [Hebrew], in *Scholarship in Jewish Studies*, vol. 2 (Jerusalem, 5758), 716–38. Epstein is the leading Mishna scholar, and his *Text of the Mishna* is considerred the basis of all scholarly work on the Mishna, its editing, and its versions.
2. The leading scholar in this field is A. Walfish. See his surveys of Mishna studies until the last decade: "From What Has Been Done in the Field of Mishna" [Hebrew], *Netuim* 8 (5762): 93–102; *Netuim* 14 (5767): 131–45. Y. Nagen has made an unusual attempt to read the Mishna as poetry, uncovering the text's parallelisms, wordplays, and literary forms. He bases his book on the scholarly insights of Walfish, who first treated the Mishna as a subject of literary study. See Y. Nagen, *The Soul of the Mishna* [Hebrew] (Otniel, 5767).

> From the time when the people of the Diaspora came up to the Land of Israel from Babylonia, there ceased to be meteors, earthquakes, violent winds, and thunder, and their wine did not sour, nor was their flax afflicted. And the sages turned their eyes to Rabbi Ḥiya and his sons. (Ḥullin 86a)

The warm reception given to Rabbi Ḥiya and his sons indicates the spirit of the times and the nature of Rebbi's leadership. The people held Rebbi in high esteem. They felt he cared for them, as demonstrated by his enactments, including his attempt to ease the laws of the sabbatical year on their behalf. But he lived in an ivory tower, remote from them. The people needed a leader they could relate to and interact with. Enter Rabbi Ḥiya. The relationship between Rebbi and Rabbi Ḥiya recalls the leadership model of Moses and Aaron. The people saw Moses only from behind, when he entered the Tent of Meeting, or through the veil on his face. But they needed a closer connection to their leader, and that is what Aaron afforded them. Thanks to Aaron, the people felt surrounded by clouds of glory and enveloped in peace.

RABBI ḤIYA'S LEARNING STYLE

Rebbi was a member of the elite. He edited the Mishna out of a sense of responsibility for the masses, lest Torah be forgotten from Israel. Rabbi Ḥiya, in contrast, sat among the people and taught them Torah directly. He was not interested in elite learning for intellectuals alone. The Talmud comments on Rabbi Ḥiya's legacy in a story about Reish Lakish, who used to mark burial caves in the Land of Israel:

> Reish Lakish would mark the sages' burial caves. When he reached the cave of Rabbi Ḥiya, it eluded him. He became disheartened. He said: Master of the Universe! Have I not expounded the Torah as Rabbi Ḥiya did? A voice came forth from heaven and told him: Indeed you have expounded the Torah as he did, but you have not disseminated the Torah as he did. (Bava Metzia 85b)

As depicted in the Babylonian Talmud, Reish Lakish knows how to interrogate the Torah's language, turning over its phrases and teasing out its meanings. He can ask a rapid-fire sequence of brilliant questions, such that no one can best him in scholarly debates. But when he fails to locate the burial cave of Rabbi Ḥiya, he assumes it is due to some fault within himself. A heavenly voice cries out that although he is an outstanding scholar, he lacks Rabbi Ḥiya's mastery as a teacher. The following source explains how Rabbi Ḥiya merited this distinction:

> When Rabbi Ḥanina and Rabbi Ḥiya were arguing, Rabbi Ḥanina said to Rabbi Ḥiya: With me you argue? Heaven forbid, if the Torah were forgotten by the Jewish people, I could restore it through my deliberations. Rabbi Ḥiya said to Rabbi Ḥanina: With me you argue? For I make sure the Torah is not forgotten by the Jewish people in the first place! What do I do? I go and sow flax. Then I weave nets from the flax, and I trap deer with these nets, and I feed their meat to orphans. Then I prepare scrolls of parchment with [the deer's] skins, and I write the five books of the Bible on them. Then I go up to the village and I teach each of five children a different one of the five books, and I teach each of six other children one of the six orders of the Mishna. Then I tell them: During the time that I return home and come back here, teach Torah to one another and teach Mishna to one another. This way, I ensure that the Torah is never forgotten by the Jewish people. (Bava Metzia 85b)

Rabbi Ḥanina, one of the leading scholars of the first generation of *Amora'im*, is Rabbi Ḥiya's study partner. Like Rabbi Ḥiya, he came from Babylonia to the Land of Israel, settled in Tzippori, and became part of Rebbi's inner circle.[3] Rabbi Ḥanina is certain that his powers of deliberation can restore any lost teachings. By dint of discipline, creativity, and insight, he is able to reach back to the wellspring of Torah. Rabbi Ḥanina therefore tells Rabbi Ḥiya not to argue with him. Rabbi Ḥiya responds coolly and confidently: *You are responsible for restoring Torah. But I am responsible for ensuring that Torah is not forgotten in the first place.* Rabbi Ḥiya works from the bottom up: He grows flax so as to weave nets in

3. B. Z. Bacher, *Legends of the Sages of Israel* [Hebrew] (Tel Aviv, 5688), 3–7.

order to trap deer, which he feeds to orphans, using the deerskin to write Torah scrolls. He brings these scrolls with him to teach children in the village. The younger ones learn Bible, and the older ones learn Mishna. Then he instructs them to teach one another. Rabbi Ḥiya's method is simple; he has no overhead costs and no budgetary constraints. He simply sits with the children and teaches them how to learn. Rebbi notices him and exclaims, "How great are the deeds of Ḥiya!"[4]

The Talmud relates a fantastical story about the relationship between Rebbi and Rabbi Ḥiya:

> Elijah often visted Rebbi's academy. One day it was Rosh Hodesh. Elijah was late and still had not come. When he came, Rebbi said to him: Why did the master come late? Elijah said to him: First I had to wake Abraham and wash his hands, and he prayed, and then I had to lay him back to rest; then I had to do the same for Isaac and then Jacob. Rebbi asked him: But you should wake them all at once! Elijah said: They maintain in heaven that the patriarchs would overwhelm the heavens with prayer and bring the Messiah before his proper time. Rebbi said to him: And is anyone like them to be found in this world? Elijah said to him: Yes, Rabbi Ḥiya and his sons.
>
> Rebbi decreed a fast. He placed Rabbi Ḥiya and his sons before the prayer stand. Rabbi Ḥiya said: He makes the wind blow. A wind blew. He said: He makes the rain fall. Rain fell. When he was about to say: He restores life to the dead, the world shook. They said in heaven: Who has revealed secrets in the world? They said: Elijah. They brought Elijah and administered sixty lashes of fire to him. Elijah came. He appeared to them as a fiery bear, entered among them, and distracted them from their prayers. (Bava Metzia 85b)

Elijah frequents Rebbi's academy. When he arrives late one morning, Rebbi requests an explanation. But even after receiving one,

4. This statement appears in a discussion about Rabbi Yishmael ben Rabbi Yose, who would test whether Rebbi valued Rabbi Ḥiya more than his father and himself.

he remains perplexed. He does not understand why Elijah cannot take care of Abraham, Isaac, and Jacob all at once so as to make it to class on time. Elijah's answer surprises him: If all three of the patriarchs rose together, their prayer might hasten the Messiah before his time. Rebbi asks if anyone similar to the patriarchs is alive in his own day, and Elijah points to Rabbi Ḥiya and his sons. Rebbi wishes to test if it is so. He schedules fast day prayers to summon the rain. Of course, Rabbi Ḥiya and his sons do not know they are being tested. Rabbi Ḥiya says, "He makes the rain fall," and the rain falls. He is about to enter into the dangerous territory of "He restores life to the dead" when suddenly the world shakes and a voice cries out from heaven: "Who has revealed secrets in the world?" Elijah is then punished.

When Rebbi asks Elijah why he does not wake all the patriarchs at once, he is told that it is forbidden to hasten the end of days. Rabbi Ḥiya, too, nearly hastens the end by bringing about the revival of the dead, though his hand is stayed at the last minute. Like Elijah, Rabbi Ḥiya is another individual within Rebbi's orbit working to draw the Messiah near.[5]

RABBI ḤIYA'S CLOSENESS TO REBBI

Several sources allude to Rabbi Ḥiya's closeness to Rebbi. The Babylonian Talmud relates that Rabbi Ḥiya used to eat at Rebbi's table (Eiruvin 73a).

Rabbi Ḥiya took it upon himself to teach the young Rav about the patriarch's habits and practices. The Babylonian Talmud relates that Rav asked Rabbi Ḥiya how Rebbi would accept upon himself the yoke of heaven. Their conversation is brief but to the point:

> Rav said to Rabbi Ḥiya: I never saw Rebbi accept upon himself the yoke of heaven. Rabbi Ḥiya said to him: O son of nobles!

5. This mysterious story contains a wealth of symbolism. For the time being, we can only wonder whether Rebbi was pleased with or jealous of Rabbi Ḥiya's power of prayer. See Y. Frankel, *Aggadic Story*, 338 note 86. Frankel is interested in the encounter between human action and the angels' limited understanding of those powerful enough to transgress natural law.

> When Rebbi passes his hands over his face, he accepts upon himself the yoke of heaven. (Berakhot 13b)

Rav wishes to witness the patriarch submit to divine rule. Does he cry, or bow down, or bend over? Rabbi Ḥiya, who is close to Rebbi, points to the moment when the patriarch places his hands over his eyes, standing otherwise completely still. As this source attests, Rabbi Ḥiya knows how to read Rebbi.

DAVID KING OF ISRAEL LIVES AND ENDURES: INTERCALATING THE YEAR

The intercalation of the year was a hallmark of the patriarch's authority and dominance, as we saw when we studied Rabban Gamliel, Rebbi's grandfather.[6] In the first assembly held after the decrees of persecution, the sages dealt with the sanctification of the new moon. During the patriarchy of Rabban Shimon ben Gamliel at Usha, they sanctified the new moon even though they were far from Jerusalem.[7] As noted, Ḥanania, the nephew of Rabbi Yehoshua, took this a step further: He tried to intercalate the years and sanctify the new moon in Babylonia. Rabban Shimon ben Gamliel prevented him, insisting this was the unique province of the sages in the Land of Israel. The following source preserves the debate about the proper site for the intercalation of the year during the Usha period:

> They do not intercalate the year except in Judea,[8] and if they do, it is deemed to have been intercalated. Ḥanina of Ono testified before Rabban Gamliel that they do not intercalate the year except in Judea, and if they do so in the Galilee, it is deemed to have been intercalated. (Tosefta Sanhedrin 2:13)

6. See *Sages* II.
7. S. Safrai, "Sites of the Sanctification of the Moon and the Intercalation of the Year After the Destruction of the Temple" [Hebrew], in *History of the Jews in the Time of the Second Temple*, vol. 1 (Jerusalem, 5754), 250–51.
8. This version appears in the Vienna manuscript. In the printed texts (based on the Erfort manuscripts) the word "except" is missing, but this is clearly a scribal error.

This seems to be a source from the Yavneh period, but the parallel version in the Jerusalem Talmud suggests otherwise:

> They do not intercalate the year except in Judea, and if they intercalate it in the Galilee, it is deemed to have been intercalated. Ḥanina of Ono testified before Rabban Gamliel that if they cannot intercalate the year in Judea, they do so in the Galilee. (Y. Nedarim 6:8 [40a])

Rabbi Ḥanina's statement refers to a period when it was impossible to intercalate the year in Judea. Another source (Mishna Gittin 6:7) teaches that Rabbi Ḥanina of Ono was one of the few surviving students of Rabbi Akiva, and he preserved traditions he had learned during the latter's imprisonment. Rabbi Ḥanina's testimony therefore dates back to the period after the Bar Kokhba revolt and the Hadrianic decrees, when it was part of the attempt to preserve rabbinic traditions. The next generation is that of Rebbi, who endeavors to restore the sanctification of the new moon to Judea and declare an end to the persecution. But something goes terribly wrong, as the Jerusalem Talmud relates:

> There was an incident involving twenty-four villages' representatives from the domain of Rebbi who came forward to intercalate the year in Lod. The evil eye entered them, and all of them died on a single occasion. From that time they relocated the intercalation of the year from Judea and permanently established it in the Galilee. (Y. Sanhedrin 1:2 [18c])

This difficult story speaks of twenty-four people who traveled to Lod to intercalate the year in a public celebration.[9] But an "evil eye" caused their deaths, and the intercalation of the year had to be relocated to the Galilee. It is hard to imagine what this "evil eye" might refer to, given that the story is dated to Rebbi's tenure and not, as we might have expected, to the Hadrianic persecutions.[10]

9. G. Alon, *History of the Jews,* vol. 2, 97; S. Safrai, "Sites of the Sanctification of the Moon," 252 note 29.
10. Though the "domain of Rebbi" could also refer to a previous patriarch, the continu-

> They considered relocating even the symbol of the intercalation from Judea to the Galilee. Rabbi Shimon said to them: Should we not leave in the land of Judea even a memorial to that rite? And behold, we find that they declared the year to be sanctified in Baalat [in Judea]. (Y. Sanhedrin 1:2 [18c])

In this source, Rabbi Shimon converses with Rabbi Ḥanina about the relocation of the intercalation. Both are young sages active at the end of Rebbi's tenure, so we cannot date this source back to the period of Rebbi's father or grandfather.[11] Perhaps the "evil eye" refers to the war between the two contenders for the position of Roman emperor in 193–194, Septimius Severus and Pescennius Niger. As noted, Judea was controlled by Niger, whereas the Galilee was loyal to Severus. The caravan of sages that Rebbi dispatched to Lod may have been attacked by Niger's followers.[12] As a result, the intercalation of the year was relocated to the Galilee, and Jerusalem lost more of its symbolic hold.

What is the "symbol" of the intercalation that the sages considered relocating? The Talmud relates that Rebbi sent the following message to Rabbi Ḥiya:

> Rebbi said to Rabbi Ḥiya: Go to Ein Tav and sanctify the month, and send me a signal that you have done so: David king of Israel lives and endures. (Rosh HaShana 25a)

Ein Tav must be located in Judea if it symbolized the connection to King David.[13] This story suggests that Rebbi viewed the patriarchy as the continuation of the royal line.[14] He sent Rabbi Ḥiya to Judea to affirm that "David king of Israel lives and endures," expressing his own aspirations to rule the Jewish people.

ation of the story clearly situates it during the patriarchy of Rabbi Yehuda HaNasi. See Y. HaLevi, *The Early Generations* [Hebrew], vol. 2, 70 note 36.

11. This point was argued at length in Ginzburg, *Interpretations and Insights,* vol. 3, 125–32.
12. S. Safrai, "Sites of the Sanctification of the Moon," 252.
13. I follow Safrai in "Sites of the Sanctification of the Moon." Other scholars locate Ein Tav in the Galilee.
14. Urbach, *Sages,* 609.

Messianic Aspirations in Rebbi's Milieu

> There was an incident in which Rebbi, Rabbi Ḥiya the Great, and Rabbi Yishmael ben Rabbi Yose were sitting and reviewing the scroll of Lamentations on the eve of the ninth of Av, which coincided with the Sabbath. They were learning from the afternoon onward. They omitted one alphabetical chapter. They said: Tomorrow we will go and complete it. When Rebbi[15] was leaving for his house, he fell and injured his finger, and he recited the following verse about himself: "The sufferings of the wicked are many" [Ps. 32:10]. Rabbi Ḥiya said to him: These things happened to you on our account, for it is written, "The breath of our nostrils, the anointed of the Lord, was caught for their corrupt deeds" [Lam. 4:20]. (Y. Shabbat 16:1 [15c])

Rebbi sits with two close colleagues on Shabbat, on the day preceding the ninth of Av. They begin studying the Scroll of Lamentations, though they do not complete it. They save the last chapter (which is structured as an alphabetical acrostic) for the next day. They know that either they will have time to finish learning on the ninth of Av, or else the Messiah will come and they will not need to continue. Rebbi then injures his finger at home. He blames himself, quoting from Psalms: "The sufferings of the wicked are many."[16] But Rabbi Ḥiya blames the generation as a whole. His comment suggests that Rebbi was destined to be the Messiah but was held back on account of the corrupt deeds of the generation. Rabbi Ḥiya thus elevates the status of the patriarch, whom he describes as "the anointed of the Lord."[17]

In another source, this same Rabbi Ḥiya attempts to temper the messianic fervor that enveloped Rebbi:

15. Rebbi's name is corrupted in the manuscripts, but I have corrected it as per the Jerusalem Talmud fragments published by Rabbi Y. N. Epstein, *Studies in the Literature of the Talmud* [Hebrew], vol. 2 (Jerusalem, 5748), 284. This also follows Lieberman, *Yerushalmi Kifshuto*, 193.
16. See Urbach's reading of this source in *Sages*, 609.
17. See Y. Frankel's reservations in *Methods of the Aggada and Midrash*, 625 note 94.

> Rebbi inquired of Rabbi Ḥiya: For someone such as me, what is the law concerning a he-goat? Rabbi Ḥiya said to Rebbi: Behold, your rival is in Babylonia. (Horayot 11b)

Rebbi's question is hypothetical, since of course no one is obligated to offer sacrifices after the Temple's destruction. He asks: If someone in his position had been obligated to bring a sin offering to the Temple, what sort of sin offering would he have brought? According to the Bible, a person who sins and wishes to atone must bring a she-goat. But if the leader of a tribe sins and wishes to atone, he must bring a he-goat. Rebbi is asking about his own status. Is he analogous to a tribal leader? Rabbi Ḥiya responds: "Your rival is in Babylonia." That is, Rebbi is not the only leader of the Jewish people; there is also the exilarch in Babylonia.[18]

Rabbi Ḥiya never publicly criticized Rebbi's messianic aspirations. The Babylonian Talmud relates that one day Rabbi Ḥiya and his sons Yehuda and Ḥizkiya ate dinner in Rebbi's home. The sons kept quiet throughout the meal. Rebbi tried to encourage them to speak up:

> Rebbi said to his servants: Overwhelm the youngsters with wine so they will say something.
>
> When they became a little drunk, they opened the discussion by saying: The Messiah will not come until two ruling families cease to exist among the Jewish people, and they are the family of the exilarch in Babylonia and the family of the patriarch in the Land of Israel. For it is stated, "And he will be a sanctuary, and he will be a tripping stone and a stumbling rock for the two houses of Israel" [Is. 8:14].
>
> Rebbi said to them: My sons, are you sticking thorns in my eyes?
>
> Rabbi Ḥiya said to Rebbi: My teacher, do not be angry. The numerical value of "wine" is seventy, and the numerical value of "secret" is seventy. When wine enters a person, his secret comes out. (Sanhedrin 38a)

18. This is the earliest explicit mention of the exilarch. See Gafni, *Jews of Babylonia*, 94.

The sons tell Rebbi that the Messiah will arrive only when the patriarch and exilarch surrender their positions. Upon hearing this, Rebbi initially responds defensively: "My sons, are you sticking thorns in my eyes?" But Rabbi Ḥiya informs him that they are merely repeating what they have heard at home: "When wine enters a person, his secret comes out."

> Rebbi was very humble. He used to say: Whatever a person tells me to do, I will do, except for what the elders of Betera did for my ancestor Hillel, for they resigned from the patriarchy and appointed him in their place. If Rav Huna the exilarch were to come here to the Land of Israel, I would place him above me, for he is from Judah and I am from Benjamin, as he is from the male line of descent from David, and I am from the female line.
>
> One time Rabbi Ḥiya the Great came up to Rebbi. He said to him: Rav Huna is outside.
>
> Rebbi's face became pale.
>
> Rabbi Ḥiya the Great said to him: His coffin has arrived.
>
> Rebbi said to him: Go and see who wants you outside.
>
> He went and did not find anyone there, and he knew Rebbi was angry with him. He did not go to Rebbi for thirty days. (Y. Kilayim 9:3 [32b])

Rebbi is depicted here as a man who prides himself on his humility. He declares his willingness to surrender his title to the exilarch, who is part of the Davidic dynasty. Rabbi Ḥiya mocks Rebbi, eager to test whether he truly means what he says. When Rebbi hears that the exilarch has indeed arrived, he blanches. He doesn't really want to surrender the patriarchy, of course. Fortunately Rav Huna arrives posthumously, so Rebbi need not abide by his word. But the tension between the patriarch and the exilarch will continue for generations, as will the tension between the two major centers of Jewish life, Babylonia and the Land of Israel.[19]

19. Ibid., 95.

TORAH: PUBLIC OR PRIVATE? AN EDUCATIONAL CONTROVERSY BETWEEN REBBI AND RABBI ḤIYA

One time, Rebbi decreed that the sages should not instruct their students in the marketplace. What verse did he expound to teach this? "Your hidden thighs are like jewels, the work of a master's hand" [Song. 7:2], which implies: Just as the thigh is kept private, so too, words of Torah should be studied in private. Nevertheless, Rabbi Ḥiya went out and taught Torah to his two nephews in the marketplace, to Rav and to Rabba bar bar Ḥana. Rebbi heard that Rabbi Ḥiya had defied his decree, and he was upset. Sometime afterward Rabbi Ḥiya came to appear before Rebbi. Rebbi said to him: Iya, who is calling to you outside? Rabbi Ḥiya understood that Rebbi had taken the matter to heart, so he took upon himself the ban of reproof for thirty days. On the thirtieth day, Rebbi sent Rabbi Ḥiya the following message: Come. Rebbi subsequently sent another message to Rabbi Ḥiya not to come....

In the end Rabbi Ḥiya came to see Rebbi. Rebbi said to him: Why did you come?

Rabbi Ḥiya said to him: Because the master sent me a message that I should come.

Rebbi responded: But I later sent a message that you should not come.

Rabbi Ḥiya said to him: I saw this first messenger, but I did not see this second messenger.

Rebbi applied to Rabbi Ḥiya the following verse: "When God favors a man's ways, even his foes will make peace with him" [Prov. 16:7].

Rebbi asked: Why did the master do this?

Rabbi Ḥiya said to Rebbi: Because it is written, "Wisdom sings out in the street" [Mishlei 1:20].

Rebbi said: If you read this verse once, you must have not read it a second time; and if you read it a second time, you did not read it a third time. And if you read it a third time, they did not explain it to you properly. The meaning of "Wisdom sings

> out in the street" accords with Rava. For Rava said: Anyone who is engaged in the study of Torah from inside, his learning will proclaim him outside.
>
> But it is written, "I did not speak in secrecy at first" [Is. 48:16].
>
> That verse speaks of the days of the public lectures.
>
> But what does Rabbi Ḥiya do with the verse "Your hidden thighs"?
>
> He applies it to charity and acts of loving-kindness. (Mo'ed Katan 16a–b)

The disagreement between Rebbi and Rabbi Ḥiya reflects two different approaches to Torah study. The first approach is that of Beit Shammai and Rabban Gamliel; the second is that of Beit Hillel and Rabbi Elazar ben Azaria, who was appointed patriarch after Rabban Gamliel's deposition. The first approach focuses on the obligation to safeguard Torah as the province of the learned elite. Torah should not be taught in the marketplace, nor should its secrets be revealed publicly. The second approach involves educating large numbers of students, so all of Israel can be privileged to study Torah. This is a deep ideological divide. Rabbi Ḥiya is very close to Rebbi, but he is not afraid to criticize his leadership style. He accepts Rebbi's decree of excommunication but without internalizing his criticism. Rebbi holds fast to his elitist approach because he feels the weight of responsibility for safeguarding Torah. Rabbi Ḥiya, in contrast, believes that Torah belongs in the public domain. Their disagreement becomes personal. When Rabbi Ḥiya comes before Rebbi, the latter mocks him by calling him "Iya."[20] But Rabbi Ḥiya does not relent, and the rift between them persists. Rabbi Ḥiya remains associated with *baraitot*, traditions "outside" the Mishna. He has no place inside Rebbi's Mishna, so he brings his teachings outside. The Babylonian Talmud is filled with his *baraitot*, thanks to which Torah is not forgotten from Israel.

20. Yonah Frankel says that Iya is a vulgar term. See Y. Frankel, "Biblical Verses Quoted in Tales of the Sages" [Hebrew], in *Studies in Aggada*, ed. Y. Heinemann (Jerusalem, 1971), 89.

Chapter Twenty-Three

The Tzippori Period: Torah and Greatness in One Place

Rebbi had been living in Tzippori for seventeen years, and he said with regard to himself: "Jacob lived in the land of Egypt for seventeen years" [Gen. 47:28], and Judah lived in Tzippori for seventeen years. (*Y. Kilayim* 9:3 [32*b*])

ANTONINUS AND REBBI

We will follow Rebbi from Beit She'arim to Tzippori, where he spent the final years of his patriarchy. If historians are accurate in dating Rebbi's death to 220 CE, then the move to Tzippori can be dated to the middle of the first decade of the third century. Rebbi came to Tzippori during Severus' reign; when Rebbi died, Caracalla was emperor.

When Severus assumed the throne in 193 CE the Jews gave him a warm reception. Inscriptions and dedications to Severus can be found in synagogues throughout the ancient world.[1] Under his rule, Jewish life

1. Levine, "The Period of Rabbi Yehuda HaNasi" [Hebrew], in *The Land of Israel from*

improved. According to the Palestinian sources, the Romans continued to rule Judea but permitted the Jews to govern their own affairs with relative freedom. Jews began to take on administrative roles, as we saw with Rabbi Elazar ben Rabbi Shimon bar Yoḥai. The Talmud depicts a close association between Rabbi Yehuda HaNasi and Severus, who is referred to as "Antoninus Caesar." In several rabbinic stories they are portrayed as fast friends. Their conversations cover a wide range of topics including family, theology, philosophy, science, and administrative matters. Even if we have reason to doubt the historicity of these sources, they testify to the sages' attempt to present Rebbi and Antoninus as equals.[2] One key story about Rebbi's relationship with Antoninus considers the patriarch's political status:

> Our teacher instructed Rabbi Afes: Write a letter in my name to our lord the emperor Antoninus. He arose and wrote: From Yehuda HaNasi to our sovereign the emperor Antoninus. Rabbi Yehuda HaNasi took and read it and tore it up and wrote: From your servant Yehuda to our sovereign the emperor Antoninus. Rabbi Afes said to him: Why do you treat your honor so lightly? He replied: Am I better than my ancestor? Did Jacob not say, "Thus said your servant Jacob"? (Genesis Rabba 75:5)

Rebbi's self-effacement upsets his secretary, who regards it as a form of submission to Roman authority. Many Jews continued to smart at the bitter memory of the Bar Kokhba revolt, and not everyone supported the new political tactic of using diplomatic means to survive under Roman rule. Rome's new policy gave rise to a tolerant and flexible leadership epitomized by the Severans, who opted for peace and cooperation in the interests of both sides.

Rebbi's conciliatory leadership style may have enabled him to strengthen his own economic position. Several sources describe his inordinate wealth, which included land, orchards, cattle, and ships.

the Destruction of the Temple to the Muslim Conquest, ed. C. Bars et al (Jerusalem, 5742), 95.

2. See, for instance, Avoda Zara 10a.

The power of the patriarchy seems to have peaked in Rebbi's time. He consolidated the religious, political, and communal order, appointed sages, and invested them with leadership roles throughout the empire, all thanks to his close association with the Roman rulers.[3] The Talmud encapsulates Rebbi's towering stature in the following maxim, which has become famous:

> From the time of Moses until the time of Rebbi, never have both Torah and greatness been found in the same person. (Gittin 59b)

REBBI'S PATRIARCHAL GOVERNMENT

During his years in Tzippori, Rebbi was on the ascendant. His palace grew resplendent, and he served as the sole, uncontested leader of the Jewish people in the Land of Israel. One source offers a rather uncomplimentary description of the administration of justice in his court:

> When a person came before Rebbi for judgment, if he accepted the verdict, it was well and good. If not, he would say to a member of his household: Show him the left side. And he would gesticulate a cutting-off from that direction. (Ecclesiastes Rabba 10:2)

Rebbi's court was rife with suspicions of conspiracy and intrigue. We sense this atmosphere from a passage in the Talmud that describes the personal petitions that the sages would append to their prayers. The prayer of the first sage who is quoted, Rabbi Elazar ben Pedat, the leading student of Rabbi Yoḥanan in the middle of the third century, typifies the others:

> May it be Your will, O Lord our God, that You cause love, brotherhood, peace, and companionship to dwell in our lot. Enlarge our boundaries with students, and cause our end to prosper with hope, and set our portion in the Garden of Eden, and establish us with a good companion and a good inclination in Your world,

3. Alon, *History of the Jews*, vol. 2, 84–158. Alon surveys the political, legal, and economic ties between Rebbi and the Roman leadership.

> and may we rise and find that the yearning of our heart is to fear Your name, and may our deeds and their fulfillment come before You for good. (Berakhot 16b)

Following this rather optimistic formulation, Rabbi Yehuda HaNasi's prayer offers a stark contrast:

> Rebbi, upon completing his prayer, would say: May it be Your will, O Lord our God and God of our fathers, that You save us from brazen individuals and from the trait of brazenness, from an evil man and an evil mishap, from the evil inclination, from an evil companion, from an evil neighbor, from a destructive spiritual impediment, and from harsh judgment and from a harsh legal adversary, whether he is a member of the covenant or not. (Berakhot 16b)

This prayer seems to have been forged in a difficult political climate. The speaker is in desperate need of divine intercession to save him from those around him, both Jews and non-Jews. At the end of Rebbi's prayer, the Talmud offers the following commentary, which may be read as sympathetic or as cynical:

> This prayer was recited even though bodyguards watched over Rebbi. (Berakhot 16b)

Rashi explains that Antoninus commanded that guards surround Rebbi to beat and avenge all who rose up against him. The Talmud's term for guards, *ketzutzei*, comes from the root of the Hebrew word for "cutting off," perhaps an allusion to men who were short or had short hair or were eunuchs.[4] We can imagine that many Jews would have recoiled

4. Although Roman law forbade castration, it may have been permissible to import eunuchs from the Persian Empire. Rabbi Yehuda HaNasi himself ruled that any slave who had been castrated had to be released (Kiddushin 25a). In Babylonia castration was legal and in fact quite common among bodyguards. So the term *ketutzei* may reflect the Babylonian reality. See Oppenheimer, *Rabbi Yehuda HaNasi*, 50–51.

from the image of a patriarch surrounded by bodyguards who were hired to do his bidding.

A non-rabbinic source from the period attests that Rebbi had autonomy when it came to capital crimes, though the Roman Empire did not generally authorize the provincial governors to rule in such matters:

> The patriarch has great power over the Jews by concession of the caesar, so he differs little from a true king. Private trials are held according to Jewish law, and some are condemned to death. And although there is not full license for this, still it is not done without knowledge of the caesar. (Origen, *Letter to Africanus* 14)[5]

Even if we have no historical documentation of executions performed by order of the patriarch, the fact that Rebbi had this authority surely inspired fear and dread.

REBBI'S "KITCHEN CABINET": THE APPOINTMENT OF OFFICIALS

Rebbi appointed the various officials in his court, avoiding factionalism. The Talmud describes Rebbi's appointment policy:

> At first each one would appoint his own disciples to the court. Rabbi Yoḥanan ben Zakkai appointed Rabbi Eliezer and Rabbi Yehoshua; Rabbi Yehoshua appointed Rabbi Akiva; and Rabbi Akiva appointed Rabbi Meir and Rabbi Shimon. He said: Let Rabbi Meir take his seat first. Rabbi Shimon's face turned pale. Rabbi Akiva said to him: Let it be enough for you that I and your Creator recognize your strengths. They went and paid honor to the patriarch. They made this rule: If a court made an appointment without the knowledge and consent of the patriarch, the act of appointment is invalid. And if a patriarch made an appointment without the knowledge and consent of the court,

5. Quotation from Alon, *History of the Jews*, vol. 2, 112. Alon rightfully dismisses those who question the reliability of this source.

> his appointment is valid. They reverted and ruled that the court should make an appointment only with the knowledge and consent of the patriarch, and that the patriarch should make an appointment only with the knowledge and consent of the court. (Y. Sanhedrin 1:2 [19a])]

According to this source, which the Jerusalem Talmud attributes to the third century sage Rabbi Abba, the method of appointing sages evolved over time. At first even those sages who were not associated with the patriarch could appoint students to positions of authority. Later, this responsibility became the province of the patriarch alone. And even later, a joint forum comprising the patriarch and the sages of the beit midrash took charge of these appointments.

Several sources describe Rebbi's appointments. Each year Rebbi would appoint two sages for a trial period. If they proved themselves worthy, they would continue in their positions; if not, they would be replaced (Y. Ta'anit 4:2 [68a]). The Talmud (Sanhedrin 5a) relates that Rabbi Ḥiya came to Rebbi to request appointments for his two nephews, Rabba bar bar Ḥana and Rav. Rebbi authorized Rabba bar bar Ḥana to instruct, to adjudicate, and even to rule on which firstborns were exempt from consecration. But he authorized Rav only to instruct and adjudicate. Rav then went to Babylonia, as documented in the epistle of Rabbi Sherira Gaon from 219 CE. Rabbi Ḥiya himself, though very close to Rebbi, was never appointed to the court, which the sages struggle to explain over an entire half page of the Talmud (Ketubot 103b). One possible reason is that Rabbi Ḥiya had many students, and Rebbi did not want to waste his time on communal matters.

In his will, Rebbi charged his son to appoint Rabbi Ḥanina bar Ḥama to a senior position in the court. The Talmud explains why Rebbi himself did not appoint him:

> And why had Rebbi not appointed him? Rabbi Drosa said: It was because the people of Tzippori cried out against him in Tzippori. And merely because the people cry out do they do whatever they want? Rabbi Elazar ben Rabbi Yose said: It was because Ḥanina answered in public.

> Rebbi was in the academy. He taught, "And if any survivors escape, they will be on the mountains, like doves of the valleys, all of them moaning" [Ezek. 7:16]. Ḥanina said to him: We read this verse as saying "roaring" rather than "moaning." Rebbi said to him: Where did you study Torah? Ḥanina said to him: Before Rabbi Hamnuna of Babylonia. Rebbi said to him: When you go down there, tell him to appoint you a sage. He realized that he would not be appointed a sage during Rebbi's lifetime. (Y. Ta'anit 4:2 [68a])

Rabbi Ḥanina bar Ḥama belongs to the transitional generation between the sages of the Mishna and those of the Talmud. He was educated in Babylonia and came to the Land of Israel at the end of Rebbi's lifetime. The Jerusalem Talmud offers two reasons he was not appointed. The first, cited by Rabbi Drosa, is political: The people of Tzippori rejected the new arrival from Babylonia and barred him from the court. The Talmud questions this explanation: "And merely because the people cry out do they do whatever they want?" Presumably it was the members of the elite leadership who objected, and thus Rebbi complied.[6] The Talmud, however, resists this explanation, positing in the name of Rabbi Elazar ben Rabbi Yose that Rabbi Ḥanina was not appointed as a result of an exchange with Rebbi. According to this source, Rebbi was once teaching a chapter from the prophecy of Ezekiel. In the middle of his teaching, he said a word that Rabbi Ḥanina thought was quoted in error. Rabbi Ḥanina pointed this out to Rebbi, who berated him and sent him back to Babylonia.[7]

Just as Rebbi opposed the appointment of certain major sages, he also granted himself dispensation to appoint his friends. For instance, he

6. Lieberman, *Studies in the Torah of the Land of Israel*, 182. Lieberman explains the appointment protocol: An announcement of the candidates was hung in a public place in order to ensure that there was no opposition. If public outcry ensued, the name would be removed from the ballot before the election.
7. It is interesting to compare this story to that of Bar Kappara, which we will discuss below. Meir points out the similarity between the two stories but does not note that both are about moaning doves, or homing pigeons. See Meir, *Yehuda HaNasi: Image of a Leader*.

appointed the grandson of Rabbi Shimon bar Yoḥai (who was also the son of Rabbi Elazar), with whom he had a complicated emotional bond. The Talmud relates that after Rabbi Elazar's death (and after Rabbi Elazar's widow refused to marry Rebbi), Rebbi came for a visit. He wished to know if anyone remained of Rabbi Elazar's family. He was taken to see Rabbi Elazar's son, a rascal of a boy who spent his time in brothels. Rebbi took him under his wing and sat him down with a study partner in the beit midrash.[8]

ECONOMIC ENACTMENTS FOR THE SAKE OF THE COMMON GOOD

During Rebbi's tenure, the Jews struggled under difficult economic conditions. The Roman government, though politically tolerant, did not cut taxes. So Rebbi sought creative ways to reduce the tax burden and permit the Jews to eat crops that were technically forbidden by halakha.

The most salient example of Rebbi's efforts to ameliorate the economic plight of the Jews was his attempt to permit the consumption of bread baked by non-Jews, the ban on which may have dated as far back as the early Second Temple period. A rabbinic tradition lists this prohibition among those decreed by Beit Shammai for the sake of separating Jews from non-Jews.[9] The Book of Daniel, too, refers to the strict avoidance of the "bread of the king" (Dan. 1:8).

The Roman government, like the Hellenistic administration before it, supplied subsidized bread to the entire population of the empire. The imperial administration built granaries in order to satisfy military and civilian demand.[10] It supplied wheat to all the windmills and regulated the price of bread throughout the empire. At the end of the second century, the Land of Israel suffered from severe droughts that led to a deep economic crisis.[11] Most of the imperial bakeries were

8. Bava Metzia 85a.
9. Y. Shabbat 1:4 (3d); Shabbat 17b. For a list of the prohibitions instituted by Beit Shammai, see Y. Ben Shalom, *Beit Shammai* [Hebrew] (Jerusalem, 5754), 252–72.
10. R. Yankelovitz, "Their Bread… Blurred Laws" [Hebrew], *Sinai* 57 (5740): 48–54.
11. D. Sperber collected all those sources referring to the severity of the economic crisis during this period. See Sperber, *JESHO* 17 (1974), 272–98.

controlled by non-Jews, a fact that serves as the backdrop for the following source:

> One time Rebbi went to a certain place and saw that bread was scarce for students. He said: Is there no baker here? The people assumed he was asking if a non-Jewish baker was available, but in fact he was asking about a Jewish baker. (Avoda Zara 35b)

Rebbi noticed that Jewish students were unwilling to buy bread. He inquired, "Is there no baker here?" That is, why weren't the students eating the bread baked in the local bakeries? The Talmud goes on to clarify that the students assumed Rebbi was asking why they weren't eating non-Jewish bread, whereas in fact he was asking why they weren't buying from a local Jewish baker. This is an obvious instance of apologetics: The Talmud is uncomfortable suggesting that Rebbi would permit eating bread baked by non-Jews. But another talmudic story clarifies that Rebbi did in fact authorize the consumption of such bread:

> One time Rebbi went out to the fields, and an idol worshipper brought him bread baked in a large commercial oven to the size of a *se'ah*. Rebbi said: How lovely is this bread! Why did the sages see fit to forbid it?
>
> [How could Rebbi ask] why the sages saw fit to forbid it? On account of intermarriage! Rather, he meant: Why did the sages see fit to forbid it in the fields? The people assumed that Rebbi had permitted non-Jewish bread. But this is not so. Rebbi did not actually permit non-Jewish bread. (Avoda Zara 35b)

Here, too, there is a disparity between the anecdote, which suggests that Rebbi was prepared to eat non-Jewish bread, and the Talmud's interpretation of his statement. According to the Talmud's narrow understanding, Rebbi meant to permit such bread only in the fields, not in the cities.

Confronted by the difficult economic and social situation and the imperial economic subsidies, Rebbi sought to legalize the consumption of bread baked in public ovens. Whether or not he did so explicitly, the people understood that such bread was permissible. Though a mishna explicitly prohibits the bread of non-Jews, the Talmud states that this is one of several "blurred laws" (Y. Shevi'it 8:4 [38a]). It seems that the sages of the generation after the Mishna deliberately relaxed this prohibition so as to prevent the situation of the Jews from deteriorating further. The Talmud relates that out of economic considerations, Rabbi Yehuda HaNasi's grandson Rabbi Yehuda Nesiya permitted the consumption of oil produced by non-Jews. His student Rabbi Simlai, who heard about this development, responded that hopefully Rabbi Yehuda Nesiya would permit their bread as well. Taken together, these sources suggest that non-Jewish bread was permitted de facto, albeit not de jure.

Rebbi is also credited with other lenient rulings intended to ease the Jews' economic burden.[12] He was concerned for the people as a whole, without favoring any particular socioeconomic group. Several sources relate that Rebbi took administrative responsibility for collecting taxes owed to the imperial government:

> Rebbi applied the law in accordance with Ben Nanas with reference to *arnona,* head taxes, and forfeiture. (Y. Ketubot 10:5 [34a])

The Talmud lists three kinds of taxes: The *arnona* was a tax on crops to feed the Roman army. The head tax was an annual tax on every member of the population. And the forfeiture was a tax on all landholders.[13] Rebbi sought to instill a sense of civic responsibility, so people would prioritize their taxes above other fiscal obligations.

Another source speaks of Rebbi's involvement with the tax authorities themselves:

> The council and the assembly were both obligated to present a payment to the government. The case came before Rebbi, who ruled: Is not the council part of the government? For what purpose, there-

12. For a list of such leniencies, see Tosefta Shevi'it 4. For instance, Rebbi also permitted the eating of vegetables immediately following the sabbatical year, though they were obviously planted illegally that year.
13. A. Golack, "Roman Taxes in the Land of Israel" [Hebrew], *Magnes Press* (Jerusalem, 5698), 97–104.

> fore, did the decree state that the council and the assembly were to make a payment? It was to specify that this party should give half, and that party should give half. (Y. Yoma 1:2 [39a])

The Roman regime imposed an additional tax on the people. The town council argued with the town assembly about who would absorb this financial obligation. The assembly wanted the funds to come from the council, and the council wanted them to come from the assembly. Rebbi ruled that each party should pay half. The Babylonian Talmud preserves a record of this incident:

> There was a royal tax that the imperial house imposed on the council and on the assembly. Rebbi said: Let the council give half, and let the assembly give half. (Bava Batra 143a)

REBBI'S RELATIONSHIP WITH THE UNLEARNED

One of the more troubling stories about the tax system during Rebbi's tenure describes the decision to exempt students of Torah from taxes:

> Rebbi opened storehouses of food to feed the poor during the years of famine. Rebbi said: Only students of Torah, students of Mishna, students of Gemara, students of halakha, or students of *Aggada* may enter. But unlearned people may not enter.
>
> Rabbi Yonatan ben Amram pushed his way into the storehouse. He said to Rebbi: Master, sustain me!
>
> Rebbi said to him: My son, have you studied Torah?
>
> Rabbi Yonatan said to him: No.
>
> Have you studied Mishna?
>
> No.
>
> If so, on what merit shall I sustain you?
>
> Rabbi Yonatan said: Sustain me as you would a dog or a raven.
>
> Rebbi relented and sustained him. After Rabbi Yonatan departed, Rebbi was sitting alone, distressed by what he had done. He said: Woe is me, for I have given of my bread to an unlearned person.

> Rabbi Shimon bar Rebbi said before Rebbi: Perhaps that man was actually Yonatan ben Amram, your disciple, who does not wish ever to benefit from the honor of Torah.
>
> They investigated the matter and found that it was indeed Rabbi Yonatan. Rebbi said: All may enter. (Bava Batra 8a)

This text describes a clear and rigid hierarchy. Rebbi opens the storehouses of food he has amassed only to those who are Torah scholars, or to those who are at least in some way connected to the world of Torah. But Yonatan ben Amram does not want to benefit on account of the Torah he has learned, so he asks Rebbi to sustain him like a dog or a raven. Both of these creatures are symbols of evil (see Sanhedrin 108b), yet God provides for their welfare: "You open Your hands, feeding every creature to its heart's content" (Ps. 145:16). Rebbi hands him a donation, then regrets it: "Woe is me, for I have given of my bread to an unlearned person." Rabbi Shimon, Rebbi's son and constant companion, recognizes Yonatan ben Amram and identifies him to his father. Rebbi promptly abandons his rigid entrance requirements and proclaims that all are welcome.

The Talmud proceeds immediately to the next story, which demonstrates that Rebbi had a consistent way of dealing with the uneducated masses. He attributed all the misfortunate in the world to *amei ha'aretz*, commoners who took no part in Torah learning. The Talmud describes the tax exemption that Rebbi granted to students of Torah:

> It is like the case of the tax imposed on the inhabitants of Tiberias to raise money for the crown. They came before Rebbi and said to him: Let the rabbis contribute along with us! Rebbi said to them: No. The people said: Then we will flee the city! Rebbi said to them: So flee! Half of them fled. The king waived half the tax. The remaining half of the people came before Rebbi. They said to him: Let the rabbis contribute along with us! Rebbi said to them: No. The people said: Then we will flee! Rebbi said to them: So flee! They all fled. A certain launderer remained. The governors imposed the entire remaining tax on the launderer. He fled, and the crown tax was canceled. Rebbi said: From here you

> see that misfortune comes to the world only because of unlearned people.[14] (Bava Batra 8a)

This section of Tractate Bava Batra (7b–8a) deals with the exemption of Torah scholars from taxes.[15] As this story recounts, the tax-paying public was furious that a sector of the population was exempt on account of religious status. This is a complicated affair, since it is the public and not individuals who shoulder the tax burden. Thus, when Rebbi refuses to compromise, half the population of Tiberias flees. When Rebbi still refuses to reconsider his tax policy, the other half of the population flees as well. To heighten the irony, the Talmud relates that only a poor launderer remained to shoulder the entire tax burden of the city. The image of the launderer, whose role is to clean dirty clothes, recalls the halakha that Torah scholars are not permitted to wear stained garments (Shabbat 114a). When the launderer flees the city, leaving no more unlearned Jews in Tiberias, the tax burden is miraculously lifted. Rebbi's reaction is quite matter-of-fact: "From here you see that misfortune comes to the world only because of unlearned people."

Rebbi seeks to promulgate the notion that a society must be built on the study of Torah. The purpose of Jewish autonomy is to allow for Torah study. Those who do not learn threaten the social order and do not deserve to receive communal funds. Rebbi wishes for Torah to become the province of all of Israel. As he sees it, there should be no one who does not study Torah, for Torah is the *raison d'être* of the Jewish people.

14. The taxes described here were special levies imposed upon the residents of Tiberias for the quartering of soldiers. Whenever a regiment moved to a new base, the local population had to pay to maintain the army. This tribute preceded the institutionalization of the *arnona* tax. See Y. Dan, "The Byzantine Administration in the Land of Israel" [Hebrew], in *The Land of Israel from the Destruction of the Temple to the Muslim Conquest*, 404.
15. On this exemption in talmudic times, see M. Bar, *The Amora'im of Babylonia: Episodes in Economic Life* [Hebrew] (Ramat Gan, 5735), 227–41. On this exemption in medieval times, see Y. M. Ta Shma, "Sages' Exemption from Taxes" [Hebrew], in *Halakha, Custom, Reality* (Jerusalem, 5756), 228–41.

REBBI RESPECTS THE RICH

Rebbi used his position as patriarch to acquaint himself with the local leadership. Although the sages forbade the study of Greek, it was the language spoken at Rebbi's table:

> Rebbi said: In the Land of Israel, why speak the Syriac language? Speak either the holy tongue or Greek! (Bava Kamma 83a)

As we have seen, it was Rebbi's grandfather Rabban Gamliel of Yavneh who instituted the study of Greek among those who had close ties to the imperial authorities. Rebbi fashioned the patriarchy into a bastion of wealth and distinction, lending prestige to the position. The following description of the seating arrangements in the patriarchal palace illustrates Rebbi's attitude toward money and status:

> Ben Bunyas came before Rebbi. Rebbi said to those present: Make room for the man of a hundred coins. Another man then came to visit Rebbi. Rebbi said to those present: Make room for the man of two hundred coins. Rabbi Yishmael ben Rabbi Yose told Rebbi: My teacher, this man's father owns a thousand ships at sea and a thousand cities on land. Rebbi said to him: If so, when you reach his father, tell him: Do not send him before me wearing these clothes. Rebbi shows respect for the wealthy. (Eiruvin 86a)

Ben Bunyas, a wealthy man, is invited to a meal in the palace. Rebbi places him in a seat reserved for major donors, called "men of a hundred coins." But then an even greater donor arrives, a "man of two hundred coins." Ben Bunyas is pushed aside. Rabbi Yishmael ben Rabbi Yose, well-acquainted with the aristocracy of Tiberias (and Rome), points out to Rebbi that he has made a mistake – Ben Bunyas is in fact worth much more, and he too should have a place at the table. Rebbi responds harshly: *When you see his father, tell him to dress his son in clothes that befit the honor of the patriarch's home.* The Talmud responds with the following summary: "Rebbi shows respect for the wealthy."

RELIGIOUS DECREES FOR THE COMING OF THE MESSIAH

The prosperity and opulence of Tzippori inspired Rebbi to try to further his own agenda for his people. He viewed this period of "Torah and greatness in one place" as a climactic moment in Jewish history. As we saw, Rabbi Ḥiya attempted to temper Rebbi's fervor by reminding him of his rival, the exilarch in Babylonia. Yet there are several indications that Rebbi regarded himself as living in messianic times. For one, he sought to institute significant changes in the observance of various holidays:

> Rabbi Elazar said in the name of Rabbi Ḥanina: Rebbi planted a sapling on Purim, bathed on the market day of Tzippori on the seventeenth of Tammuz, and sought to abolish the ninth of Av. But the sages did not agree with him. Rabbi Abba bar Zavda said to Rabbi Elazar: Rabbi, that was not the case. It was a year when the ninth of Av fell on the Sabbath, and it was postponed until after the Sabbath, and Rebbi said: Since it is postponed this year, let it be postponed altogether. But the sages did not agree with him. Rabbi Elazar applied this verse to him: "Two are better than one" [Eccl. 4:9]. (Megilla 5b)

We have already encountered Rabbi Ḥanina bar Ḥama, who was acquainted with Rebbi during the patriarch's final years in Tzippori. He relates that Rebbi sought to change the people's observance of Purim and the seventeenth of Tammuz, as well as to abolish the ninth of Av commemoration altogether. According to Rebbi, the Jewish people had entered a new era. Although still under Roman dominion, the Jews had prospered in their own land (at least in the Galilee), so there was no reason to continue fasting on the ninth of Av, as had been the custom since the Temple's destruction. The other sages disagreed, a reminder that even the power of the patriarch was held in check.

The *Amora'im* of the Land of Israel refused to accept Rabbi Ḥanina's testimony about Rebbi. Presumably they sought to avoid the dangerous implications of such a teaching. Rabbi Abba bar Zavda instead taught that Rebbi attempted to abolish the ninth of Av only during a year when it fell on the Sabbath and was therefore postponed until Sunday. But Bar Zavda's account clearly smacks of apologetics.

The *Tosafot* comment on this source:

> This is difficult. How could it be that Rebbi would abolish the ninth of Av altogether? For as we say, "Anyone who eats and drinks on the ninth of Av will not be privileged to witness the consolation of Jerusalem" (Ta'anit 30b). And furthermore, no court can repeal the ruling of another court unless it is superior to that court in wisdom and number. (*Tosafot* on Megilla 5b)

The challenges raised by *Tosafot* are interesting in two senses. First, the statement that "Anyone who eats and drinks on the ninth of Av will not be privileged to witness the consolation of Jerusalem" is actually a teaching of Rabban Shimon ben Gamliel, Rebbi's father. And second, *Tosafot's* claim that "no court can repeal the ruling of another court unless it is superior to that court in wisdom and number" is based on the implicit assumption that a later court cannot possibly eclipse an earlier one. But this scenario is exactly what Rebbi represents. He views himself as the harbinger of a new era in Jewish history.

Ritva (Rabbi Yom Tov ben Avraham Asevilli, fourteenth century Seville) tried to understand Rebbi's motivations in seeking to abolish the ninth of Av:

> In the time of Rebbi, our holy sage, there was no persecution but also no peace. And we learn in Tractate Rosh HaShana [18b] that in any era in which there is no persecution and no peace, the people may decide whether or not to fast, as decreed by the prophets. For if there is peace – meaning that Israel resides securely in its land – and no persecution, then they rejoice. And if there is persecution, then they fast. But if there is no peace but also no persecution, they decide whether or not to fast. Therefore Rebbi bathed on the seventeenth of Tammuz. He may have even eaten, since he had the option of not fasting. But the Talmud speaks of bathing because this is a more public act. (Ritva, *Insights on Tractate Megilla*)

Commentators from the third generation of *Amora'im* until the Middle Ages tried to come to terms with how Rabbi Yehuda HaNasi could abolish the fasts commemorating the destruction of the Temple, uprooting such a foundational tradition. But it seems clear that Rebbi's attempts to redefine these significant days of the Jewish calendar reflect his sense that he was living during a redemptive era. Even the sapling he planted on Purim bespeaks a desire to revoke a diasporic festival in recognition of the autonomy of the Jews in their own land.[16]

REBBI AS THE COUNTERPART OF HEZEKIAH KING OF JUDAH: "GOD WISHED TO MAKE HIM MESSIAH"

In rabbinic tradition, the biblical Hezekiah is a symbol of missed opportunity. He reigned during the Assyrian king Sennacherib's mission to the Land of Israel in 701 BCE. Sennacherib laid waste to all of Judea, as immortalized by Isaiah: "Fair Zion is left like a booth in a vineyard, like a hut in a cucumber field, like a city beleaguered" (Is. 1:8). But miraculously, Hezekiah survived. According to one talmudic story, God wished to make Hezekiah into the Messiah and Sennacherib into Gog and Magog (see Sanhedrin 94a). Tragically, this plan was revoked because Hezekiah failed to express gratitude for all the good God had shown him. This story resonated with Rebbi and his compatriots.[17]

A rabbinic source compares Rebbi to Hezekiah:

> Rabbi Yehoshua ben Zeruz, the son of Rabbi Meir's father-in-law, testified before Rebbi that Rabbi Meir ate a vegetable leaf grown in Beit She'an. Rebbi therefore exempted the entire area of Beit She'an from the tithing requirement on his account. Rebbi's brothers and the other members of his father's household gathered around him and said to him: Beit She'an is a place regarding which your fathers and your fathers' fathers acted prohibitively. Will you now act permissively in its regard? Rebbi expounded

16. Rabbi Tzaddok HaKohen of Lublin, *Maḥshevot Ḥarutz* 20. And see Urbach, *Sages*, 609.
17. M. Aberbach, "Hezekiah King of Judah and Rabbi Yehuda the Patriarch" [Hebrew], *Tarbiz* 53 (5744): 363–71.

> for them this verse: "And he [Hezekiah] crumbled the copper serpent that Moses had made, for until those days the children of Israel had burned incense to it. And he called it Nehushtan" [II Kings 18:4]. Rebbi said: Is it possible that Asa came to power and did not destroy it? That Jehoshafat came to power and did not destroy it? Asa and Jehoshafat destroyed all the idols in the world! Rather, his [Hezekiah's] forefathers left him a place in which to distinguish himself. This is true of me as well; my forefathers left me a place in which to distinguish myself. (Ḥullin 6b)

Hezekiah king of Judea did what no man since Moses had dared. Moses had erected a copper serpent in the desert to serve as a sort of charm: Anyone bitten by the serpent would be ḥealed by it. According to the Mishna in Rosh HaShana, the serpent was supposed to direct the people's attention to God, though this was not always the case. For generations, Jews were led into sin on account of this serpent, but no one dared destroy it. Then Hezekiah came along and crushed the serpent. Like Hezekiah, Rebbi felt he was entering a new historical moment in which he would distinguish himself as a leader of his people.

Chapter Twenty-Four

Rebbi and Bar Kappara

Rebbi and his court were not immune to criticism and attack. We have already seen how Rabbi Ḥiya challenged Rebbi's messianic leanings and his pedagogical approach. Now let us consider one of the more colorful members of Rebbi's circle, Rabbi Elazar HaKappar, also known as Bar Kappara. In the Jerusalem Talmud he appears as the leader of a beit midrash of his own, where he taught mishnayot that differed from those found in Rebbi's Mishna. In the Babylonian Talmud, in contrast, he is depicted as Rebbi's student.[1] Academic scholars have written extensively about the halakhic evidence cited by Bar Kappara (as well as Rabbi Hoshaya Rabba), who drew on his own unique traditions.[2] In this chapter we will discuss Rebbi's encounters with Bar Kappara.

1. Meir studied the sources on Bar Kappara, distinguishing between the Babylonian and Palestinian traditions. See Meir, *Yehuda HaNasi: Image of a Leader*, 154–66.
2. Epstein, *Text of the Mishna*, 236–37; S. Lieberman, *The Talmud of Caesarea* [Hebrew] (Jerusalem, 5791), 9.

THE WEDDING FEAST

The Invitation

> Rebbi made a wedding for his son Rabbi Shimon [and did not invite Bar Kappara]. He wrote on the wedding hall: Two hundred forty million dinars were spent on this wedding hall. Yet they did not invite Bar Kappara. Bar Kappara said to Rebbi: If this wealth is the lot of those who transgress His will, then the lot of those who perform His will should be all the more so! Rebbi then invited Bar Kappara. Bar Kappara said: If this is the lot of those who perform His will in this world, then their lot in the World to Come will be all the more so! (Nedarim 50b)

This opening scene is prefaced by a discussion about wealth and prosperity. Rebbi comments, "Our ancestors said, 'We have forgotten prosperity,' but we have never even seen it." This leads to the story of Rabbi Shimon's extravagant wedding. Only Bar Kappara, the study partner of the groom, was left off the guest list. Presumably he was not sufficiently well connected to merit an invitation to the patriarchal court. Someone proceeds to write on the wall of the wedding hall the first graffiti in Jewish history: "Two hundred forty million dinars were spent on this wedding hall. Yet they did not invite Bar Kappara."[3] We are given no background information on Bar Kappara, but it seems that his omission from the guest list elicits a public protest. Bar Kappara then speaks up for himself, offering the following barb: "If this wealth is the lot of those who transgress His will, then the lot of those who perform His will should be all the more so!"[4] The graffiti does the trick, and Rebbi invites Bar Kappara to the wedding. When Bar Kappara receives the invitation, he responds, "If this is the lot of those who perform His will in this world, then their lot in the World to Come will be all the more

3. The parallel version in Leviticus Rabba includes some variants. There Bar Kappara himself writes the following graffiti: "After his rejoicing comes death. Of what purpose is his rejoicing?"
4. The phrase "those who transgress His will" is generally reserved for those who commit egregious sins. See Genesis Rabba 65 on Yakum Ish Tzerurot.

so!" That is, he declares that the benefit he will derive from attending the wedding feast will pale in comparison to the benefit he expects in the World to Come.

The Talmud continues with the following cryptic and ominous statement:

> Any day on which Rebbi laughed, misfortune would befall the world. (Nedarim 50b)

What is the curse associated with Rebbi's laughter? Elsewhere in the Talmud, Rebbi states that "misfortune comes into the world only because of unlearned people" (Bava Batra 8a). Perhaps Rebbi associates levity with the uneducated. He may feel that as patriarch, he cannot afford to laugh. He must conduct himself with restraint and authority, as befits his dignified position. Perhaps this is the reason Rebbi initially refrains from inviting Bar Kappara, as we might conclude from his explicit request when Bar Kappara arrives at the wedding hall:

> Rebbi said to Bar Kappara: Do not bring me to levity, and in return I will give you forty measures of wheat. Bar Kappara said to Rebbi: I accept, but note, master, that I will take as large a measure as I wish. (Nedarim 50b–51a)

Rebbi worries that Bar Kappara may make him laugh, suggesting that this fellow was some sort of court jester. Rebbi promises a reward if only Bar Kappara will refrain from doing so. The Talmud relates how Bar Kappara accedes to Rebbi's terms:

> Bar Kappara took a large basket and coated it with pitch to make sure that not a single grain of wheat should fall through the holes. He then turned the basket upside down and went and said to Rebbi: Let the master apportion out to me the forty measures of wheat that you owe me. Rebbi laughed and said to him: Did I not warn you not to make me laugh? Bar Kappara said to him: I am merely taking the wheat that I have a claim on! (Nedarim 51a)

The otherwise austere Rebbi cracks a smile in spite of himself, then immediately regains his composure and censures Bar Kappara. This concludes the first scene.

Coming Apart at the Wedding

In the next scene, Bar Kappara turns to Rebbi's daughter:

> Bar Kappara said to Rebbi's daughter: Tomorrow I will drink wine accompanied by your father's dancing and your mother's singing. (Nedarim 51a)

The Talmud then offers us a rare window into a fancy wedding feast in the patriarchal court. This is a difficult scene to imagine. To convey the impact of Bar Kappara's behavior on those present, the Talmud introduces the figure of Ben Elasa:

> Ben Elasa was the son-in-law of Rebbi and a very wealthy person. He was invited to the wedding of Rabbi Shimon, Rebbi's son. (Nedarim 51a)

Ben Elasa is familiar from other sources as a well-connected, well-dressed, and well-mannered dandy. The Talmud relates that he wore his hair in the "Lulian" style, as did the high priest. Ben Elasa feels comfortable in aristocratic circles, but he is no scholar. As soon as he comes on the scene, Bar Kappara begins putting on a show:

> Bar Kappara said to Rebbi: What is the meaning of the word abomination (*to'eiva*) [in the verse "You shall not lie with a man as one lies with a woman; it is an abomination" (Lev. 18:22)]. Bar Kappara refuted any meaning that Rebbi would suggest. Rebbi said: You explain it! Bar Kappara said to Rebbi: First let your wife come and pour me a cup of drink. She came and poured him a drink. Bar Kappara said to Rebbi: Arise and dance before me, and in return I will tell you my explanation. Bar Kappara said: This is what the Merciful One is saying: It is an abomination (*to'eiva*) because you are straying with this cohabitation (*to'eh ata bah*).

> When it was time for another cup of wine, Bar Kappara said to Rebbi: What is the meaning of the word perversion (*tevel*) [in the verse "A woman shall not stand before an animal for mating; it is a perversion" (Lev. 18:23)]. Rebbi said to Bar Kappara as cited previously. Bar Kappara said to Rebbi: Do for me as you did earlier, and in return I will tell you the explanation. Rebbi did. Bar Kappara then said to Rebbi: *Tevel hu* means, is there any spice (*tavlin*) in this cohabitation? Why is this cohabitation different from other cohabitations?
>
> Bar Kappara further said to Rebbi: What is the meaning of depravity (*zima*) [in the verse "Do not uncover the nakedness of a woman and her daughter... it is depravity" (Lev. 18:17)]. Bar Kappara said to Rebbi: Do for me as I asked before. Rebbi did so. Bar Kappara said to him: *Zima* means, this child – whose is he (*zo ma hi*)? (Nedarim 51a)

This conversation is a strange hybrid of learned discourse and vulgarity. Bar Kappara's questions are legitimate because they deal with Torah matters: The words abomination, perversion, and depravity all appear in the biblical verses about forbidden sexual liaisons. But of course his questions are laden with sexual innuendo. Moreover, by the time Bar Kappara begins addressing Rebbi, the wedding guests have had their fill of wine, which has reduced their inhibitions. Bar Kappara, who has already prepared Rebbi's daughter the night before, stages his performance, asking his provocative questions about biblical interpretation. Rebbi tries his hand at answering, but Bar Kappara refutes him each time. Bar Kappara then tries to make Rebbi dance and his wife pour him wine – the very levity Rebbi sought to avoid. The more the drink flows, the more heated the atmosphere, as is familiar to us from descriptions of ancient Roman banquets. It was the Roman custom to break into a more festive, lighthearted atmosphere at the end of the meal and to go from house to house singing bawdy songs.[5] Precisely to avoid such an atmosphere, the sages famously stipulated that it is forbidden to travel

5. Lieberman, *Yerushalmi Kifshuto*, 521. Y. Tabori, *Passover for the Generations* [Hebrew] (Tel Aviv, 5756), 367–77.

from house to house on the Seder night, lest the Seder, too, devolve into a drinking party.

Ben Elasa, the patriarch's son-in-law, watches from the sidelines, incensed:

> Ben Elasa could not tolerate Bar Kappara's behavior. He and his wife arose and departed from there. (Nedarim 51a)

Throughout the Talmud, Ben Elasa is never quoted as speaking words of Torah. He is depicted as a Greek prince, and as someone who married into the patriarchal family for the sake of his social status. But when he witnesses the patriarchal couple making fools of themselves in public, even he can tolerate it no longer. He gets up and leaves, taking his wife with him.

This concludes the drama as depicted in Tractate Nedarim. But the Jerusalem Talmud paints a fuller picture of what transpired between Bar Kappara and Ben Elasa.

Bar Kappara's Cryptic Note to Ben Elasa

> Rebbi had high regard for Ben Elasa. Bar Kappara said to him: Everyone submits questions to Rebbi, but you do not submit questions to him. He said to him: What should I ask him? He said to him: Ask: Who looks down from the heavens, searching from the corners of her house, all the winged creatures fear? "The young men saw me and withdrew, the aged rose and stood ... and laid their hands on their mouth" [Job 29:8–9]. Lo, they cry in woe. He who is taken is taken in sin.

Upon hearing this riddle, Rebbi turned and saw Bar Kappara laughing. Rebbi said: I do not recognize you, O sage. And Bar Kappara realized he would not be appointed as an official in Rebbi's court for the rest of his life. (Y. Mo'ed Katan 3:1 [81c])

The Jerusalem Talmud offers no background to this story. We are told only that Rebbi held Ben Elasa in high regard. In the previous section we encountered Ben Elasa at his brother-in-law's wedding. Perhaps it was a few days later that Bar Kappara, responsible for the levity at the wedding, tried to provoke the patriarch's son-in-law by asking him why he did not ask Rebbi about his conduct at the wedding. Ben Elasa is embarrassed: "What should I ask him?" Bar Kappara suggests a riddle based on a verse from Job and on this passage from the Book of Proverbs:

> From the window of my house, through my lattice, I looked out and saw among the simple, noticed among the youths, a lad devoid of sense. He was crossing the street near her corner, walking toward her house in the dusk of evening, in the dark hours of night. A woman comes toward him dressed like a harlot, with set purpose. She is bustling and restive; she is never at home. Now in the street, now in the square, she lurks at every corner. She lays hold of him and kisses him; brazenly she says to him: I had to make a sacrifice of well-being; today I fulfilled my vows. Therefore I have come out to you, seeking you, and have found you. I have decked my couch with covers of dyed Egyptian linen; I have sprinkled my bed with myrrh, aloes, and cinnamon. Let us drink our fill of love till morning; let us delight in amorous embrace. For the man of the house is away; he is off on a distant journey. He took his bag of money with him and will return only at mid-month. She sways him with her eloquence, turns him aside with her smooth talk. Thoughtlessly he follows her, like an ox going to the slaughter. (Prov. 7:6–21)

We can begin to make sense of Bar Kappara's riddle in light of this passage. He instructs Ben Elasa to ask about who "looks down from the heavens." He is invoking the principle that every time the Hebrew word for "look down" (*hashkafa*) appears, it has negative connotations.[6]

6. Tanḥuma, *Ki Tissa* 14. The midrash cites several examples: "And looking down toward Sodom and Gomorrah and all the land of the plain, he saw the smoke of the land rising like the smoke of a kiln" (Gen. 19:28); "At the morning watch the Lord looked down upon the Egyptian army from a pillar of fire and cloud and threw the Egyptian army into a panic" (Ex. 14:24); "Through the window Sisera's mother looked down and whined" (Judges 5:28); "Two or three eunuchs looked down toward him" (II Kings 9:32); "From the window of my house, through my lattice, I looked down"

Bar Kappara's riddle also speaks of something that "searches from the corners of her house," which evokes Proverbs' description of the harlot who looks down through her window in the hope of finding a client. Bar Kappara emphasizes that she searches from the corners, an intimate description of someone peering deep into the recesses of the home. Perhaps he is criticizing Rebbi, who was unable to confine his learning to the corners of his house and instead wore it on his sleeve. The riddle continues with "All the winged creatures fear," a possible reference to the sages fearful of the prostitute who wants them to flock to her.

The next line of Bar Kappara's riddle, "The young men saw me and withdrew, the aged rose and stood," is a reference to a verse from Job: "When I passed through the city gates to take my seat in the square, young men saw me and hid, elders rose and stood. Nobles held back their words; they clapped their hands to their mouths. The voices of princes were hushed; their tongues stuck to their palates" (Job 29:7–10). When the patriarch passes by, everyone comes to a halt out of respect and fear. Bar Kappara's riddle continues, "Lo, they cry in woe. He who is taken is taken in sin." This line is based on a verse from Amos: "Assuredly, thus said the Lord, my Lord the God of hosts: in every square there shall be lamenting, in every street cries of woe; and the farmhand shall be called to mourn, and those skilled in wailing to lament" (Amos 5:15). Bar Kappara seems to be implying that the patriarchal house is a source of wailing and woe. He conveys his criticism through Ben Elasa, the condescending son-in-law. Rebbi is aware of Bar Kappara's mockery even if his son-in-law is oblivious. He responds harshly to Bar Kappara: "I do not recognize you, O sage." Bar Kappara understands from Rebbi's reaction that as a consequence of his behavior, he will never be appointed to the patriarch's court.

THE BABYLONIAN VERSION OF BAR KAPPARA'S DISMISSAL

The Babylonian parallel to this story appears in the context of a discussion about the laws of excommunication:

(Prov. 7:6). The only positive connotation appears in "Look down from Your holy abode, from heaven, and bless Your people Israel" (Deut. 26:15).

> Rebbi said: No ban of excommunication lasts less than thirty days, and no ban of reproof lasts less than seven days.... Rav Ḥisda said: Our ban of excommunication [in Babylonia] is equivalent to their ban of reproof in the Land of Israel. But is their ban of reproof only seven days long? For Rabbi Shimon and Bar Kappara were once sitting and learning together when a difficulty arose about a certain passage. Rabbi Shimon said to Bar Kappara: We need Rebbi's explanation for this matter. Bar Kappara said to Rabbi Shimon: And what could Rebbi have to offer on this matter? Rabbi Shimon went and relayed this to his father. Rebbi grew angry. When Bar Kappara next came before Rebbi, Rebbi said to him: Bar Kappara, I have never known you. Bar Kappara realized that Rebbi had taken the matter to heart, so he took upon himself the ban of reproof for thirty days. (Mo'ed Katan 16a)

The three key players are Rabbi Shimon ben Rebbi, his friend Bar Kappara, and Rebbi. As noted, Bar Kappara studies with the patriarch's son. We don't know their ages, but they seem to be young students who learn independently. At a certain point in their studies Rabbi Shimon says, "We need Rebbi's explanation for this matter."

Rabbi Shimon was very close to his father. Although it was his older brother Gamliel who was supposed to be the next patriarch, everyone knew Shimon was the true scholar. Rabbi Shimon and his father would try to best one another in matters of Torah. Rabbi Shimon would also question his father's version of the Mishna. The Jerusalem Talmud relates that "Rebbi would sit and teach Rabbi Shimon" (Y. Avoda Zara 4:4 [43d]). Elsewhere in the Jerusalem Talmud we find Rebbi sending Shimon to bring dried figs from a barrel. Shimon asks if the figs are forbidden for use on Shabbat. His father responds by teaching him the laws of *muktzeh* (Y. Ma'asrot 1:8 [49b]).

Rabbinic *Aggada* includes several stories about Rabbi Shimon, including his marriage and the birth of his daughter.[7] He remains unwaveringly loyal to his father. And he is jealously protective of his father's

7. His marriage is discussed in Y. Beitza 5:2 (63a). The birth of his daughter is discussed in Genesis Rabba 26:4 and Bava Batra 16a.

honor in the face of those who threaten to undermine it. This kind of relationship is common among the families of prime ministers, chief rabbis, and other major leaders.

When Rabbi Shimon relates Bar Kappara's words to Rebbi, Rebbi's response is harsh: "I have never known you." Here, too, Bar Kappara is shown to the door.

BAR KAPPARA RELOCATES

In the 1970s, archeologists excavating the city of Devora in the Golan Heights found a doorpost with the following inscription: "This is the beit midrash of Elazar HaKappar." The discovery of this beit midrash on the far side of the Jordan River and not on the western shores of the Sea of Galilee calls into question Bar Kappara's proximity to the patriarchal court.[8]

It is fitting that the doorpost of Bar Kappara's beit midrash has been preserved for posterity given his teaching in *Avot deRabbi Natan*:

> Rabbi Elazar HaKappar would say: Do not be like the uppermost doorpost, which men cannot touch with their hands, or like the highest step, which swallows faces. And do not be like the middle step, which bruises feet. Rather, be like the threshold on which everyone treads. Although in the end the whole edifice may crumble, the threshold will remain in its place. (*Avot deRabbi Natan*, recension A, ch. 26)

The Talmud depicts Bar Kappara as a harsh critic of Rebbi's aristocratic court. He tries to temper the patriarch's austerity with a degree of levity. Elsewhere we are told that Bar Kappara taught:

> What is a brief text on which all the essential principles of Torah

8. D. Orman, "Jewish Inscriptions from the Village of Dvora in the Golan" [Hebrew], *Tarbiz* 40 (5731): 21–23. On the identification of Elazar HaKapar as Bar Kappara, see Y. Barilel, *Introduction to the Mishna*, vol. 1 (Frankfurt am Main, 5636), 243–44. For a review of the literature, see D. Orman, "On the Question of the Location of the Beit Midrash of Bar Kappara and Rabbi Hoshaya Rabba" [Hebrew], in *A Nation and Its History*, 163–72.

> are based? "In all your ways acknowledge Him, and He will direct your paths" [Prov. 3:6]. (Berakhot 63a)

Bar Kappara did not consider Rebbi's fortified palace to be the proper expression of the service of God. He tried to teach Rebbi that despite his role as patriarch, he was still just one of the people.

Chapter Twenty-Five

Parting from the Patriarch

THE PATRIARCH'S SUFFERING

The Talmud recounts that Rebbi moved from Beit She'arim to Tzippori not for political reasons, but on account of health problems that plagued him in his final years.

> Rebbi was living in Beit She'arim, but when he fell ill, he was brought to the elevated city of Tzippori, because its air was salubrious. (Ketubot 103b)[1]

For most of his years in Tzippori, he suffered from painful physical ailments:

> And of these years [that Rebbi lived in Tzippori], he spent thirteen years suffering from a toothache. Rabbi Yose ben Rabbi Bun said: Throughout these thirteen years, no pregnant women died or miscarried in the Land of Israel. And why did he have a

1. Y. Neeman, "From Beit She'arim to Tzippori: On the Reasons for Rabbi Yehuda HaNasi's Relocation from Beit She'arim to Tzippori" [Hebrew], *HaMa'ayan* 36 (5756): 38–42.

> toothache? One time, as he was passing by, he saw a calf about to be slaughtered. It cried out and said to him: Rebbi, save me! He said to it: You were created for this purpose. And how was he finally cured? He saw people about to kill a nest of mice. Rebbi said: Let them be, for it is written, "and His compassion extends to all His creatures" [Ps. 145:9]. (Y. Kilayim 9:3[32a])

Though Rebbi enjoyed prosperity and abundance in Tzippori, his body betrayed him. Rabbi Yose ben Rabbi Bun, one of the last of the *Amora'im* of the Land of Israel, describes Rebbi's physical distress as a sort of sacrifice for the sake of the general welfare. Rebbi bore all the suffering of the people upon himself, such that the world was fruitful and bountiful while he alone suffered.

The Talmud juxtaposes two vignettes from the beginning and end of Rebbi's illness. In the first, Rebbi encounters a calf that pleads with him to be spared from slaughter. Rebbi answers brusquely, "You were created for this purpose." He is unwilling to consider bending the law on account of individual suffering. But after years of discomfort and distress, Rebbi's attitude changes. He spares a nest of mice because "His compassion extends to all His creatures."

Rebbi also suffered from stomach problems, which are described in quite colorful detail:

> The stableman of Rebbi's house was wealthier than Shevur Malka, king of Persia. When he threw fodder to the animals, the noise they made was so loud it would travel three *mil*. The stableman would schedule himself so that he threw the fodder at the same time as Rebbi entered the bathroom, in order to drown out his cries. Nevertheless, Rebbi's cries drowned out the cries of the animals, and even the seafarers heard him. (Bava Metzia 85a)

This source, albeit richly imagined, dramatizes the enormity of Rebbi's distress. Several other rabbinic sources describe Rebbi's dietary practices: He ate small vegetarian meals and frequented the privy at regular intervals.[2] It seems that his stomach trouble caused infection and intestinal blockage.[3]

THE WILL

Rebbi's last will and testament is mentioned in both the Jerusalem and Babylonian Talmuds:

In the Jerusalem Talmud

> Rebbi commanded three things at the time of his death: Do not remove my widow from my house; do not eulogize me in the towns; and those who took care of me in life shall take care of me in death. (Y. Kilayim 9:3[32a])

The Jerusalem Talmud considers each of these three instructions in turn. First, why did Rebbi have to instruct that the sages not remove his widow? A mishna in Ketubot (12:3) explicitly states that a widow may not be evicted from her husband's home. The Talmud explains that since Rebbi lived in the seat of the patriarchy, the authorities were liable to transfer the house from the widow's control to that of the local government. Rebbi therefore orders that his wife be allowed to remain in her home, living under the same conditions to which she was accustomed when they lived there together.

Rebbi next charged that he not be eulogized in the towns. The Talmud explains that he gave this charge "on account of dispute." According to the commentary of the Penei Moshe, "If they were to eulogize him in the towns, many from the neighboring villages would come, the land would not be able to contain them, and dispute would ensue." That is, Rebbi was concerned that the locals would fight over the right to house

2. Small meals: Y. Pesaḥim 9:1 (36c); vegetables: Avoda Zara 11a; privy: Y. Shabbat 18:11 (17a).
3. A. Devorchki, "Rebbi's Sickness in Light of Modern Medicine" [Hebrew], *Medicine* 139 (Elul 5760): 232–35.

his coffin while he was being eulogized. He sought to avoid the administrative chaos that would result from such a dispute. According to the commentary of the Korban HaEda, the townspeople would fight over who had the honor of eulogizing Rebbi, whereas the city was subject to a centralized government that would maintain order. Either way, it seems clear that Rebbi preferred one central ceremony.

The final charge, "Those who took care of me in life shall take care of me in death," is elaborated upon by Rabbi Ḥanania of Tzippori: "Such as Yose Efrati and Yosef Ḥofnayim." This is a reference to the *ḥevra kaddisha*, the group of people who prepare the body of the dead for burial. Rebbi wishes that those who cared for him in life will prepare him for death.

The Jerusalem Talmud adds two other charges, quoted in the name of Ḥizkiya:

> Rebbi also ordered: Do not give me many shrouds, and let my coffin be open to the ground. (Y. Kilayim 9:3[32a])

Despite his lavish aristocratic lifestyle, Rebbi wishes to be buried like everyone else.[4]

In the Babylonian Talmud

> When Rebbi was about to die, he said: I need my sons. His sons entered into his presence. He said to them: Take care that you show respect for your mother. The light shall continue to burn in its usual place, the table shall be laid in its usual place, and my bed shall be spread in its usual place. Yosef Ḥofni and Shimon Efrati, who attended me in my lifetime, shall attend me when I am dead.... He said: I need the sages of Israel. The sages of Israel entered into his presence. He said to them: Do not lament me in the towns, and resume learning after thirty days.... My son Shimon is a sage and my son Gamliel is patriarch, and Ḥanina ben Ḥama shall preside at their head.... He said to them: I need

4. B. M. Bialik, "Rabbi Yehuda HaNasi's Will" [Hebrew], *Batzron* 26 (5725): 14–21.

> my younger son. Rabbi Shimon entered into his presence, and he entrusted him with the orders of wisdom. He said to them: I need my older son. His older son entered into his presence, and he entrusted him with the orders of the patriarchy. He said to him: My son, conduct the patriarchy with men of high standing, and cast bile among the students. (Ketubot 103a)

Rebbi remains in control until his final breath. He understands that the centralized organization of his patriarchy cannot endure after his death. To avoid a dispute about his succession, he proposes a division of power. His son Shimon will be responsible for Torah learning ("the orders of wisdom"), and his son Gamliel will be the political leader ("the orders of the patriarchy"). He reminds Gamliel that the patriarchal role requires acting with authority and commanding respect.

THE DAY OF HIS DEATH

Rebbi endures great physical distress even on his dying day. The Talmud describes the drama of that day:[5]

> On the day Rebbi died, the rabbis decreed a public fast and offered prayers for divine mercy and said: Whoever says Rebbi is dead will be stabbed by a sword. Rebbi's handmaid ascended to the roof and prayed: Those above desire that Rebbi join them, and those below desire that Rebbi remain with them. May it be the will of God that those below overpower those above.
>
> When she saw how often he went in to the privy, painfully taking off his *tefillin* and putting them on again each time, she prayed: May it be the will of God that those above overpower those below.
>
> As the rabbis continued praying incessantly, she took a jar and threw it down from the roof to the ground. They stopped praying for an instant, and the soul of Rebbi departed to its eternal rest.
>
> The sages said to Bar Kappara: Go and investigate. He went and found that Rebbi's soul had departed. He tore his

5. This story has many parallels. See Meir, *Yehuda HaNasi: Image of a Leader*, 300–37.

> garments and turned the tear backward. He opened with: The angels and the mortals were grasping at the holy ark. The angels overpowered the mortals, and the holy ark was captured. They said to him: Has his soul departed? He said to them: You said it, not I. (Ketubot 104a)

In the tense final hours before Rebbi's death, the world battles for his soul: "Whoever says Rebbi is dead will be stabbed by a sword." There is no room for compromise, because life without Rebbi is inconceivable. Rebbi's maidservant, responsible for nursing the ailing master, decides to partake in the war for his soul. She climbs up to the roof and informs the heavens of the declaration of war, praying, "May it be the will of God that those below overpower those above." But then she returns to Rebbi and observes his pain up close, perhaps remembering the prayer recited upon going to the bathroom: "If one of them should open or be blocked, it would be impossible to exist and stand before you for even an hour." She decides to reverse her prayer: "May it be the will of God that those above overpower those below." This is the story's climax.[6] The sages below, still praying fervently for Rebbi, know their prayer has the power to prevent the heavens from seizing his soul. The maidservant, too, understands that so long as the sages continue to pray, her own prayer stands no chance. At this point, she takes a jar and throws it down from the roof. The jar crashes to the ground, and for a moment the sages are silenced. Rebbi dies, and the battle is over.

Now Bar Kappara comes back on stage. He has spent the previous few years in the village of Devora, building his own beit midrash after Rebbi excommunicated him. In the moment of reckoning, only Bar Kappara could voice the terrible truth. Only he who understood that Rebbi was a flesh-and-blood human being could convey to the patriarch's disciples that he, too, was mortal. In a garment that is torn but with the tear concealed, he offers a powerful eulogy, comparing Rebbi to the Ark of the Covenant, which everyone wants to grasp: "The angels and the mortals were grasping at the holy ark. The angels overpowered

6. This source is invoked in conversations about the ethics of praying for a loved one who is wracked by pain.

the mortals, and the holy ark was captured." The students fear they have understood his words. They ask tentatively, "Has his soul departed?" The moment they say it, they know it is true.

THE END OF PIRKEI AVOT

The identification of Bar Kappara with Rabbi Elazar HaKappar returns us to the final mishna of the last chronological chapter of *Pirkei Avot*:[7]

> He [Rabbi Elazar HaKappar] used to say: Those who have been born will die, and those who are dead will be revived. Those who live are destined to be judged, that men may know and make known and understand that He is God, He is the maker, He is the creator, He is the discerner, He is the judge, He is the witness, He is the plaintiff, and it is He who in the future will judge, blessed be He, in whose presence is neither guile nor forgetfulness nor respect of persons nor taking of bribes; for all is His. And know that everything is according to the reckoning. And let not your evil nature assure you that the grave will be your refuge: for despite yourself you were fashioned, and despite yourself you were born, and despite yourself you live, and despite yourself you die, and despite yourself you are destined to give an account and reckoning before the supreme King of kings, the Holy One, Blessed Be He. (Mishna Avot 4:22)

7. The first four chapters of Avot are organized chronologically from the Second Temple period until Rebbi's patriarchy. The fifth chapter is organized literarily, and the sixth chapter is a *baraita*.

About the Author

Rabbi Dr. Binyamin Lau is an Israeli community leader, educator, and rabbi. He is the rabbi of the Ramban Synagogue in Jerusalem, the founder of the Moshe Green Beit Midrash for Women's Leadership at Beit Morasha's Beren College, and a research fellow at the Israel Democracy Institute. Rabbi Lau also serves as a consultant for a number of leading organizations, is widely published, and is frequently cited in the media. He studied at Yeshivat Har Etzion and Yeshivat HaKibbutz HaDati, and received a PhD in Talmud from Bar-Ilan University.

The fonts used in this book are from the Arno family

Other books in *The Sages* series by
Rabbi Dr. Binyamin Lau

Volume I: The Second Temple Period

Volume II: From Yavneh to the Bar Kokhba Revolt

Maggid Books
The best of contemporary Jewish thought from
Koren Publishers Jerusalem Ltd.